The Rise of
Canadian Business

Graham D. Taylor

OXFORD
UNIVERSITY PRESS

OXFORD
UNIVERSITY PRESS

70 Wynford Drive, Don Mills, Ontario M3C 1J9
www.oupcanada.com

Oxford University Press is a department of the University of Oxford.
It furthers the University's objective of excellence in research, scholarship,
and education by publishing worldwide in

Oxford New York

Auckland Cape Town Dar es Salaam Hong Kong Karachi
Kuala Lumpur Madrid Melbourne Mexico City Nairobi
New Delhi Shanghai Taipei Toronto

With offices in

Argentina Austria Brazil Chile Czech Republic France Greece
Guatemala Hungary Italy Japan Poland Portugal Singapore
South Korea Switzerland Thailand Turkey Ukraine Vietnam

Oxford is a trade mark of Oxford University Press
in the UK and in certain other countries

Published in Canada
by Oxford University Press

Library and Archives Canada Cataloguing in Publication

Taylor, Graham D., 1944–
The rise of Canadian business / Graham D. Taylor.

Includes bibliographical references and index.
ISBN 978-0-19-542549-9

1. Canada—Commerce—History—Textbooks.   2. Industries—Canada—History—Textbooks.
3. Business enterprises—Canada—History—Textbooks.   4. Canada—Economic conditions—1867—Textbooks.
I. Title.

HF3224.T393 2008   330.971'05   C2008-903011-7

1 2 3 4 – 12 11 10 09

This book is printed on permanent (acid-free) paper ∞.
Printed in Canada.

Contents

Introduction

A generation ago, writing a history of Canadian business would have been both harder and easier: harder, because of the absence of primary sources and research-based analyses of businesses in this country. Few companies maintained archives, and many of those that did limited public access to them, a situation that remains a challenge for historians today. Reliable statistical information on industrial activities in Canada was equally difficult to procure, particularly for the period before Confederation. Although some companies—the chartered banks in particular—had commissioned histories of their institutions, few were written by professional historians, and they provided at best limited glimpses of the inner workings of these enterprises.

But writing such a history a generation ago would have been easier, too, in that the pattern of Canadian business evolution seemed much more clear-cut, owing largely to the pioneering research and analysis undertaken in the 1920s–1940s by a small number of economists, notably Harold Innis and his followers. The views of the 'Innis school' had a pervasive influence on the writing of economic and business history in Canada for many years. Even today, the basic concepts formulated by Innis in his studies of the fur trade, the fisheries, and the Canadian Pacific Railway undergird the work of many scholars, some of whom characterize themselves as 'political economists' and contrast their approach to the theoretical model building of 'neo-classical economists'.

Although Innis's ideas were complex and his writing tended to be opaque, the main thrust of his 'staple thesis' was straightforward. Since the earliest European settlements in the 1500s, the economy of Canada was based on the extraction and exporting of a series of raw materials or 'staples': fish and furs in the period before 1830; timber in the early to mid-nineteenth century; wheat and mineral products from the 1890s through World War II; oil and pulpwood towards the end of the twentieth century. The country's economic infrastructure and virtually its entire business community were harnessed, directly or indirectly, to the development of these staples, and fortunes rose and fell with shifts in foreign demand for them. The transportation network, the banking system, merchant communities, and isolated 'company towns' were all by-products of the staples trade. Political arrangements, social structures, and relations between Native Canadians and European settlers were in turn shaped by the needs and constraints of the staple system.

The fundamental role of staples in the Canadian economy also determined the country's international position and the internal structures of its business institutions. Canada was basically a resource hinterland, supplying raw materials to developed commercial and industrial nations abroad, and dependent on them for capital, technology, and management as well as manufactured products. In economic terms, even after it achieved a measure of political independence Canada was vitally tied to foreign metropolitan centres: France and England in the early years of European settlement, Britain in the nineteenth century, and the United States in the twentieth century. Although in the early 1900s Canada acquired a modest domestic manufacturing base, the country remained largely dependent on foreign imports of finished products and continued to rely on exports of raw and semi-processed goods for its economic growth. Canadian banks and commercial houses functioned principally as middlemen in the staples export trade and maintained close ties with larger counterparts in the financial centres of London and New York. Much of Canada's manufacturing sector (as well as its mining and forestry industries) was controlled by businesses headquartered abroad: Glasgow, London, Chicago, Detroit. Despite the relatively high standard of living achieved by Canadians in the twentieth century, the country did not develop a diversified, self-sustaining economy, and its businesses remained, directly or indirectly, under the control of foreign interests.[1]

Persuasive as this interpretation was (and still is, in some quarters), it rested on a precariously small base of documentation: the histories of a handful of large enterprises, most notably the Hudson's Bay Company and the Canadian Pacific Railway. Since the 1960s, studies of Canadian businesses have proliferated, revealing a more complex picture of the country's commercial and industrial system. Dozens of books and hundreds of articles and papers chronicled the careers of entrepreneurs, case histories of companies, the evolution of government policies affecting business, the social and political roles of business figures, and trends in trade, investment, labour relations, and technological developments.

Although these studies represented a wide range of viewpoints and perspectives, their appearance reflected a broader trend, particularly in the United States and Britain, but eventually spreading to many other industrialized nations. This approach was based on an interest in the organization and evolution of businesses, not simply as anonymous 'firms' responding to the fluctuations of supply and demand as they appeared in economists' models, but as personalities and institutions with unique identities whose activities significantly influenced the social and political world in which they operated.

Before World War II, the study of business organizations and practices was carried out by a few researchers, mostly resident in business schools in the United States. Among the most noteworthy of these was a Canadian, Norman S.B. Gras, who taught at Harvard Business School where the 'case study' method of instruction was particularly congenial to historical approaches. During the 1920s and 1930s Gras developed a general framework to explain the evolution of capitalism in Europe and North America, derived in part from the work of German economic historians such as Werner Sombart and Gustav Schmoller at the turn of the century. But the utilitarian environment of business education, oriented towards training professional managers, imposed limits on the range of issues Gras and his colleagues addressed, focusing their attention on administrative and financial aspects of business organizations rather than the broader social, political, and cultural settings in which businesses developed.

During the 1940s and 1950s the interests of historians of business began to broaden. Some set out deliberately to challenge the popular stereotype of the business tycoon as a modern-day 'robber baron', a view that had flourished in the Great Depression and reflected widespread public distrust of the large corporations that had emerged at the turn of the century, particularly in the United States and Canada. Self-consciously presenting themselves as defenders of capitalism in the Cold War era, these writers lauded corporate empire builders such as John D. Rockefeller and Henry Ford as 'industrial statesmen' whose achievements laid the groundwork for economic prosperity in the mid-twentieth century.

Another group undertook to more clearly link the study of business institutions with the social sciences. At Harvard University, Arthur Cole and others, inspired in part by the ideas of an Austrian economist, Joseph Schumpeter, focused on the concept of 'entrepreneurship', seeking to determine how social institutions and cultural values as well as economic factors stimulated or retarded individual enterprise in different countries. Others traced the historical development of large corporations and investigated their impact on the market system. By the mid-1970s the work of Alfred D. Chandler Jr and others, on the rise of 'managerial capitalism' in the United States, stimulated research on this subject in Europe and Japan and ancillary analyses of the consequences of the rise of big business on government policies, labour relations, the development and diffusion of new technologies, and political ideas.[2]

In general, the post-war business historians elaborated on and fleshed out the framework of evolution enunciated by Gras, indicating a clear set of stages of institutional changes that took place in the 'capitalist' world, with some distinctive regional and national variations. Between the fourteenth and seventeenth centuries, basic techniques of commercial organization and market transactions were developed by merchant communities in Western Europe, spreading through trade and colonization to North America and outposts in other parts of the world. During the late 1700s and 1800s some merchants diversified into specialized fields such as banking and insurance; others applied their capital and organizing techniques to industrial production. Around the turn of the twentieth century, finance capitalists and some ambitious industrialists orchestrated consolidations of many smaller and diverse enterprises into large corporate systems and developed methods of communications and control to run these giant operations, ushering in the era of 'managerial capitalism'. Beginning in the late 1800s, some corporations that had functioned primarily within national boundaries began to expand their production and marketing activities into global systems. At the same time, national governments, which had hitherto functioned principally as guarantors of property rights and private market transactions, began to intervene more directly in the market system through tax and regulatory measures and public ownership.

More recent work by business historians has extended beyond and to some extent modified this basic paradigm of development. A greater appreciation has emerged of the complexity and innovative nature of pre-industrial merchant communities not only in medieval Europe but also in other societies, particularly in the Islamic world and East Asia. The persistence of small enterprise, even in situations where large corporate organizations seem to dominate, has been highlighted, particularly since the 1980s when big businesses lost their control over markets, undergoing 'downsizing' and 'deconglomeration' in the face of emerging new technologies and international competition. Perhaps the most significant theme to emerge in recent years has been a deeper historical exploration of the concept of 'globalization'. Even though the term was coined only towards the end of the twentieth century, historians have traced the origins of the process of global integration as far back as the 1500s, although the greatest emphasis has been placed on developments in the nineteenth century when technologies such as the railway, steamship, and telegraph provided businesses with new capabilities for integrating operations on an international scale comparable to the dramatic changes in computer and telecommunications technology in the past two decades. This research has also yielded the insight that the process of globalization is not irreversible, as the experiences of the early to mid-twentieth century demonstrated how vulnerable business systems could be to forces of war, nationalism, and social upheaval.[3]

This book examines the history of business in Canada in the context of these general themes and the framework of capitalist evolution developed by business historians here and abroad since the 1970s. This is not an explicit rejection of the staple system approach or an attempt to replace it with a single dominating explanation: for much of its history, Canadian business has been shaped by the critical role that the staples trade has played and continues to play in the nation's economic life. But this book does seek to show how Canada's position as a staple-producing country interacted with its emergence as part of the capitalist world from the 1500s. While in many respects

Canada was indeed a resource hinterland, at the same time it developed a diversified commercial system and an indigenous industrial sector; by the mid-twentieth century it also served as a base for multinational banks and corporations. The configuration of business development in Canada may not be unique (there are suggestive parallels, for example, in the history of Australia and some South American countries), but it is distinctive and deserves its own detailed account.[4]

In this account three dimensions of Canada's business evolution are highlighted:

1. *Changing patterns of business organization.* In Canada, as elsewhere, basic objectives of enterprises—profitability, growth, and survival—have remained fairly consistent; but the means of achieving those ends have varied over time, in response to changing markets, the advent of new technologies, alterations in political and social arrangements, and other factors. Changes in business structures—the movement from general to specialized activities in merchant communities, for example, or the emergence of joint-stock corporations—have in turn had an impact on government–business relationships and the growth (or decline) of communities and regions.

2. *The particular character of Canadian business arrangements.* In many respects these patterns of change and stability in business organizations resemble developments elsewhere in the capitalist world. At the same time, Canada has some distinctive features that have produced a special configuration of business arrangements. These include, of course, the harvest of staples for export, but also the persistent tensions among regions in a sprawling, underpopulated country divided along cultural and linguistic as well as economic and geographic lines; a legal system that has placed constraints on the operations of private enterprises even though the degree of constraint has varied over time; and, at least over the past century, a political system that has uneasily tried to balance 'national' interests against regional and continental economic pressures.

3. *The international setting of Canadian business.* Since the earliest period of European settlement, Canada has been part of a transatlantic (and more recently global) business environment, not only in terms of trade, capital flows, and the migration of people, but also in the diffusion of technology, ideas, and business practices. Canadian staples producers have faced competition in other remote hinterlands as well as shifting markets in the industrial heartlands of Europe and the United States. Events in financial centres—London, Tokyo, New York—have repercussions in Canadian capital markets. Technological developments have created opportunities for some industries while spelling the ruin of others. New methods of production, concepts of labour relations, and ideas about government regulation and other matters have been imported, along with foreign industrial products.

These processes have not been entirely one-sided. Canadian businesses have developed specialized techniques in shipbuilding, the mining industry, even in automated machine production. Merchant fleets from Atlantic Canadian ports competed vigorously in the global carrying trade in the nineteenth century, and Canadian firms operated in utilities, mining, oil and gas, and manufacturing in the United States, Europe, Latin America, Africa, and Australia from the early twentieth century.

ORGANIZATION OF THE BOOK

After an opening chapter, which relates the history of business in Canada to 1885, the book is divided into three sections. Part I (Chapters 2–6) examines 'The Age of Business Consolidation, 1885–1930'. In the late nineteenth century both economic and technological factors contributed to the growth of companies that could encompass national markets, usually at the expense of firms serving local and regional needs. These smaller firms were merged into larger entities or simply disappeared. The same process was occurring in many countries in Europe, as well as in North America, and in some cases (as in Canada) this consolidation occurred simultaneously with the rapid development of industrial capabilities. Canada's particular experience was shaped by the presence of foreign businesses, particularly British and American, and the great demand for its natural resources to fuel industrial development, a circumstance that made this period, or at least up until the outbreak of World War I, a 'golden age' (literally and figuratively) for the country's economy.

Part II (Chapters 7–10) considers 'The Age of the Activist State, 1930–1988'. Two factors in particular impelled governments in the capitalist industrial nations to play an active role in the market system in the twentieth century: the imperatives of wartime mobilization—for the two world wars and the protracted era of Cold War; and the need to deal with the social distress and upheaval that came in the wake of economic crises, particularly the Great Depression of the 1930s. Although Canada has a reputation as being more 'statist' than countries such as the United States, its experience paralleled that of the US, Britain, and other industrial nations in many respects. By the 1960s–70s, governments at both the federal and provincial levels were pursuing interventionist policies to promote economic development and restrict foreign control of business. A combination of developments—the revival of political conservatism, the impact of globalization, and a period of sustained inflation that no government seemed able to control—helped bring an end to this era.

In Part III (Chapters 11–13) we explore 'Canada in the New Era of Globalization, 1980 to the Present'. In the nineteenth century, global integration had been promoted by technologies such as the railway and the telegraph and new forms of business organization to exploit them. This development was disrupted first by war and then by protectionist economic policies in the mid-twentieth century, but the trend towards global markets for goods, labour, and money revived in the 1980s, accelerated by the end of the Cold War and the emergence of technologies such as the personal computer, satellite telecommunications, and the Internet. Canada, whose growth had been largely shaped by transatlantic and international trade since its origins, shared in this experience, both as a recipient of foreign capital and as a participant in emerging global markets. In the early years of the twenty-first century, Canadian business faced the challenges posed by trends towards corporate integration on an international scale but also encompassed a diverse community of enterprises serving its domestic and foreign markets—features that have been present throughout the history of Canada.

The chapters included in Parts I and II of this book originally appeared as my contribution to *The Concise History of Business in Canada*, published by Oxford University Press in 1994, which I co-authored with Peter Baskerville; these chapters have been updated and revised in varying degrees to reflect new scholarship. Chapter 1 and the chapters in Part III are largely new material, both to carry the story of Canadian business beyond the time of the Canada–US Free Trade Agreement, and also to reflect my perspectives more generally. Some readers may feel that this book might more accurately be entitled 'The Rise *and Fall* of Canadian Business', particularly in light of the recent foreign takeovers of such venerable Canadian enterprises as the Hudson's Bay Company, Alcan, Algoma Steel, Inco, Falconbridge, and Abitibi. This subject is dealt with at the end of Chapter 13.

CHAPTER 1

The Road to Craigellachie: Business in Canada to 1885

It is one of the best-known photographs in Canadian history—second only, perhaps, to the snapshot of Paul Henderson's winning goal in the final game of the Canada–Soviet Union hockey series in 1972. Although the grainy sepia film obscures the surroundings, that morning of 7 November 1885 in a remote corner of Eagle Pass in British Columbia was cold and murky: a snowfall the night before had blocked a trainload of dignitaries, including Canada's Governor General, from arriving in time for the ceremonies.

In the centre of the picture a weather-beaten man with a white beard and a tall stovepipe hat leans over the rails, hammer poised to drive 'the last spike' of the Canadian Pacific Railway. This is Donald Smith, a leading figure in the Montreal-based syndicate that handled the financing of the enterprise. Smith embodied in many respects a link between the past and the future of the business world: he began his career in Labrador as a fur trader for the venerable Hudson's Bay Company, and later he would be involved in the creation of the company known today as British Petroleum (BP), one of the world's largest oil multinationals. Looming behind him is another full-bearded, top-hatted Scot, Sandford Fleming, who had spent much of the previous quarter-century carrying out surveys and designing plans for transcontinental railways. To his right, in a shorter hat

and with a smaller beard, stands William Van Horne, an American railroad manager, recruited from Chicago three years earlier to supervise the railway construction through to completion, five years ahead of schedule. Van Horne would remain in Canada, eventually becoming head of Canadian Pacific and later orchestrating the construction of railways in the Caribbean and Latin America.

Surrounding these figures is an array of railway workers in derby hats and slouch hats, many of them Irish, along with Americans, English, Scots, Germans, and Scandinavians. Present but unseen were the Chinese workers, mostly from Kwangtung province, who were assigned some of the most dangerous construction tasks. Unseen as well were the Métis and Native Canadian residents of the region the railway was opening up to settlement: they had been suppressed a few months earlier in what the Canadian government referred to as the 'Northwest Rebellion'.

Absent from the picture are some key figures in the project. George Stephen, Smith's cousin, president of the Bank of Montreal and the designer of the financial syndicate, was in London persuading Baring Brothers to market bonds for the railway. Earlier in the project's life, when investor support seemed to be fading, Stephen rallied his partners, quoting the motto of his family's Scottish clan: 'Stand fast, Craigellachie.' In his honour, Van

Donald Smith prepares to drive the last spike on the CPR line, Craigellachie, BC, 1885. (Glenbow Archives NA-1494-6)

Horne bequeathed the name to the spot where the last spike was driven. Also absent was Canada's Prime Minister, Sir John A. Macdonald, who had steadfastly promoted the Canadian Pacific for almost two decades, been driven into political exile as a result of scandals over the financing of the project, then returned to office in 1879 committed to completing it. By 1885 the Canadian government had provided over $25 million in cash subsidies, along with a 25-million-acre land grant, emergency loans totalling $27.5 million, and assorted other benefits to the railway company, accounting for almost 60 per cent of the costs.

Generations of Canadians celebrated the building of the Canadian Pacific Railway in song and story—even an epic poem and a televised mini-series. In recent times, more skeptical attitudes have emerged. 'The construction of the Canadian Pacific Railway was a national achievement only in a certain, limited sense', Michael Bliss observed in *Northern Enterprise*, his history of Canadian business, noting the important role

of foreign capital and management in the project. Even more critical is 'The Canadian West Project', a website maintained by Library and Archives Canada that comments that the driving of the last spike was 'an anticlimactic gesture', going on to make the argument that 'the price of building the transcontinental railway was high . . . not to mention the displacement of Canada's First Nations and the lost lives of many immigrant laborers.'[1]

Craigellachie did not necessarily mark a turning point in Canadian history except in a symbolic sense. Nevertheless, it did represent the physical linking of western Canada with Ontario and Quebec—the Intercolonial Railway, connecting Quebec and the Maritimes, designed and largely built by Sandford Fleming, was completed in 1876. These two projects were in many respects more critical to the economic development of Canada than the establishment of Confederation had been in 1867.

From the perspective of the present, other features of the transcontinental railway project resonate through the history of business in Canada: the presence of Scottish businessmen in key positions; the role of British (and American) capital and (primarily) American management; the reliance on immigrant labour from across the globe; and the involvement of government in supporting, albeit sometimes half-heartedly, a project of 'national' significance, whose longer-term objective was economic growth through the expansion of Canada's export trade. Even before Canada as a country existed, it was part of an international network of trade and finance; and the businesses that evolved here were either directly tied to foreign owners or partners or derived from models of successful organizations in the larger world of capitalist development in which Canada played a significant part.

COMMERCIAL BEGINNINGS

John Cabot (Giovanni Caboto), an Italian contemporary of Columbus, is traditionally identified as the first European explorer to encounter land, probably Newfoundland, that is now part of Canada, in 1497 (although Norse settlers had been in this same region several centuries earlier). Cabot's objective was economic—to find a northern passage to the wealth of Asia—but in practical terms his critical discovery was 'a sea swarming with fish'. Some historians maintain that Cabot had been preceded there by fishermen working for merchants in Bristol on the west coast of England, who had begun moving into the Grand Banks from the 1480s after being excluded from the fisheries around Iceland. Whether that is accurate or not, the main result of Cabot's voyages was the opening of the Newfoundland cod fisheries to exploitation, not just by the English, but also by French, Portuguese, and Spanish fishers. For the most part they did not require access to land, as the fish were preserved through heavy salting on shipboard. But the English were at a disadvantage, because of their limited access to salt, and by the mid-1500s they were establishing seasonal settlements in Newfoundland, catching

fish near the shore and preserving them through dry-curing. By the end of the century English fleets from Bristol and French from Normandy and Brittany had come to dominate the fishery; and both were probing further into the continent, the French into the Gulf of St Lawrence and the Bay of Fundy, the English in a more southerly direction.

By the early 1600s when Champlain was exploring the St Lawrence region, a market had emerged in Europe for hats made of fur pelts and the European beaver population had been decimated, creating a fortuitous opportunity for trading in furs with the Aboriginal people that he encountered. By the middle of the century the fur trade had become the primary activity of settlers in the colony of New France despite efforts by government officials dispatched there to foster agricultural and industrial pursuits. The Dutch and later the English also entered the fur trade, advancing on the French from both the south, where they formed an alliance with the Iroquois to control the flow of the trade from the Ohio Valley, and from the Hudson's Bay region in the north. Although the demand for fur pelts fluctuated and the destruction of the beaver population required the constant geographic expansion of the trade into the interior of Canada and eventually the west coast, the fur trade remained a central feature of the country through the first quarter of the nineteenth century.

By that time a third staple had emerged to drive Canadian exports. Since the 1500s English power was based on its navy and merchant marine, which in turn depended on a steady supply of timber. Having depleted their homeland, the English turned to supplies from Scandinavia, but during the long period of war from 1793 to 1815, this source was either cut off or undependable. On the other hand, the region around the Bay of Fundy and the St Lawrence, now securely under British control, provided vast, untapped stands of hardwood suitable for ships, and so a vigorous trade developed that eventually embraced much of northern and eastern Ontario as well as Quebec and New Brunswick. Although the coming of iron steamships in the late 1800s brought an end to that market, demand for lumber for housing and other products sustained the forestry industry.

Merchants were the key figures in the development of these staples. Explorers could claim lands in the name of their monarchs and kings might award trading monopolies to court favourites, but the financing and organization of trade were carried out by merchants both in Europe and North America. There had been merchants in virtually every society historically, and by the 1400s commercial groups clustered in market towns and ports had achieved some degree of political as well as economic independence. In this same period merchants were adopting innovative practices: the use of bills of exchange expanded the mobility of capital, and the development of double-entry bookkeeping enabled merchants to run businesses over long distances. The advent of this 'commercial revolution' was perhaps as significant in promoting the global expansion of Europe as the development of improved navigation instruments and square-rigged sailing vessels.

Merchants were in competition with one another, but the conditions of trade fostered a good deal of collaboration: few merchants were wealthy enough or had the inclination to accept the risks of underwriting new ventures and voyages alone. In the sixteenth- and seventeenth-century fisheries, for example, a ship's captain would in effect sell shares in each voyage to members of his crew, those who provisioned the ship, and merchants prepared to lend money for outfitting, and they in turn might share the risk with other merchants who would insure them against loss. A merchant might at any time have dozens of different investments out, often with different partners.

By the 1700s, conditions in the transatlantic trading world were more stable, although every venture ran the risk of storms, piracy, war, or pilfering by employees or partners. In these circumstances some merchants were prepared to make more permanent arrangements to facilitate trade with particular destinations: this usually involved stationing an agent or 'factor' overseas, preferably a family member or someone equally trustworthy, if possible. Clusters of merchant communities would become more focused on a particular line of trade: in the Newfoundland fisheries, for example, the ports of Bristol and Plymouth were major scenes of activity on the English side in the sixteenth and seventeenth centuries, competing with French merchants based in Rouen, La Rochelle, and Nantes. Although London, with its large pools of capital, became the major merchant centre in England by the eighteenth century, there were still opportunities for other ports to establish trading niches. Merchants in the Channel Islands of Jersey and Guernsey, for example, carved out a place in the fishery of the Gaspé region of the St Lawrence River, which they dominated for more than a century. By the late 1700s Glasgow was emerging as a major port for shipbuilding and trade, and young Scotsmen went forth to North America, the Caribbean, and later Australia and New Zealand to make their fortunes.[2]

New France provides an example of this dynamic at work. Although faced with recurrent challenges (and eventual conquest) by the English, from the 1680s through the 1760s the thriving fur trade and the colony's need for supplies attracted the merchants of Rouen and La Rochelle, who largely controlled this trade. One of the largest merchant houses in Rouen, Robert Dugard, formed a partnership in 1729 called the Société du Canada with four other families and, after several exploratory voyages, dispatched two young cousins, François Havy and Jean Lefebvre, to handle their business in Quebec. In addition to dealing with local suppliers of furs, Havy and Lefebvre developed an occasional trade with the West Indies, invested in fishing and sealing expeditions in the Bay of St Lawrence, and for a time engaged in shipbuilding, taking advantage of a royal bounty offered in one of the government's regular if unsuccessful efforts to promote industry in New France. By the 1740s the Dugard enterprise accounted for between 10 and 20 per cent of the colony's trade. In the ensuing War of the Austrian Succession, however, after losing several ships to English privateers, Dugard and his associates pulled out of the Canada trade. Havy and Lefebvre stayed on, and Havy went back to France, in effect as an agent in reverse for the partnership. For a time their fortunes seemed to be improving, when Havy married into a wealthy family of Bordeaux; but the French loss of Quebec in 1759 led Lefebvre to return to France, winding up business affairs in North America.[3]

The end of this story could be seen as a demonstration of the 'decapitation' of French Canada's business leadership in the wake of the English conquest, and, indeed, many of the representatives of French merchant houses departed in the 1760s, soon to be replaced by American and Scottish traders. But the economic growth stimulated by the fur trade had spawned a congeries of small operators in the interior of North America. From the beginnings of New France in the early 1600s there had been efforts by the government and merchants at home to set up a monopoly over the fur trade, but the circumstances of that trade worked against this aim. The French, like the English, depended for pelts on Native suppliers, and on the agents who were sent out to deal with them, the coureurs de bois. These 'runners of the woods' were apt to do trading on their own account on the side, and to rebel at efforts to rein them in—Pierre Radisson and Médard Chouart de Groseilliers, the two Frenchmen who enabled the Hudson's Bay Company to get a foothold in the fur trade in the 1670s, were classic examples: Radisson later defected from the English company because he wanted a better deal.

The Hudson's Bay Company, although in many respects a logical outgrowth of the innovations associated with the commercial revolution, was itself something of an anomaly, one of a handful of chartered joint stock corporations that emerged in the seventeenth century, beginning with the Dutch and English East India companies. These precursors of the modern multinational corporation were intended to reach a larger audience of potential investors than the merchant community, although merchants tended to dominate the inner workings of these enterprises. By offering

limited liability to shareholders, they could appeal to people (especially landowners and aristocrats) with little commercial experience, and they were usually promoted as serving a greater purpose than mere profit, although that, too, was to be provided. The East India companies were set up to break the Iberian (and Catholic) stranglehold on trade with Asia, for example, as later the Hudson's Bay Company would challenge the alleged French monopoly of the North American fur trade. They were bequeathed by the Crown with special powers that would perhaps inspire the envy of twenty-first-century multinationals: they could operate armed forces, impose their own laws, and govern territories. In the early 1700s joint stock companies lost favour with the investing public in the wake of speculative crashes associated with what became known as the 'South Sea Bubble' and the 'Mississippi Bubble', and the British Parliament banned them for more than a century.

The Hudson's Bay Company thus had political as well as commercial interests in its early years, and several of the initial investors were prominent aristocrats and political figures in Restoration England. But it was, at least for a few years, wildly successful as a commercial venture. Chartered in 1670, in the following decade it paid out 50 per cent dividends over several years, reflecting in large part both the buoyancy of the market and the fact that the company was able to penetrate the hitherto untapped area around Hudson's Bay, far from the more heavily exploited St Lawrence and Great Lakes region.

By the end of the century, however, the French had rebounded, the dividends disappeared, and on several occasions over the ensuing 50 years French forces were able to dislodge Hudson's Bay traders from their posts, at least temporarily. Nevertheless, the company survived and would continue for more than 300 years.

In contrast to the fishery and timber trade, the fur trade required interactions by Europeans with Native Canadians. Although they had very different ideas about property rights and the appropriate distribution of wealth in their communities, the Aboriginal people of North America were prolific traders and experienced negotiators, and well aware of the value of their goods to Europeans: there had been brutal struggles over control of access to the trade in the Great Lakes region in the 1500s. Whatever else the Hudson's Bay Company factors may have done poorly, they seem to have managed trade relations with the Native people reasonably well. Radisson had assembled what amounted to price lists for beaver pelts, designated in terms of trade goods such as muskets, pots and pans, and so on (including alcohol, although the factors were urged to discourage excessive drinking), and these lists were regularly updated to reflect current economic conditions. On their side, Native leaders sought to preserve prized positions in control of trade routes, and employees of the Bay were not encouraged to get involved in tribal politics.

The Hudson's Bay Company directors in London were, however, realistic enough to allow their employees a certain amount of trading on their own account. In return they expected obedience to their decrees, and the company operated in a relatively centralized fashion, given the constraints of poor communications and the lengthy turn-around time of a trading cycle, usually running up to two years from the time a ship bearing trade goods left England until its return, hopefully laden with furs. Factors submitted regular reports on conditions relating to the availability and quality of pelts, Native preferences in items of trade, obstacles to trade, and the operations of French competitors.

Centralization had its benefits, but the structure of the company and its cautious policies left it vulnerable to the challenge mounted by more vigorous, entrepreneurial rivals in the late 1700s. After the conquest of New France, aspiring fur traders flowed into Quebec from the American colonies, England, and Scotland (especially the latter) to take over the role abandoned by French merchants, forming partnerships with the coureurs de bois. By the 1770s a variety of trading enterprises were operating out of Montreal in the Ohio Valley and beyond the Great Lakes into the areas claimed by the Hudson's Bay Company, which disdained them as 'Cursed Scots pedlars'.

In 1779 leading Montreal fur merchants, including Isaac Todd, Joseph Frobisher, James McGill, and Simon McTavish, pooled their interests to form the North West Company, petitioning the new British government in Quebec for a monopoly on the fur trade of the 'North West', in effect directly challenging the Hudson's Bay Company. For the next 40 years the two companies clashed, mostly in terms of trade, but sometimes in violent confrontations, culminating in 1816 when a party of Nor'Westers attacked a settlement on the Red River (near present-day Winnipeg) that had been set up by the Earl of Selkirk, a major shareholder in the Hudson's Bay Company, as a model community for impoverished Scottish immigrants. Although the Selkirk Grant had almost no connection to the fur-trading activities of the Hudson's Bay Company, their rivals viewed it, with some justification, as the first step in the displacement of fur trapping to make way for agriculture.

The Nor'Westers proved far more adept in competition in the fur trade itself: figures like Alexander Mackenzie and Peter Pond ranged deep into the wilderness of western Canada to exploit new sources of furs. But serious weaknesses ultimately undermined their position. Opening new areas for trade extended the already stretched logistics of the North West Company, aggravated by the costs of proliferating trading posts. The company itself was unstable, basically an assembly of partnerships that shared profits but had little co-ordination. By the 1790s new competitors from Montreal were entering the field, including Mackenzie after a squabble with McTavish, the dominant figure in the company in Montreal. In the aftermath of the Selkirk episode, it was apparent to both the directors of the Hudson's Bay Company and their rivals that the competition was damaging everyone, increasing supplies and costs even as demand for furs was levelling off. In 1821 the two companies merged, and the Hudson's Bay Company was the apparent victor, as its name graced the merger and its centralized model of organization prevailed.

In the aftermath, a Bay man, George Simpson, took charge, and like many post-merger chief executives since, he instituted a housecleaning, closing down hundreds of posts (mostly at the expense of the former Nor'Westers). Called 'The Little Emperor', Simpson perpetually travelled around his domains, inspecting the books and assessing the factors at remote posts. His judgements were not always flawless: Donald Smith, then an employee in Labrador, was given a bad report for 'slovenliness', although it did not impede his future success. In any case, by the 1830s dividends of 20 per cent annually were flowing back to investors, and Simpson was credited with the turnaround.

By this time new competition was emerging from the south. As early as 1811 the New York merchant John Jacob Astor had invaded Bay territory on the Pacific coast, setting up a post he named Astoria. This foray was turned back, but Simpson continued to face challenges from the Russians as well as the Americans along the coast, while American traders from Minnesota were probing into the Red River region, setting up a rival trading post on the US border at Pembina. But an even greater threat to the entire fur-trading system came in the late 1840s as the California gold rush lured prospectors and speculators further north into the Puget Sound area. American settlers had already moved into the Oregon Territory south of the Columbia River, which Britain ceded to the United States. By this time Simpson had recognized that the traditional fur trade was in decline, and set out to diversify the company's operations and promote the colonization of Vancouver Island. But these efforts were half-hearted and ultimately the British government took over the region, renamed British Columbia in 1858. In that same year Parliament in London stripped the Hudson's Bay Company of its exclusive trading privileges, which by this time were fictional anyway. After Simpson's death a year later it was only a matter of time before the company would cease to operate as a territorial government; and its commercial future was equally uncertain.

While its history is filled with melodrama and adventure, the Hudson's Bay Company was of limited significance in the greater scheme of things. In 1783 Britain seriously contemplated abandoning its claim to 'all the furs of Canada' to acquire the sugar island of Guadeloupe in the Caribbean. The average value of the fur trade at its peak was less than that of the Newfoundland fishery. Nevertheless, it was an important factor in the development of northern and western Canada, particularly during the years of competition between the Hudson's Bay Company and the North West Company, and the profits of the trade helped make Montreal the centre of Canadian business until well into the twentieth century. Perhaps not least, the company remains, albeit much changed, an enduring monument to the joint stock corporation.[4]

NETWORKS AND COMMUNITIES

'The mercantile firm depended on credit', Douglas McCalla, a leading historian of nineteenth-century Canadian business, has pointed out:

> Because trust was central to the granting of credit, easiest and earliest access to it in expansionary times and preferential treatment in contractions went to those on whom the creditor considered he could rely most fully, that is, to people whose characters he knew and to those personally recommended or guaranteed by those he knew and trusted. Thus the commercial world was structured not only in competitive yet mutually supportive business communities of individual cities, but also, in some respects more importantly, along international chains of personal connections.[5]

In British North America, the business environment was shaped by the interaction of merchants clustered in scattered communities from the Atlantic coast to the Great Lakes with the networks they maintained to metropolitan centres in Britain and, to a lesser extent, the United States.

London was, of course, a central entrepôt in the Atlantic world for the movement of capital and technology, as well as goods. But for Canada, fishing ports such as Bristol also had been significant, and in the latter part of the eighteenth century a vigorous new centre, Glasgow in Scotland, emerged as a source of capital, trading opportunities, and, not least, an influx of entrepreneurs who left an enduring imprint on Canadian business development. Until the early 1700s Scotland had been an economic backwater, but by the middle of the century improvements in education as well as in the physical infrastructure of its ports had transformed it into a commercial powerhouse with a nascent industrial base in textiles and iron goods as well as shipbuilding. At the same time the 'clearances' of the Highlands promoted large-scale sheep herding, which tied in directly with the textile industry and generated a massive population movement off the land into factories or overseas. Among those who departed were Donald Smith, who went to Canada, and Andrew Carnegie, who made his way to the United States, where he later became that country's largest steelmaker.

The Scottish immigration included aspiring merchants as well as poverty-stricken crofters. Traders from Scotland made their way into the North Atlantic fisheries and the West Indies and focused particularly on establishing a foothold in the Virginia tobacco trade until the American Revolution cut off their access. At this point the lure of the fur trade led Scottish merchants to Montreal, where they soon outpaced the American traders who had migrated there after the fall of New France. Scots like McTavish, McGill, and William MacGillvray played a major role in the formation of the North West Company, but they and their fellow-countrymen also invested in a range of commercial and financial undertakings, including shipbuilding, flour milling, sugar refining, gas lighting, insurance, and banking as well as general wholesale trade. As the hinterland for Montreal expanded, the Scots extended their networks westward: Robert Hamilton, for example, after serving his apprenticeship with a fur company, was set up in business as a 'forwarding merchant' in distant Queenston in the Niagara region of Upper Canada by Isaac Todd and James McGill, two of Montreal's wealthiest merchants. By the early 1800s Hamilton was handling most of the local merchandise trade in the Niagara Peninsula, while his partner, Richard Cartwright, a Loyalist émigré from New York, played a similar role in Kingston, with Todd and McGill as their main suppliers and creditors.

In this same period Scottish merchants were setting themselves up in Halifax as suppliers to the naval forces stationed there, as well as outfitting fishing fleets and handling much of the carrying trade with the West Indies and Britain. In New Brunswick, Scottish merchants had installed themselves in Saint John by the 1780s on the eve of the dramatic growth in demand for square timber for shipping. With capital from their family bases in Glasgow, Allen Gilmour, Robert Rankin, and others set up large lumber mills in the Miramichi region in the early 1800s, expanding into northeastern Quebec and diversifying into shipbuilding by the 1820s: between 1815 and 1860 the Maritimes accounted for 20 per cent of all ship tonnage produced for Britain.

Scottish merchants were successful in part because they were entrepreneurial and energetic, but also because of the widespread networks they created and sustained, forming partnerships, employing each others' family members, pooling resources, drawing capital from Glasgow, and, not least, leveraging economic power into political influence. William Forsyth, for example, who was a major figure in the Glasgow-based 'Halifax circle' from the 1780s, built up a carrying trade with West Indian ports based on his contacts with local Scottish agents of merchants he knew and dealt with in Glasgow. When he contemplated moving into the timber trade, Forsyth befriended John

Wentworth, the 'surveyor general of the King's woods' who later became lieutenant-governor of Nova Scotia, and who ensured that Forsyth received a steady flow of contracts for naval supplies. This, in turn, enabled him to set up a long-term arrangement with William Davidson, a New Brunswick lumber merchant (and fellow Scot) who built 600-ton ships for Forsyth's West Indies fleet as well. Unfortunately for Forsyth, Wentworth was ousted in 1808 and the merchant returned to Scotland a few years later. But his career demonstrated the benefits that accrued from being part of the Glasgow network. It is not surprising that in later years Samuel Cunard (see box, p. 10), who was not Scottish, would look to Glasgow when he set out to expand beyond the confines of the Maritimes.[6]

The years from 1775 to 1815 comprised an era of persistent if not continuous warfare in North America and Europe: the American Revolution from 1775 to 1783; the wars of the French Revolution and Napoleonic period beginning in 1782; and the war with the Americans from 1812 to 1815. These struggles produced disruptions for merchants, from periodic invasions to the constant predations on commerce by the warring powers. At the same time, war created opportunities for merchants to provide supplies to military forces and even engage in smuggling and privateering on the side.

After 1815, however, came decades of peace that for Canada continued with only minor outbreaks for an entire century. In these circumstances, business communities took a more stable form. While not abandoning their overseas networks, merchants tied their futures to their own locales, and some merchants began to specialize in particular areas such as banking, insurance, and manufacturing. Nevertheless, peace was not without its hazards. The Maritimes experienced a difficult period of adjustment from wartime conditions in the 1820s; the central Canadian provinces confronted social and ethnic tensions that boiled over in the 1837 Rebellions. Technological changes, particularly in transportation and

industry, presented opportunities for the enterprising but threatened rapid obsolescence for those who failed to adapt. Looming over all of British North America was the explosive growth of the American economy to the south at a time when Britain, preoccupied with its own industrial development, seemed indifferent to the fate of its colonies. Faced with these conditions, political and business leaders began to look for ways to promote their own economic growth, increasingly through linkages across the continent.

In the years after Confederation, as their economy stagnated, Maritimers were inclined to view the early and middle decades of the nineteenth century as a 'golden age' when their trading ships plied the seas from the Caribbean to China and local shipbuilding thrived. More recent economic historians have painted a somewhat more subdued picture: except for the boom in the timber trade, the actual pace of growth was not much higher in the early 1800s than later in the century, and the limited resource base inhibited population growth and industrial development. The timber trade stimulated shipbuilding in New Brunswick, enriching investors in Nova Scotia as well, but it has been characterized as an 'enclave industry' with relatively few spinoffs into other areas of manufacturing, and went into a steep decline after the 1870s with the coming of steel ships. The other major export of the Maritimes in the mid-1800s was coal from Nova Scotia; in this case, however, the industry was largely dominated by a British-controlled firm, the General Mining Association, until 1857, and although it built an iron foundry, there was little development of this industry until the 1880s.

For the merchant elite in Halifax one of the major changes after 1815, aside from the loss of lucrative wartime contracts, was a significant shift in the carrying trade. During the 1830s, largely as a result of the abolition of slavery, the sugar plantation economy of the West Indies, which Maritime traders had provisioned in exchange for sugar and rum, went into a sharp decline. Although there was a shift in exports to other

SAMUEL CUNARD, 1787–1865

For most of his life, Samuel Cunard was a typical, although very successful, general merchant in the small colonial city of Halifax, Nova Scotia. Then, at age 52, he plunged into a new career, building and running steamships across the Atlantic from Britain to the US east coast. Within seven years the Cunard Line was the dominant transatlantic transportation company, a position it retained for decades; and today, the Cunard name remains, operating the *Queen Elizabeth II* and *Queen Mary II* cruise vessels. Samuel Cunard's career exemplified the capabilities that merchants in Maritime Canada had developed by the nineteenth century from their experience operating in the high-risk environment of the North Atlantic trade.

Samuel Cunard's parents were Loyalists who left the US (under some duress) at the end of the American Revolution. His father, Abraham Cunard, worked as a carpenter for the British military in Halifax, meanwhile acquiring property, including wharves that his sons were able to use when they embarked on careers as traders in timber and supplies for the British Navy. Although the company set up in 1812 was named A. Cunard & Co., Samuel, who was born in 1787, was soon to be the leading figure. The company was involved in the West Indian trade, and as timber demand increased, Sam's brother, Joseph, went into developing lumber mills in the Miramichi region in New Brunswick in the 1820s. Samuel acquired a stranglehold on the market for imported tea from the East India Company for the Maritimes and Newfoundland. In 1826, he proposed to take on mining of coal in Cape

The Cunard fleet in its heyday in the 1940s. The Cunard Line still operates luxury ocean cruisers, including the *Queen Elizabeth II*, the *Queen Mary II*, and the *Queen Victoria*.
(www. lategreatliners.com/uk_cunard_postwar.htm)

Breton, but this move was blocked by British interests who subsequently established the General Mining Association that monopolized this operation. Nonetheless, Cunard's influence was strong enough to persuade the British group to offer him the position of agent for the GMA, and he helped them surmount financial problems during an economic downturn in 1837 while bailing out his brother's troubled timber operations in New Brunswick. Meanwhile, he accumulated large landholdings in Prince Edward Island, which later made him a political target as a non-resident proprietor charged with creating 'Ireland on a small scale' there.

By this time Samuel Cunard exercised political as well as economic power in Nova Scotia, serving for a time on the executive council of the lieutenant-governor of the colony; but he believed that the changes in trade arrangements with the West Indies and the decline of the timber trade would seriously hamper opportunities for further growth—his own and that of his country. One of his early investments had been in a vessel commissioned to carry mail between Halifax and Boston, which provided a regular source of revenue to his company, and in the early 1830s he was involved in what turned out to be a premature venture to establish steamboat service between Halifax and Quebec. Despite the disappointment of this latter enterprise, Cunard retained an interest in the development of steam-powered vessels, and in 1839, when he learned that the British government was contemplating establishing a steamship line for transatlantic mail service, he set off to acquire the contract for it.

At that time the dominant steamship operator in Britain was the Great Western, whose ships had been designed by the prominent engineer, Isambard Brunel. Cunard's opportunity arose when the Great Western in effect rejected the demands of the British Admiralty that the service be set up within six months. Using contacts he had acquired through running mail services in North America, Cunard came up with an alternative proposal that would not only meet the Admiralty's timeline but promised to provide weekly rather than monthly services. With the contract in hand, Cunard then made his way to Glasgow: although not a Scot, his connections with Scottish-born merchants in Halifax provided him entrée with the business community there. There he negotiated an agreement with Robert Napier and John Wood, who had designed fast steamships for the India trade.

As might be expected, Cunard's ambitious undertaking experienced growing pains. The cost of the ships Napier designed was higher than what Cunard had anticipated, requiring delicate renegotiations with the Admiralty and the taking on of some new partners in Glasgow. Predictably, unexpected mechanical and weather problems plagued the line in its first year of operations, requiring Cunard to suspend weekly service during winter months, and the Admiralty cut his subsidy, aggravating the company's financial woes. Nevertheless, within a few years the Cunard Line had acquired a reputation for reliability and safety, and by the mid-1840s it had staved off competitors for the transatlantic mail and established a foothold in passenger service that would become increasingly important as the tide of immigration from the British Isles to North America expanded over the next two decades.

As his business activities became increasingly tied to running the shipping service, Cunard's ties to Halifax diminished. By 1858, he had moved permanently to Britain where, in 1859, he was granted a baronetcy by Queen Victoria. He died six years later, in 1865. His heirs lived on estates in England and New York, and the Cunard Line stopped serving Halifax in 1877. But Cunard left a mark on both sides of the Atlantic as a Maritime entrepreneur who had made his way into the upper echelons of British and international business in the mid-nineteenth century.

Sources: Phyllis Blakeley, 'Sir Samuel Cunard', Dictionary of Canadian Biography Online, at: <www.biographi.ca>; Stephen Fox, *Transatlantic: Samuel Cunard, Isambard Brunel and the Great Atlantic Steamships* (New York, 2003), chs 2–5; Kay Grant, *Samuel Cunard: Pioneer of the Atlantic Steamship* (London, 1967).

parts of British North America, trade ties grew more significantly with the United States, and until Confederation the economic orientation of Nova Scotia in particular was towards New England. This situation gave the Maritime business leaders a very different perspective from their counterparts in Montreal and Upper Canada that would complicate the process of Confederation and affect Maritime attitudes about the benefits of being part of Canada.[7]

In *The Commercial Empire of the St. Lawrence*, a pioneering book on Canada's economic history, Donald Creighton maintained that Montreal's merchant aristocracy of this era generated a vision of a nation based on the St Lawrence River and the Great Lakes, linked through a canal system that would enable Montreal to dominate not just the lightly settled region of Upper Canada but also the burgeoning markets of the American Midwest. To accomplish this goal, they set out to construct a canal system that would bypass the St Lawrence rapids. In the end their aims were frustrated by lack of capital and the internal politics of Quebec—the completion of the St Lawrence canals was delayed until the 1840s—and the trade of the American interior fell to Montreal's great rival, New York City; but the concept of Canada designed along an east–west axis and extending to the Pacific would endure and give shape to the emerging Dominion.

Later historians have questioned the consistency with which the Montrealers pursued this vision or, indeed, whether it ever was likely to be achieved: New York completed the Erie Canal, which gave it direct access to the Midwest in the mid-1820s when Montreal's merchants were just beginning to look beyond the fur trade. Nevertheless, the strategy of western expansion was logical at that point: as the fur trade declined, the timber trade in the Ottawa region was taking off. Although enterprising Americans, such as Philemon Wright, had already set themselves up as lumber barons there, Montreal was the obvious port for transshipment to Britain—Wright himself built a timber slide at Chaudière Falls in 1820, which facilitated transportation of squared logs to Quebec.

But the pull of the growing American market was hard to resist. The career of Mossom Boyd, 'the Lumber King of the Trent' in Upper Canada, typified the experience of entrepreneurs in this region during the mid-nineteenth century. After emigrating from Ireland in the 1830s, Boyd acquired a sawmill at Bobcaygeon in the Kawartha Lakes region and began shipping squared timber for British shipping to Quebec via a series of canals and linked waterways along the Trent River system, emulating J.R. Booth, who used the Rideau Canal system to exploit the forests of the Ottawa Valley. By the 1850s, however, Boyd found a more promising market selling boards to the United States, where residential building based on 'balloon-frame' construction was booming. Canal and rail connections linked his sawmills to Lake Ontario, and the Erie Canal in New York carried his products to the eastern seaboard. Eventually Boyd set up an agency in Albany to handle his growing business there, effectively creating a vertically integrated cross-border enterprise that lasted through the end of the century.

By the 1840s wheat was also becoming a major staple export from Upper Canada. For a time, merchants in Montreal were able to dominate this trade as well, which offset the declining returns from Quebec agriculture, although they faced growing competition from the burgeoning towns of Kingston, Hamilton, and Toronto. The completion of the Welland Canal between Lake Erie and Lake Ontario in 1829 boosted the growth of direct trade between these Upper Canadian centres and the American Midwest—although the project's investors, led by a St Catharines merchant, William H. Merritt, incurred substantial debts in the process. The canal was ultimately taken over by the provincial government in 1841, a process that was to reappear throughout Canada's history.[8]

At this point the relatively stable conditions in which British North America had evolved over the previous quarter-century underwent dramatic changes. The first transformation involved a shift in British policies towards its North American colonies in terms of both political organization and, more critically for business interests, trade. The second development was the introduction of the new technology of rail transportation that would disrupt existing patterns of trade but also seemed to offer prospects of dramatic economic growth, albeit at what would prove to be extravagant costs. Both of these changes would propel the scattered regions towards closer ties and ultimately a more consolidated economic system, in which business interests would reap the benefits of tying their fortunes to the new nation of Canada.

TIES THAT BIND

Beginning in the 1650s, the English government enacted a series of laws regulating trade with other countries and with its own colonies. The Navigation Acts required that all goods brought to English ports must be carried on English ships, and the Staple Act extended this provision to the colonies. Other laws imposed high duties on imports where they were not excluded altogether, and introduced incentives to encourage domestic manufacturing of previously imported goods, at the same time banning or discouraging manufactures in the colonies. England was not alone in developing these regulations: France, the Netherlands, Spain, and Portugal, among the major trading nations of Europe, had similar measures in place by the middle of the eighteenth century.

For the most part these Acts were introduced on a piecemeal basis to respond to particular concerns,

but economic historians have tended to lump them together under the rubric 'mercantilism', as the prevailing way of thinking in Europe about trade issues. Underlying these policies were some basic beliefs: the purpose of economic activity, particularly in trade, was to generate wealth that would strengthen the military and political power of the sovereign. Since the world's sum total of wealth was assumed to be fixed, one nation's gain would occur at the expense of the others—hence the emphasis on boosting exports and reducing imports to a minimum. To that end, colonies could help the mother country by providing items for re-export, of which sugar was particularly preferred, followed (at quite a distance) by furs and fish.

An early critic of this approach to trade was Adam Smith (a Scotsman), whose *Inquiry into the Nature and Causes of the Wealth of Nations* was published in 1776, the same year (as Americans fondly note) that the United States declared independence from Britain. Smith questioned most of the assumptions underlying mercantilist doctrines, arguing that wealth of a nation was based on the standard of living of its citizens, which in turn was most efficiently served through the natural operations of the marketplace, untrammelled by government intervention. Although he was subsequently lauded (or excoriated) as the 'father of capitalism', Smith's main target was the panoply of trade regulations: he advocated the elimination of all restrictions, enabling each country to make and trade what it could best produce through specialization and economies of scale.

For many years Smith could be dismissed as a prophet ahead of his time, for during the period of virtually endless wars from 1793 to 1815 there was even more government intervention into trade, including restrictions on imports of foreign timber and food, together with measures to encourage their production at home and in the colonies. Many of these measures persisted long past the end of the Napoleonic Wars, kept in place by strong lobbies maintained by their beneficiaries. The colonies of British North America were among these beneficiaries: the Navigation

Acts gave Maritime merchants preferential access to the British West Indies, particularly after the American Revolution removed (at least legally) their New England rivals from the scene. The bounties on timber from the colonies undergirded expansion of production in New Brunswick and the Canadas. The Corn Laws, which restricted access of foreign wheat and flour to the British market, benefited the grain farmers of Upper Canada and the Montreal merchants who processed and exported their products.

By the 1840s support for the Corn Laws and, indeed, for virtually all of the mercantilist system was waning in Britain. Textile and iron manufacturers wanted to open foreign markets to their exports, and to see the costs of food and other basic needs at home reduced. The value of colonies (except possibly India) was questioned, in economic and political terms. The government of Sir Robert Peel in Britain used the crisis of famine in Ireland as an opportunity to repeal the Corn Laws in 1846. The timber bounties and restrictions disappeared shortly thereafter, as did the Navigation Acts.

These developments pitched the colonies of British North America into a period of upheaval. The province of Canada, only recently united, was badly divided. Merchants in Montreal, who not only saw the value of their timber trade dwindle but also the prospective loss of investments in flour mills, agitated for a time for annexation to the United States, an ironic about-face for a group who had until then regarded the Americans as rivals. They were joined in this quest by the lumber barons of New Brunswick. In the former Upper Canada the impact was not as great, since produce could now be shipped directly into the US for export rather than through the circuitous (and sometimes icebound) St Lawrence route, a practice that was encouraged by the American government. Although the Maritimers lost their advantageous position in the British and Caribbean trade, the change boosted a trend towards trading with the United States, and their views of the future, too, were mixed.

The British government eventually exhibited greater sensitivity towards colonial concerns (particularly after a Montreal mob, allegedly led by prominent merchants, burned down the colony's Houses of Parliament in 1849). The new Governor General of Canada, Lord Elgin, encouraged the creation of a customs union across British North America, but this initiative got nowhere; indeed, up through the present the country is characterized by interprovincial trade barriers, even in the era of international free trade agreements. Failing that, Lord Elgin negotiated a Reciprocity Agreement with a less-than-enthusiastic United States government. The treaty, signed in 1854, provided for reciprocal free entry of many natural products in both directions, which was particularly beneficial to Canadian farmers and processors. On the other hand, it gave Americans access to the east coast fisheries, a source of grievance to Maritimers, who considered (not for the last time) that their interests had been sacrificed on behalf of central Canadians.[9]

By most historical accounts the Reciprocity Treaty worked well, at least until the end of the American Civil War, and contemporaries certainly shared this view. A downturn in the US economy in the late 1850s affected trade relations, but demand for Canadian supplies picked up during the war, although political relations soured over allegations that Canada tacitly supported the Confederacy. At the same time, the economic ups and downs in British North America were affected by a long-delayed boom in railway construction. The first steam-driven railway had begun operations in Britain in 1825, and this new form of transportation spread to the US only a few years later. But the capital costs of both rails and rolling stock were beyond the capacity of most investors in British North America: a short line was opened in 1836 between the St John River and La Prairie, across the St Lawrence River from Montreal, but for many years thereafter railways appeared only in the prospectuses of promoters. Merchants were reluctant to tie up capital for the long term required for construction, and in the uncertain economic environment of the 1840s there were few foreign investors.

In these circumstances the government became the lender (or subsidizer) of first resort for railway promoters. In 1849 the United Canadas introduced a Guarantee Act under which the province would cover the interest costs of new railways, which inaugurated a building spree that culminated with the construction of the Grand Trunk Railway, completed in 1859, that linked up many shorter local lines to create a route from Montreal to Sarnia on Lake Huron, while its competitor, the Great Western, ran from the US border at Buffalo to Windsor, opposite Detroit. The Grand Trunk also linked up in the east with a line that ran to Portland, Maine, providing the Maritimes with access of a sort to central Canada. Much of the capital for these projects initially came from American investors, and the engineering and construction work, too, was carried out by American managers, a precursor of the development of the Canadian Pacific Railway two decades later.

The railway boom of the late 1850s had some valuable spinoffs: it promoted industrial development as railways needed rail supplies, machine shops, and repair facilities. In the 1860s the Grand Trunk built large repair shops near Montreal, and the Molson family diversified from brewing beer into building locomotives in Kingston. Casimir Gzowski, who was the chief designer of the Grand Trunk system, was a partner in the Toronto Rolling Mills in 1860; George Stephen, a Montreal merchant who had diversified into textile manufacturing, invested in the Montreal Rolling Mills and the Canadian Locomotive & Engine Company in Kingston. These were not particularly impressive establishments in comparison with the British and American factories, but they represented the beginnings of an industrial system.

By the mid-1860s, however, for the public and the government, the railways, greeted initially as harbingers of a new era of prosperity and progress, were increasingly seen as burdens on the citizenry, run by sharp operators who bribed politicians, manipulated contracts, and fleeced

investors. Certainly, governments at various levels were obliged to absorb the costs of underwriting these ventures: 45 municipalities in the Canadas, including Hamilton and Toronto, effectively defaulted on debts incurred to help finance railways, and the province had to absorb them, in addition to covering costs under the Guarantee Act. Its debt levels more than doubled during the railway boom, with the Grand Trunk accounting for 50 per cent of these obligations. In 1864 half of the province's revenues had to go towards servicing this debt.[10]

As the euphoria over railways subsided, trade issues again came to the fore. Trade with the United States had increased during the Civil War, offsetting to some extent the effects of the end of the railway boom; but the Republican government that had come to power in Washington, and crushed the rebellion, was dominated by industrialists who now set out to impose protectionist tariffs. These were chiefly directed against Britain but inevitably affected Canada, despite the fact that its northern neighbour was primarily an exporter of natural products. In 1866 the US government cancelled the Reciprocity Treaty and businesses in British North America once again faced the difficult choices posed in the 1840s.

Discussions about Confederation had begun before the abrogation of Reciprocity Treaty, but that event probably had an impact on the movement towards a federal state that would become Canada. The issue of railways was also a factor, although it was not a prominent feature in the debates. For many years the Maritimers had clamoured for an Intercolonial Railway that would link them to Montreal, but the capital requirements were beyond the reach of local investors or the provincial governments; the end of reciprocity with the US, however, renewed these demands. For politicians in the Canadas, Confederation could lead to a restructuring of debts that would help alleviate the burden of financing the Grand Trunk, and also open the way for new projects, particularly if the new entity could be enlarged to embrace the territories extending to British Columbia. While some historians have seen business leaders as playing a decisive role in Confederation, Bliss argues that 'the man in the merchant's counting-house or the bank cashier's cage had little reason to be enthusiastic about politicians' and promoters' schemes for grandiose, expensive projects.'[11] Certainly, the wide-ranging promises that were made to entice the outlying provinces to join Confederation—the Intercolonial line to the Maritimes and (later) a transcontinental railway to the Pacific—represented a potential bonanza for railway contractors and their backers.

The first government of the new nation, under the Conservative leader John A. Macdonald, set about carrying out these promises. The North-Western Territory and Rupert's Land were purchased from the Hudson's Bay Company in 1870. Meanwhile, in Montreal, Hugh Allan, who like Samuel Cunard had developed a transatlantic steamship line, assembled a syndicate that included several Americans involved in a US transcontinental line, the Northern Pacific Railroad. These plans unravelled, however, in 1873 when it was revealed in Parliament that Allan had contributed funds, at Macdonald's solicitation, in support of the Conservatives in the previous election, presumably in return for the transcontinental railway contract. In the wake of the 'Pacific Scandal', Macdonald resigned as Prime Minister and the opposition Liberals came to power. Although the Liberals under Alexander Mackenzie were also supportive of a Pacific railway, little progress was made for the rest of the decade. Construction of the Intercolonial Railway was also plagued with delays and cost overruns until Sandford Fleming, who had designed the route, took charge of the project and completed it in 1876, a railway that was wholly funded by the government.

The 1870s proved to be a hard decade. After many years of economic growth in the industrial economies of Europe and North America, a downturn in 1873 ushered in an equally long era of stagnation. In Canada, as elsewhere, there was much debate over solutions to this quandary. Both Macdonald and later the Liberals had trekked to Washington to try to persuade the US government to restore reciprocity, but to no avail. In this context, Macdonald staged a political comeback in 1878, offering a 'National Policy' for Canada that would include protective tariffs to help foster industrial growth combined with a renewed effort to complete the Pacific railway, which in turn would promote population growth by attracting settlers to the Canadian prairies.

The advent of the National Policy has engendered several debates among historians. Was it a coherent program of interlinked policies, an early form of government planning for the economy? Economic historians in the mid-twentieth century were inclined to see it in this fashion, and projects such as the National Energy Program of the Trudeau era were sometimes characterized as a new 'National Policy' for Canada. Michael Bliss has argued that a main aim of the National Policy was to attract US investment into Canada rather than promote homegrown industry. Others have noted that Macdonald was something of a latecomer to embracing protective tariffs, and speculated that he still hoped to restore reciprocity with the US, using the threat of higher tariffs for leverage.

Were Canadian manufacturers in danger of being swamped by larger American competitors? The hard times of the 1870s lent credence to these fears. But economic historians Kris Inwood and Ian Keay have argued that while Canadian manufacturers were smaller and more localized than American firms, they were reasonably competitive within their own markets. But, like their American counterparts, they recognized the potential benefits of protectionism and organized to lobby for high tariffs. In 1859 Alexander Galt, the finance minister of the government of the United Canadas, introduced a measure that significantly raised duties on some manufactured goods not covered under the Reciprocity Treaty. Although Galt was motivated in part by the need to raise public revenues to offset the growing costs of railway construction, he was also under pressure from prominent protectionists such as Hamilton's Isaac Buchanan. The 'Galt Tariff' was effectively used by American critics of reciprocity (and American manufacturers) in making their case to cancel the agreement.

In the mid-1870s Montreal industrialists joined forces with Maritime coal and iron interests in pressing for tougher measures. The Conservatives leaped on the bandwagon when it became clear that the Liberal government in power was not responding to the pressure. Once in power, the Conservatives used tariff legislation to reward industrial groups that had supported them, such as the textile makers, while ignoring the entreaties of those who, like the lumber barons, had failed to shift their political loyalties in a timely fashion.[12]

Although much anti-American rhetoric surrounded the introduction of the National Policy tariffs, foreign, including American, capital was also welcomed in the development of that other great national project, the Pacific railway. In 1880, the Macdonald government negotiated a contract with a syndicate headed by George Stephen, president of the Bank of Montreal, who had significant holdings in the railway and iron industries. Behind the scenes was Stephen's cousin, Donald Smith, who would succeed him as president of the bank. Stephen's other associates in this group were two former Canadians now in business in the US: Norman Kittson, who had set up the Pembina trading centre in Minnesota that challenged the Hudson's Bay Company in the Red River area in the 1860s; and James J. Hill, an ambitious railway promoter. The partners had previously acquired a near-bankrupt line, the St Paul & Pacific Railroad in Minnesota, and resuscitated it. Hill in particular had his eye on extending this line north to the Red River and linking it with the proposed Canadian transcontinental railway. At Hill's suggestion, William Van Horne was brought up from Chicago to supervise construction.

In addition to the physical challenges Van Horne faced in pushing construction through the Canadian Shield and the Rockies, the syndicate confronted financial difficulties and sometimes less than reliable support in Ottawa. The Grand Trunk Railway was a consistent opponent of the Canadian Pacific group, and exerted influence both politically and financially. Bond sales boomed at first, stimulated by speculators in the prospective development of the land granted to the railway, but by 1883 this market was exhausted, and the syndicate's members were drawing heavily on their own assets to support the project; Hill and several other prominent backers withdrew. The government, under criticism for the generosity of the original contract, was reluctant to extend further assistance, although several emergency short-term loans were eventually approved. Providentially (for the railway), the Northwest Rebellion broke out in the spring of 1885, and Van Horne was able to use the existing trackage to transport troops to the Saskatchewan frontier to suppress it—he later suggested building a monument to Louis Riel for salvaging the Pacific railway. A new bond issue was authorized and a five-year moratorium on debt repayment was approved in June 1885. The ceremony at Craigellachie took place five months later.

Canada in 1885 was a nation in transition. The basic structure of Confederation was in place, but the territories north and west of Manitoba to British Columbia remained largely unsettled and unorganized. The Canadian population of 4.5 million was mostly clustered along the coasts and river valleys of the interior. The country's business system, however, was surprisingly well developed and sophisticated. Capital was scarce, and ambitious projects like railways depended on access to foreign sources, but the merchant communities of the Maritimes and central Canada had erected a complex network of financial institutions to facilitate the country's commercial activities. The staples trade, particularly in lumber and wheat, was still critical to the health of the economy, but there was a wide range of industrial activity: flour milling, furniture making, breweries and distilleries, sugar refining, shoemaking, kerosene refining, and farm machinery production, to mention the largest fields of endeavour. Although the iron and steel industry was only beginning to develop, in part in response to railway construction, textile manufacturing—the other gauge in the nineteenth century of industrialization—was well ensconced in the Montreal area and the National Policy was already spawning new and ambitious (sometimes overly ambitious) factories elsewhere. Canada's business enterprises were small in comparison to those found in the United States or Germany, but the country's business elite had a familiarity with the intricacies of international trade and finance that would stand them in good stead over the next four decades when the Canadian economy entered an era of sustained growth, accompanied by some wrenching social and economic changes.

PART I

THE AGE OF
BUSINESS CONSOLIDATION
1885-1930

CHAPTER 2

Commanding Heights

In the late nineteenth century the investment banker emerged as the virtual embodiment of capitalism. In the editorial caricatures of the new mass-market newspapers, he appeared as the 'bloated plutocrat' replete with pinstripe trousers, black coat, diamond stickpin, and top hat. In the works of radical social critics, 'finance capitalism' represented an advanced form of concentrated economic and political power: from their position on the 'commanding heights' of the economy, investment bankers consolidated industrial monopolies and maintained their control through interlocked directorates of commercial banks, manufacturing firms, and the older merchant houses.

From the 1880s through World War I the great finance capitalists of the era—J.P. Morgan in the US, the Rothschilds in England and Europe, Hikojiro Nakamigawa in Japan—were the most visible elements in a complex process of industrial growth and business consolidation. The networks of rail and wire erected in the late nineteenth century presented opportunities for commercial and industrial entrepreneurs to exploit national and industrial markets. The development of new technologies in chemical, electrical, and metallurgical processing enhanced the capabilities of manufacturers to expand production while reducing unit costs, achieving economies of scale. But the expansion of marketing and manufacturing required substantial capital investment. In the early nineteenth century the relatively modest capital needs of manufacturers came from savings of individual entrepreneurs or partnerships, augmented by short-term commercial loans and reinvestment of savings. These sources were insufficient to cover the heavy initial costs of large-scale manufacturing and distribution. To meet these needs a wider capital market had to be tapped, and new financial institutions emerged to mobilize money on the scale required.

The mechanisms for mobilizing large-scale capital varied widely across the industrializing world. In Germany and Japan, national governments encouraged big commercial banks to move directly into financing long-term investment in railways, manufacturing, and export trade ventures and often to exercise proprietary control over these enterprises. In the US, where commercial banking had become more decentralized since the 1830s, a different, more informal pattern emerged. After the American Civil War, a small number of investment houses appeared. They were often linked to but functionally separate from commercial banks, and located for the most part in eastern seaboard cities where they could tap foreign, principally British, money markets. These investment houses, such as Jay Cooke's in Philadelphia and Morgan's in New

York, would underwrite entire issues of stocks and bonds for railways—and after the 1890s, industrial enterprises—reselling the securities to investors in New York and London. Unlike the German or Japanese banks, however, these investment houses acted primarily as middlemen rather than exercising direct control over the companies they financed.

In Britain a more complex system of capital financing had developed by the late nineteenth century. In contrast to the US, where banking across state lines was legally banned and small local banks proliferated, commercial banks in Britain established branches throughout the country, and by the end of the 1880s a few large institutions dominated the scene. British entrepreneurs used these banks for a variety of services. These banks generally did not engage in long-term investment or underwrite security issues; but British businesses could go into the stock and bond markets for these needs, tapping the savings resources of the wealthiest nation of the age. A variety of financial agents, stock and bond brokers, and portfolio managers facilitated securities issues, which were marketed to assorted savings institutions, investor syndicates, and wealthy individuals. The availability of capital for investment and the large number and variety of investors enabled British firms to expand without significantly altering the prevailing pattern of small and medium-sized industrial enterprises well into the twentieth century. At the same time, the size of the London money markets attracted capital seekers not only from the United States but also from Canada and other Dominions of the British Empire.[1]

FINANCE CAPITALISM IN CANADA

The Canadian financial community developed mechanisms for capital mobilization that represented a unique configuration of institutional arrangements, influenced by the patterns of the metropolitan centres of the Atlantic economic community, but also reflecting its colonial heritage and the particular needs of an under-populated, resource-rich economy. Completion of the Intercolonial Railway linking the Maritimes and central Canada in 1876 and of the Canadian Pacific Railway in 1885 offered the prospect of a national market to aspiring entrepreneurs, and the National Policy tariffs promised protection to domestic manufacturers. By the mid-1890s, the potential resources of the western and northern interior regions were becoming visible to Canadian and foreign observers.

It is important to keep a sense of perspective about the pace and scale of Canadian capital development. Even in the early 1900s, most capital formation was carried out by individuals through reinvestment of earnings or by small-scale partnerships. Although growing, Canadian urban centres were small by international standards: in 1890 the combined population of 400,000 of the two largest cities, Montreal and Toronto, was less than half the size of Chicago in the United States and only slightly larger than Dusseldorf, a medium-sized German industrial city. Most business enterprises in the country were small proprietary firms operating in local markets, and the emergence of large consolidations in some industries over the next two decades did not wholly transform this pattern.

The major holders of Canadian savings—approximately 60 per cent of the total in 1890—were the chartered commercial banks. Authorized by the Bank Act of 1871, these banks, like their British counterparts, were allowed to establish branches throughout the country, and the Act set substantial capital reserve requirements, thus restricting competition in the field. Business slumps in the late 1870s and early 1890s further reduced their numbers. Between 1890 and 1920 the number of chartered banks shrank from 41 to 18, while the survivors extended a network of more than 4,600 banks across Canada. Smaller proprietary banks serving local communities steadily gave way to the national joint-stock enterprises that could more readily ride the fluctuations in the business cycle. In the aftermath

Banks in the pre-Confederation era printed their own money. This is a one-dollar note issued in 1857 by the Molson Bank established by John and William Molson. The Molson Bank merged with the Bank of Montreal in 1925. (National Currency Collection, Currency Museum, Bank of Canada, Gord Carter)

of the Depression and World War II, the pressures towards amalgamation continued, leaving only the 'Big Five'—the Royal Bank of Canada, the Bank of Montreal, Canadian Imperial Bank of Commerce, Toronto-Dominion Bank, and the Bank of Nova Scotia—by the end of the century, albeit with a growing number of new domestic and foreign competitors.

The oldest of these institutions, and the largest until well into the twentieth century, was the Bank of Montreal, founded in 1817. In its early years the BMO faced significant competition not only from other local banks but also from British-owned entities such as the Bank of British North America. Under the leadership of two ambitious 'cashiers', Benjamin Holmes and Edwin King, who were the effective chief executives, the Bank of Montreal was able to install itself for a time as a de facto central bank, handling government Treasury deposits, managing financial flows from British investors in Canadian canals and railways, bailing out other banks in crisis situations, and playing a significant role in shaping banking legislation, including the critical element of branch banking. Two of the key figures in the financing of the Canadian Pacific Railway—George Stephen and Donald Smith—presided at various times over the BMO, reflecting its role in shaping the country's economy during the nineteenth century.

By the middle of the nineteenth century other challengers arose, reflecting in part regional business opposition to the dominant position of both Montreal and the BMO. In 1866 William McMaster led a group of Toronto merchants in setting up the Canadian Bank of Commerce with branches throughout Ontario, expanding into British Columbia and the Maritimes in the early 1900s. The Atlantic region also sired several of what were to become the nation's largest banks. The Bank of Nova Scotia, established in 1832, set out to exploit opportunities in the West in the years following completion of the CPR, setting up branches in Manitoba and nearby Minnesota, and subsequently moving aggressively overseas. Of later vintage was the Merchants' Bank of Halifax, which received a federal charter in 1869, restricting its activities primarily to the Maritimes for its first 25 years, but then, like the BNS, leaping into operations in British Columbia and the Caribbean, and relocating to Montreal, ambitiously rechristened the Royal Bank of Canada. By the latter part of the twentieth century the RBC laid claim to being Canada's largest bank.[2]

The chartered banks, reflecting their origins and the influence of the British commercial banks with which they did business, were principally oriented to serving the needs of merchants for short-term credit to finance inventories and shipping costs. As they advanced into the western farming communities, the banks extended credit on a seasonal basis to wheat growers, but only to cover operating costs. The banks' own charters barred them from lending on real estate, which would tie up capital on a long-term basis, thus keeping them out of the mortgage business.

In the late nineteenth century, savings and loan companies emerged to finance farms and residential construction, benefiting from the expansion of cities and filling a need that the commercial banks were unable to handle. By the 1890s almost 20 per cent of Canadian financial assets were held by mortgage loan companies. The banks responded to this challenge by moving into the savings deposit field, offering rates competitive with the mortgage companies, but well into the twentieth century they remained relatively minor participants in the residential construction market.

The mortgage and loan companies provided a source of longer-term credit than the commercial banks, but only in a specialized area. By the early 1900s another source of domestic finance capital was developing with a more liberal approach to the longer-term credit needs of the economy. Between 1870 and 1890 Canadian life insurance companies made inroads against foreign-owned firms in the domestic market, controlling over 60 per cent of the business by 1890 with assets of over $20 million. By 1900 assets had doubled, and by 1914 they had reached $120 million. The earnings of this booming service industry initially moved into mortgage financing; but the life insurance companies also diversified into railways and other corporate securities, either directly or through loans to brokers and other securities underwriters. Tables 2.1 and 2.2 provide snapshots of the control of Canadian capital in 1901 and 1929, indicating that, although by 1929 the banks still were the major players in the financial field, other institutions had grown significantly and were among the leading asset-holding entities.

The life insurance companies eventually exhausted their market at home, which was initially directed primarily at the urban middle class. The whole field was something of a novelty in the mid-nineteenth century. Merchants were accustomed to purchasing marine insurance and local businesses provided an obvious market for insurers against fire and theft. During the 1840s and 1850s British and American companies had begun selling life insurance policies in Canada,

TABLE 2.1

DISTRIBUTION OF ASSETS, CANADIAN FINANCIAL INSTITUTIONS, 1901 AND 1929

Year	Banks (%)	Insurance (%)	Other* (%)
1901	75	6	19
1929	50	13	37

*Includes savings and loans, trust companies, etc.

TABLE 2.2

THE 10 LEADING FINANCIAL INSTITUTIONS RANKED BY ASSETS, 1901 AND 1929

1901	1929
1. Bank of Montreal	1. Royal Bank of Canada
2. Canadian Bank of Commerce	2. Bank of Montreal
3. Merchants Bank of Montreal	3. Canadian Bank of Commerce
4. Dominion Bank	4. Royal Trust Co.
5. Canada Life Insurance Co.	5. Public Utility Investment
6. Bank of Nova Scotia	6. Bank of Nova Scotia
7. Imperial Bank	7. National Trust Co.
8. Bank of Toronto	8. Toronto General Trust Co
9. Molson Bank	9. Canada Life Assurance Co.
10. Royal Bank of Canada	10. Dominion Bank

Source: Compiled from *Canadian Annual Financial Review* (Toronto, 1901, 1930).

appealing to Victorian sentiments about family responsibilities. By the 1870s Canadian companies like Sun Life of Montreal, Confederation Life, and Manufacturers Life had emerged (Manufacturers Life highlighted that the Prime Minister, Sir John A. Macdonald, was president of the company as evidence of its solid reliability). Once the domestic market was saturated, many of these companies sent sales agents abroad, relying on links with the Caribbean and East Asian markets that their merchant predecessors had initiated, becoming in the process, along with the banks, the earliest Canadian multinationals.[3]

Although mortgage companies, life insurance firms, and other smaller institutions such as trust companies—which at this time catered to a small but wealthy clientele—attracted an increasing proportion of Canadian savings, the chartered banks continued to command the bulk of the country's domestic capital resources through World War II. In *The History of Canadian Business, 1867–1914*, the political economist Tom Naylor advanced the argument that the dominant position of the chartered commercial banks in Canada, with their preference for short-term lending principally for merchants and staple exporters, stunted Canadian manufacturing by diverting depositors away from local private banks and loan companies that were more inclined to support fixed capital investment. The chartered banks were more likely to invest abroad, particularly in the United States and Britain, than in home-based industries. As a result, Canada's manufacturers remained small and inefficient, vulnerable to foreign competition without tariff protection and equally vulnerable to foreign takeovers that the National Policy encouraged.[4]

Naylor's arguments have been challenged by Canadian business historians as based on faulty premises and inadequate evidence. In developing his thesis, Naylor treated railway investment, in which large chartered banks such as the Bank of Montreal played a major role, as distinct from industrial investment—even though both types of activity required substantial amounts of fixed initial capital; and railways not only stimulated the manufacture of iron and steel, but also developed their own machine shops and factories to produce locomotives and rolling stock.

While commercial loans may have constituted the bulk of the business of chartered banks, as business activities became more diversified, so also did the portfolios of bank loans. An examination by James Frost of the policies of the Bank of Nova Scotia, for example, provides evidence on both sides of the controversy. Established in the 1830s, the BNS extended branches through the Maritimes in the late 1880s and by the early twentieth century had become a national institution with its head office in Toronto. Through the 1880s the BNS invested substantially in Maritime industries, but shifted its emphasis thereafter to investment outside the region, in Caribbean utilities and US real estate among other fields. Although the bank's directors appear to have become disenchanted over the prospects for industrial growth in the Atlantic Canada region during the depression of the 1890s, they continued to underwrite some manufacturing ventures there as late as 1910, particularly in the coal and steel industries.[5]

The lending and investment policies of particular financial institutions, however, provide a somewhat misleading picture of the structure of Canadian finance. While chartered banks, mortgage houses, and life insurance and trust companies functioned as separate organizations, they were interlinked by ownership ties into a few cohesive 'communities of interest' that initially formed in the various regional metropolitan centres in the 1880s and 1890s. The most important groups were in Montreal and Toronto; by the 1920s they had extended their financial tentacles throughout the country, eclipsing other aspirants in the Maritimes and western Canada.

Montreal was the site of the first such assemblage of finance capitalists, who retained a dominant position in the field through the 1930s. Under George Stephen and Donald Smith (Lord Strathcona), the Bank of Montreal played a central role in financing the CPR; the fruits of that venture helped underwrite expansion into a variety of industrial, commercial, and financial ventures. By the early 1900s the Bank of Montreal/CPR group held substantial investments in, and colonized the boards of (among others) Sun Life, the largest insurance company in Canada; Consolidated Mining and Smelting, a direct spinoff of the CPR; Ogilvie Flour Mills and Lake of the Woods Milling Co., which dominated that market and controlled networks of grain elevators across the prairies; Montreal Loan & Mortgage Co.; and numerous cotton mills, fire and marine insurance companies, trust companies, and ventures in emerging fields such as pulp and paper production.

In Toronto, the central figure of the turn-of-the-century financial community was George Cox.

Beginning his career in Peterborough, Ontario, where he became president of the Midland Railway and founded Central Canada Savings & Loan (while also serving as mayor), Cox moved to Toronto in 1888 where he presided over the Imperial Bank of Commerce and Canada Life Assurance, second only in their respective fields to the Bank of Montreal and Sun National Trust. Through links with enterprising railway and industrial entrepreneurs such as William Mackenzie and Joseph Flavelle, Cox and investors associated with him were also involved in meat-packing, hydroelectric power and urban tramways, iron and steel, cement manufacturing, and retail merchandising.

Although an element of rivalry existed between the established financial centre of Montreal and the growing industrial metropolis of Toronto—enlivened in the first decade of the twentieth century by railway competition between the CPR and the Canadian Northern Railway, which had financial ties with the Bank of Commerce—members of both groups joined forces from time to time in investment ventures. The relationship of Herbert Holt and William Mackenzie is instructive in this regard. Holt began his career as a subcontractor for the CPR, then consolidated electric utilities in Montreal, and eventually became president of the Royal Bank of Canada—which, like the Bank of Nova Scotia, had moved from its original base in the Maritimes, and during Holt's era (although not necessarily through his exclusive leadership) developed into the largest bank in the country, surpassing the Bank of Montreal by 1929. Although maintaining his ties with the CPR group and operating from a Montreal base, Holt also took an interest in Latin American utility ventures promoted by Mackenzie (another CPR veteran), who had joined Cox in Toronto, developing electric utilities in that city before moving on to direct Canadian Northern's challenge to the CPR in the West.

Montreal and Toronto were the major centres of high finance in Canada, but other regionally oriented groups congregated in some of the older commercial cities of the East. In Halifax, for example, John F. Stairs, scion of a long-established merchant family, sought to build a Maritime-based financial domain. An advocate of the National Policy, Stairs envisioned an industrial future for his region, based on its position on the transatlantic trade routes and its coal reserves, and energetically promoted ventures in sugar refining, textile production, and iron manufacturing. His ambitions were cut short by his sudden death in 1904. Even before that point, however, financial interests from Boston and Montreal had begun to move into the Maritimes, and the shifting locus of regional control was signalled by the departure of Stairs's protege, Max Aitken, to Montreal in 1907.

Another group remained outside the orbit of the metropolitan financial centres: French-Canadian banks in Quebec. Although initially dependent on anglophone capital, by the late nineteenth century these banks had large savings reserves from French Canadians, had established modest branch operations across the province and in French-speaking communities in the Maritimes and the West, and were dominated by francophone directors. They provided commercial loans to businesses in these communities and, through affiliated trust companies, invested in local industries, although out of necessity a greater part of their investment went into non-francophone Quebec firms. The larger chartered banks of Montreal did not seek to impinge on these activities, and anglophone shareholders in the 'French' banks were content to leave the French-Canadian managers to their own devices.

Although small and localized operations in comparison with the powerful institutions of Toronto and Montreal, the francophone banks were sufficiently important in the Quebec economy to induce the provincial government to support a merger in 1924 of the two largest entities, the Banque d'Hochelaga and the Banque Nationale, to protect the interests of francophone depositors and businesses dependent on their credit. The leading figures of the French-Canadian banking community in the early twentieth century, F.L. Beique and Joseph-Marcellin Wilson of the Banque d'Hochelaga, were tied in with the anglophone financial community of Montreal through Holt and Joseph Forget.

By the end of the first decade of the twentieth century the aspirations of financial groups outside central Canada were declining, with Montreal and Toronto bankers entrenched as the heart of finance capitalism in the country. Ensconced in awe-inspiring neo-classical bastions of marble and masonry along King Street in Toronto and Saint James Street in Montreal, a group of no more than 40 or 50 men—bankers, lawyers, and securities brokers—presided over a financial community with assets of over $1.6 billion.

The ties that bound this elite were essentially personal and social rather than institutional: links forged by shared experiences, values, and kinship. Common to more than half of them was a Scottish heritage: 25 per cent were immigrants, a larger proportion second- or third-generation Scots. The overwhelming majority were Anglican or Presbyterian, with a rising number of Methodists. Members of the same private clubs, their children attending a select circle of boarding or day schools, they encountered one another regularly at charitable events, weddings, graduations, funerals, and other social occasions as well as in the boardrooms of the numerous companies whose fortunes they commanded.

The financial elite of Canada at this time had evolved from small, close-knit merchant communities in an underdeveloped colonial society, isolated from one another and from their transatlantic political masters and trading partners for long periods of time due to poor communications and transportation, and thus they had been very much dependent on ties of kinship and mutual personal trust to survive. The telegraph, steamship, and railway were breaking down these barriers by the end of the nineteenth century, and the corporate structures this elite was erecting introduced an element of bureaucratic formality into business activities; but for the money men of Montreal and Toronto, many of them born a decade or more before Confederation, the older patterns of personal loyalty persisted.[6]

MONEY MARKETS AND MERGERS

Given the informal nature of their business relationships, personal contacts among Canada's financial elite played a major role in the processes of capital mobilization. In the absence of institutional arrangements such as investment banks, financiers formed private syndicates to underwrite large capital outlays, drawing on the assorted agglomerations of savings at their disposal. In exchange, the syndicates took large quantities of corporate bonds with some common stock thrown in as a bonus, to be sold later if and when the undertaking became profitable. The securities would then be marketed through specialized companies affiliated with the syndicates: in Toronto, for example, Cox relied on the brokerage house of A.E. Ames, which was presided over by his son-in-law, and Dominion Securities, run by another protege, E.R. Wood. The Bank of Montreal fielded securities through Louis J. Forget, one of the few French Canadians to successfully breach the anglophone financial bastions in Quebec, and several other brokerage houses. Both the Bank of Montreal and the rising Royal Bank worked closely in the great merger movement of 1909–13 with Max Aitken's two organizations, Royal Securities and Montreal Trust.

The immediate sites of activity were the stock exchanges in Montreal and Toronto. Both had emerged in the mid-1870s; as might be expected, neither was particularly impressive in comparison with the metropolitan exchanges of New York and London, which absorbed the largest security issues, government and railway bonds. The Toronto exchange was located, until 1913, on the second floor of the Ames brokerage house, with Cox as its landlord. Nevertheless, the exchanges did benefit from the growth of the economy between 1900 and 1914 and the diversification of financial institutions. Trust, insurance, and loan companies provided call loans to brokers and investors, and even the chartered banks entered the market in a small way, although they preferred lending to investors in New York where the volume of businesses ensured greater liquidity in times of crisis as, for example, in the short but sharp market panic of 1907 and the slump engendered by the outbreak of war in Europe in 1914.

The Montreal and Toronto exchanges competed for business, probably to the detriment of both, although there was a certain amount of regional specialization. The Toronto exchange did a much larger volume of business in shares of non-banking financial companies and speculative mining ventures than Montreal, which had a virtual stranglehold on railway stocks traded in Canada. But Toronto mounted a strong challenge in the first decade of the twentieth century to Montreal's hitherto dominant position, acquiring over 50 per cent of shares in banks by the end of that period and competing vigorously in the growing field of hydroelectric utilities. Nevertheless, Montreal remained the leading securities market in Canada through World War I, particularly in the lucrative bond trade.[7]

But Canadian exchanges picked up only the odds and ends of the market. The big money was sent—or came from—elsewhere. The larger brokers like Ames traded heavily on the New York exchanges, and promoters of major underwriting ventures like James Dunn and Aitken headed for London. Virtually all federal and provincial government bonds were marketed outside Canada, and the large railways followed suit. In 1913 the bulk of CPR shares were held by British investors, with Canadian participation at about 13 per cent. The Grand Trunk remained an even more British undertaking, and Canadian Northern, the Canadian 'West's own product', was critically dependent on inflows of capital from London. The industrial mergers of 1909–13 were carried out by Canadian financial entrepreneurs using mostly British money. Of these, perhaps the most flamboyant was Max Aitken (see box, p. 30).

The pre-war merger movement, the dramatic expansion of government securities issues to finance Canadian participation in World War I, and rather exaggerated expectations about the growth prospects of the 'new staples'—newsprint

and metals—in the 1920s all contributed to the development of more specialized and diversified techniques of financial underwriting. By this time a number of companies were emerging that labelled themselves investment banks, such as Nesbitt Thomson and Wood Gundy. Their clients were increasingly found in Canada: the British investment market never fully recovered from the losses of World War I, and the Americans tended to focus on particular areas such as mining and petroleum and to use US brokers or to invest directly in Canadian firms, especially in manufacturing. Canadian brokers coaxed hitherto private family firms, such as Massey-Harris, to go public and spun off specialized investment companies that held large quantities of common stocks as well as bonds in a variety of industries.

A second merger boom, larger than the pre-war episode, took shape in 1925–9, generating 315 consolidations accumulating assets of nearly $1 billion, three times the size of earlier mergers. The economic collapse of 1929–32 destroyed many of these speculative endeavours and chastened the survivors; market activity stagnated through the Depression and World War II. But mutual funds made an appearance in the 1930s, representing a less risky opportunity for small investors; and trust companies became more significant on the financial scene, managing a growing body of public and private pension funds in the 1940s and 1950s. The investment community remained small, but the instruments of capital mobilization became more diverse, responding to both the growth of the Canadian economy and the broadening of the market for securities among middle-class investors.[8]

WEALTH AND POWER IN CANADA

How powerful were the finance capitalists in this era of dramatic economic development and industrial consolidation? To be sure, they had at their disposal vast reservoirs of money— 'other people's money', as their critics pointed out—and used their strategic position in the investment process

MAX AITKEN (LORD BEAVERBROOK), 1879–1964

'The little fellow with the big head'—this was how Bank of Montreal president Edward Clouston described Max Aitken following their first encounter in 1904. Clouston was probably referring to Aitken's physical characteristics, but to other contemporaries it would have been an apt description of the brash young promoter's massive ego. Restlessly ambitious, Aitken alternately intrigued and exasperated the financial leaders of Halifax, Montreal, and London in the first decade of the twentieth century. Yet his achievements matched his ambitions. In Britain, where he settled in 1910, Aitken became Lord Beaverbrook, one of that nation's leading press barons, held cabinet posts during both world wars, and left a $40 million estate at his death in 1964. In Canada, his legacy—besides a $12 million Beaverbrook Foundation supporting universities and museums—included major industrial consolidations and, more significantly, a host of innovative techniques for mobilizing large blocks of capital.

Born in 1879, son of a Scots Presbyterian minister, Aitken grew up in the isolated hinterland of New Brunswick where he formed early links of friendship with two other ambitious young men: James Dunn, who like Aitken would become a major figure in Canadian and British finance and ultimately salvaged Algoma Steel; and R.B. Bennett, later to become one of Canada's leading corporate lawyers and then Prime Minister of Canada. After several years of adolescent aimlessness, Aitken wound up in Halifax in 1902 where he began a career as a stock and bond salesman for John F. Stairs. His success in these endeavours—and his penchant for simultaneously doing business on his own account—induced Stairs and his associates to set up Royal Securities Co. under Aitken in 1903. Following Stairs's unexpected death a year later,

Max Aitken, 'the little fellow with the big head', in 1905. (McCord Museum 11-156536)

Aitken chafed under restraints placed on him by other investors in Royal Securities, and he sold out his interest in 1907 and moved to Montreal, where he bought Montreal Trust Co. In 1909 he sold Montreal Trust to the Royal Bank of Canada and resumed control of Royal Securities.

Up to 1909 Aitken's promotional activities had focused on electric utility ventures in Latin America and on consolidating industries in the Maritimes. Riding a tide of investor optimism as the economy recovered from the Panic of 1907, he turned his attention and skills to mergers in the industrial heartland of central Canada. During one frantic year, 1909–10, Aitken assembled a series of major consolidations, including

Canada Cement, Canadian Car & Foundry, Canadian Consolidated Rubber, and the Steel Co. of Canada (Stelco). A multi-millionaire at age 30, he then left Montreal, seeking greater worlds to conquer across the Atlantic. In Britain he became a press tycoon, hobnobbed with political leaders during both world wars, and was appointed Minister of Aircraft Production and later Minister of Supply for the British government by Winston Churchill during World War II. In 1917 he was knighted as Lord Beaverbrook (in those pre-Conrad Black days, Canadians could accept such titles without surrendering their Canadian citizenship).

'I created all the big trusts in Canada', Aitken later boasted to Churchill. This was a characteristically exaggerated claim, but he was a major figure in the transformation of the Canadian financial scene. When he began his promotional career, the market for Canadian securities was small, the instruments of capital mobilization limited, and even the most prominent bankers had little experience in underwriting the large flotations required to finance corporations that could operate on a national scale. During his apprenticeship in the Maritimes, Aitken developed sales techniques for luring small investors into the market; and along with Dunn and other financial entrepreneurs, he created a network of contacts in the larger and more varied London investment community. With a broader view of economic possibilities than any of his contemporaries, Aitken assessed both the market prospects and internal capabilities of the companies he assembled. Since he rewarded himself with large quantities of bonus stock from these mergers, his aim was to create logically coherent business structures that would dominate their markets, and his expectations were generally borne out.

Finally, Aitken both inspired and trained a new generation of financial investment specialists who refined, elaborated, and expanded on his techniques. Among the recruits to Royal Securities in its early years were C.H. Cahan, later a minister in the cabinet of Conservative Prime Minister R.B. Bennett; Arthur Nesbitt, who later established a major investment and brokerage house; Ward Pitfield, whose descendants included the founder of Pitfield McKay Ross, and one of Pierre Trudeau's closest government advisers. Aitken's chosen successor at Royal Securities, Izaak Walton Killam, assembled even larger (though less durable) mergers in the 1920s when he became known as the 'mystery man of high finance'. When Killam died, he left an estate four times the size of Aitken's, and a tax bill sufficient to help establish the Canada Council.

Sources: Christopher Armstrong and H.V. Nelles, *Southern Exposure* (Toronto, 1988), 107–47; G.P. Marchildon, *Profit and Power: Beaverbrook and the Gilded Age of Canadian Finance* (Toronto, 1996)

to increase their profits. From the proceeds of these investments they enriched themselves and their families, procured lucrative employment opportunities for their children, in-laws, and cronies, and erected tasteless late Victorian era palaces: Henry Pellatt's pseudo-Gothic castle in Toronto remains a classic example of this form of conspicuous consumption. But did they exercise real control over the multitude of companies whose boards they populated, and did they determine the long-term direction of the industrial economy?

Much of the recent scholarship on the role of investment bankers in other countries suggests that their domination of the corporate empires they assembled was transitory and incomplete. Most of the merger titans of the turn of the century, like the conglomerates of the 1960s or the corporate takeover artists of the 1980s, were interested primarily in short-term profits, not enduring responsibility for these enterprises. The few who sought to translate financial leverage into operational control of companies or whole industries, like Morgan in the United States, experienced mixed fortunes. Many of their corporate agglomerations collapsed under the weight of excessive debt; control of those that survived passed into the hands of professional managers, who could be periodically purged but represented a permanent feature of life in the upper echelons of twentieth-century capitalism. Finance capitalists thus represented a phase in the evolution of the corporate economy, playing a significant role in the mobilization of capital and creation of large-scale enterprises, but they were a group whose influence was ultimately hedged about by other contending forces in the industrial system: managers, government regulatory bodies, unions, and financial competitors with innovative techniques for tapping a larger and more diverse capital market.

Was this the case in Canada? Opinions differ, both on the question of the extent of influence of the finance capitalists over the economy and the durability of their power. Certainly, there has been an enduring popular conviction that Canadian business has been dominated by a close-knit elite whose seat of power shifted from Montreal to Toronto but otherwise remained intact. Western agrarians complained mightily about the political as well as economic influence wielded by the Montreal/CPR clique at the turn of the century. In the 1930s the Social Credit leader of Alberta, 'Bible Bill' Aberhart, inveighed against the 'fifty big shots' who ruled the country. Forty years later the journalist Peter C. Newman popularized the concept of a 'Canadian Establishment'—admittedly a somewhat broader group, encompassing bankers, lawyers, holding company titans, and a sprinkling of industrialists—perpetuating their domination through interlocked directorships, cultivating each new generation through their private schools and social networks. The corporate managers whose significance bulks large in contemporary portrayals of the American business system were dismissed as 'the frightened men in corner offices', constantly harried by the bottom-line demands of their investors.

In academic circles, the notion that an entrenched financial elite dominated Canadian business found a secure niche among political economists and sociologists who generally rejected the view that 'managerial capitalism' displaced the finance capitalists, or that wealth and political influence had become more widely distributed and competitive in the industrial world of the twentieth century. As noted earlier, Naylor traced the roots of this financial oligarchy back to Confederation, while others, such as Wallace Clement, explored the linkages between Canadian and American financial leaders who formed a 'continental corporate elite'.

This interpretation provided a certain intellectual respectability for widely shared popular opinions in Canada, but has encountered criticism from several directions. The Quebec sociologist Jorge Niosi challenged the assumption that the turn-of-the-century financiers established lasting domination over the corporate entities they sired or that the Canadian economy was dominated by a single cohesive elite. Although Niosi's 'ruling class' was small and concentrated in central Canada, it was never fully entrenched, as new groups emerged in the twentieth century—professional managers, Jewish and French-Canadian financial and industrial entrepreneurs, western Canadian oilmen—to undermine the power of the old Anglo-Scots establishment. Similarly, Canadian business historians have drawn a more complex picture. In *Northern Enterprise*, Michael Bliss dismissed the economic power of the finance capitalists and professional managers—and, for that matter, virtually all groups that were aspiring to control the Canadian market—as transitory at best. Assailed by public critics of big business and frustrated in their attempts to perpetuate family dynasties, many of the financial barons of the early twentieth century succumbed to the remorseless pressure of competition, changing markets, unforeseen or irresistible economic disasters, or their own misjudgements.[9]

Regardless whether they exercised substantial and enduring domination over the Canadian business scene, did the country's finance capitalists focus on certain sectors of the economy while neglecting others, particularly manufacturing? On this point, there is more agreement. As noted earlier, the large chartered banks preferred the short-term commercial loans over long-term fixed commitments of capital, although they provided an increasing volume of call-loan money to investors in the twentieth century. Canadian investors, in turn, preferred to channel their money into the securities of financial institutions and electrical utilities at home and abroad, particularly in the US and Latin America. British portfolio investment in Canada, much of which flowed through the hands of financial syndicates in Montreal and Toronto, tended to concentrate on government bond issues, railways, and the mining industry. During periods of investor optimism, as in 1909–13 and the late 1920s, some of this money went into industrial investment, particularly to finance mergers, but in general industrial securities (if railways and utilities are excluded from this definition) were embraced with less enthusiasm.

Canadian industrial ventures were not, however, starved for capital. A substantial amount of direct investment—establishment of Canadian affiliates by foreign firms—flowed into the country in this era. The asset value of this direct investment more than doubled between 1897 and 1913, by which time it represented almost one-third of the total value of publicly owned corporate stock in Canada. The largest volume of this investment came from the United States, totalling $254 million in 1910, of which 43 per cent was in manufacturing (including pulp and paper processing) and a large part of the balance in mining and smelting. From British sources came another $120 million in direct investment, almost 50 per cent of which was in manufacturing and mining.[10]

There were, then, distinctive patterns of investment and, consequently, of ownership in the various sectors of the Canadian economy apparent by World War I. Banks, financial institutions, and utilities were financed by Canadians through domestic and British sources, and these companies for the most part remained in Canadian hands. Industrial and mining ventures depended more heavily on foreign direct investment, and the extent of foreign ownership in these sectors was proportionately greater.

These distinctions were of little consequence to most contemporaries. Domestic or foreign capital, portfolio or direct investment, all of it was welcome to help finance Canadian economic growth in the early years of the twentieth century. In the 1970s and 1980s, as Canadians worried over the consequences of a branch-plant economy for their industrial competitiveness and national economic independence, the origins of these problems were traced back to this era and the indifference of Canada's financial elite towards industrial investment, a view advanced in particular by the political economists. But the argument rested on the assumption that these attitudes were unique to Canada's finance capitalists; this was not necessarily the case. In Britain, for example, many of the chartered banks and the largest private merchant banks, Baring Brothers and Rothschilds, were wary of industrial investment, preferring to finance commercial undertakings and back government bonds. In Japan, the banks that sprang from the established merchant houses like Mitsui were equally reluctant to finance industrial ventures. Even in the US, the big investment banks pursued security, not risk: railroad and industrial mergers were promoted when they seemed likely to dominate or monopolize markets; the small entrepreneur with a bright idea had to look elsewhere for initial capital. The common thread is that finance capitalists in general were cautious men, trusting only the judgement of their close associates, looking for a sure thing and skeptical of innovation.

The turn-of-the-century finance capitalists of Canada and other countries deserved much of the opprobrium heaped upon them by contemporaries and historians. They formed tight exclusive groups hostile to those not of their own social background. To enhance their personal wealth or power, they helped themselves freely to the savings of thousands placed in their trust. They formed investment syndicates that engaged in insider trading, deceptive marketing of securities, and other practices of questionable legality even in their own time. To augment their short-term profits, they saddled companies with burdens of long-term fixed debt that often drove these enterprises to ruin, leaving bankruptcies and unemployment in their wake. They rarely supported innovative entrepreneurship, and siphoned scarce capital resources to sectors of the economy that were already operating at excess capacity. At the same time, these financiers performed tasks of capital mobilization that were beyond the means of individual businesses and many governments; assembled an international network of institutions that could channel money from established commercial centres to promote development of remote hinterlands; and developed increasingly diverse techniques for financing large and complex corporate organizations that would populate the heartland of the industrial world through the late twentieth century.

CHAPTER 3

Networks of Progress

Two technologies—one old and one new—occupied much of the attention of financiers, political leaders, and the general public in Canada in the early twentieth century. By that time railways had become associated with big business, economic progress, and national unification, and the period 1900–13 witnessed a dramatic overexpansion of Canada's rail network. In this same era the emerging technologies of electric power generation and distribution offered prospects of cleaner, safer cities, improved urban transportation, and more dispersed and diversified industrial development. Rail lines and electric power grids linked the scattered cities of Canada, encouraged the growth of new commercial and industrial centres, opened the resource-rich northern hinterland for exploitation, and could at least potentially alleviate the harshness and isolation of rural life.

The development of both technologies involved the erection of organizations of unprecedented size and complexity, characterized by large fixed capital costs, sophisticated technical capabilities, and bureaucratic structures. While communities initially welcomed the economic and social benefits bestowed by these organizations, those who controlled them were soon perceived as exploiters, gouging the public with high or discriminatory rates, enriching their owners with 'monopoly profits', and exercising behind-the-scene political influence. Consequently, the railways and utilities were among the first industries to become targets of political reform movements, and government intervention in the form of regulation and public ownership began to emerge early in the twentieth century. By the end of the 1920s, the Canadian railway, communications, and electric power networks comprised a well-developed 'public sector' at the federal as well as provincial and municipal levels, a sector that contested, though it did not fully displace, the large private corporate enterprises that had established these systems.

ELECTRICAL UTILITIES

Of all the technological achievements of the late nineteenth century, the development of the electrical industry was probably the most publicized, due in no small measure to the vigorous self-promotion of its pioneers, particularly Thomas Edison. Although the inventions of Edison and other Americans received the most attention, technical improvements in the field took place in many countries and electrical technology diffused rapidly in the period 1875–95. During these years French and German researchers designed commercially viable electrical generators; the harnessing of electric power for lighting proceeded from the experiments of Edison and Elihu Thomson in the US and Joseph Swan in Britain. Edison established the first central generating station for the distribution of electricity via direct current in New York in 1881. Five years later another American, George Westinghouse, developed the alternating current system that made it possible to transmit electric power over long distances. In 1887 Frank Sprague introduced the first electrified street railway, in Richmond, Virginia. In the early 1890s an American investment syndicate, using Swiss-designed turbines, erected the first large-scale electric generating plant at Niagara Falls, providing power for lighting and streetcars in Buffalo, NY, as well as energy for the metallurgical and chemical industries that quickly clustered in the region.

While these technical feats enthralled the public, organizational developments of no less significance shaped the future of the electrical industry. In 1892 the two largest competitors in the field, Edison and Thomson-Houston, merged to form General Electric Co. and four years later negotiated a patent-sharing arrangement with Westinghouse. Meanwhile, Samuel Insull, a British immigrant to the US who had been Edison's personal secretary, devised the financial and organizational techniques for developing regional electric power grids, creating a Chicago-based system that dominated the American Midwest through a structure of holding companies and interconnected transmission lines.

The companies that distributed electric power developed independently of the electrical equipment manufacturers, but in the early years of electrification in Canada, as in the US, the equipment makers initiated the establishment of distributing firms (which by the 1890s were designated, along with telephone, telegraph, and railway companies, as 'utilities') in order to create a market for their products. During the 1880s salesmen from Edison and Thomson-Houston encouraged local entrepreneurs to set up companies, preferably with exclusive franchises or long-term contracts with municipal or provincial governments, to

distribute electric power for streetcars, public lighting, and domestic household uses. Since the initial costs of installing these systems were substantial, the equipment companies preferred not to participate directly, or at most to hold minority interest in the ventures, but they could provide a variety of inducements to attract investors. While the capital costs of utilities were high, operating costs, once the system was in place, were relatively modest and the profit potential was substantial.

Participants in investor syndicates could be lured into underwriting bonds through liberal distribution of bonus stocks at below-par value, with the expectation that their market value would rise dramatically once the company was launched. Stock and bond salesmen also played upon the sense of public excitement generated by the inventive achievements of Edison et al., and the expectation that electrification would usher in a new era of scientific progress and economic growth, creating what historians Christopher Armstrong and H.V. Nelles called a 'theatre of science'.[1]

Electrical equipment salesmen were not alone in adopting this strategy: American Bell of Boston, which secured the telephone patent of Alexander Graham Bell, also followed this route into Canada. In 1880 the Bell Company secured the services of Charles Sise, a transplanted New Englander involved in the Canadian insurance field, who assembled an investment syndicate to merge competing telephone systems in Montreal. Sise, who went on to run the company and extended Bell Canada into Ontario and the Maritimes, also took an interest in electrical utilities. In 1884 he participated in the formation of Royal Electric Co. in Montreal, a firm that established a central station for municipal lighting and also a plant to manufacture equipment under licence from Thomson-Houston Co.[2]

In Toronto another Thomson protege, J.J. Wright, established a distributing company with financing organized by Henry Pellatt, a securities broker linked to the Cox group. In 1892, when

Edison and Thomson-Houston merged in the US, Frederic Nicholls, another Cox associate, established Canadian General Electric, which in its early years was an independent Canadian-owned venture that manufactured electrical equipment under licence from the Americans; CGE was absorbed by the American firm after Nicholls died in 1923.

The development of these Canadian ventures in the 1880s and early 1890s took place in a highly competitive context. Rival American patent-holders in various technologies jockeyed for market position; meanwhile, the older utilities such as gas companies fought to hold their existing position in the markets for public and domestic lighting, and some began to diversify into the electrical illumination field. Mergers in the electric equipment industry in the US in the 1890s did not translate immediately into consolidations in the utilities, but the introduction of alternating-current technology and long-distance power transmission opened the way for larger-scale enterprises to exploit regional markets.

This trend towards larger formations in the Canadian electric utility field can be seen in the growth of electric streetcar systems—more generally called tramways or traction companies—in urban communities. The tramway market attracted the interest of a new group of entrepreneurs. Railway building contractors, whose business had flourished in the era of CPR construction in the 1880s, faced diminished prospects in the following decade and turned their attention to related undertakings. The construction of urban street railways seemed a logical step for men like William Mackenzie, James Ross, Donald Mann, Herbert Holt, and others who had honed their contracting skills on the CPR project, and they could anticipate a sympathetic hearing from financial syndicates accustomed to raising large sums of capital for steam railways.

The market for electrified city tramways was also apparent. Horse-drawn railways had appeared in Canadian cities in the 1860s, but after 30 years their limitations were painfully evident. Expensive to operate (in Montreal, for example, the system required stables and feed for over 1,000 horses), unreliable in bad weather, and restricted largely to city centres, these systems served a relatively small market: in 1892, only 10 per cent of the Montreal population and 25 per cent of Toronto's. Electrification would dramatically cut operating costs and permit the extension of lines over much larger distances.

A central figure in the rapid expansion of electric tramways (and much else) in the 1890s was William Mackenzie, who would later figure prominently in the railway expansion in the West. Combining stalwart Presbyterian virtue with gregarious optimism and hard-driving ambition, Mackenzie was a prototype for the expansionist-minded business figures who flourished on the Canadian scene at the turn of the century. After learning the contracting trade on the CPR line Mackenzie returned to his home in Kirkfield, Ontario, in the early 1890s, dabbling briefly in Tory politics before discovering a more interesting and lucrative outlet for his considerable energies.

That opportunity was provided by the imminent bankruptcy of several of Toronto's horse-drawn tramways in 1892. Forming a syndicate of former associates from his CPR construction days (including William Van Horne, now the president of that line), Mackenzie merged the companies, refinanced them with $2 million in bonds secured with an exclusive franchise from Toronto's city council, and acquired controlling interest in the stocks of the new Toronto Railway Co. at a cost of only $10,000 in cash.

The success of the Toronto street railway encouraged Mackenzie and his associates to undertake similar ventures in Winnipeg, Montreal, and Saint John, NB. Mackenzie also spread his interest into municipal lighting through investments in gas companies in Vancouver and Halifax. By 1895, according to Armstrong and Nelles, Mackenzie had come close to 'assembling a de facto national utilities conglomerate', with visions of expanding his empire into the British utility market. This last venture proved to be a fiasco, however, and by this time Mackenzie had turned to another suitably grandiose project, the Canadian Northern Railway. He continued to take an interest in utility investments, particularly in Latin America after 1900, but his imperial visions were increasingly focused on developing a transcontinental rival to the CPR.

Canadian railway entrepreneurs were not the only ones to find the undeveloped electric traction market in Canada attractive. Henry M. Whitney, a Boston capitalist who had established electric railways in that city, took an interest in reorganizing the Halifax system as a sideline to his investment in Cape Breton coal mines in the early 1890s. Perhaps the most significant result of this project was that Whitney brought with him a talented and ambitious young engineer, Frank Pearson, who would play a major role in organizing Canadian utility companies in Latin America. On the other side of the continent a British investment syndicate led by R.M. Horne-Payne acquired a number of foundering utility companies in Victoria, Vancouver, and New Westminster, BC, and reorganized them into BC Electric Railway Co. The name was misleadingly narrow, for BCER effectively controlled the province's utility industry, and the charter it received from the British Columbia legislature gave the company exclusive rights to provide services to municipalities that had not even been established.

As the BC example indicates, utility promoters were very adept at exploiting the Canadian federal system to procure the most advantageous corporate charters. As in the US, municipalities were initially the preferred jurisdiction since they were most likely to welcome providers of local services with few strings attached, and councillors could be bought relatively cheaply. After the first flush of enthusiasm for utilities wore off, however, municipal governments could prove troublesome; happily for promoters, municipal powers were subject to provincial laws. In provinces like BC this situation could work to the advantage of the promoters, but in other cases—particularly in Ontario by the early 1900s—provincial legislators took a more restrictive view of the powers to

be granted private enterprises in charters. But the federal government also had chartering authority, and an adroit promoter (or his legal adviser) could select the jurisdiction most likely to adopt a liberal approach to such matters. When Charles Sise was organizing Bell Canada, for example, he was careful to secure both a federal charter to permit the establishment of a system that could operate across provincial boundaries and special laws in Ontario and Quebec to enable Bell to erect its poles and lines with minimal interference from municipal authorities.

The structure of BCER also indicates a broader trend in the erection of Canadian utilities. Traction companies were indeed profitable, but in order to be cost-effective and reliable they established their own central generating stations. Since these stations produced electric power in excess of the volume required for running street railways, particularly during off-peak hours, the traction companies sought customers in other markets, including public lighting as well as industrial and household uses. This strategy led logically to moves to amalgamate tramways and other electric utilities at the municipal level. By 1900 the development of alternating-current technology, through which large areas could be provided power from a single or a few large generating sources, opened the way for amalgamation of utilities on a regional or provincial basis.

Montreal was the scene of one of the first dramatic large-scale consolidations of electric utilities. Through the 1890s rival groups of financiers had engaged in a complex struggle for control of various gas, electric power, and traction companies in the city, culminating in the creation of Montreal Light, Heat and Power Co. in 1901, built around the base of Royal Electric Co. Although the organization of MLH&P was engineered by financiers James Ross and Louis Forget, the figure who was to dominate the company was its hired manager, Herbert Holt.

Holt, like Mackenzie, had entered the utilities field from a background as a CPR contractor, but in other respects the two contrasted remarkably:

Mackenzie was an optimistic, exuberant risk-taker; Holt was a dour, cautious technocrat. While Mackenzie created nation-spanning rail and utility empires that ultimately collapsed with melodramatic flair, Holt steadily erected an edifice of interconnected companies that made him the most powerful Canadian capitalist of his time, presiding over the giant Royal Bank as well as a multitude of utility and industrial ventures. By the time he died in 1941 Holt had become the symbol of Montreal's secretive, arrogant anglophone elite.

In 1901, however, the success of Holt and MLH&P was by no means a sure thing. In Montreal it faced strong competition from Lachine Rapids Hydraulic Co. Although Holt's company had a large power site at Chambly, in 1902 Lachine Rapids Co. brought a more formidable ally onto the scene, negotiating an agreement to purchase power from a huge project developed on the St Maurice River by Shawinigan Water & Power Co. The Shawinigan venture, which had been established in 1897 by American interests (joined by the ubiquitous L.J. Forget), was primarily intended to provide electric power to industries encouraged to locate on the St Maurice River, notably a Canadian affiliate of the American aluminum company, Alcoa. But Shawinigan produced far more power than could be absorbed locally and the Montreal market was attractive.

Although Holt had earned a reputation for ruthless cost-effective management, his strategy for dealing with these challenges involved co-operation rather than price competition. In 1903, MLH&P bought Lachine Rapids Co., and four years later Holt negotiated a comprehensive agreement with Shawinigan to share the Montreal market, and completed a long-term supply contract that enabled MLH&P to expand its distribution network and solidify its position in the city and its environs. Over the next three decades the two companies worked in tandem to turn back challengers to the Montreal market.

Similar pressures towards consolidation and oligopoly in the utilities field were at work in Ontario in this period, but events there unfolded in a dramatically different fashion. At about the same time as the Montreal merger, utility financiers in Toronto, their confidence bolstered by successful ventures abroad, turned their attention to the hydro-power potential of Niagara Falls. By 1903 all but one of the major sites for power generation on the Canadian side of the Falls were occupied by American companies. Mackenzie, joined by Nicholls of CGE, as well as Pellatt and the Cox group, formed Electrical Development Co. (EDC) to acquire this last site, which would not only expand their supplies for Toronto utilities but also be in a position to market surplus power throughout southern Ontario.

Even before Electrical Development began work on the site, however, opposition surfaced both in Toronto and in the smaller cities of the region. In Toronto, high utility rates and the refusal of the tramway to extend lines into the burgeoning suburbs had antagonized domestic consumers. Hostility towards the utility barons of Toronto was even greater in the nearby aspiring industrial towns like Berlin (now Kitchener), Waterloo, and Guelph, which feared that EDC would establish a monopoly that would thwart their future growth. From both quarters a movement for public control of electrical utilities gained strength; the provincial opposition Conservative Party took up the cause and swept into office, vowing to block expansion of EDC. The key figure in this movement was Adam Beck (see box, p. 40).

The public power movement was not restricted to Ontario; indeed, by the 1920s, except in Quebec and British Columbia, the private utilities faced some form of government intervention either through regulatory measures or Crown corporations, or both. On the prairies, government ownership appeared first at the municipal level: in 1905 Winnipeg authorized the establishment of a public hydroelectric system that went into competition with Mackenzie's company. By that time the small cities of Saskatchewan had set up municipally owned operations. During this period as well, both of these provinces and Alberta had 'nationalized' their telephone systems,

ADAM BECK (1857–1925) AND ONTARIO HYDRO

The streets of Berlin (now Kitchener), Ontario, festooned with electric lights in readiness for the opening of the Niagara power station on 11 October 1910. (Hydro One Networks Inc.)

The virtual founding father and dominant figure of the Ontario Hydro Electric Commission in its early years, Adam Beck was also the first of a long line of Crown company entrepreneurs—including Sir Henry Thornton of Canadian National Railways in the 1920s and Wilbert Hopper of Petro-Canada in the 1970s—who flourished in twentieth-century Canada. Officially the bureaucratic chieftains of government-owned corporations, they acted more like Rockefeller, Carnegie, and other private business empire builders of nineteenth-century America.

Beck began his career in the 1880s as a businessman, manufacturing wood veneers and cigar boxes in London, Ontario, a small but ambitious commercial and industrial city that was already the hub of Canadian petroleum refining, included two breweries (Carling's and Labatt's), and aspired to become a major financial centre as well. Like his future rival, William Mackenzie, Beck was restlessly competitive, in sports as well as business; and, like Mackenzie, he dabbled in local politics, though with greater success. In 1900 he was elected mayor of London and two years later became a Conservative member of the Ontario legislature.

As mayor of London, Beck attended a meeting in nearby Berlin, Ontario, in early 1903 instigated by opponents of Mackenzie's Electrical Development Co. Reflecting the alarm of small-town southern Ontario businesses at the prospect of a Toronto power monopoly, Beck also quickly recognized the political opportunities presented by the issue for his own ambitions and those of his party. Within a year he emerged as the leading advocate for public control of the province's hydroelectric power, which the Tory leader, Richard Whitney, made the centrepiece of his successful election campaign in 1905. As a reward for his efforts, Beck was appointed chairman of a committee to investigate Ontario's hydro power needs and resources.

Beck dominated the inquiry and assembled a bipartisan coalition to support its proposal for a provincial hydro commission that would regulate rates charged by private power companies and sell electric power 'at cost' to municipalities in Ontario. A curiously hybrid entity—it was, in theory, owned by the municipalities as a public corporation but was financed by the provincial government, which also enforced its regulatory decrees—the Ontario Hydro Electric Commission, with Beck at its head, commenced operations in 1910.

Although the attempt by the Electrical Development Co. to secure control of all available water power from Niagara Falls had been foiled, Ontario Hydro depended entirely at this point on private suppliers, and Mackenzie's company was still the largest supplier. Beck's strategy for overcoming this problem was in the tradition of robber-baron entrepreneurship. Ontario Hydro embarked on a vigorous campaign to promote electric usage, offering cheap rates to industries and domestic users.

The Commission relied on government subsidies to cover the difference between its costs and sales prices; and with an assured market, Ontario Hydro proceeded to develop its own power sites, culminating in the early 1920s with the construction of the largest power station of its time, at Queenston. Meanwhile, Beck used the regulatory powers of the Commission to control the rates of its private competitors. By 1921, Ontario Hydro had ousted EDC from its major market, the Toronto utility system, and Mackenzie's financial empire lay in ruins. Before the end of the decade Ontario Hydro controlled over three-quarters of the electric power generated in the province.

Beck died in 1925, embroiled in disputes with the province's political leaders, who were increasingly troubled by the autonomy and influence of what was supposed to be an arm of government. Although Ontario Hydro's independence was reined in after Beck's time, few politicians cared to challenge directly the power of this large, technologically complex organization whose channels of influence percolated across the province. Adam Beck's legacy thus embraced both an enduring tradition of public ownership in the Canadian utility industry and a classic example of bureaucratic imperialism.

Sources: Christopher Armstrong and H.V. Nelles, *Monopoly's Moment: The Organization and Regulation of Canadian Utilities, 1830–1930* (Philadelphia, 1986); W.R. Plewman, *Adam Beck and Ontario Hydro* (Toronto, 1947).

more or less with the acquiescence of Bell Canada, which did not intend at that time to burden itself with the costs of developing rural services.

During the 1920s the electrical utilities of Manitoba and Saskatchewan were knitted into province-wide systems. In Alberta and the Maritimes, private electric utility companies maintained a firm hold on the most lucrative urban markets, leaving the rural and small-town hinterland to the modest public systems. In Calgary, Halifax, and Saint John, consolidations of utility companies were orchestrated by financial groups in Montreal between 1910 and 1930. None of them, however, aspired to control regional markets in the style of MLH&P and Shawinigan; and in none of these situations did an Adam Beck emerge with visions of building a public power empire.[3]

Public ownership of utilities limited the aspirations of private entrepreneurs in Canada, but it was only one factor. As early as 1898 electric utility promoters had discovered another promising market for their skills and capital resources,

Canadian tramways in Brazil: a Brazilian Traction freight car in São Paulo, 1905. (Eletropavlo Archives)

and in the early years of the twentieth century investments in Latin American utilities to some extent diverted their energies. Political leaders in these underdeveloped climes proved, if anything, to be more accommodating than their Canadian counterparts towards foreign capitalists bearing the latest technologies. Canadian businessmen were small players in this region—British, Americans, and Germans were acquiring mining and petroleum concessions and aggressively marketing their industrial wares from Mexico to Chile and Argentina—but they found lucrative niches in the utility markets of the burgeoning cities of Latin America and the Caribbean.

The earliest venturers in this direction were Mackenzie and James Ross of Montreal. Blocked in their effort to establish a foothold in British tramways, the two promoters encountered a more congenial welcome in Jamaica in 1897. Their modest success lured another railroader, Sir William Van Horne, into the Caribbean. The

master builder of the CPR retired from active management of that enterprise in 1899, but at age 56 his energies were undiminished, and Van Horne spotted an alluring opportunity to develop electric railways in Cuba, recently liberated from Spain. Together with some CPR cronies, American streetcar promoters, and his old rival, Jim Hill, Van Horne organized a Cuban venture in 1900.

The Cuban railway was not particularly successful, but it helped alert Canadian utility entrepreneurs and financiers to the possibilities of larger undertakings in the region. A key figure in this process was Halifax-based Frank Pearson. In 1899 Pearson turned up on Mackenzie's doorstep in Toronto with a prospective concession in hand to develop electric street railways in São Paulo, the centre of Brazil's coffee trade. He had already hawked it unsuccessfully to American investors, who found it too small, and to his Halifax associates, who found it too expensive. Mackenzie embraced the opportunity and sent Pearson off to explore the prospects of amalgamating all of the city's utilities. With the Cox group, Mackenzie then set up São Paulo Railway, Light and Power Co. with the usual distribution of bonds and bonus stock to the Canadian promoters.

Success in São Paulo led to a larger undertaking in 1904 in Brazil's capital city, Rio de Janeiro. Eight years later Mackenzie and Pearson reorganized the two operations under a holding company, Brazilian Traction, Light and Power Co., capitalized at $120 million. The largest Canadian multinational enterprise of the era, this company dominated Brazil's utility industry and was variously dubbed 'The Light' or 'the Canadian Octopus' by citizens of the host country. After World War II the Brazilian government began to undermine The Light's monopoly, ultimately buying out the foreigners for $380 million in 1978. At that point the company in Canada was reorganized as Brascan, a conglomerate that eventually passed into the hands of the Bronfman family.

The Brazilian ventures whetted the appetites of other Canadian observers. In 1901 Pearson discovered another prospective utility market in Mexico, which interested his Halifax colleague, John Stairs, then attracted Ross and Van Horne, and ultimately Pearson roped in some Toronto investors and the Sperling Group in Britain, which was involved in BC Electric. Mexican Light & Power was incorporated in 1902; three years later Pearson added the Mexico City trolley lines to the portfolio. Initially highly profitable, the Mexican utility ventures fell on hard times after 1912. Threatened by marauding armies during the Mexican Revolution and devastated by the loss of Pearson, who went down with the *Lusitania* in 1915, Mexican Light & Power was threatened with nationalization in 1921. It survived these vicissitudes and by the end of World War II was supplying over half the country's electric power. In 1960 the Mexican government took over all foreign-owned utilities, although, oddly, Mexican Light & Power's charter remained in Canada.

The Halifax utility financiers had to share control of the Mexican venture virtually from its inception, but Stairs and his protege, Max Aitken, had already begun exploring other Latin American projects, including electric railways in Cuba (carefully leaving the big ventures to Van Horne), Puerto Rico, Trinidad, and British Guiana. After Aitken went on to greater things, his protege, I.W. Killam, continued to accumulate properties through Royal Securities, including utilities in Calgary, Newfoundland, Bolivia, El Salvador, and Venezuela, organized into a holding company, International Power, in 1926. These were not truly big operations—International Power was only one-tenth the size of Brazilian Traction—but they maintained a traditional Maritime link with Latin America, and their profits cushioned Killam when his schemes to consolidate the Canadian pulp and paper industry collapsed in the Great Depression. While bigger fish like Mackenzie floundered amid financial woes at the end of their careers, Killam went to his grave in 1955 one of the wealthiest men in Canada.

The Canadian utility ventures in Latin America indeed represented, as their chief chroniclers, Armstrong and Nelles, have put it, 'a curious capital flow'. Aside from Maritime trade with the West Indies, there was no historical tradition linking Canada to the region. The Canadians did not have any particular technological edge over others in the field: they simply brought together mostly American technology and mostly British capital, exploiting a modest vacuum neglected by their larger counterparts. Although the earnings from these utility ventures enriched some promoters, the enterprises did not leave any lasting mark on Canadian business development, aside from providing Canadian engineers with some international experience. A few lawyers and clerks monitored these operations in Canada on behalf of the investors. Unlike the Canadian mining and manufacturing companies that moved overseas in the more recent past, these 'utility multinationals' were a rather more ephemeral presence, at least in the Canadian context, reflecting primarily the wide-ranging ambitions of a handful of enterprising contractors and financiers and the mobility of international capital in the era that preceded World War I.[4]

RAILWAYS

While the emerging field of electric utilities attracted adventurous investors, the established technology of steam railroads remained a staple element of the Canadian and foreign securities markets in the decades preceding World War I. Although the opening of the Canadian Pacific Railway did not immediately people the prairies with wheat farmers, by 1897 the company had weathered its early financial troubles. At the same time, opposition in the West to the CPR's monopoly stimulated provincial politicians to encourage expansion of the railway network, which in turn enticed entrepreneurial railway promoters into the region. As the Canadian economy recovered from the depression of the mid-1890s the groundwork was laid for a new boom in railway construction.

Between 1900 and 1914 railway mileage in Canada more than doubled, increasing from 17,824 to over 40,000 miles, reflecting not only expansion in the West but also the opening of lines into northern Ontario and Quebec and a thickening of the central and eastern networks of branch and feeder lines. By 1910 two new transcontinental systems were in the works, liberally endowed with government bond guarantees, subsidies, and land grants. Meanwhile, the CPR responded by expanding its own system and diversifying its activities into ocean transportation, hotels, and mining. This orgy of railway promotion, which far exceeded the capacity and needs of the economy, began to disintegrate even before the outbreak of war in Europe in 1914 cut the flow of overseas investment.

During the war the Canadian government was obliged to keep the nation's rail lines running but also had to confront the long-term problems of rationalizing an overbuilt and overcapitalized network. Amid bitter debates over the dangers of monopoly versus the hazards of public ownership,

the government took over the two new (bankrupt) transcontinental lines, Canadian Northern Railway and Grand Trunk Pacific, and consolidated them into Canadian National Railways between 1918 and 1923; this was the country's first major experiment with Crown corporations (they were to become a far more pervasive feature on the Canadian business scene after World War II). During the 1920s the CPR and CNR embarked on a new round of competition that benefited shippers and rail passengers but proved ruinous in financial terms for both companies. Exhaustion and retrenchment marked the Canadian railway environment in the Great Depression, signalling the end of an era of expansion that stretched back to the years before Confederation and had been a major factor in the political and cultural life as well as the nation's economy for almost a century.

For many Canadians, 7 November 1885 had marked the fulfillment of the 'national dream', the completion of the nation's transcontinental railway line. For William Van Horne, General Manager of the Canadian Pacific Railway, it had been another business day: a beginning rather than an end. This hard-headed approach to their tasks was characteristic of the dominant figures of the CPR, Van Horne and Thomas Shaughnessy, and the managers they assembled to operate this complex enterprise. Cautious, attentive to details, and competitive, the CPR managers weathered a decade of financial and political difficulties over the 1885–95 period, and steadily erected a formidable and diversified system of rail lines and associated undertakings that enabled the company to surmount strong competitive challenges from the Canadian Northern and the Grand Trunk during the ensuing 20 years. After World War I the CPR, unloved but profitable, remained the dominant carrier of commercial and passenger traffic in Canada with offshoots in mining, urban real estate, and oceanic shipping lines.

The immediate problem for the CPR after the 'last spike' had been driven at Craigellachie, BC, was to rebuild and improve the existing line, which had been hastily laid to satisfy the expectations of politicians and bondholders. In addition, branch and feeder lines, essential for increasing traffic and revenues, had to be fleshed out. Finally, there was the threat of competition, particularly from James J. Hill's Great Northern Railway as it extended westward from Minnesota, to goad the CPR to expand services and offset complaints from Manitoba over the company's monopoly.

But expansion required financing and the debt-burdened line could not anticipate a rapid infusion of revenues from its western traffic or sales from its huge land grant. Settlers did not at once pour into the Canadian prairies; indeed, western settlement lagged until the late 1890s when the federal government mounted a vigorous campaign to boost immigration to Canada. In the interim the American Great Plains, with numerous competing railway lines, attracted more migrants; and the harsh economic depression of the early 1890s withered the confidence of investors as well as aspiring farmers.

Nevertheless, the CPR did expand, more than doubling its rail mileage between 1886 and 1896. This growth was not without pain: in 1894 earnings were insufficient to cover capital costs and in the following year the CPR cut dividends by half, leading its former president, George Stephen, to urge fellow shareholders to sell their securities. The company survived the crisis, but this experience reinforced management's financial caution and preoccupation with cash flow during the decades of prosperity that followed.

Pressures for expansion were hard to resist. Manitoba farmers had been resentful of the CPR's freight-rate policies even before completion of the line, and several times during the 1880s the province sought to issue new railway charters to encourage competition. The federal government under Sir John A. Macdonald vetoed the Manitoba legislation, but by 1888 the CPR decided to give up the monopoly clause in its charter 'in the interests of peace in the northwest', as Stephen put it (and in exchange for further government guarantees of its bonds).

An American line, Northern Pacific, had extended into Manitoba in the 1880s, but the CPR was able to negotiate a rate agreement with that company to avoid a price war. The major threat to the CPR in the 1890s was posed by Hill's Great Northern; and to complicate matters for Van Horne, Hill was involved in assorted railway ventures in the US with Stephen and Donald Smith, who still held blocks of shares in the CPR. By 1893 the Great Northern had reached the US west coast and the government of British Columbia was prepared to charter a line that would link the Kootenay mining region in the eastern part of the province with Hill's railway.

To meet this challenge Van Horne decided to build a new line from Alberta well to the south of the original CPR route. To do this, the CPR would have to go through the Crowsnest Pass of the Rockies, a costly undertaking that would require a new infusion of government assistance. In 1896, however, a federal election brought the Liberals to power under Wilfrid Laurier, long-time critic of the CPR's monopolistic tendencies, freight rates, and Tory political connections.

Fortunately for Van Horne, other Liberal politicos, especially Clifford Sifton of Brandon, Manitoba, Laurier's Minister of the Interior, were anxious to promote western settlement and the CPR remained the major instrument to achieve this aim. After some dickering, the government and the company concluded the Crow's Nest Pass Agreement of 1897, under which the CPR would receive the cash subsidies it needed in return for concessions over freight rates, particularly on the eastbound grain traffic from the prairies to central Canada. This concession was to remain in effect for an indefinite period, and in fact the Agreement established the base rate for western railways for almost a century.

Although the CPR had surmounted its financial difficulties by 1899, Van Horne decided to step down as president, his enthusiasm sapped by years of bickering with fellow directors as well as politicians. Even before his formal retirement, his successor, Thomas Shaughnessy, had emerged as the key figure in the company. Like Van Horne, Shaughnessy was an American; his talents, however, lay in organization and financial management rather than construction. Shaughnessy, a prototype of the professional corporate manager of the twentieth century, thus represented an ideal candidate for running the CPR during the era of consolidation and measured growth that came after 1900.

Under Shaughnessy the modern organization of the CPR took shape. As the company's chief financial officer in its difficult early years, he emphasized cost controls and maintained a centralized system for monitoring budgetary allocations and earnings while adopting the decentralized system of operational management pioneered by American railroads in the nineteenth century, under which regional division chiefs exercised autonomy over such matters as traffic control, with regular assessments by headquarters of their financial performance. The physical plant of the line was regularly upgraded, larger and more technically advanced locomotives and other equipment were introduced, and rolling stock was increased to handle the growing volume of grain traffic after 1900.

Shaughnessy was particularly committed to reorganizing the company's debt structure. The financial traumas that wracked the CPR in 1894-5 were to be avoided. In contrast to its future Canadian railway rivals (and many other Canadian firms in the early twentieth century), the CPR had always relied on equity rather than debt financing (except for government-backed bonds). In the early 1890s the cash-strapped firm had departed from this practice to raise funds for expansion; Shaugnessy was determined to eliminate this debt as quickly as possible. After 1906 the CPR was able to finance more than three-quarters of its capital needs from reinvested earnings and sales of common stock. Consequently, the capital market crunch of 1913-14 that ruined its rivals, Canadian Northern and the Grand Trunk, left the CPR relatively unscathed.

Diversification also helped to cushion the CPR against the perils of an overbuilt railway system in this era. The company had never been exclusively a transportation enterprise: earnings from sales of its land grants had been intended from the outset to contribute to its revenues. But Shaughnessy regarded the land grants as a 'drag on the company' because of the costs incurred in improving the land through irrigation works to attract settlers. Other activities were more promising.

Under Van Home the CPR had begun to diversify: hotels were established along the main rail route, notably the Banff Springs resort erected in 1888. By the end of the century the company had investments in urban real estate as well. Steamship services were inaugurated in 1886, and within 20 years CPR ships were plying the Atlantic and Pacific oceans as well as the Great Lakes and the BC coast (where they carried Klondike-bound prospectors during the gold rush of 1897-8). In 1898 the company acquired a mineral smelter at Trail, BC, along with a mining railway, an unsought investment that would turn into one of the CPR's most lucrative industrial subsidiaries, Cominco. Under Shaughnessy the company also promoted exploration of the petroleum potentialities of its western lands. While the combined earnings of these various activities in the period 1900-30 were far less significant for the company than revenues from rail traffic and land sales, they presaged the later evolution of the CPR into a diversified holding company. The divisional structure inaugurated by Shaughnessy provided the organizational versatility needed to hold together its increasingly wide-ranging operations.

The success of the CPR under Shaughnessy was due in part to its organizational and diversification strategies, but also reflected the improving economic conditions in Canada after 1896, the federal government's immigration policies, and the expansion of the wheat belt in the West. Shaughnessy did not neglect the basic mission of the CPR to promote western development; indeed, under his management the company's westward orientation became more pronounced. Van Horne had devoted considerable attention in the 1890s to developing an eastern network for the CPR through a 'short line' running from Montreal to Saint John, New Brunswick, via Maine, in addition to the Crowsnest Pass line in the West. Shaughnessy, however, increasingly focused on the prairies, double-tracking the main line through the region as well as building more feeder lines, expanding repair and industrial operations in Winnipeg and Calgary, and increasing western rail mileage by 6,000 miles between 1903 and 1912, by which point more than half the company's tracks ran west of the Great Lakes. While this westward tilt by the CPR was not surprising, given the explosive growth of the prairies during the wheat boom of the first two decades of the twentieth century, Shaughnessy's actions were also prompted by the emergence of two major competitors in the region, whose spectacular rise and fall punctuated the Laurier era and left the country with its first major experiment with government ownership of a national enterprise.[5]

Canada's second (more precisely, its third) venture in transcontinental railway building began modestly in Manitoba in 1895. As noted earlier, Manitobans were unhappy over the CPR monopoly in the West even before completion of that line, and they remained unmollified when the company surrendered its monopoly clause in 1888. While Jim Hill was probing northward from Minnesota in the early 1890s, the Manitoba provincial government began hawking a charter to build a line from Winnipeg to Hudson Bay, promising bond guarantees, land grants, and subsidies.

The Hudson Bay project attracted the attention of Donald Mann, yet another CPR subcontractor at loose ends. Mann got in touch with his erstwhile partner, William Mackenzie, whose aspirations to build a utility empire were temporarily stalled. Mackenzie and Mann took on the Manitoba charter but they were not particularly interested in constructing a line through the province's northern wilderness. Instead, they began piecing together a series of short lines from Lake of the Woods to the Saskatchewan border between 1896 and 1901, picking up some federal government support in the process.

At this time, Mackenzie and Mann moved carefully, building not just railways but a base of local support that would stand them in good stead in their subsequent, more ambitious undertakings. They selected routes that had good development prospects and constructed a network of feeder lines to ensure that their main line would ultimately carry substantial traffic at rates that would be competitive with the CPR. To control costs, they built their lines to standards appropriate to anticipated use: heavily travelled sections were well constructed while those sections covering unsettled areas were laid down quickly, to be upgraded if and when traffic increased. Rather than importing labour, they employed people in the local communities, and their construction 'had something of the air of a barn-raising about it; everyone was allowed to pitch in and do what they could.'

Up to 1899 these activities had created what historian Ted Regehr characterized as 'unconnected projections of steel' lacing Manitoba with profitable but as yet unintegrated lines. In that year, Mackenzie and Mann reorganized their venture as the Canadian Northern Railway and began to unveil plans to extend into Saskatchewan and the North-West Territories. Two years later they scored their first major coup, acquiring the Manitoba branch lines of the Northern Pacific Railway, which gave them direct access to a transcontinental main line in the United States. Between 1901 and 1903 Mackenzie and Mann accumulated more bond guarantees and land grants from the Manitoba government, which enabled them to market Canadian Northern securities in London and New York. With over $14 million in new capital, they were now prepared to build a prairie line that would compete directly with the CPR. As in the case of Mackenzie's utility ventures, neither of the promoters had put up their own money: one-third of the capital raised was guaranteed by governments at various levels, which ensured Canadian Northern's attractiveness to foreign investors. Mackenzie's Toronto associate, George Cox, brought in the Bank of

Commerce, and the insiders rewarded themselves as usual with bonus stocks.

Besides making money, what did Mackenzie and Mann have in mind for Canadian Northern? At this time, in 1903, they seemed most intent on consolidating their prairie network and advancing with caution, as had been the case in their early years in Manitoba. Both Regehr and Mackenzie's most recent biographer, R.B. Fleming, suggest, however, that as early as 1900 they were contemplating development of a transcontinental line to ensure an adequate traffic flow from east to west; but this was a long-term plan, not to be attempted until the western system was complete.[6]

Canadian Northern's success as a regional carrier, however, lured another player onto the field. Up to 1902 the Grand Trunk Railway, reflecting the conservatism of its London-based board of directors, had concentrated on exploiting the central Canadian market, forgoing new ventures to keep earnings and dividends high. The depression of the early 1890s cut into the Grand Trunk's revenues, leading to a management shakeup in 1895: Sir Charles Rivers-Wilson, a British diplomat with experience in financial reorganization, was brought in as president, and he in turn recruited a battle-hardened American railroader, Charles M. Hays, to be general manager. Rivers-Wilson and Hays devoted their early years at Grand Trunk to rebuilding the company's earnings on its established lines, but Hays had his eye on the western market.

Rivers-Wilson, who met Mackenzie in London in 1902, seems to have been inclined towards developing a co-operative arrangement between the Grand Trunk and Canadian Northern to challenge the CPR, but Hays proposed a takeover of Canadian Northern. Cox and Laurier were both enlisted to assist in the process, but merger talks deadlocked as Mackenzie and Mann refused to accept the terms. Hays now determined to build a western line, or at least to threaten to do so, in order to put pressure on Canadian Northern: 'railroading', as Regehr put it, 'in the American tradition' of aggressive and ruthless competition.

Laurier had his own reasons for endorsing this scheme. Although the Crow's Nest Pass Agreement had harnessed the CPR's western freight rates, the Prime Minister wanted to strengthen the regulatory capabilities of the newly established Board of Railway Commissioners. To that end, competition between two (or better yet, three) strong transcontinental lines seemed desirable, and would also enhance the government's policy of encouraging western settlement. Consequently, he was receptive to a proposal from Hays for cash subsidies and a land grant to the Grand Trunk to support a Pacific line. But a political Pandora's box had now been opened and other interested parties gathered round to voice their demands. Quebec MPs wanted more rail service in their province; Maritimers clamoured for yet another line to the Atlantic coast; others demanded improvements in local Grand Trunk rail facilities. Meanwhile, advocates of Canadian Northern, including Sifton, insisted that pledges of support for that line be honoured.

Hays balked at meeting all these demands, and Laurier's cabinet was split over the issue. As usual, a 'compromise' was worked out, in May 1903. Under this complicated proposal, the Grand Trunk would form a wholly owned subsidiary, the Grand Trunk Pacific Railway Co., which would construct a line from Moncton, NB, to Winnipeg; this 'Eastern Division' would be owned by the federal government but leased to the Grand Trunk upon completion. A 'Western Division' from Winnipeg to the Pacific coast would be built, owned, and operated by the Grand Trunk Pacific. An array of land grants, subsidies, and bond guarantees up to $100 million would be provided, but assorted safeguards were imposed, including the requirement that the construction of the Eastern Division would be subject to supervision by a government commission. The entire system would be called the 'National Transcontinental'.

In the parliamentary debates that ensued, this messy proposal was subjected to further criticism. The Conservative leader, Robert Borden, introduced an alternative under which the government would take over the CPR from Lake Superior west and lease carrying rights to all railways on equal terms. In the end, however, Laurier was able to push through his plan. In early 1904 Hays, despite his own reservations, persuaded Rivers-Wilson and the Grand Trunk board to accept it, and the nation's second transcontinental venture was launched. What had begun as a negotiating ploy by Hays had been transformed through political pressures and the momentum of events into a huge but poorly conceived and ultimately disastrous undertaking.

In 1904, however, the outlook was bright, and even Mackenzie and Mann displayed little outward concern about the future; but they did initiate steps to extend Canadian Northern's links to eastern Canada. They were inadvertently assisted by the appearance of the National Transcontinental scheme, which persuaded smaller railway promoters and investors in Quebec that their own ventures were imperilled; and Mackenzie and Mann proceeded in the East as they had on the prairies, acquiring at bargain prices short lines that could be knit into a trunk system to connect with the Canadian Northern line in the West.

Both Canadian Northern and Grand Trunk steadily expanded their systems between 1904 and 1907. At that point a sudden speculators' panic spreading from Wall Street to the London money market led to a short but sharp business recession. Mackenzie and Mann retrenched and survived the slump; Hays took advantage of the situation to delay the assumption by the Grand Trunk of the Eastern Division of the National Transcontinental. Hays was convinced that the contracts for work on that division had been let at excessively high costs due to the political influence of the government-appointed supervisory board. A Royal Commission established in 1911 to investigate this issue tended to bear out Hays's suspicions, indicating that over $70 million of the $160 million project had been wasted on extravagant construction. But in 1907 Hays's actions soured an already deteriorating relationship between the Grand Trunk and the Liberal government in Ottawa.

Sunny days reappeared in 1909, however, and the orgy of railway construction resumed as the full effects of Sifton's western settlement policy took hold. Mackenzie and Mann now felt confident enough to unveil plans to complete their own transcontinental line, floating new security issues of over $130 million in London. They were hailed as public heroes and knighted in 1911. Canadian Northern sprouted branch lines in all directions: the initial and long-neglected Hudson Bay route was revived, lines were run deep into the Alberta backcountry, and further link-ups with American railroads were in progress. Meanwhile, Hays went on a building and buying spree in the United States with plans to construct lines in New England and New York. He appears to have been contemplating an even more dramatic move in 1912, unloading the Grand Trunk Pacific onto the government and building an alternative western line from Chicago. At this point he booked passage across the Atlantic on the *Titanic* and his schemes went down with him on that vessel's fateful voyage.

Even before this tragedy, the railway boom was beginning to run out of steam. In 1910 labour unrest, which was reaching a peak of intensity in North America, swept across the Canadian railways, affecting both operating lines and construction projects. Time was lost in settling these disputes (or battling the unions, as Hays chose to do). Inflationary pressures drove up the costs of labour and materials; and the money markets, especially in Europe, were growing jittery over recurring war scares.

In 1911 the federal election removed Laurier and the ever-generous Liberals from power, and the new government of Robert Borden was determined to bring some order to what many Tories regarded as an uncontrolled railway building and borrowing spree. As noted above, one of their first acts was to set up a Royal Commission to investigate cost overruns in the Eastern Division. Although the Commission exonerated the Grand Trunk of responsibility for these problems, members of Borden's cabinet, including the Minister of Railways, Frank Cochrane, were now floating proposals for government acquisition and rationalization of the debt-burdened projects.

Mackenzie and Mann were the first to encounter the winds of change in Ottawa. Unable to raise more long-term funding in London, in 1913 they reluctantly approached the Canadian government for $30 million in new subsidies and loans to complete the Canadian Northern's western lines. Borden and Cochrane agreed to provide half this amount, but demanded that the government receive an equity position in the company. Mackenzie grudgingly accepted the terms, but interest charges on short-term debt accumulated in New York quickly dissipated this infusion of funds and Mackenzie was back at Borden's door in less than a year, this time requesting $96 million to complete the entire transcontinental project. Again the government agreed to provide bond guarantees for half this amount, but required Mackenzie and Mann to reorganize all their far-flung enterprises under the Canadian Northern umbrella, transfer a much larger bloc of voting stock in the company to the government (raising its equity to 40 per cent), and secure the balance of funds from private sources.

The outbreak of war in Europe in the summer of 1914 now engulfed the hapless pair: the British government banned the export of capital, choking off that source, and the New York securities market, plunged into chaos by that action, was equally unreceptive to the Canadian promoters. In 1915 Wall Street bankers agreed to consider a loan to Canadian Northern but proposed a full examination of the properties and demanded that the Canadian government guarantee any new bond flotations.

Meanwhile, Cochrane had been vainly pressing the Grand Trunk to take over the Eastern Division as required under the 1903 Railway Act. Hays was gone, but his successor, Alfred Smithers, was equally obdurate on this point and also wanted $30 million in Canadian government bond guarantees to continue work on the Grand Trunk Pacific. At this point Borden decided to buy time by creating yet another Royal Commission to try to sort out the railway problem. Although the head of the Commission was A.H. Smith of the New York Central Railroad, the dominant figure was Henry Drayton, chairman of the Canadian Board of Railway Commissioners and, like Cochrane, a strong advocate of government control if not ownership of all the nation's railways, including the CPR. Not surprisingly, in their 1917 report Drayton and the third member of the commission, W.H. Acworth, recommended that the government take over both the Canadian Northern and the Grand Trunk Pacific (along with its parent, the Grand Trunk). Smith dissented, arguing that the Canadian Northern was a viable entity, a view shared by the Wall Street bankers' review completed in 1916.

In July 1917 Borden, who had endorsed the idea of a government-owned western line back in 1903, moved quickly to take over Canadian Northern. This decision precipitated an emotional interview with Mackenzie, who, disconsolate over the mortal illness of his wife as well as the disintegration of his business empire, 'completely broke down with audible sobs which were most distressing'.[7] Action on the other elements of the Royal Commission report was delayed as the Prime Minister fought out the election on the conscription issue. With a strong majority for his 'Union' government, Borden proceeded towards a complete takeover of the Grand Trunk properties, beginning with the Grand Trunk Pacific line in 1919. In 1923 Grand Trunk was fully amalgamated with Canadian Northern as the Canadian National Railways.

Although contemporary public opinion tended (as did Shaughnessy of the CPR) to assign blame for the debacle on all the railway promoters, historians have been more discriminating. The Canadian Northern, by most accounts, was a soundly built line and served the needs of the West, not least by pressuring the CPR to expand its own operations in the region. Mackenzie and Mann may have been overly optimistic in attempting to create a transcontinental system, but their failure was due more to circumstances beyond their control: the outbreak of war in 1914 cut off the flow of capital 'when they were within sight of their goal', and the refusal of the Board of Railway Commissioners, under pressure from western farmers and other shippers, to allow freight rates to rise despite war-induced inflation cut into their operating revenues. By contrast, the National Transcontinental/Grand Trunk Pacific is seen as an ill-conceived, wastefully built system that ultimately dragged down the otherwise reasonably sound Grand Trunk Railway. Hays, in particular, built 'castles in the air' and antagonized politicians of all persuasions; his successors performed equally poorly in defending the venture before the Royal Commission.

There have been some differences among historians over the motives and objectives of the Canadian government in dealing with the railway crisis. Traditional accounts see the Borden administration as reluctant nationalizers, taking over the bankrupt lines because no other option seemed possible— or no other option that would not have imperilled the Bank of Commerce and other financial institutions that had invested heavily in the railway ventures during the pre-war boom. Regehr and John Eagle, however, have argued that Borden and his ministers embraced public ownership as a step towards a rationalization of Canada's transportation system that would provide more equitable service in the West and reduce the role of foreign investors in an essential sector of the nation's economy. Although this argument may impute a longer-term approach to economic planning than seems appropriate for politicians of the era, there certainly were other examples of government-owned railways in Europe for them to emulate; even in the US, the rail system was placed under government control, albeit only for the duration of the war. Borden, as noted above, had advocated government ownership of the western lines as early as 1903, and during the 1920s he professed regret that the CPR had not been integrated with the other railways to form a single nationalized system.[8]

Such an amalgamation did not come to pass, however, and the nation's railway system instead came to resemble the utilities industry, with a combination of publicly and privately owned enterprises. By 1920 the Intercolonial Railway had been folded into the Canadian Northern/Grand Trunk system, despite the protests of Maritimers, to form the federal government's first major Crown corporation, Canadian National Railways. Sir Joseph Flavelle, the meat-packing millionaire who had headed Canada's Imperial Munitions Board during World War I, was the first chairman of the CNR; the chief operating officer was David B. Hanna, who in 1921 encountered what was to be one of the line's most troublesome features: the inevitable complications that partisan politics introduced in running the CNR.

In 1922, Hanna, a veteran manager from Canadian Northern, fell afoul of the new Liberal regime of Mackenzie King and resigned. To replace him, King recruited Sir Henry Thornton. An American by birth, Thornton had begun his railway career with the Long Island Railroad, a commuter line, then moved to Britain shortly before World War I to run the Great Eastern Railway. Thornton's talents in organizing passenger service led to his appointment as Inspector-General of Transportation for the British War Office. He came to Canada in 1923 with a formidable reputation, and assurances from the government that there would be no further political interference.

Thornton's tasks were equally formidable. The CNR comprised over 200 assorted railway lines and carried $1.3 billion in debt: in 1922, earnings were insufficient to cover the service charges on the debt. Canadian railway workers had pressed successfully during the war for wage rates equal to those of their counterparts in the US; then the Board of Railway Commissioners reduced freight rates in 1920–1 in response to the post-war recession. Finally, in the post-war era the automobile was emerging for the first time in Canada as a serious rival to railways in the transportation field.

The CPR faced many of these same problems, but did not carry a significant debt load, and Shaughnessy's successor, Edward Beatty, maintained his company's earnings by cutting expenditures on equipment maintenance, living for a time off the accumulated assets of the Shaughnessy era.

Nor did Beatty have to face the sniping that the Conservative Party, now in opposition, directed towards Thornton—and the CPR contributed to the chorus, pointing out repeatedly that the CNR's access to public funds gave it an unfair advantage over the private line.

Despite these problems, in his early years at CNR, Thornton was successful in at least restoring the public image of the government enterprise. Attentive to labour relations—in 1925 he introduced proposals for an employee pension plan—he was also able to bring some internal order to the sprawling CNR system with its heterogeneous management drawn from previously rival companies. Thornton diversified the company into radio broadcasting, introducing *Hockey Night in Canada* in 1924; he was mindful of technological changes as well, bringing the first diesel locomotive into Canada in 1929. Not all his ventures were successful: an effort to revive western 'colonization' proved abortive, as the tide of population was moving off the land in the 1920s. Nevertheless, Thornton could point in 1928 to an increase in surplus operating revenues, from less than $4 million when he took over to $58 million within five years.

The revival of CNR's fortunes brought Beatty back into active competition in the late 1920s. Both sides indulged in hotel-building binges in the major cities as well as in the growing resorts, such as Jasper Park on the CNR line. Resplendent palaces such as the CPR's Royal York Hotel in Toronto and the CNR's Hotel Vancouver were erected, neither of which earned enough to cover costs of construction for many years. A new round of railway construction also ensued, focusing on Saskatchewan, with almost 2,000 new miles laid. The CNR also built, at long last, the Hudson's Bay Railway that Mackenzie and Mann had promised to the Manitoba government more than 30 years earlier. In the buoyant economic times of 1926–9 these various commitments seemed worthwhile if costly, but for Thornton in particular, they were to prove the sources of undoing.

The onset of the Depression caught both companies in a financially overextended position and both suffered severe losses in operating revenues. The CNR's surplus dwindled to less than $10 million by 1930 and the company ran a $60 million deficit in 1931–2. But Thornton's problems were aggravated by the departure of the Liberals from power in Ottawa in the election of 1930. The new Tory leader, R.B. Bennett, had been one of the CPR's chief attorneys and had vigorously criticized Thornton and the Crown corporation for years. The CNR's accounts were subjected to a thorough investigation by a parliamentary committee in 1931 and by a Royal Commission the following year. Thornton's personal expenditures and salary came under fire, and amid allegations of extravagance and mismanagement, he was forced to resign in 1932. A year later he was dead.[9]

Beatty pushed for an amalgamation of the two lines, under CPR control, or alternatively for the government to take over running all the money-losing rail services, leaving the CPR with its more profitable divisions, particularly Cominco. The Liberals' return to power in 1935 stymied these proposals, and the new Minister of Transport, C.D. Howe, reorganized CNR management. By this time, the era of the railway as the major transportation mode in Canada was passing. The combined effect of the Depression and the shift to motor vehicles cut freight and passenger sales by half for the Canadian railways. Although World War II resuscitated the lines, the CPR continued to pursue its strategy of diversification into air transportation and eventually into oil and gas, telecommunications, and other novel fields, transforming itself into a conglomerate. The CNR was restrained by its public-service position from pursuing ancillary ventures to this degree, but it expanded investment in communications and urban real estate, with the CN Tower in Toronto providing a suitable symbol: few tourists who visit it would be likely to immediately associate this edifice with a company that began as a railway builder for farmers on the Canadian prairies.

CHAPTER 4

Gifts of Nature

For both domestic and foreign investors, much of the attraction of railroad and utility securities reflected confidence that the development of Canada's infrastructure would open the way for rapid exploitation of the country's natural resources. While both supplies of and demand for Canada's traditional staples were apparently declining in the late nineteenth century, new resources were being discovered that would serve the needs of industries, especially in the United States, and thus provide export markets considered essential for economic revival and long-term prosperity.

Looking back from the perspective of the present, the exploitation of Canada's 'treasure house of resources' may seem to have been a mixed blessing. The rapid development of the country's mining and forestry frontiers in the early twentieth century did indeed generate wealth and create jobs, but left a residue of environmental problems and littered the northern interior region with isolated, vulnerable single-industry settlements. Harnessing the 'new staples' to a continental market perpetuated Canada's role as a resource hinterland, and the linkages forged by American corporate investment were, if anything, much tighter than the older economic ties with Britain.

But for Canada's turn-of-the-century business and political leaders, foreign investment, natural resource exports, population growth,

industrialization, and economic prosperity were all part of the same package. This vision of development provided Canadian business people with hope for the future in the depressed 1890s, and their optimism grew over the next decade as Canada, in its emerging role as supplier of essential materials, shared in the industrialized world's long boom that preceded the outbreak of World War I. Sir Wilfrid Laurier reflected that confidence, while taking political credit for his role in the process, when he predicted in 1910 that the twentieth century would 'belong to Canada'.

THE WHEAT BOOM

The opening of the prairies for agriculture was, of course, the most obvious example of the interconnection of staple exports and economic growth. The depression of the early 1890s delayed prairie settlement, but by the end of the decade world wheat prices were rising, transportation costs were falling as western rail networks proliferated, and the Canadian government embarked on a vigorous campaign to stimulate immigration to the region through homesteading and subsidized travel costs for settlers. Wheat production tripled between 1904 and 1914, at which point it was Canada's major export commodity, accounting for almost 15 per cent of total exports, principally directed to the British market. Despite the slump in world wheat prices from overproduction in the 1920s, Canada's share of global wheat exports rose from 14 per cent in the pre-war era to almost 40 per cent on the eve of the Great Depression.

The 'wheat boom' of the period from 1901 to World War I was a highly visible element in Canada's development, but economists differ over its significance in accounting for the nation's economic growth in this era. Estimates of the contribution of the wheat boom to real per capita income growth for the decade 1901–11 have ranged from a low of 8 per cent to a high of close to 40 per cent. To some extent these variations reflect differences in calculating the 'linkages' between prairie agriculture and other sectors of the economy. These linkages were numerous and in effect diffused the impact of the wheat boom throughout much of the Canadian business system, although the degree to which this single staple affected overall economic development remains a matter of controversy.[1]

The most direct links were formed in the grain-handling and marketing arrangements that emerged in tandem with prairie settlement. Along the rail lines various companies erected grain warehouses to store wheat for farmers for a fee. At Fort William/Port Arthur on Lake Superior (later renamed Thunder Bay), the major transshipment point for prairie wheat destined for eastern Canadian and export markets, large terminal elevators provided bulk storage. The railway companies owned most of these terminal elevators directly— CPR built the first one in 1884—and dominated this phase of the process until co-operatives and government-owned elevators entered the field in the late 1920s. The 'country' or line elevators were independent of the railways from whom they leased the land and who set basic design guidelines for storage facilities. By 1900 there were over 400 line elevators and they continued to proliferate, reaching a peak of 5,733 by 1930 with storage capacity of 5 million tons.

The line elevator business attracted a variety of groups. During the 1890s grain merchants operating out of Winnipeg entered the field, as did some Ontario-based firms, notably James Richardson and Sons of Kingston, which remains one of the largest family enterprises in the business. It was also one of the few big companies presided over by a woman: Muriel Richardson took charge of the firm after her husband's death in 1938 and ran it for the next quarter-century. Meanwhile, two Montreal flour milling firms, Ogilvie and Lake of the Woods, established footholds in Manitoba line elevators as part of their strategy of vertical integration. After 1900 both also established western mills, and Ogilvie erected a terminal elevator at Fort William. Ontario mills began developing their own prairie elevator networks during this decade, and by 1912 almost half of Canada's wheat exports took the form of processed flour. The Canadian Northern Railway promoters, Mackenzie and Mann, invited American capital into the field: in 1906 Frank Peavey, the 'Grain King of Minneapolis', set up an elevator network on the Canadian Northern route; within three years he had elevators along the CPR line as well.

After World War I, mergers steadily reduced the number of line elevator companies and the amalgamated firms moved to integrate line and terminal elevator systems. By the end of the 1930s the number of private firms in the field had diminished by 50 per cent from the 1914 total. Long before this process of amalgamation began, however, western wheat farmers had been agitating against what they regarded as 'monopolistic' behaviour by line elevator syndicates in collusion with the CPR. In 1897 the railway had begun dealing only with warehouses maintaining mechanized grain elevators. At this point only three firms controlled almost half the elevator capacity, and CPR interests were linked to the two milling firms that occupied much of the rest of the market. Furthermore, the line elevator companies functioned as middlemen in the marketing of grain; in addition to storing wheat, they were often the major or the only buyers available to farmers. The Winnipeg Grain Exchange, established in 1887, was heavily populated with

Muriel Richardson, president from 1939 to 1966 of James Richardson & Sons Ltd, one of Canada's largest grain merchants. (Courtesy Department of Archives and Special Collections, University of Manitoba)

wheat pools and elevator networks that within another decade controlled almost half the country's elevator capacity.[2]

On the supply side, western wheat farmers depended heavily on Canadian manufacturers for a wide range of consumer goods as well as production equipment, thanks in large part to the National Policy tariffs, another source of their discontent. The most direct beneficiaries of these arrangements were the makers of farm equipment. From the middle of the nineteenth century a number of technological improvements in farm implements appeared, from cream separators and seed drills to steam-driven threshing machines. Of particular significance for western wheat producers, as beneficial as the new strains of wheat, were the steel plow and mechanical reaper, which enhanced the efficiency of planting and harvesting in Canada's short growing season. Many of these innovations originated in the United States, and Canadian farm equipment manufacturers, who had liberally borrowed and adapted American designs up to 1870, became ardent protectionists, lobbying for import duties that peaked at 35 per cent in 1883 as large US firms such as McCormick extended northward.

In 1871 there were over 250 farm implement firms in Canada, most of them congregated in southwest Ontario close to the old agricultural heartland as well as the nascent iron mills of Hamilton. Unlike many other protected industries, however, small-scale competitors were rapidly winnowed out, particularly during the depression of the early 1890s. In 1891, when the two largest companies—Massey of Toronto and Harris of Brantford—merged, they controlled over half the market.

Both Massey and Harris were family firms that had emerged in the 1850s. In the ensuing decades they had pursued parallel and competitive lines, developing their own sales agencies, persistently searching for innovations on the American scene, licensing and then refashioning these products for the Canadian market. The Massey firm was the senior partner in the amalgamation, with a

brokers connected to the elevator companies; after 1903 and until World War II, dealers on the exchange could trade in grain futures to provide a hedge against grain price fluctuations.

The shift from warehouses to elevators helped cut transportation costs by reducing the turn-around time for cargo pickups, and the operations of the Grain Exchange provided a certain degree of stability to the market. But prairie farmers saw the lion's share of these benefits passing to eastern and Winnipeg business interests. The following two decades witnessed the rise of a powerful agrarian political movement in the West, a series of provincial and federal government investigations and attempts to regulate the grain trade, and the emergence by the 1920s of the co-operative foothold in the European market thanks to years of exhibiting at international fairs. During the debates preceding introduction of the National Policy of 1879, Hart Massey, the architect of his company's development since the 1860s, had broken ranks with other Canadian farm implement manufacturers, arguing that higher tariffs would raise production costs for his industry and weaken Massey's competitive export potential. After the Massey-Harris amalgamation, Massey renewed lobbying for tariff reduction, and duties on imported farm equipment were cut to 20 per cent in 1894.

This level remained high enough, however, to attract a formidable competitor in 1903 when the McCormick Co., reorganized by J.P. Morgan as International Harvester with almost 90 per cent control of the US market for binders and reapers, established a subsidiary in Canada. In the meantime, Massey-Harris had erected a strong sales network on the prairies, enlarged its manufacturing plant, and moved into the European market, which by 1901 accounted for more than one-third of its total sales. Export sales and development of overseas manufacturing, especially in France, provided a needed cushion for Massey-Harris because International Harvester's sheer size and production capabilities dwarfed the Canadian firm: by the mid-1920s Harvester held a 40 per cent share of the Canadian market and had moved with greater dispatch and efficiency into production of mechanized tractors.

In addition to competition in its home market from Harvester and slumping sales overseas in the early 1920s, Massey-Harris suffered from a lack of leadership: Vincent Massey, the last direct descendant of the founding families, was more interested in politics and diplomacy than running the firm. In 1927 Massey-Harris was reorganized as a public joint-stock company. The ensuing Great Depression, which virtually destroyed the company's export business, took Massey-Harris to the brink of bankruptcy in 1931, but under James Duncan, who had managed Massey's French plant in the 1920s, the company was able to stagger through

the slump.[3] While the wheat boom of the early 1900s (and its subsequent collapse in the 1920s) had a direct impact on suppliers such as Massey-Harris and the grain marketing industry, its effects permeated the rest of the economy, and the aggregate of these indirect linkages greatly exceeded in macroeconomic terms the income generated by specific industries directly serving the farming sector. The fortunes of western urban businesses— wholesalers, small local merchants, savings institutions with heavy investment in prairie real estate—rose and fell with the wheat market. In the early 1900s railway construction, which in turn stimulated expansion of affiliated industries such as iron and steel, was intended primarily to provide capacity for hauling immigrants to the prairies and their wheat in the opposite direction; and as in the 1840s the inflow of foreign capital to finance railways percolated into other quarters.

But the western wheat boom provides only part of the explanation for the country's remarkable economic growth in this era. Even in the case of industries directly related to agriculture, as the Massey-Harris example indicates, some production was destined for export. As the economy diversified and urban populations expanded, merchants, manufacturers, and other businesses served these markets; by 1911 the proportion of the labour force involved in agriculture was little more than one-third of the total, and by 1931 this had diminished to less than 30 per cent. Even at the peak of the wheat boom in the second decade of the twentieth century, with the western rail network essentially complete, farm products accounted for only one-quarter of the total volume of freight, with minerals providing another 25 per cent and forestry products slightly less.

The prairie wheat fields unquestionably provided a major staple export for Canada between 1890 and 1930 and stimulated the growth of the West with its major grain entrepôts across the region and its overbuilt railway networks, not to mention enriching financiers in central Canada and Britain. Certain features of the wheat trade distinguish it from other 'new staples' of this era. First, the major market for wheat lay in Britain and later continental Europe, in contrast to minerals and forestry products that largely flowed southward to the United States. Wheat was thus very much a 'traditional' transatlantic staple, with Canadians competing with American producers, bolstering the older ties with Britain. Western farmers longed for cheap American manufactured goods and resented eastern control of the transport and marketing of their wheat, but the 'regional alienation' of that era did not reflect the pro-American tilt of more recent western protest movements.

Second, and to some extent for related reasons, American direct investment played a somewhat less significant role in the wheat boom than in the development of other natural resources. Canadian rail expansion into the West was largely financed with British capital. The American presence in the line elevator field was fairly substantial in the early years of the century, comprising about 50 per cent of capacity in 1911, but that proportion diminished after the 1920s: by World War II, US interests held only about one-fifth of the total. American farm equipment companies like International Harvester crossed the tariff barrier to set up branch plants in Canada, but this was part of a general trend in manufacturing, particularly after the defeat of reciprocity in 1911.

MINING

The emergence of Canada as a major player in the North American mining industry by the 1920s was the result of the fortuitous convergence of shifts in demand for and supplies of minerals after the 1880s. During the 'First Industrial Revolution' of the early nineteenth century the major ore required had been coal for generating steam power and the charcoal residue needed for iron production. British North America had few known reserves of coal outside Nova Scotia and little if any of the hard, fast-burning anthracite that fuelled American industrial growth. In any case, most of the Maritime coal flowed south to New England while central Canadians imported

coal from Pennsylvania and Ohio. When prospects for developing Nova Scotia's coal mines and integrating them with iron and steel manufacturing beckoned in the 1890s, it was a Boston capitalist, Henry M. Whitney, who in 1893 took the initiative in consolidating the Cape Breton coal fields into the Dominion Coal Co.

The technologies associated with the 'Second Industrial Revolution' of the 1880s–1920s, by contrast, required a wide range of special metals, many of which had to be extracted and refined through complex, capital-intensive techniques. The most dramatic applications were in the military field, stimulated by the international arms race that culminated in World War I. Nickel alloyed with steel provided hard armour-plating for the dreadnoughts and other warships developed by the navies of the Great Powers; during the war, tanks and other armoured vehicles were introduced. Zinc and copper were combined to make brass casings for lead bullets, produced in vast quantities in the war. At the same time, civilian commercial uses flourished: nickel-steel alloys produced corrosive-resistant steel coated with zinc for general industrial purposes, in particular in the automotive field. Motor vehicles also used fibred asbestos for brake linings and clutch facings, and asbestos blended with cement was used for heavy-duty pipes and construction materials. The electrical equipment industry required large amounts of lead for batteries and copper wiring for transmission lines. Even precious metals—gold and silver—had industrial uses, though the major gold booms of Canada in the 1890s and 1930s were more notably tied to the use of the metal for currency.

The rising demand for industrial minerals coincided with the opening of the Canadian northern and western interior by railway construction and the development of hydroelectric capacity that was harnessed to the smelting and refining of metals. The Canadian Shield, stretching across northern Quebec and Ontario, hitherto regarded as useless real estate and a barrier to agricultural settlement, was discovered to possess vast reserves of a range of minerals. A substantial portion of the wealth generated by the mining booms between the 1890s and 1930s was siphoned off by Montreal and Toronto financiers to help under-write ancillary ventures and industrial consolida-tions that solidified central Canada's position as the economic heartland of the country.

The Canadian West, however, was the scene of the first sustained sequence of development. It centred on the Kootenay Valley in south-central British Columbia. During the 1880s American miners had begun exploiting massive copper deposits in Montana and silver-lead deposits in Idaho and Washington. Some of them began looking northward, among them F. Augustus Heinze, a Columbia University-trained geolo-gist who by the early 1890s was embroiled in a struggle among the 'copper kings' of Butte, Montana, for control the industry. To outflank his rivals, Heinze in 1894 established a smelter at Trail, BC, to process locally mined copper and silver ores; in the following year Heinze secured a charter to build a narrow-gauge railway to connect the Trail smelter to the mine sites.

At this point the CPR entered the picture. Alarmed by the prospect that Heinze might extend his railway from Trail to link up with Jim Hill's Great Northern Railroad, Van Horne and Shaughnessy in 1898 decided to buy not only the railway but also the Trail smelter—an inadver-tent first step towards diversification by the CPR, which also in the long run transferred control over the development of the region from Amer-ican to central Canadian business interests.

At the turn of the century, however, the Trail smelting operation was only one of a number of mining ventures in the Kootenay region. By this time the most readily accessible sources of copper, silver, and gold had been played out and the CPR faced the problem of having a large smelter with no supplies of ore. Shaughnessy's strategy to deal with this problem was twofold. Using its growing financial resources CPR began buying up other mines, culminating in 1906 with the establishment of Consolidated Mining and Smelting Co. (a name

later shortened to Cominco). At the same time, technical specialists were brought in to develop new processes for separating, purifying, and refining the often intermixed ores encountered by miners as they moved further underground.

The 1910 acquisition and subsequent devel-opment of the Sullivan Mine at Kimberley, BC, was the key to Cominco's eventual domination of the region's mineral industry. The Sullivan Mine consisted largely of mixed lead and zinc ores, both of which had potential commercial value but had defied various technical efforts by smaller local smelters to separate them. Cominco acquired a promising separation process and began erecting a zinc refining plant at Trail in 1914. At this point the outbreak of war stimulated demand for both metals for shell casings, and the Cana-dian government undertook to finance Comin-co's research and development. As it happened, a completely satisfactory zinc refining process was not brought on stream until the early 1920s; but Cominco had both the technology and capacity to fully exploit post-war civilian markets. To provide necessary electric power Cominco had also taken over a local power system in 1917, providing the company with a fully integrated operation. During the 1920s more than half of BC's mineral output came from Cominco's lead and zinc production. Given its economies of scale, Cominco generated profits even through the Depression and deployed the earnings from its Sullivan Mine base to diver-sify into fertilizers, iron and steel, and direct investment in East Asia after World War II.

The CPR was not the only railway to invest in the mining industry—Mackenzie and Mann acquired coal mines in BC to supply Canadian Northern—but the most important impact of railway development was to open up mineral regions of northern Ontario. Even before the CPR completed its transcontinental line this process was underway. In 1883 residents of Sudbury, Ontario, a settlement about 80 kilometres north of Georgian Bay that had just been reached by the CPR line, discovered traces of what appeared to be copper ores. Although the samples by the

Geological Survey of Canada were not very promising, a few prospectors filtered into the region. Among them was Samuel Ritchie, originally from Cleveland, Ohio, who had earlier been involved in unsuccessful efforts to develop iron ore sites at Marmora, near Peterborough in eastern Ontario. Despite pessimistic reports on the Sudbury ores, Ritchie and others were encouraged to purchase land for mineral exploration by the provisions of Ontario's General Mining Act of 1869, which imposed virtually no constraints on mining development, offered mineral rights on Crown lands for $1 per acre, and did not require royalty payments. By 1886 Ritchie had assembled claims to all unpatented land in Sudbury and organized the Canadian Copper Co. with $2 million from business associates in Ohio.

Initially, this enterprise seemed fated to go the way of Ritchie's iron ore venture. As in the case of the Sullivan Mine's lead-zinc deposits, the copper from Sudbury was intermixed with nickel and other minerals—the result, apparently, of the intense heat created by a meteorite that had formed the vast oval bowl of Sudbury Basin in prehistoric times. Nickel was an ore of little known commercial value and there was no established technology to efficiently separate it from copper, although refining experiments were underway in Britain. Ritchie had already contracted for copper refining with a New Jersey company, Orford Copper, and he persuaded Orford's owner, Col. Robert Thompson, to try to develop a separation technique. Meanwhile, stimulated by reports from Britain on the potential military value of nickel, Ritchie began lobbying the US Navy for contracts to supply nickel-plated armour.

By 1895 Orford had perfected methods of separating and refining the Sudbury ores, and a different but equally effective technique for purifying nickel had been developed by the Anglo-German chemist, Ludwig Mond. Meanwhile, there were major changes on the business side. In 1891, Ritchie, whose penchant for risk-taking alarmed his backers—he envisioned erecting a diversified industrial empire encompassing iron- and

steelmaking at Sudbury as well as mining at Copper Cliff—was ousted from the management of Canadian Copper. Thompson at Orford Copper had persuaded his erstwhile colleagues in the US Navy to award him an exclusive contract for refined nickel, and then used this coup to secure the bulk of Canadian Copper's output, buttressed by a significant equity share in the mining firm. The Orford/Canadian Copper combination turned back challenges from several British- and American-backed competitors (including a short-lived riposte from Ritchie), and reached an agreement with its only real international rival, the French company Société le Nickel, which had mines in the Pacific, to divide world markets.

A more substantial challenger entered the field in 1899 when Ludwig Mond acquired mines in the Sudbury region, shipping output to his refinery in Wales. Growing military demand for nickel soon brought a much bigger player onto the scene. In 1901 J.P. Morgan consolidated US Steel Co., the largest merger of its time. Charles Schwab, who headed the new amalgamation, advised absorption of a nickel producer to ensure a reliable flow of supplies. Thompson, facing renewed competition from Mond, was amenable, and in 1902 Morgan orchestrated consolidation of Orford, Canadian Copper, and assorted other producers into International Nickel Co. (later Inco), capitalized at $24 million.

Mond, whose refinery began production that same year, remained outside the amalgamation, and over the next 30 years his enterprise maintained a strategy of advanced research, diversification of product lines, and aggressive marketing that outpaced Inco's performance. By 1925 Mond's mining output virtually equalled that of Inco, and earnings from his operation had risen from one-fifth to one-half those of the American giant. But Mond generally avoided direct competition with Inco in the American market, and Inco's connection with Morgan helped thwart other potential entrants. Francis Clergue's venture into nickel in 1903 was easily suppressed when that ambitious empire-builder failed to secure American financing. In 1910 Fred Pearson, the peripatetic hydro-power promoter, formed a syndicate (that included, as usual, Mackenzie and Mann) to set up British-American Nickel Corporation using a new refining process developed in Norway. But Pearson was rebuffed by American bankers, and the onset of war in Europe blocked British sources of capital. After the war another Canadian group, which included John R. Booth, the Ontario lumber baron, and former Prime Minister Sir Robert Borden, tried to revive the venture but was driven from the field by a price war initiated by Inco and Mond. In 1928 Sir Alfred Mond, Ludwig's son, sold the family's nickel interests to Inco in order to devote more attention to his chemical enterprise. Although at the end of the 1920s another nickel company, Falconbridge, was assembled by Thayer Lindsley, an American geologist with Canadian backers and using the Norwegian process, the Inco–Mond merger left the American firm in virtual control of both the Sudbury field and the North American market.

The heavy capital costs and complex technology involved in extracting and refining nickel from Sudbury Basin established the conditions under which development would occur through large-scale corporations, although government policies encouraged the process as well—inadvertently before 1891, through mining regulation that permitted accumulations of claims on easy terms. After the Sudbury experience the Ontario government established a graded land price system and attempted, with limited success, to introduce royalty fees along with more formal procedures for establishing mineral claims. Both the provincial and federal governments also set out deliberately to attract foreign capital and foreign mining experts; there were no institutions in Canada for mining education until the mid-1890s, and governments were always balancing the need to regulate (and raise revenues) against the need to promote economic development.

The American orientation in the Sudbury fields was more fortuitous. Ritchie's early arrival on the scene and hasty commitment to the New Jersey refiner, before he realized the technical problems involved in nickel production, were events not dictated by fate or forces of nature. Once the Morgan interests moved in, the integration of Canadian nickel production into the American steel industry proceeded steadily. At this point a degree of Canadian nationalist (or at least anti-American) sentiment surfaced, focusing not on the presence of foreign direct investment, which was generally regarded as desirable, but on the fact that virtually all refining and processing of nickel was carried out in the US, depriving Canadians of potential jobs and business opportunities. Not surprisingly, this theme was promoted by Ritchie after his ouster by Canadian Copper, as well as by steelmakers in Hamilton and Sault Ste Marie, Ontario, who were interested in developing their own integrated industry.

In 1897, emboldened by popular discontent over a highly protectionist American tariff law, these groups lobbied in Ottawa for an export duty to be placed on unrefined nickel. Frustrated by inaction at this level, they turned to the Ontario government in 1900, urging it to use its licensing powers to compel the nickel companies to establish the 'manufacturing condition' in that field, similar to the province's undertaking for forestry products. Canadian Copper and Mond both resisted such pressures, threatening to close down Sudbury operations and draw their supplies of ore from New Caledonia, the French mine in the Pacific.

Although the government backed down, the issue simmered on through the next decade. The onset of war in Europe provided advocates of Canadian nickel refining with new ammunition. American neutrality in the war and the expansion of Inco's refineries in New Jersey fed rumours that the US company was supplying armour plating material to Germany, thus providing aid and comfort to Canada's foes. Although there was little evidence that significant quantities of nickel were running through the British blockade, Inco's owners (including the intensely pro-British J.P. Morgan) slowly succumbed to pressures from the Ontario and Canadian governments.

Prime Minister Borden hinted that subsidies might be provided to Pearson's group, British-American Co., to build a refinery in Canada. In 1916 Inco announced plans to erect a refinery at Port Colbourne, close to the hydro facilities of Niagara Falls. Although the post-war slump temporarily closed all Inco's refineries, the company shifted the bulk of its nickel smelting to Canada in the 1920s.

The CPR had opened Sudbury Basin for exploitation in the 1880s as an unanticipated by-product of its construction towards the Canadian prairies. Twenty years later a very similar sequence of events opened northeastern Ontario for mineral development, although the results were very different. Throughout the last two decades of the nineteenth century, land speculators in Ontario and French-Canadian missionaries in Quebec campaigned for construction of a railway between Lake Nipissing and James Bay to open that region—the agricultural fringe of the Clay Belt—to settlement. By 1900 some Toronto business interests joined the chorus, anticipating that rail access to Hudson Bay would reduce their dependence on Montreal for shipping transatlantic goods; some even dreamed of linking Toronto to the Klondike via James Bay. Reflecting these various ambitions, the Liberal regime of George Ross in Ontario committed itself in 1902 to build a government-owned line, christened the Timiskaming and Northern Ontario Railway (later the Ontario Northland Railway).

By 1903 the line had been laboriously completed to Long Lake on the Ontario–Quebec border, about 160 kilometres north of Lake Nipissing. At this point workers on the line discovered veins of what proved to be pure silver. Within a short time there was a silver rush centring on a settlement named Cobalt, since that metal was found intermixed with the silver; Long Lake was renamed Cobalt Lake. By 1906 several thousand prospectors and their camp followers clustered at Cobalt, thanks to easy access via the railway (in contrast to the Klondike); silver-mine stock promoters from Toronto could trundle potential investors up for a day's viewing of the site.

In contrast to Sudbury Basin, and like the Klondike (see box, p. 62), Cobalt was a 'poor man's camp'. Although the Ontario government tightened its regulatory procedures under the 1897 Mining Act, requiring a 'proved discovery' before licensing a claim, the intent of the measure was at least in part to streamline processing of claims and resolve disputes over claims, which, to put it mildly, were frequent and spirited. By 1914 much of the silver was gone, but in the interim small prospectors could pry out the ores fairly easily without having to worry overmuch about separating mixed ores.

The Cobalt silver boom was short-lived but it spawned a number of millionaire prospectors who used their earnings to finance further ventures and to stake promising proteges. In 1909 gold discoveries at Porcupine, northwest of Cobalt, attracted the attention of the Timmins brothers, who had developed one of Cobalt's early claims. Acquiring a site at Porcupine, discovered by a fellow prospector, Benny Hollinger, the Timminses set up Hollinger Gold Mines, drew on their Cobalt profits to buy neighbouring claims, and laid out a townsite. Another set of brothers, Gilbert and Charles Labine, migrated from Cobalt to briefly join forces with the Timminses in the Hollinger mine, then moved westward, eventually opening the Eldorado gold mine in Manitoba—which proved to be more significant for its uranium deposits, leading to its acquisition by the Canadian government in 1944. The Labines used the proceeds from this sale to finance further lucrative mining ventures in Saskatchewan and Alberta in the 1940s. The Timmins and Labine brothers were only a few of the cohort of mining entrepreneurs who fanned out across the Canadian northern interior to exploit gold fields at Kirkland Lake and Red Lake in Ontario and more remote mining sites after World War I, their explorations made easier by small bush aircraft and the systematic topographical research of the Geological Survey of Canada.

For the most part, the smaller operators at Cobalt and other mines were content to take

THE KLONDIKE GOLD RUSH

Curiously, Canada's best-known mining boom, the Klondike gold rush of 1897–8, had relatively little impact on the country's economy and business community. Canada had experienced modest gold rushes through the nineteenth century, most notably on the Fraser River and in the interior region of Cariboo and the Kootenays in British Columbia in the 1860s. Another short-lived bonanza was discovered at Silver Islet on Lake Superior in the mid-1870s. It yielded $3.2 million in silver ore over a 14-year span, much of which flowed into the hands of a Detroit businessman, Alexander Sibley, who had acquired the venture from its despondent Montreal founders shortly before the strike.

Gold prospectors, many of them Americans, moved slowly from British Columbia into the Yukon wilderness in the 1880s, and the Canadian government had only just established its authority in the region when gold was discovered in the summer of 1896. The feature that made the discovery so attractive to the thousands of 'amateur' prospectors who poured into the Yukon across Chilkoot Pass was that it was 'placer gold', which, at least initially, could be found along the bottoms of rivers and creeks and panned rather than mined.

By 1898 over $8 million in gold had been brought out in this fashion. Latecomers had to start tunnelling underground but the technology remained relatively straightforward, although the vast majority of those who ventured to the Klondike never fulfilled their hopes. Those who exploited the prospectors—suppliers of equipment and transportation and the array of gamblers, saloon keepers, and other camp followers who congregated at Dawson City— probably found more reliable sources of income than the gold seekers themselves.

Large-scale mining operations were not a major feature of the Klondike gold rush. In 1899 a British entrepreneur, A.N.C. Treadgold, persuaded the Canadian government to provide him with a large consolidated concession to permit more systematic mining operations. But the Treadgold concession stimulated a populist outcry among the small miners and was abandoned in 1904. Two years later the government imposed new regulations to encourage larger ventures, and the Treadgold claim was taken over by a subsidiary of the US mining multinational, Guggenheim. Several other big firms mined the area for copper, but by 1914 most of the gold was gone, and Dawson shrank to a small outpost for government officials and mine employees.

The Klondike gold rush had some spillover effects: in 1899 an Anglo-American group built a rail line, eventually acquired by the CPR, to link the Yukon to the BC inland waterway, contributing to a dispute between the US and Canada over the boundary of the Alaska panhandle. But little in the way of long-term development came about in the region until the 1970s, by which time 'black gold'—the oil deposits of the Beaufort Sea—was the major lure.

The Klondike also helped fix in the public mind (not just among Canadians) the notion of Canada as a 'storehouse of resources' awaiting exploitation. The silver strike at Cobalt in northern Ontario in 1904, followed by gold discoveries at Porcupine and Kirkland Lake in the same region, fuelled this perspective and lured northward other mining entrepreneurs, such as Benny Hollinger, Noah Timmins, and Harry Oakes. But success in mining could also be achieved without venturing out of Toronto or Vancouver: J.P. Bickell, a broker in mining stocks, took over

The Hudson's Bay Company advertised supplies for the Klondike gold rush.
(Hudson's Bay Company Archives, Archives of Manitoba D. 26/34 fo. 21d N7815)

the McIntyre Porcupine mine as his first step towards fame and fortune.

The examples of Bickell and Oakes stimulated many an unwary investor to enter the world of 'penny' mining stocks where risky or fraudulent ventures abounded. Even before the Klondike rush, speculators were sinking their savings into uncertain mining enterprises in Rossland, British Columbia, and the inevitable scandals that followed laid the groundwork for provincial measures in Ontario and elsewhere to try to impose some restraints on the marketing of high-risk shares. But until the late 1920s there were few regulations on the books and these were laxly enforced. But the urge to speculate has been a constant element in the mining field, and the temptations to fraud have been equally persistent, as exemplified by the Bre-X gold mine scandal of 1997.

Sources: Christopher Armstrong, *Blue Skies and Boiler Rooms* (Toronto, 1997); Harold Innis, *Settlement and the Mining Frontier* (Toronto, 1936); Morris Zaslow, *The Grand Opening of the Canadian North 1870–1914* (Toronto, 1971).

out surface ores and ship them off in a relatively unrefined form. Eventually, however, the surface veins were played out and heavier equipment was needed. At this point metal mining became more capital-intensive and technologically demanding, and larger companies entered the scene, often consolidating a number of smaller claims and integrating mining and refining operations much like Cominco in British Columbia and Inco in Sudbury, albeit on a smaller scale. After World War I the pace of this expansion accelerated, driven by industrial demand for metals and a buoyant market for mining securities.

In 1922 two American mining engineers, S.C. Thompson and H.W. Chadbourne, set up a New York-based syndicate to develop some promising gold fields in Rouyn township on the western border of Quebec. On the advice of their Canadian lawyer, James Murdoch, the syndicate incorporated in Ontario as Noranda Mines to provide limited liability to the partners, and Murdoch became president. Noranda included both American and Canadian investors, among them the Timmins brothers. Recognizing that the copper sources of Rouyn were more abundant than its gold, Murdoch drew on capital from Hollinger Mines to set up a smelter near the mine and by 1930 had established a refinery in Montreal. By the end of World War II, Noranda had acquired a brass factory and mining ventures in Central America; its copper output and vertical integration made Noranda second only to Inco in the Canadian mining industry. As in the case of Cominco, Noranda devoted much attention to technological improvements, developing its own high-speed ore roasters, as well as drawing on American and British processes through joint ventures.

Noranda was only one of a number of Canadian mining enterprises that integrated forward into refining, relying often on proximity to Canadian hydroelectric facilities and introducing technological innovations to achieve larger-scale production at lower per-unit cost: in 1927, for example, Hudson Bay Mining and Smelting was set up to develop copper-zinc deposits at Flin Flon in

Manitoba. In that same year Falconbridge Nickel appeared at Sudbury.

Sources of capital and corporate control varied. Inco, which dwarfed all other Canadian mining entities in 1929 (particularly after its merger with Mond Nickel), was essentially an Anglo-American operation with a research unit in New Jersey and rolling mills in the US and Britain (see Table 4.1). While its near-monopoly position in the nickel industry declined after World War II, the company followed Falconbridge and Noranda into overseas direct investment. Cominco, the second largest firm in 1929, was controlled by CPR until 1986. The other major companies represented a mixture (sometimes an intermixture) of American and Canadian capital. The Ontario Northland rail link-up of Toronto to the Cobalt–Porcupine–Kirkland Lake region and the integration of the mining exchange into the Toronto Stock Exchange ensured that Toronto-based groups would play a major role in financing Canadian metal mining: Canadian historian J.M.S. Careless commented that the 'opulent suburbs of Toronto spell out a veritable progression of northern mining booms.'[4]

FORESTRY PRODUCTS

Between the mid-1880s and 1930 the forestry industry in Canada went through two overlapping cycles. With the rise of steamships the demand for squared pine timber declined, and that development, aggravated by the disappearance of good pine through overcutting, eroded the position of the Maritimes, especially New Brunswick, in the industry by World War I. At the same time, railways not only opened up new areas in Ontario and the West for logging but also provided a market for rail ties. The growth of cities in central Canada and the American Midwest provided another booming market, with the burgeoning rail network around the Great Lakes favouring timber development along the Ottawa River and Georgian Bay. Completion of the CPR in 1885 stimulated the rise of the lumber

TABLE 4.1

MAJOR CANADIAN MINING COMPANIES, 1929

Company	Assets	Ownership
International Nickel	$182 million	47% US; 31% UK
Cominco	$55 million	Cdn (CPR)
Hollinger Mines	$36 million	Cdn
Hudson Bay Mining & Smelting	$28 million	85% US
Noranda Mines	$21 million	65% Cdn; 30%US
Asbestos Corporation	$21 million	Cdn
Granby Consolidated Mining & Smelting	$17 million	majority US
Dome Mines	$13 million	majority US
McIntyre-Porcupine Mines	$12 million	majority Cdn
Mining Corporation of Canada	$9 million	Cdn

Sources: Compiled from: *Canadian Annual Financial Review* (Toronto, 1930); ownership data from E.S. Moore, *The American Influence in Canadian Mining* (Toronto, 1941); H. Marshall et al., *Canadian-American Industry* (New Haven, Conn., 1936).

industry in British Columbia, particularly along the Fraser River, with Vancouver as its terminus and a centre for sawmilling. Much of this lumber went to the Canadian prairies, but the opening of the Panama Canal in 1910 provided BC fir and cedar products with new urban markets on the American east coast.

Meanwhile, a substantially new industry emerged after 1900 with the rapidly growing demand for pulpwood, using hitherto largely untapped stands of spruce, to be made into newsprint. By 1930 pulpwood accounted for over 40 per cent of total forestry production by value and processed and unprocessed pulpwood for over half of all timber exports by value. The Great Depression severely damaged both the traditional Canadian lumber industry and the pulp and paper industry, but newsprint emerged after World War II to become Canada's major export commodity, outpacing wheat as well as mineral and petroleum exports.

Although both construction lumber and newsprint flowed in the same direction—southward to the U.S. market—in other respects there were significant differences between these two major components of Canada's forestry products industry. Traditional lumber production did not require major initial capital outlays, and although the introduction of steam-driven sawmills and log draggers at the end of the nineteenth century contributed to the growth of larger, integrated operations, there was still room in the industry for smaller firms. As late as the mid-1920s the average capital cost of a sawmill was less than $100,000. Even the larger companies were run by individual proprietors or families: most notable among these was John R. Booth, the 'lumber king' of the Ottawa Valley who in the 1880s financed his own railway, the Canadian and Atlantic, to link his lumber tracts to Parry Sound, and later developed a Great Lakes steamer fleet to carry milled wood to Chicago. In Quebec, the descendants of William Price expanded his timber empire in the Saguenay region. On the west coast in the 1890s James Hendry established BC Mills, Timber & Trading Co., which operated sales agencies as far afield as Australia and Britain. Hendry also pioneered in the production of an early version of prefabricated housing for prairie farmers. As might be expected, the ubiquitous Mackenzie and Mann dabbled in this industry as well, establishing Canadian Western Lumber Co. in 1910 and erecting at Fraser Mills what was touted as 'the largest sawmill in the British Empire'. By this time foreign investors were entering the BC lumber trade: in 1909 Brooks-Scanlon, a Minneapolis-based family firm, built a large mill at Powell River that eventually became part of H.R. MacMillan's 'empire of wood'. A more exotic entrant was Vancouver Timber & Trading Co., set up by a German nobleman, Alvo van Alvensleben, which reputedly included the Kaiser among its aristocratic shareholders; this enterprise was seized as 'enemy' property and its assets auctioned off in World War I.

In contrast, the pulp and paper industry required huge stands of woodland and large amounts of chemicals and hydroelectric power to operate high-speed continuous production mills. Although some of the larger individual lumber producers, including Booth and the Price brothers, moved into this field in the early 1900s, the substantial capital investment needed—by the 1920s an average paper mill cost several million dollars—encouraged the formation of large-scale joint-stock corporations and syndicates, attracting the interest of financiers in Montreal, Toronto, New York, and London as well as publishers and manufacturers in the US and Britain seeking to control the flow of paper supplies through direct investment. Overexpansion of the industry after World War I led to periodic crises and eventual rationalization of competing firms into a few large vertically integrated enterprises combining wood-cutting, milling, pulp-processing, and paper-making that dominated the market by the 1940s.

The development of an integrated Canadian pulp and paper industry was, to some extent, a by-product of government measures to protect the established lumber-milling industry. By the 1890s the focus of the lumber trade in Ontario had shifted from the Ottawa Valley to the Georgian Bay region. At this point conditions of relatively free trade in both logs and milled lumber prevailed between the US and Canada, and both American loggers and Canadian lumber millers exploited the situation. The Americans, and some small Canadian loggers, floated giant rafts of unmilled logs from Ontario to sawmills in Michigan, while larger Canadian lumber entrepreneurs like Booth competed directly with US sawmills for the lucrative Chicago construction market. Depression in the 1890s intensified competition, and in 1897 the American lumber industry successfully lobbied in the US Congress for restoration of import duties on milled lumber while permitting duty-free entry of logs, provisions that were incorporated in the so-called 'Dingley Tariff'.

Ontario lumbermen turned naturally to the Dominion government for help in maintaining their US market position, but the Laurier regime proved reluctant to act on this specific case, hoping to negotiate a broader reciprocal trade agreement. Sawmillers then put pressure on the provincial governments in Ontario and Quebec to take action. In both provinces most of the land available for cutting was Crown property with timber rights leased by the government: in 1900 Ontario passed an Act requiring all licensees to process wood from Crown lands in Canadian mills. Quebec was slower to respond, but by 1910 it imposed a similar restriction; New Brunswick and British Columbia followed in 1913.

The intent of the Ontario government of George Ross in initiating this measure in 1900—as in the case of the less successful concurrent efforts to promote nickel refining at Sudbury—was to encourage the 'manufacturing condition' in the province's natural resource sector. Although Ontario lumber interests supported this measure, their long-term aim was to regain access to the US market. When the Laurier government introduced a similar manufacturing requirement on federal

Crown lands in 1907, the latter objective may have been the key consideration, for by this time the attitude of the US government, hitherto stalwartly protectionist, was beginning to change. American lumber producers remained adamant on the need for high import duties on milled wood, but they now confronted a more formidable domestic foe: the American newspaper publishers' lobby.

In the late nineteenth century the American newspaper business had been transformed. The growth of big cities and the spread of literacy created a demand for newspapers at the same time that technological developments such as the rotary press enabled publishers to increase their output and reduce costs. Entrepreneurial publishers like William Randolph Hearst and Joseph Pulitzer exploited the opportunity, establishing mass-circulation newspapers and magazines designed to attract this growing audience with stories that emphasized drama and human interest. Newspapers had traditionally been organs of political parties and commercial interests, but the new mass-circulation media could exercise a much broader influence on public opinion, as well as amassing great wealth for their owners: Hearst, for example, took credit (with considerable exaggeration) for having pressured the US government to go to war with Spain in 1898.

A crucial link in the growth of mass-circulation newspapers was the technological revolution in papermaking that occurred in this era. Traditionally, paper was made from reconverted waste materials, such as rags and straw, which placed limits on supplies; in the mid-1800s new processes emerged in Germany and the US for processing paper from low-grade wood such as spruce or hemlock. The simplest process involved the mechanical grinding or chipping of logs. A more refined product was produced by cooking the pulped wood in a solution of calcium bisulphide, leaving cellulose fibres. The fibres would be pressed into paper sheets or newsprint through steam-heated rolling machines: the most common was the Fourdrinier machine patented in England in the early nineteenth century. The mechanical and sulphite pulping processes were most commonly used in Canada and the US for papermaking; other chemical processes were later introduced to produce a finer quality paper or a tougher paper that could be used for packaging material. After World War II, Canadian papermakers began to diversify into production of this latter 'kraft' paper, which by the 1980s became an important component of the industry as demand for newsprint slackened.

Since the Dingley Tariff imposed protective duties on imported paper as well as milled lumber, American newspaper publishers in the early 1900s faced problems not only of high current costs but long-term decline of reliable sources of supply of newsprint. By 1907 they were actively lobbying for reduction of duties to provide access to the cheaper and largely undeveloped pulp and paper resources of Canada. Reduction of duties on Canadian newsprint and milled lumber was a central feature of the Reciprocity Agreement negotiated by the Laurier government and the Taft administration in the US in 1911. Although the broader trade agreement was stillborn when the Liberals lost the 1911 federal election in Canada, US duties on newsprint were virtually eliminated two years later.

The US tariff reductions of 1913 and the manufacturing requirements of provincial and federal licensing arrangements in Canada between 1900 and 1913 were followed by a dramatic growth of the pulp and paper industry. Newsprint production in Canada increased from less than 200,000 tons to over 4 million tons per year between 1913 and 1929; at the end of that period over 90 per cent of the output was exported, principally to the US although Britain and other markets absorbed a portion from Quebec and the Maritimes.

The extent to which this expansion was the result of government trade and regulatory policies has been a matter of some controversy. Historians have generally assigned these measures a significant, if not necessarily critical role in setting the stage for the growth of the Canadian newsprint industry. Economist Trevor Dick, on the other hand, has argued that Canada's resource endowments were the major factors promoting growth.

By the eve of World War I, Canadian reserves of timber for newsprint were more plentiful than American supplies, so that market forces would have brought them into play sooner or later. Furthermore, since every stage of the pulp and paper process required massive inputs of water and electric power, the availability of large hydro sites in Canada and their proximity to the timber lands indicate, according to Dick, that cost considerations rather than government policies determined the location of newsprint manufacturing facilities.[5] It may be worth noting that after World War II, the US newspaper industry began drawing more heavily on supplies from the southern states, which had experienced major expansion of hydroelectric facilities in the 1930s and have large, relatively unexploited timber lands.

In addition to the rapid development of vertically integrated firms, the period between 1912 and 1930 was punctuated by spasmodic phases of amalgamation, first in 1912–13, then in the immediate post-war period, and finally in the late twenties. Although in some cases these amalgamations reflected the growth of successful single firms, more frequently the mergers were orchestrated by Toronto and Montreal financiers such as I.W. Killam, A.J. Nesbitt, and Herbert Holt, exploiting optimistic securities markets. As in the case of hydroelectric utilities, these mergers were financed through large bond issues, with the promoters picking up bonus stock; bonded debt in turn left these apparent industrial giants vulnerable to sudden downturns in newsprint prices, as occurred in 1921 and again in 1929–32; bankruptcies, reorganizations, and rationalizations then ensued.

The largest of these boom-and-bust cycles came at the end of the 1920s. After World War I the provincial governments in Quebec and Ontario became increasingly generous in their forestry leasing policies in order to entice companies into the hinterland. Buoyed by the recovery of the North American economy from the post-war recession, American, British, and Canadian newsprint manufacturers expanded their operations so that by 1926–7 production capacity had increased 10 times over its level in 1920. By this time the larger firms began to worry about overcapacity and sought to control a potential price slide by voluntary agreements among sales agencies. When these efforts proved futile, a wave of amalgamations swept the industry, encouraged by security promoters in the bull market atmosphere of the time. Between 1926 and 1930 six gigantic mergers consolidated dozens of mills, controlling more than two-thirds of the industry's productive capacity. Two of the largest—Canada International Paper, a subsidiary of the American firm International Pulp & Paper, and Canadian Power & Paper, controlled by a Montreal syndicate led by Holt—were respectively the third and fifth largest industrial corporations in Canada in 1929.

Almost all of these mastodons carried far too much debt and lurched into bankruptcy when the Great Depression decimated investor confidence and newsprint markets. By 1932 four of the six leading firms were in receivership, including long-established companies like Abitibi Paper and Price Brothers, as well as the parvenu groupings. The only ones that escaped were companies tied to large foreign newspaper chains through long-term contracts, and smaller firms owned directly by newspapers, like Ontario Paper Co., a subsidiary of 'Colonel' Robert McCormick's *Chicago Tribune*.

Until the Great Depression the pattern of control of the largest newsprint firms resembled that of the mining industry: a mixture of foreign-owned (mostly American) and Canadian enterprises. During the 1930s two US firms dominated the devastated industry. But some British and European companies entered Canada in these years: Bowater Corp. acquired large timber reserves in Newfoundland, the Maritimes, and Quebec to supply the London press lords Beaverbrook and Rothermere. Domestic entrants also appeared, usually lumber companies diversifying into pulp and paper as their best sources of construction-quality timber diminished: the most notable of these was H.R. MacMillan in British Columbia, who began his career as a government forester. Following World War I, he went into business as a lumber exporter; by 1930 he had acquired several sawmills to guarantee supplies for his British buyers. Subsequently, he moved into newsprint, absorbing other BC firms, and emerged by the 1960s as one of the largest lumber and paper manufacturers in North America.

The larger Canadian newsprint companies did integrate cutting, pulping, and papermaking operations, but for the most part they did not diversify product lines. After the removal of US import duties in 1913, many American paper manufacturers shifted into fine paper and heavy-duty kraft products; American newsprint multinationals also rationalized operations, with their Canadian branches producing newsprint exclusively. In terms of technology, there was not a great deal of innovation in the industry from the late nineteenth century to the 1940s, and pulp and papermaking equipment was largely purchased from a small number of British and American-owned firms. While the newsprint companies represented large agglomerations of capital with integrated operations to achieve economies of scale in production, as single-line producers they remained vulnerable to market shifts; the frequent boom-and-bust cycles in the industry may have worked against the development of managerial capabilities even in well-established firms.[6]

CHAPTER 5

Nation Builders

While the technological achievements of the Second Industrial Revolution—electric lighting and power, the automobile, the airplane, the skyscraper—commanded the greatest public notice, business enterprises were experiencing organizational transformations of equal if not more lasting significance. The new technologies themselves and the expansion of national and international markets linked by steamships, rail, and telecommunications contributed to business firms' growth in size and complexity. The problems of running large or far-flung enterprises in turn stimulated innovations in company organization and administration.

This process of organizational change—the American business historian Alfred Chandler Jr has called it the 'managerial revolution in business'—was most advanced in the US. There, the rapid completion of a national railway system and the growth of immigration in the years immediately following the Civil War established the underpinnings for a large national market. Entrepreneurs such as Gustavus Swift, Andrew Carnegie, and John D. Rockefeller moved quickly to exploit this market, using the new technologies to achieve economies of scale in production and to develop national distribution networks, and new legal devices for corporate organization to integrate raw material extraction, manufacturing,

transportation of goods, and marketing. As previously isolated local and regional markets became accessible, other businessmen sought to protect themselves by informal arrangements such as cartels and, later, through amalgamations with competitors. By the early twentieth century, the American business community was characterized by large-scale enterprises, the product of these processes of vertical and horizontal integration, which reduced costs by eliminating middlemen.

Although many contemporary observers regarded such large enterprises as business juggernauts exercising monopoly or near-monopoly control over the economy, the people involved in running these firms found it difficult to exercise control over organizations' increasingly complex workings. Traditional methods of cost accounting, supervising workers, monitoring the flow of materials, maintaining product quality, and selling goods in distant markets often proved inadequate; production bottlenecks, disruptions in the workplace, unforeseen shifts in consumer demand, and an array of related problems confronted even the most technologically advanced or prudently financed firm. In many cases these large enterprises, created to exploit a costly technology or national market, carried a heavy debt load while shareholders and bondholders clamoured for a quick return on their investment.

In the United States the railroads of the mid-nineteenth century pioneered techniques of managing large-scale enterprises: they were the first to have a body of salaried managers whose local supervisory authority was co-ordinated by a central office (using the telegraph system for that purpose). This management system also monitored operations through standardized and regular statistical and financial reports. Building on this base, the large industrial and commercial enterprises of the early 1900s introduced a variety of measures to control costs, expand output, and enhance co-ordination and communication within their organizations. The most publicized of these innovations—the introduction of an assembly-line form of mass production associated with the auto manufacturer Henry Ford, and the techniques of 'scientific management' of workers and workplace design developed by Frederick Taylor and his associates—were but two of a wide range of organizational changes characterizing American industry in this era. New methods of advertising and marketing products and services were developed to cater to an increasingly urbanized society. The organizational capabilities developed by US firms generated versatility and flexibility, enabling them to move quickly and effectively into foreign direct investment and to diversify their product lines and markets, achieving what Chandler calls 'economies of scope'.[1]

In other industrializing countries, similar processes of integration and managerial rationalization were taking place. In Germany, economic and political unification and technological advances in chemicals and metallurgy contributed to the late-nineteenth century growth of large-scale enterprises. In the United States, the Sherman Antitrust Act of 1890 banned cartels, so that industrial integration was shaped principally by mergers of smaller firms into large joint-stock corporations. In Germany, however, cartels were encouraged by the state so that large-scale industries often were dominated by confederations of nominally separate firms. Nevertheless, the need for better instruments of communication

and control of production and marketing encouraged close co-ordination among firms. In Japan, vertical and horizontal integration was carried out by family-based trading companies such as Mitsui and Mitsubishi, which invested in a wide range of interconnected industrial and financial enterprises and recruited managers from the samurai class as well as from merchant families.

In Britain, on the other hand, the processes of integration and rationalization were slow to take hold. Family firms and proprietorships from the earlier industrial era, particularly in established fields such as textiles, tended to remain small and independent. Capital requirements for these enterprises were relatively modest and financial services readily available, so that the pressures for cost control were correspondingly less severe than in the United States. Market linkages to both local and overseas customers were already in place, reducing the incentive for innovation. Existing labour relations (and, perhaps, cultural attitudes of businessmen) tended to inhibit technological changes. Although British businesses joined in the merger mania of the early 1900s, these larger corporate enterprises clustered in the new industries of the time, such as chemicals or automobiles; even in these companies older traditions of organization persisted: management structures remained rudimentary and systems of internal communication and co-ordination loose and informal.

How does Canada fit into this picture? Did Canada experience a 'managerial revolution' similar to the US or Germany, or did it more closely follow the pattern of the mother country, Britain? Views on the subject vary considerably, depending on the perspective of the observer and the time period observed. Canadian labour historian Craig Heron, for example, perceives a 'second industrial revolution' in place by the early 1930s, albeit with some special Canadian features: most of the major financial, manufacturing, and extractive sectors of the economy were dominated by a handful of large integrated firms with headquarters in central Canada. Political economist Glen Williams describes a more diffuse pattern: small and medium-sized manufacturers persisting in a wide range of industries serving the domestic market, their inefficiencies protected by the National Policy tariffs. These views are not necessarily incompatible, but they indicate the difficulties in describing the processes of change in Canadian business in this era.[2]

Certainly, big businesses did emerge. In 1930 about 600 firms produced over $2 billion worth of goods, accounting for almost 60 per cent of total manufacturing output by value. One-quarter of all employees worked in firms with over 500 people, of which 68 per cent were grouped in 11 industries. Growth occurred both through individual firm expansion and through consolidation by merger. Between 1900 and 1930 there were over 500 mergers in Canada, absorbing almost 1,200 firms. Mergers clustered in particular industries: consolidations in utilities, iron and steel, and wood products accounted for more than one-quarter of the total number of firms absorbed. Although most mergers involved horizontal integration, about one-fifth of the consolidations in iron and steel, wood products, and food processing produced vertically integrated enterprises.

The pattern of big business shifted markedly between the early years of the twentieth century and 1930, as indicated in the rankings of the top 20 non-financial corporations by assets in 1909 (on the eve of the first big merger movement) and in 1929 (Table 5.1). Although the national railway lines remained the largest enterprises in Canada throughout this period (CNR, a Crown corporation, was second only to CPR in assets in 1929), most notable are the rise of the extractive industries (mining and forestry products) and the relative decline of utilities vis-à-vis manufacturing in these years. Virtually all the manufacturing and extractive firms appearing in the 1929 ranking were at least in part vertically integrated. The CPR and the Hudson's Bay Company (see box, p. 76) had diversified investments in a range of fields.

'Bigness' is, of course, a relative term. The accumulated assets of the 30 largest non-financial corporations in Canada in 1909, for example, did not equal the asset value of the American giant, United States Steel Corporation. For Chandler, however, size alone was not a sufficient determinant: some degree of vertical integration, the organizational capabilities to effectively manage such large agglomerations, and the capacity to develop strategies for long-term development rather than simply responding to market changes must also be considered.

In Canada in the 1900–30 period, most companies that advanced in this direction were linked to export markets. Vertical integration was undertaken by flour millers, newsprint and mineral processors, and some export-oriented manufacturing firms such as Massey-Harris. Another (and related) feature of these large integrated firms was the significant and increasing role of foreign direct investment. In 1909, 11 of the top 30 non-financial corporations were wholly or partly foreign-owned, and this number increased to 15 by 1929. Foreign direct investment, mostly American, tended to concentrate in the mining, forestry, and petroleum industries; but there were British as well as American firms in fields such as automobiles, electrical equipment, and chemicals, which represented the 'high-tech' industries of the day. The Canadian firms in these industries were in effect integrated into larger corporate structures that a later era would designate as 'multinationals'.

REVOLUTION IN RETAILING

Even before industrialization took firm hold in Canada, traditional patterns of distribution and sales of goods were changing, and between the 1880s and the 1930s the transformation of wholesale and retail trade proceeded apace. The decline of both the general wholesaler and the small retailer and the growth of chain stores and mail-order catalogues, brand-name packaging, and the advertising industry were all part of this transformation. A number of social and economic developments contributed to this 'revolution in retailing'. The growth of cities enlarged markets,

TABLE 5.1

CANADA'S 20 LEADING NON-FINANCIAL CORPORATIONS*
(RANKED BY ASSETS)

1909	1929
1. Canadian Pacific Railway	1. Canadian Pacific Railway
2. Grand Trunk Railway	2. International Power & Paper
3. Canadian Northern Railway	3. Imperial Oil Co.
4. Minnesota, St Paul & Sault Ste Marie Railway	4. Abitibi Paper Co.
5. MacKay Co.	5. Minnesota, St Paul & Sault Ste Marie Railway
6. Lake Superior Corp. (Algoma)	6. Bell Telephone Co. of Canada
7. Atlantic Railway	7. Shawinigan Water & Power
8. Commercial Cable Co.	8. MacKay Co.
9. Dominion Iron & Steel Co.	9. Canada Power & Paper
10. Montreal Light, Heat & Power	10. Dominion Steel & Coal Co.
11. Canada Cement Co.	11. Montreal Light, Heat & Power
12. Dominion Coal Co.	12. International Nickel
13. Amalgamated Asbestos Co.	13. Price Brothers
14. Bell Telephone Co. of Canada	14. Duluth, South Shore & Atlantic Railway
15. Canadian Car & Foundry	15. Twin City Transit Co.
16. Dominion Power & Transmission	16. Duke/Price Co.
17. Montreal Street Railway	17. Imperial Tobacco Co.
18. Ontario Power Co.	18. Massey-Harris Co.
19. Granby Consolidated Mining	19. Hudson's Bay Co.
20. British Columbia Electric Railway	20. Steel Co. of Canada

*Excludes proprietary companies without public shares (e.g., Eaton's), Crown corporations (e.g., CNR), and companies with exclusively foreign assets (e.g., Brazilian Traction Co.).

while improvements in city transit systems encouraged established merchants to build bigger stores in the downtown commercial centres.

Urban workers, both blue-collar and white-collar, earned year-round cash incomes and had neither the time nor space to produce their food or clothing at home; rising incomes, particularly for the middle class, promoted a wider consumption of 'luxury' products. The railway network helped make possible direct linkages between manufacturers and retailers, and provided urban merchants access to rural communities. Standardization of products and product quality by manufacturers abetted the efforts of enterprising retailers seeking to build national market systems. For such entrepreneurs there were models to observe and improve upon, for large retail department stores and chains were appearing in all of the industrialized countries. When Timothy Eaton was developing his Toronto-based retailing empire in the 1880s and 1890s, for example, he could and did study the pioneering efforts of companies like Macy's and Montgomery-Ward in the US and Whiteleys in Britain.

General wholesale merchants still dominated the flow of trade through the country; indeed, they were the first to exploit the new opportunities for a national market presented by railway expansion. Wholesalers in Montreal and Toronto, using their financial resources for discount bulk purchases directly from manufacturers, deployed cohorts of drummers across the prairies and into the Maritimes to sell a wide range of dry goods and other manufactured products to local wholesale or retail merchants. While the Maritimes had large general wholesalers who drew on transatlantic suppliers, for the most part wholesale merchants and retailers outside central Canada ran relatively small establishments serving local markets, purchasing goods on credit from the general wholesalers and extending credit on fairly long terms to their customers. Credit sales were particularly entrenched in rural communities due to the seasonal nature of farming and fishing. In larger towns there was a certain degree of specialization among retailers, while in rural Canada general stores carrying a wide range but limited stock of goods predominated.

By the 1880s, however, a larger and distinctively different kind of retail establishment was emerging in the bigger towns and cities of central Canada. Eaton was only one of a number of entrepreneurial retailers of his time, although in certain respects he had a broader vision of the potential

Eaton's catalogues, beginning in 1884, spread the marketing operations of the Toronto retail firm into remote corners of Canada (a French-language edition began in 1928) and popularized consumer holiday spending sprees. (Eaton Catalogue de Noel, 1953–1954, F 229-231-0-12, Archives of Ontario. Used with permission of Sears Canada Inc.)

market than did his rivals. Timothy Eaton had worked with his brothers in wholesaling ventures in small-town Ontario in the 1850s and 1860s before moving to Toronto to set up a dry goods store in 1869. His experience as a wholesaler made Eaton leery of credit sales, and the widely advertised policy of his new store was 'cash only' and a fixed price for all goods. With a steady flow of cash, Eaton could avoid debt (the company did not have to resort to large-scale borrowing until the 1920s, when it expanded branch operations outside Ontario) and the volume of business enabled him to hold frequent 'bargain days'.

Unlike his competitors, who tended to focus on the upscale, middle-class market, Eaton targeted his sales towards lower-income buyers while stressing quality: like Sears in the US, Eaton guaranteed refunds for goods that were unsatisfactory, and worked hard to ensure that there would be few unsatisfied customers. To that end, by the 1890s Eaton developed direct links with manufacturers, reducing costs over the long term by cutting out the wholesalers. By the end of that decade Eaton had buyers in London, Paris, New York, and even Japan. During this same time he also began to manufacture some goods in-house, particularly clothing, and eventually a wide range of products, including horse harnesses, furniture, and camping equipment.

Eaton also took steps to establish internal controls over his increasingly complex business. During the 1880s the store began grouping related products for display into 'departments', which not only helped shoppers locate goods but also streamlined the management of records of procurement, inventory, accounts, and sales. Eventually, there were departments for groceries, drugs, and electric appliances as well as the traditional dry goods and home furnishings. Cash registers, adding machines, electric lighting, and a pneumatic tube communications system increased the speed and efficiency of sales processing and accounting in the store.

Naturally, much attention was devoted to enhancing marketing and sales. Advertisements became less cluttered, more oriented to piquing the reader's interest than simply to conveying information. As early as 1884, Eaton began issuing a catalogue of goods for circulation through the Toronto metropolitan region. The mail-order catalogue quickly became a major part of the business, providing Eaton with customers deep in the heart of rural Ontario and eventually across the country. By 1903 Eaton had to set up a separate warehouse for mail orders; seven years later it became a separate division within the firm. Initially, mail orders were handled through the

postal service, but by 1916 the volume of business was so great the post office could no longer handle it, so Eaton's began establishing mail-order outlets.

The Toronto store also established a full-scale branch in Winnipeg in 1905, although branch stores did not become a major part of Eaton's expansion until the 1920s under Timothy's grandson, Robert Y. Eaton, when new stores were established in Montreal, Hamilton, Halifax, and the major cities of the Prairie provinces. In 1930, with assets over $110 million (which would make it the twelfth largest non-financial company in the country) and a sales turnover of $172 million, Eaton's was the most successful of Canada's department stores, but it was by no means alone. Robert Simpson's store, virtually next door to Eaton's in downtown Toronto, quickly followed the lead into cash sales, departmentalization, direct purchasing, vertical integration into manufacturing some goods, and mail-order sales. Other large cities also featured large local department stores, usually family enterprises like Eaton's: Woodward's in Vancouver and Ogilvy's and Dupuis Freres in Montreal were among the most successful and enduring examples. But none of these stores were to move beyond their local markets or develop mail-order businesses on the scale of Eaton's and Simpsons.

The rise of the department store eroded the market position of small specialized retailers in the cities, and the growth of mail-order catalogue sales undermined the role of the general stores in small-town and rural Canada. By World War I another set of players was entering the field: the chain stores, ranging from general merchandise companies like the American-owned Woolworth's, which moved into Canada in the early 1900s, to grocery chains (soon to be dubbed 'supermarkets'), which appeared in the 1920s: Loblaw's and Dominion Stores in Ontario and Quebec, Safeway in western Canada, and others. General merchandise or 'variety' stores resembled department stores, achieving economies through direct bulk

THE HUDSON'S BAY COMPANY IN TRANSITION

It may not be the oldest business enterprise in existence, but the Hudson's Bay Company does lay claim to being the longest surviving business corporation, dating back to its charter from King Charles II in 1670. This longevity may have less to do with the strategic brilliance of its leaders than forces of size, inertia, and the mistakes of overly ambitious rivals. Nevertheless, its history was largely intertwined with the development of British North America through its first two centuries, during which time its land claims expanded to encompass much of what would become northern Quebec, Ontario, and the prairies.

From the late 1770s, the Hudson's Bay Company was challenged by its more aggressive Montreal-based competitors, the North West Company, whose adventurous partners, such as Alexander Mackenzie and Peter Pond, probed deep into the Alberta and British Columbia frontier. But the loose internal structure of the Nor'Westers undermined their ability to mobilize capital for the longer term, and in 1821 a forced amalgamation took place, with the HBC as the dominant element. Under the leadership of George Simpson, from 1821 to 1860 the company expanded and intensified the exploitation of the fur trade even as its traditional markets were going into decline. In 1870 the HBC sold a huge portion of its western territories to the new government of Canada, although it retained title to the best acreage for future sales after the CPR opened the region to settlement.

Thanks to its vast real estate and resource holdings, the HBC continued to play an important role in northern and western development and to provide healthy dividends to its shareholders after 1870. But for more than a generation senior management was sharply divided over the best strategy for long-term development. In London two factions squabbled over whether to diversify into the general merchandise trade or to focus on land sales and immigration. Both sides agreed that the fur trade was a 'dying industry', but Canadian officers of the company argued that the fur trade could be resuscitated and sustained through the introduction of new management techniques, improved technology, and the development of 'fur ranching' to supplement trapping.

As it turned out the fur trade was not on the verge of disappearance, although market demand had shifted from the traditional beaver and muskrat fur to fox, lynx, and mink. The advent of the bush plane and wireless radio after World War I opened the Canadian North to new competitors in the trade, particularly from the US. The divided Bay Co. leadership was slow to respond and gradually lost ground from the 1920s on. Meanwhile, however, the company had developed a network of general stores in the North and gathered a windfall supplying gold seekers bound for the Klondike at the turn of the century.

In 1887 the Bay had opened its first urban outlet in Vancouver, but it moved fairly slowly into this market. By 1914 there were stores in other cities of BC and Alberta and the company recruited a manager from the British department store, Harrod's, to run this unfamiliar operation. In the 1920s, the Bay opened a large store in Winnipeg but the timing was poor: Eaton's was already there and the wheat boom was collapsing. The Bay suffered serious losses in its foray into retailing and kept a low profile for a time thereafter, remaining principally in the North and West until the 1960s. In another curious example of missed opportunities, the HBC leased its mineral rights in western Canada in 1929 to an Oklahoma oilman, E.W. Marland, founder of Continental Oil.

Even as it was developing retail stores in urban centres of Canada, the HBC continued to run its northern trading posts, such as this one at Cameron Bay, NWT, well into the twentieth century. (Library and Archives Canada C-033945)

As its rival retailers, Simpsons and Eaton's, fell by the wayside in the 1970s–80s, the HBC emerged as Canada's improbable leading department store. Controlled for a time by Ken Thomson, the HBC absorbed Simpsons and the discount retailer Zellers. In 1987 the HBC pulled out of the fur auction business, although it resuscitated fashion fur sales a decade later. In 2006, the HBC was acquired by a South Carolina financier, Jerry Zucker. This event provided the occasion for lamentations over the loss of a Canadian icon to foreign ownership, although it is worth noting that until 1970 the Hudson's Bay Company was under predominantly British control, and only in 1934 did a British governor of HBC bother to visit Canada.

Sources: Peter C. Newman, *Merchant Princes* (Toronto, 1991); Arthur J. Ray, *The Canadian Fur Trade in the Industrial Age* (Toronto, 1990).

buying from manufacturers, but they tended to locate in smaller cities and towns and to focus on volume sales of low-price goods, as indicated by their nickname, the 'five and dimes'.

The chains were seen as a particularly insidious threat by local wholesalers and small retailers since they encroached directly on traditional rural and small-town markets: resistance to the chains took political as well as economic forms, particularly in the grocery business, and persisted well into the 1930s. As historian David Monod has noted, not all small retailers were simply resistant—a 'progressive' element of shopkeepers sought to adapt to the new circumstances, introducing more up-to-date accounting practices and the advertising techniques of the larger chains, among other innovations. They formed their own business associations, such as the Fair Trade League, which set out on the one hand to limit the market power of the chains but also to spread the gospel of modern marketing and organizational change in the small business sector. These activities crested in the Depression years, when small retailers' associations presented testimony before the Royal Commission on Price Spreads and rallied behind the concept of 'retail price maintenance'. By the time of World War II, however, much of the political force of this movement had dissipated into various splinter parties.[3]

MANUFACTURING PATTERNS

While large retailers like Eaton were integrating back into manufacturing, the process also worked the other way, particularly in food processing. In the 1920s flour mills such as Ogilvie and Lake of the Woods began establishing bakeries to market their own brands in Canada. Long before this time large meat packers had moved into retailing. Among the most innovative of these entrepreneurs was William Davies, one of a number of pork slaughterers in Toronto in the 1880s when the city gained its reputation as 'Hogtown', drawing supplies from the large agricultural hinterland of southern Ontario and packing salt-cured bacon

for export, principally to Britain. Davies and his partner Joseph Flavelle expanded operations in the 1890s, introduced assembly-line techniques pioneered by American packers like Swift, and began retailing fresh and preserved meat through their own stores in Ontario and Quebec in the early 1900s. Flavelle became one of the wealthiest men in Canada and an influential figure in the Conservative Party.

Even during the 1880s, long regarded as a period of stagnation for the Canadian economy, the level of capital investment in manufacturing doubled. The depression of the mid-1890s slowed growth in some areas, particularly in construction-related and consumer goods; but between 1896 and the eve of World War I expansion was general and more or less continuous, reflecting the buoyant economy. Manufacturing output by value almost quadrupled between 1891 and 1915, and the number of factories tripled from the turn of the century to World War I.

Ontario had perhaps the most diversified manufacturing base. In the 1880s the province's main industries were involved in processing agricultural products and lumber. By 1910 foundries, machine shops, iron and steel fabricating mills, and clothing manufacturers accounted for almost one-quarter of Ontario's industrial output by value, although meat packers, flour mills, dairies, and bakeries, along with logging and mining, continued to be central to the economy. In Quebec food and beverage processing remained the dominant area of manufacturing from the 1880s through World War I: Ogilvie and other large flour millers moved their centres of operations westward following the railways, but sugar refineries took the place of flour mills in Montreal in the 1880s. Cotton textiles became the most important of the new industries to emerge in Quebec in this era: by 1900 the textile and clothing manufacturing fields comprised the second largest industrial group in the province.

The Maritimes also experienced rapid industrial development between 1880 and 1900, especially in the cotton textile industry as mills proliferated in the towns of New Brunswick and Nova Scotia. Two industries—sugar refining, and coal, iron, and steel—were seen as particularly promising. Maritime access to the Caribbean encouraged the growth of sugar refining, and by the mid-1880s the region had 60 per cent of the capacity in this field. The coal mines of Nova Scotia and the proximity of iron ore from Newfoundland enticed foreign as well as local investment in the iron and steel industry.

For contemporary observers and many historians, a key factor in industrialization was the National Policy, combining protective tariffs for domestic manufactured goods and the development of a national market through the construction of railway systems. Economic historians are less certain of the direct connections between industrial growth and the National Policy, particularly before 1900; and, as will become apparent, there were some significant gaps in the protectionist bastions. Canadian manufacturers catering to the domestic market, however, entertained few doubts on the subject. Whenever the National Policy faced a challenge—in 1891 from advocates of 'unrestricted reciprocity' with the US, and in 1911 when Laurier negotiated a reciprocal trade agreement that encompassed natural products but seemed to open the door for reductions in rates on manufactured goods—the Canadian Manufacturers' Association could be counted on to sound the tocsin and bankroll the party of protectionism.

Opponents of the National Policy, particularly among western farmers, assailed protectionism as an instrument of monopolistic big business, much as American populists condemned the protective tariff in that country as the 'mother of trusts'. In the Canadian context, however, the relationship between the National Policy and the rise of big business is more complex. In the immediate aftermath of the introduction of the National Policy in the 1880s and 1890s, small competitive firms proliferated in many of the 'protected' industries, and in at least some of these industries small-scale, localized production and marketing persisted well into the twentieth century. Even in those fields where large national enterprises emerged, the patterns of integration and managerial organization were uneven and incomplete. The evolution of two industries whose fortunes were linked closely with the protective tariff system—cotton textiles and steel—indicates the difficulties of generalizing about this relationship.

TEXTILES

In Britain and the United States, small-scale enterprises predominated in the cotton textile industry until at least the period after World War I, when integrated chemical firms producing synthetic fibres moved into the field. The basic technologies of factory production of both cotton and woollen textiles were well established in those countries by the early 1800s, and as a primarily labour-intensive industry, barriers to entry of new firms were relatively low. The diversity of products, in terms of both quality and range, also worked to the benefit of small manufacturers catering to special market niches. Furthermore, as would-be Canadian textile makers in the late nineteenth century discovered, the latest technology was readily available from equipment manufacturers: in many newly industrializing nations, textile factories made an early appearance, reducing the export markets for established firms in Britain and the United States.

In Canada, however, at least in the cotton textile field, big businesses appeared fairly quickly and established a stranglehold over the market for more than half a century. Prior to the National Policy, Canadian textile manufacturing was mainly in woollen fabrics and centred in Ontario. These woollen mills relied generally on water power and were dispersed, serving local markets; their products were of coarse quality. During the 1860s and early 1870s there was a trend towards larger factories to serve an expanding market. The National Policy actually retarded this process by allowing the smaller producers to hang on in a protected market. The introduction of imperial preference under Laurier in 1897, which opened Canada to much-desired British fine woollens, undermined this element of the domestic textile industry.

Cotton textile manufacturing emerged in Quebec and the Maritimes in the 1870s and 1880s. Both regions had readier access than Ontario to overseas supplies of cotton, and merchants in these communities (as in New England in the early 1800s) found textiles to be a logical field for diversification. The National Policy, which raised *ad valorem* rates from 17 per cent to 30 per cent for imported cotton products, persuaded Montreal dry goods wholesalers such as Andrew Gault and David Morrice to integrate back into textile production. In Nova Scotia and New Brunswick a more diverse group of import merchants and shipbuilders chose to move into cotton manufacturing as their traditional sources of wealth from the West Indies trade declined, and the Intercolonial Railway offered prospective markets in central Canada.

As in the woollens field, the National Policy initially produced a spurt of competitive expansion by small cotton cloth manufacturers, leading to a crisis of overproduction by the mid-1880s. The Montreal manufacturers urged cartel arrangements to stabilize prices, but two of the largest mills, both in New Brunswick, held out and the scheme collapsed. By the early 1890s the Montrealers had shifted to a strategy of consolidation, abetted by the depression that fell particularly harshly on their financially overextended competitors in the Maritimes. A second round of mergers came in the period between 1897 and 1905 as Canadian manufacturers faced increased competition from British cotton imports under imperial preference.

It was not the National Policy, then, but rather its attenuation that stimulated the growth of large horizontal combinations in the Canadian cotton textile industry. The big textile firms displayed some other curious features. Dominion Textile Co., the largest of these entities after its 1905 amalgamation with four other companies operating 12 mills, and possessing $10 million capital,

specialized in 'grey and white cottons'. Just behind it came Canadian Colored Cotton Mills, which in addition to its own Quebec operations acted as sales agent for several of the larger remaining Maritime companies in that particular line. Third was Montreal Cotton Co., which produced linings and dyed goods. This de facto division of markets has been described by business historian Barbara Austin as 'complementary monopolies'. In effect, it was a cartel in everything but name.[4]

The role of strong personalities and personal contacts among them may have been a major factor in creating this structure. During the 1880s and 1890s, Andrew Gault presided, separately, over two of the major firms—Dominion Cotton Co. (the predecessor to Dominion Textiles) and Montreal Cotton Co.—and was linked indirectly, by marriage, to the Morrice family, who controlled Canadian Colored Cottons. Gault's death in 1904 precipitated the formation of Dominion Textiles as a corporate entity, orchestrated by Montreal financiers. Several of these figures, including Holt and Louis Forget, were directors of Dominion Textiles, but the dominant figure over the next 40 years was Charles B. Gordon. Although Gordon eventually became president of the Bank of Montreal, he was by training a textile manufacturer and retained Gault's connection with Montreal Cotton, which was later absorbed into Dominion. The major new entrant in the white goods field was created by another strong-willed figure, Charles Whitehead, who had briefly been Dominion's general manager before departing to set up his own enterprise, Wabasso Cotton Co., in 1907. Whitehead chose to specialize in fine cottons, in competition with British importers rather than with the Canadian 'big three', so the market division arrangement remained more or less intact. Whitehead ran Wabasso until his death in 1953.

Under forceful leaders like Gordon and Whitehead, the large textile firms were centralized and rationalized. Marginal mills were closed down, and production increasingly centred in Quebec. Given the tariff wall and cartel-like structure of the industry, however, few of these firms moved towards full integration into marketing or more elaborate managerial organization. As their founders aged, the companies tended to become tradition-bound, reluctant to develop new markets or introduce new technologies, although Dominion did move gingerly into synthetic fibres. As protectionist measures actually increased in the Great Depression, there were few incentives for change before the abandonment of import duties in the 1950s.

IRON AND STEEL

The development of iron and later mass-production steel manufacturing was a central feature of industrialization in nineteenth-century Europe and North America. Indeed, although iron and steel were essential for a wide range of producer and consumer goods—machinery, ships, rails and rolling stock, stoves and pots, etc.—for many industrializing countries, developing primary manufacturing capability in this field took on a symbolic quality, demonstrating that the nation was truly modern and progressive. The introduction of new technologies such as the Siemens-Martin open-hearth furnace and the rolling mill in the mid-1800s made it possible to produce steel on a mass-production basis. By the 1890s entrepreneurs such as Andrew Carnegie in the US and Friedrich Krupp in Germany had assembled organizations integrating mining, smelting, and metal fabricating with primary steel production that were among the largest corporate enterprises in the world.

Aspiring Carnegies in Canada, however, faced formidable obstacles. One problem was lack of resources: in the late nineteenth century accessible iron ore deposits were modest. Although the large reserves of Labrador were discovered in 1895, transportation costs from this remote region were prohibitive until after World War II. Substantial coal supplies existed in British Columbia and Nova Scotia, but were of relatively poor quality for efficient use in iron and steel-making because of their high sulphur content.

Finally, and most critically, the domestic market for primary iron and steel, at least up to the early 1900s, was too small to support production on the scale required to justify the substantial capital investment that an integrated steel industry needed. US tariffs barred them from that lucrative market; Canadian secondary iron and steel fabricators could satisfy their supply needs from the growing American industry, and during the debates over the National Policy in 1879 they successfully blocked the imposition of protective tariffs in this field. Despite these obstacles, entrepreneurs in Nova Scotia began to expand iron-making capacity in the early 1880s, supported by government bounties. In 1887, partly in response to Maritime complaints, some primary iron products were brought under the National Policy umbrella. But tariff protection was only gradually extended: steel rails were not included until 1903, and even in the 1920s Canadian steel manufacturers were lobbying with limited success for across-the-board coverage at 20 per cent rates. At that point more than half the structural steel and sheet metal consumed in Canada was imported.

There were charcoal furnaces and iron foundries in Canada long before the time of the National Policy, but for the most part they operated on a small scale, serving local markets, and depended on diminishing ore deposits: the St Maurice forges in Quebec, in existence since 1737, were finally closed in 1883. The first 'modern' iron and steel manufacturer appeared in New Glasgow, NS, at about the same time. Several local merchants and blacksmiths joined forces to establish the Nova Scotia Steel Co. in 1882. Encouraged by federal bounties and the 1887 tariff revisions, in 1889 they expanded operations to produce a range of primary iron and steel products, established feeder rail lines to the Intercolonial, and by 1894 had acquired control of iron ore deposits at Bell Island in Newfoundland. In 1900 the company continued on this path of vertical integration by purchasing the old General Mining Association coal properties on Cape Breton Island, and reorganizing as Nova Scotia Coal & Steel, capitalized at

$7 million. NS Coal & Steel was owned by Maritime merchants and financiers—John Stairs was a director—and focused primarily on the regional market, expanding carefully under an experienced manager, Thomas Cantley. By 1909 the company's assets had doubled and central Canadian investors were eyeing it as a potential merger target.

NS Coal & Steel's success lured other players onto the field. In 1899 the Boston traction magnate, Henry Whitney, who had established the Dominion Coal Co. in Cape Breton six years earlier, set up Dominion Iron & Steel Co. (Disco), which, like NS Coal & Steel, would procure iron ore from Newfoundland and integrate its operations with Dominion Coal to sell primary steel products to central Canada and, perhaps, the European market as well. After several early blunders—presaging the future experiences of this unhappy enterprise—Whitney sold out his interests in Dominion Steel to a group of Montreal financiers, led by James Ross and including Donald Smith and William Van Horne. Meanwhile, in Ontario several new enterprises were being established. In 1895 a group of merchants and secondary iron manufacturers in Hamilton set up the Hamilton Steel & Iron Co., which merged with Ontario Rolling Mills four years later. Although this company, unlike the two Maritime firms, had no control over coal and ore supplies, which were imported from the US, from the outset it linked primary production with fabrication and was oriented towards developing a diversified line of products.

The most dramatic—or melodramatic—episode in the early history of the Canadian steel industry took place at Sault Ste Marie in Ontario. Here, a young American entrepreneur, Francis Clergue, had appeared in 1893, offering to take over the city's debt-ridden electric power plant and link it to a nearby pulp and paper mill. Over the next several years, Clergue's enterprises in the area proliferated: in 1897 he acquired a mine that seemed to possess promising iron ore deposits, built a short rail line between the mine and Sault Ste Marie,

and, in 1901, established Algoma Steel Co. But Clergue's ambitions did not stop at this point. Like Sam Ritchie in Sudbury a decade earlier, Clergue envisioned creating an integrated and diversified industrial empire, embracing chemical and nickel production as well as newsprint and steel. A talented promoter, Clergue persuaded American investors to contribute to the $15 million venture, unveiled in 1902 and christened the Consolidated Lake Superior Corporation.

Clergue's vision exceeded his managerial abilities. The ore from the Helen Mine proved to be of poor quality, coal and pig iron had to be brought in from distant sources, the Algoma mill had a Bessemer converter rather than the more efficient open-hearth technology, and transportation costs to the southern Ontario market were higher than projected. Within two years the Lake Superior Corp. teetered on the brink of bankruptcy, and Clergue's backers removed him from the scene. Before his departure, however, Clergue had spearheaded a successful lobbying campaign to bring steel rails—Algoma's major product—under tariff protection, and the company's fortunes were revived by the railway boom of the Laurier era.

The pre-World War I boom and the war itself stimulated moves towards consolidation in the Canadian steel industry between 1910 and 1920. In 1910 Max Aitken orchestrated the formation of the Steel Co. of Canada (Stelco), combining Hamilton Steel & Iron with four secondary steel fabricators in Ontario and Quebec, capitalized at $25 million. Much of the capital was raised by Aitken from British investors, and the board included the usual prominent Montreal and Toronto financial figures such as Holt and Edmund Osier of the Dominion Bank. But the firm was managed by experienced steelmakers: initially by Charles Wilcox and Robert Hobson from the Hamilton enterprise and later by Ross McMaster, whose father had run Montreal Rolling Mills before the merger.

Aitken had organized Stelco only after failing to consolidate the Nova Scotia iron and steel industry. In 1909 he had been able to recombine Dominion Coal and Dominion Steel (which had been separate since Whitney's departure), but NS Coal & Steel rebuffed his overtures. By 1917, however, the New Glasgow–Halifax group had been replaced by New York-based investors. Over the next few years a byzantine struggle for control of the Nova Scotia industry, involving American, British, and central Canadian financial interests, culminated in the creation of the British Empire Steel Corporation (Besco) in 1921, combining Dominion Coal, Dominion Steel, NS Coal & Steel, Halifax Shipyards, and assorted other steel-consuming enterprises.

The chief figure in the merger, Roy Wolvin, a Montreal shipbuilder and financier, seems to have believed, mistakenly, that the Canadian government intended to underwrite a large expansion of the country's merchant marine fleet after the war. Like many mining and newsprint agglomerations that sprang up at this time, Besco, capitalized at $500 million, carried a fair amount of 'watered' stock (new shares issued without corresponding assets). More critically, Besco was launched at a time when international steel markets were weak. This situation hurt all Canadian producers, but Besco was particularly vulnerable because of its relatively high production costs and peripheral position in the central Canadian market.

By the 1920s these three companies—Algoma, Stelco, and Besco—controlled most of the country's domestic primary iron and steel output and a large proportion of secondary manufacturing as well, although there were some strong competitors in this part of the market, notably Dominion Foundries & Steel. Dofasco was established in Hamilton in 1913 by the Shermans, a Cleveland family who managed it carefully, introducing state-of-the-art facilities and diversifying product lines regularly. In the 1960s, Dofasco moved back into the primary steel industry, the first Canadian firm to use the basic oxygen process that replaced the open-hearth technology. The 'big three' did not monopolize the primary market either, since

more than half the country's supplies came from abroad; even after World War II over one-third of Canada's primary iron and steel was imported.

But the uneven tariff protection was only one factor affecting the Canadian steel industry. None of the 'big three' was a fully integrated operation. Two of these firms experienced so many problems, ranging from inadequate resources to bad management, that they survived only through periodic injections of government largesse in the form of contracts or direct subsidies. Although Algoma performed reasonably well through World War I (thanks to rail and munitions contracts), much of its earnings were absorbed by debt payments on the original Lake Superior venture, and new capital raised in the war had to go towards replacing the Bessemer converter. Algoma's absentee owners were reluctant to seek new financing, fearing loss of control of the enterprise (and their dividends), so the company failed to diversify, remaining primarily a producer of steel rails.

When this market collapsed in the 1930s, Algoma careened back into bankruptcy. At that point it fell into the hands of James Dunn, a financier who, like his fellow New Brunswicker Max Aitken, had made his millions as a promoter of Canadian utility companies and similar ventures on the London money market. Returning to Canada in the Depression, Dunn salvaged Algoma by ruthlessly writing down its bonded debt, reorganizing its management, and using political connections to procure rail contracts that would carry it until full-scale diversification could be carried out. Although Dunn ultimately saved Algoma and made his mark as an industrialist, the company—facing high transport costs and dependent on external supplies of its raw materials—continued to rely largely on government assistance through World War II.

Meanwhile, Besco staggered through the 1920s from one crisis to another. By 1921 Wolvin's expectations of a post-war shipbuilding boom had glimmered away, and hopes for a transatlantic market never got off the ground as European steel producers, operating at excess capacity, cartelized to block North American competition. Increases in east–west rail freight rates reduced Besco's competitive position in the home market as well. To meet his debt obligations, Wolvin sought to reduce operating costs by imposing severe wage cuts in Besco's steel mills and coal mines, a move precipitating some of the bitterest labour conflicts of the era, and leaving a legacy of hostility and distrust that poisoned worker–management relations through the 1960s. Wolvin's harsh measures failed, and in 1926 Besco collapsed into receivership. Reorganized in 1928 as Dominion Steel and Coal Co. (Dosco), the company was now under the control of Herbert Holt and the Royal Bank. Although nursed back to moderate health by the end of the decade, Dosco remained, like Algoma, primarily a producer of steel rails, even more distant from central Canadian markets and dependent on government contracts to survive.

Stelco, by contrast, weathered the post-war recession and performed well through the 1920s, doubling its sales volume and more than quadrupling net profits between 1921 and 1930. In part, Stelco's success could be attributed to its strategic location in central Canada's industrial heartland, but there were other factors, not least among them good management. During World War I the company applied its retained earnings to updating its equipment and acquired iron and coal mines in the US to ensure its supply needs. Oriented from the outset towards secondary manufacturing, Stelco under McMaster in the 1920s continued its strategy of diversification in such products as sheet steel, machine parts, and steel rods, which were in demand by the growing Canadian auto industry. With a substantial amount of its output accounted for by fabricated materials, Stelco also benefited from the existing tariff structure and declined to join its rivals in lobbying for new duties except on products where it faced threats from US Steel. Although Stelco suffered in the Depression, its diversity and careful use of its

financial resources in the 1920s left the company the strongest in the industry.[5]

A FOREIGN PRESENCE

While the role of the National Policy in creating large integrated industrial entities in Canada is not entirely clear-cut, there does seem to be a strong relationship between the tariff system and the growth of foreign direct investment, particularly from the US. Between 1879 and 1887, 37 American 'branch plants' sprang up in Canada, and this number increased to 66 by 1900. Provincial measures such as Ontario's pulpwood processing requirement brought more direct investment across the border in the first decade of the new century, and the defeat of reciprocity in 1911 stimulated a new round of American entrants. By 1914, US direct investment in Canada exceeded $600 million, making Canada the largest recipient of American capital, over one-third of which went into manufacturing enterprises (Table 5.2). During World War I the pace of American direct investment in Canada slowed, but between 1919 and 1929 the capital flow doubled, about half going into manufacturing. In 1929 the US Commerce Department estimated that there were over 1,000 firms in Canada that were wholly or partially owned by Americans. Between 1890 and 1913, direct investment flowed in from Britain as well, particularly in the utilities field, but the British generally preferred portfolio investment, which entailed earnings without the responsibilities of managing enterprises.

Americans usually wanted to exercise some control over the companies they established in Canada, and after World War I American capital inflows grew steadily, surpassing British direct and indirect investment levels by 1926. This influx of American direct investment was not an accidental by-product of the National Policy. The architects of the protective trade system recognized that Canada desperately needed foreign capital and erected the tariff wall deliberately to entice

TABLE 5.2
DIRECT US INVESTMENT IN CANADA, 1914, 1919, AND 1929
($ MILLIONS US)

	1914	1919	1929
Total	618	814	1,657
Manufacturing	221	400	820
Mining/Oil	184	230	373
Utilities*	77	91	318
Sales	27	30	38
Misc.	109	63	108

*Includes railways.

Source: Mira Wilkins, *The Maturing of Multinational Enterprise* (Cambridge, Mass., 1971), 31, 189. From data from US Department of Commerce Bureau of Foreign and Domestic Commerce, American Direct Investments in Foreign Countries Trade Information Bull. 731 (1930), 'American Direct Investments Abroad–1936' (1938), and 'American Direct Investments in Foreign Countries–1940' (1942); and Cleona Lewis assisted by Karl T. Schlotterbeck, *America's Stake in International Investments* (Washington, DC: The Brookings Institution, 1938).

American manufacturers to leap across and set up branch plants that would 'keep jobs at home'. Similarly, the Patent Act of 1872, which contained a 'working clause' requiring patentees to establish manufacturing plants in Canada within two years, was intended to bring foreign technology into the country. The central objective was economic growth, and the questions of where the capital came from or who owned the factories operating in Canada were hardly raised. Certainly up through World War I the US, the world's largest debtor nation in 1913, had based its own dramatic industrial expansion on a steady inflow of foreign direct as well as portfolio investment.[6]

But the National Policy was only one factor in the process. From the 1890s on, Canada's mineral and forestry resources attracted investors from abroad. In the service sector, US and other foreign firms found it desirable to form affiliations with Canadian businesses that had well-established contacts in their local communities. Even in manufacturing, Canadian trade measures were only one consideration for foreign enterprises establishing branch plants. In the US many of the large integrated industrial firms that emerged in the early 1900s adopted a decentralized multidivisional structure in their domestic operations that was logically extended into a branch plant system when they moved into foreign markets. An examination of the expansion of American companies in Canada in two important (and related) industries—automobiles and petroleum—indicates the complex nature of the process of direct investment in this era.

Few businesses have been as well and fully chronicled as those in the automotive industry. While the basic technology and earliest manufacturing in the field developed in France and Germany in the 1880s and 1890s, American entrepreneurs, notably Henry Ford and William Durant, transformed the automobile into a major commercial product, combining assembly-line production and mass-marketing techniques on an unprecedented scale between 1910 and 1920. During the following decade US automakers expanded sales and operations overseas, and those that survived the Great Depression consolidated the American position of domination in the industry until the 1970s. Much as the railway had exemplified industrial progress in the nineteenth century, the automobile became the symbol of the Second Industrial Revolution and of America's pre-eminent economic role in the twentieth century.

Not surprisingly, given these circumstances, the Canadian automobile industry was rapidly submerged. Of the 40-odd auto manufacturers established in Canada between 1898 and 1933, only a handful were 'Canadian' in the sense of being locally owned and using Canadian technology, and few of these survived for long. More than half of the total were under foreign ownership from the outset, and by 1933, 70 per cent were branch plants of American firms.

Various explanations have been presented to account for the weakness of the indigenous auto industry. Short-sighted bankers have come in for the usual round of abuse for ignoring budding Canadian Henry Fords; the underdeveloped state of paved roads, particularly in rural areas—due in part to the opposition of farmers to the taxes required to pave them—was an impediment to the growth of an already small market. Most Canadian auto manufacturers were drawn from the carriage and wagon industry. In the US, automakers more frequently began their careers building bicycles, which familiarized them with the precision designing required for motor vehicles. In Canada the bicycle industry had fallen into the hands of a monopoly, Canada Cycle and Motor Co., at an early stage, blocking the dissemination of such skills. This particular situation reflected a broader problem: the absence of mechanical engineers and skilled machinists generally in Canada. According to legend, R.S. McLaughlin had to turn to an American manufacturer, Durant, when the engineer he hired became too ill to work and there were no other trained designers for him to fall back on.

One factor that contributed to the early arrival of Americans on the Canadian auto scene was proximity. Most American automakers were concentrated in the Midwest, particularly around Detroit. Aspiring auto entrepreneurs on the other side of the border tended to congregate in southern Ontario; only a few auto manufacturers surfaced in Quebec and the Maritimes, and none lasted. While the tariff might lure Americans northward, they did not have far to go, and in many cases the initiative came form the Canadian side.

In 1904, Gordon McGregor, a carriage maker near Windsor, Ont., crossed the border to call on Henry Ford. Ford, who had yet to win fame and fortune with his Model T, accepted McGregor's proposal to set up a company (in which Ford held 50 per cent interest) to manufacture Ford's autos in Canada; and, more significantly, to have exclusive rights to sell Ford products throughout the British Empire, except in Britain where Ford had another potential partner. The 35 per cent duty on auto imports into Canada—an extension of National Policy tariffs on carriages—may have been a factor, but from Ford's vantage point, access to the 'imperial' market through a Canadian company that was virtually next door to his Detroit factory was a major attraction. Ford Canada held what in current parlance would be a 'mandate' to make and sell Ford cars on four continents. Three years later another Ontario carriage maker, R.S. McLaughlin, struck a deal with Durant to build and sell Buicks in Canada. When Buick and Durant's other enterprises became part of General Motors Corporation (GM), McLaughlin's Oshawa-based enterprise acquired its Canadian manufacturing and marketing rights; and in 1921, when Britain extended special preferential duty remissions to Canada, GM gave McLaughlin the 'mandate' to the British imperial market. By the early 1920s between one-third and one-half of Canada's auto production was exported, principally to other parts of the Empire. By this time many of the Canadian automakers, including those who had made licensing agreements with American manufacturers, had disappeared: GM and Ford accounted for 60 per cent of the country's output.

The Canadian auto industry has been called 'a creature of the tariff',[7] but it would perhaps be more precise to say that it was a creature of the various preferential trade agreements made between Britain and Canada between 1900 and 1920. The Canadian protective tariff structure did, however, have a major impact on the production arrangements made by American firms and their Canadian affiliates. Since import duties on auto parts and materials were considerably lower than the duty on the final product, the Canadian plants specialized in assembly operations. Also, despite the export orientation of the Canadian firms, their production runs were much smaller than those of their parent companies. Despite their inability to achieve economies of scale, the Canadian companies were cushioned by the 35 per cent tariff rate. By the mid-1920s, however, consumer discontent over the price differentials between American- and Canadian-made autos led the Liberal government of Mackenzie King to roll back the tariff to 20 per cent. At the same time the government introduced a 50 per cent 'Canadian content' provision on auto parts and materials, in effect playing off the big assembly firms against the suppliers. Although tariffs on assembled vehicles were raised again in the Depression, this proved to be a temporary measure. But the Canadian-content requirement remained.

Despite their fulminations over changes in Canadian duties, the big American automakers did not dismantle their Canadian operations, in part because up to World War II these factories served markets that maintained barriers against direct US imports. There was, however, no particular incentive for them to significantly improve the production capabilities of their Canadian affiliates, which remained miniature and relatively inefficient replicas of American auto plants.

The Canadian-content requirements encouraged the growth of domestic auto parts manufacturers, mostly in Ontario; but the combined forces of these regulations and the Depression drove most of the remaining smaller auto producers out of business in Canada in the 1930s, so that the parts industry was tied to a handful of US-owned giants. By this time McGregor, McLaughlin, and other Canadian partner-investors had passed from the scene, and the Canadian automaking companies were effectively wholly owned subsidiaries of the Americans.[8]

Canadian trade policies also contributed to the entry of foreign firms in the petroleum industry; but here again other factors helped ensure that they would acquire a commanding position in the field, at least up through the 1960s. In the case of the largest of these companies, Imperial Oil, the corporate structure that emerged was probably influenced more by US antitrust laws than by anything that happened in Canada.

In the nineteenth century, petroleum was used primarily as a base for fuel for illuminating homes and streets: kerosene, the refined product used for this purpose, was developed by a Nova Scotian, Abraham Gesner, in the 1840s. With the advent of electric lighting towards the end of the century that market died. Providentially, the development of the internal combustion engine, which by 1914 had become the major power source for automobiles, not only salvaged the fortunes of the petroleum industry but ensured that it would become one of the largest and most lucrative fields of enterprise in Canada and in the world.

As in the case of iron ore, Canada's large deposits of oil and natural gas in the West and off the east coast were either unknown or inaccessible in the nineteenth century. Some deposits of crude oil, however, were being worked in south-central Ontario from the 1860s, at the same time that the larger fields of western Pennsylvania were being opened. A number of small oil-drilling companies surfaced at Oil Springs and Petrolia, and nearby London, Ontario, became the local centre for refining. As in the US, competition in the industry in the early days was fierce, and several efforts by refiners to establish cartels to control production and prices in the 1870s proved short-lived. In 1880, Joseph Englehart, an emigrant from Cleveland, Ohio, the refining capital of the US industry, joined with several London merchants to set up Imperial Oil, which took over much of the refining capacity in the region. One holdout, however, was McColl and Anderson, a partnership that continued to operate as one of the few Canadian-owned independent oil companies for more than 70 years. Imperial controlled only about one-third of the production of Ontario's oil and gas output through the late 1880s, but it established a distribution network in the prairies and moved into the more profitable Toronto and Montreal markets in the years 1888–90.

Meanwhile, in the US the industry was being consolidated by John D. Rockefeller. After acquiring control over the major refineries in Cleveland, Rockefeller created a huge vertically integrated enterprise, Standard Oil, absorbing or eliminating most of his competitors. By 1890, Standard Oil controlled over 90 per cent of the US market and had begun moving into foreign markets, including Canada.

In 1885 the Canadian government imposed import duties on both crude oil and refined kerosene. The tariff on crude oil, at six cents per gallon, was not at a 'protected' level—and in fact, Canadian refiners were soon to need crude imports to supplement the limited output from the Petrolia fields—but it was supplemented by 'inspection fees' charged on imports and a 50-gallon quota on bulk imports of crude and refined oil. Between 1889 and 1896 Standard Oil set up three separate subsidiaries in Canada: in part, these were intended to circumvent the tariff restrictions, but they also represented part of the American company's strategy of forward integration, establishing direct distributing outlets to the Maritimes, Quebec, and Ontario.

In 1893 the restriction on bulk imports was lifted, and four years later the Laurier government introduced moderate reductions of the duties on refined products. In 1898 Imperial Oil's Canadian owners sold their company to Rockefeller, and in the following year the other Standard subsidiaries were merged with it. The new American-owned Imperial controlled virtually the entire Canadian market. While prospective changes in Canadian trade laws may have provided the occasion for the Standard takeover, this was not the only factor involved. Throughout the 1890s Imperial had faced serious difficulties raising capital to expand operations in order to compete with the Standard subsidiaries. The quality of crude oil from the Petrolia fields was poor and Imperial did not have the technology to overcome the problem. By the mid-1890s Petrolia output had peaked and Imperial was increasingly dependent on imported crude, much of it from Standard's American fields. The alternative to the Standard takeover might well have been the elimination of Imperial from the market. Like many of Standard's competitors in the US, Imperial's owners decided to merge instead.

In the years immediately following the Standard takeover, from 1899 to 1910, Imperial Oil existed as a company in name only: its refineries were largely closed down and the few that remained in operation were managed by another Standard subsidiary in Buffalo, New York. Many of the previously quasi-independent sales agencies were eliminated, and the entire marketing and distribution network was run from Standard's headquarters in New York City. In 1904, the Canadian duties on imported crude were removed, and Standard constructed a line to supply the Canadian market from its fields in Cygnet, Ohio. During this period, Standard/Imperial faced little competition for the Canadian market. A handful of small producers continued to operate in Petrolia, and two refining enterprises appeared between 1902 and 1909, both controlled by American 'independents' in Ohio. In 1910, however, Standard still held over 80 per cent of the market and had extended its distribution network across the prairies to the west coast.

In that year the Anglo-Dutch company, Shell—Standard's major rival in international petroleum markets—announced its intention to establish a subsidiary in Canada, to be supplied from fields in the Dutch East Indies. At the same time, Standard Oil faced an even graver threat on its home front. Assailed by reformers since the 1890s as the virtual embodiment of a 'predatory monopoly', Rockefeller's empire became the target of US government antitrust action in 1907. Four years later the US Supreme Court upheld a decree ordering the dissolution of the Standard Oil 'trust'. In the ensuing division of the American corporation, Imperial passed into the hands of the Standard Oil Company of New Jersey. More significantly, Imperial's role was re-evaluated: it was now to be both a Canadian bastion against Shell and a vehicle for some of Jersey Standard's overseas investments that would be more secure from the potential scrutiny of US antitrust officials.

Accordingly, Jersey Standard dispatched its most vigorous executive, Walter Teagle, to take charge of reorganizing Imperial. In the words of John Ewing, Imperial's historian, 'Teagle . . . took Imperial from the vassalage in which it had been since 1898 and gave it at least the status of a free man.'9 Control of sales and distribution was shifted to Toronto and the network continued to expand, particularly in the West, to meet the challenge from Shell. The original Imperial refinery at Sarnia, Ontario, increased production with a steady supply of crude via the Ohio pipeline, and five new refineries were established between 1914 and 1923. The company's capital base was significantly enlarged in 1917, from $15 million to $50 million. A subsidiary, International Petroleum, was set up to develop oil fields in South America, and in 1918–19 another subsidiary commenced exploratory work in Alberta and

the Northwest Territories. This last undertaking was prompted by the news that Shell was negotiating with the Canadian government for access to mineral concessions in the West. Shell did not, in fact, carry out any substantial exploration before 1939; but Imperial acquired a concession from the CPR and began drilling for oil in Alberta in the 1920s. Altogether, Imperial spent over $18 million in exploration and drilling before striking a gusher at Leduc, Alberta, in 1947.

Although Imperial had been resurrected as a vertically integrated concern, it was very much a part of Jersey Standard's global system, as Teagle made apparent when he took charge of the parent company in 1918. Imperial's South American fields shipped oil principally to the American west coast and Caribbean markets, and its own supplies came largely from Jersey Standard's own fields up to the 1950s. More than 90 per cent of the company's net income between 1921 and 1939 was distributed to shareholders, with Jersey Standard as the main beneficiary. Aside from Shell, Imperial's main competitor in this period was McColl-Frontenac, which focused on the central Canadian market; in 1938, it was taken over by the American giant, Texaco, so that by World War II Canada's three major integrated oil companies were all foreign-owned entities. There were a few smaller drilling companies operating in Alberta, and in the Maritimes K.C. Irving began to build a regional distribution system in the 1930s, benefiting from public discontent over Imperial's near-monopoly position there—although Irving also bought much of his crude from the US company. Ironically, the emergence of a vigorous indigenous group of entrepreneurs in the industry did not come until the 1950s, stimulated in large measure by Imperial's ultimate success in its long and expensive search for oil in the Canadian West.

CHAPTER 6

Integration and Disintegration

The emergence of big business was never a painless process. Thousands of small enterprises succumbed to the rigours of competition, driven from the field or absorbed into larger, stronger firms. 'Rationalization' eradicated the roles of those who had functioned as middlemen in industries undergoing vertical integration, and new managerial structures challenged both the status and living standards of skilled artisans. Not surprisingly, this was an era punctuated by political upheavals, pitting small businesses against the new corporate organizations, and by chronic labour unrest where the underlying issue was often not wages and working conditions but control of the workplace. In Canada these dislocations also took on a regional dimension: local industries in the West and the Maritimes confronted the centralizing strategies of Toronto- and Montreal-based corporations. For the small retail merchant in Winnipeg, the independent kerosene jobber in Montreal, the machine parts manufacturer in Amherst, or the iron puddler in Hamilton, the advent of the large integrated corporation threatened disintegration of their livelihoods and sometimes of their entire communities.

Those who were so threatened did not, however, meekly accept their fate; and although the triumph of big business is often seen as the era's prevailing theme in Canada, it was not a total victory. Skilled craft unions resisted the full-scale introduction of 'scientific management' and mechanization in industry with considerable effectiveness at least up through World War I; and in many fields industrialists continued to depend on skilled workers. Small and medium-scale family-owned enterprises persisted in the industrial as well as commercial and service sectors of the economy, where consolidation could not produce economies of scale. Small-business owners resorted to trade associations and similar organizations to defend the status quo, often through pressure on local and provincial governments. Farmers adopted 'modern' business practices and also joined co-operatives and commodity marketing 'pools' that could compete more effectively with large corporate enterprises: here, too, governments played a role in responding to the pressures from small producers to constrain big business through regulatory measures imposed on the railways and grain merchants. The extent to which workers, farmers, and small businesses were able to 'countervail' the power of the large corporations through economic and political pressures has been the subject of continuing debate among historians and social scientists in the US and Europe, as well as in Canada. It seems reasonable to say, however, that the struggles for control of the workplace and the marketplace that accompanied the rise of big business in the early twentieth century helped lay the groundwork for more activist and interventionist roles for government in the 50-odd years following the coming of the Great Depression.

CONTROLLING THE WORKPLACE

The Second Industrial Revolution transformed traditional relationships between employers and their workers in several critical ways. The sheer growth in size and scale of firms in industries where consolidation and integration took hold made it impossible for owners, even of proprietary or family firms such as Massey-Harris, to maintain effective and regular face-to-face contacts with their employees. Layers of salaried supervisors or 'managers'—a term rarely used in the nineteenth-century business world—emerged to handle these and other routine tasks of administration. In corporate organizations, such as the CPR, salaried executives with little or no proprietary interest in the firms they worked for determined strategies and policies, subject at most to the sporadic intervention of major shareholders. By the early 1900s 'management' had become a recognized element in large industrial organizations, and no small part of the tasks of management encompassed establishing and enforcing rules and procedures under which work was conducted in the enterprise.

For larger integrated companies (and smaller ones aspiring to that status), reaping the benefits accruing from economies of scale in production required managers to devote constant attention to achieving 'efficiency' by controlling the costs of production and increasing the productivity of workers. Concepts of cost accounting, which enabled manufacturers to determine and monitor the cost per unit of production, migrated via branch plants and industrial journals from the US into Canada in the early 1900s. Productivity—higher unit output per input of capital, labour, and technology—could be increased by introducing labour-saving machinery, redesigning jobs

to reduce 'waste', offering various incentives to workers to increase output, or a combination of these techniques, developed in their most elaborate form by the American engineer, Frederick W. Taylor, and his fellow advocates of 'scientific management'.

The extent to which employers comprehended and embraced these ideas is a matter of some debate. The American labour historian Harry Braverman, in *Labor and Monopoly Capital*, argues that scientific management was a central element in a concerted effort by corporations to use technological and administrative methods to reorganize the workplace, reducing the autonomy (and pay rates) of skilled craft workers and replacing them with 'machine tenders' whose working environment was dominated by white-collar managers. Others have maintained that, despite the widespread publicity surrounding 'Taylorism' in the early 1900s, few employers adopted these ideas completely—although many did introduce specific techniques such as the piece-rate system and bonus incentives. Even skilled workers were willing to accept some of these innovations, particularly measures that reduced the arbitrary power of foremen and introduced more formal work rules, although they also bitterly and often successfully contested the imposition of more comprehensive schemes.

In Canada, many businesses embraced cost-accounting procedures and a few experimented with more elaborate scientific management plans. In 1910 the CPR brought in Henry L. Gantt, one of Taylor's disciples, to reorganize production in its locomotive repair shops in Montreal, later extending the system to its other facilities. The Canadian Manufacturers' Association encouraged its members to follow suit, publishing articles on scientific management in its journal, *Industrial Age*. It is difficult to determine how deeply the movement took hold or how enduring the changes were among Canadian employers. The experience of Knechtel Furniture Co. of Hanover, Ontario, indicates the rather mixed record of scientific management. A family firm established in the

1880s, Knechtel brought in 'efficiency experts' from Chicago in the early 1920s who introduced a quota and bonus pay scheme endorsed by the United Brotherhood of Carpenters, which, like many Canadian craft unions, was an offshoot of an American organization. Resentful of what they perceived as a challenge to their competence as craftsmen, the employees engaged in covert opposition and eventually staged a strike in 1923. Knechtel subsequently abandoned the scheme and there were no further experiments with wage incentives until the 1950s. Similar episodes of effective worker resistance to ventures in scientific management occurred throughout this period, even at the larger corporate-owned operations such as the Canadian General Electric plant in Hamilton. To some extent, the limited impact of these techniques, particularly in industries such as furniture-making where proprietary firms were well-entrenched, reflected uneasiness on the part of the owners themselves over derogating their authority in labour relations to 'college boys' with no experience on the shop floor.[1]

Another route through which reorganization of the workplace proceeded, possibly with greater impact than the complicated planning operations of Taylor and his followers, involved introduction of new machines and machine processes, particularly in the branch-plant industries. Ford, for example, transferred his assembly-line system to the Canadian plants shortly after developing it at Highland Park in 1910–13. The American-owned mining and newsprint companies introduced continuous-flow processes into the new mills established in Ontario and Quebec in the 1920s.

The introduction of labour-saving technologies in these 'new' industries did not precipitate confrontations with displaced skilled workers. Mechanization was more troublesome in older established fields, such as iron production. A range of jobs, both skilled and unskilled, was eliminated or downgraded as the larger mills moved to open-hearth operations in the early 1900s, in the face of dozens of strikes and slowdowns that sometimes affected the entire workforce, as happened at Dominion Steel in 1904 and NS Coal & Steel in 1915. Nevertheless, as late as the 1930s a variety of skilled jobs persisted, particularly in the rolling mills, and the new technologies required trained machinists, electricians, and crane operators who exercised more autonomy than assembly-line workers. In this industry, the workplace had been reorganized, but it remained a complex system in which informal patterns of bargaining underlay the formal structure of managerial authority.

Although the degree of management control varied among industries and among firms within industries, the enlarged scale of industrial operations and elaboration of formal systems of management generated a massive increase in administrative paperwork and a growing body of clerical workers to deal with it. Between 1900 and 1930, white-collar worker numbers rose from 2 per cent to 7 per cent of the total Canadian workforce, and during the first two decades of the twentieth century clerical jobs increased at almost three times the rate of job creation for workers generally. Initially, this growth occurred in the larger consolidated firms where increases in administrative overhead could be absorbed and offset by gains in productivity and reduced labour costs. The introduction of new technologies—adding machines and tabulators, stencils and mimeographs, vertical files and intercoms—not only improved the efficiency of office operations in larger firms but also enabled smaller enterprises to adopt 'modern' business methods without incurring substantial new administrative costs.

The recruitment of women into this emerging clerical workforce reflected these advances in the mechanization of office tasks and the employers' interest in controlling the costs of administration. Between 1890 and 1930 the proportion of women in clerical jobs in Canada rose from 14 per cent to almost half the total. In the late nineteenth century, women constituted only about 10 per cent of wage-earning workers, although in certain industries, notably cotton textile manufacturing in Ontario, the proportion was significantly larger. The expansion of white-collar clerical jobs in the early 1900s provided women with an entry into full-time paid employment. At the same time, employers generally paid them less than their male counterparts, in keeping with prevailing social mores on the status of men as 'heads of households' and the main income earners of their families. Scientific management techniques were probably more accepted in office organization than other areas of work, with increasing numbers of routine tasks such as bookkeeping, typing, and filing assigned to lower-paid female clerks. This picture can be overdrawn: both male and female white-collar workers (including unskilled transient workers) earned higher than average wages throughout this period, although the gap narrowed during the 1920s. Secretarial and other office work was hardly unskilled labour: these jobs required literacy and training in running office equipment. The conditions of work were generally cleaner and safer than shop floors, not to mention mines and sawmills. Opportunities for advancement into management, however, were far more constricted for women than for men, both in administrative work and in retail sales, another area of growing employment of women by the 1920s.[2]

Both corporate managers and small business proprietors were preoccupied with cost control and improving efficiency, but some of them recognized that a discontented worker could be a less productive worker and a potential labour union recruit. One response to these dangers was adoption of a variety of measures that have been termed 'welfare capitalism', ranging from Christmas bonuses and annual company picnics to pension annuity plans and 'profit-sharing' schemes for workers. Many of these initiatives represented extensions of policies followed by paternalistic employers in the nineteenth century, but they also reflected the influence of newer concepts of scientific management, seeking to stimulate greater productivity by encouraging worker loyalty to the firm. Employees would be encouraged to purchase stock in their companies on an installment payment basis in the hope that

this would give them a vested interest in boosting profits. Measures of this sort did not always work out as expected: president Walter Teagle of Imperial Oil, for example, was outraged to discover that employees who had purchased shares in the company under a program introduced in 1915 were 'speculating', i.e., selling their stock as the market value increased during World War I. Most employers preferred arrangements under which profit-sharing took the form of bonuses calibrated to reward employees who had rendered faithful service for many years.

In the early 1900s mining and forestry enterprises in the northern and western interior began developing planned communities that reflected both their economic requirements and 'welfare' ideas. The early mining towns, like Sudbury, with rail links to urban centres had grown more or less spontaneously as grubstakers and mine workers attracted by good wages (or at least steady jobs in the depressed 1890s) swarmed into these areas. Sometimes mining companies would erect primitive bunkhouses for their workers, but there was little deliberate planning involved. After 1900 big firms began establishing more stable communities of company-built houses on well-laid-out streets, with parks and playgrounds: Copper Cliff, developed by Inco after 1910 to replace an earlier shantytown, was a typical example, as was Arvida in Quebec (see box, p. 94). Meanwhile, corporations and entrepreneurs like the Timmins brothers, extending their operations deep into the wilderness, adopted similar town-planning methods to attract and retain workers in these remote settlements.

The larger, mostly foreign-owned firms also experimented with various forms of employee representation committees during and after World War I. Although at their peak in 1920 these 'industrial councils' boasted 145,000 members (about 8 per cent of all industrial workers but equal to 50 per cent of all unionized workers), they clustered in a relatively small number of companies, mostly US branch plants, that were also engaged in 'welfare' activities. The model

ALCOA AND ARVIDA, QUEBEC: A 'PLANNED' COMPANY TOWN

Arvida, Quebec, erected from the ground up by the then Canadian subsidiary of Alcoa in the 1920s, was a prime example of a 'planned town'. In 1901 the Pittsburgh Reduction Co. (later the Aluminum Co. of America) established a plant on the St Maurice River in Quebec, purchasing electricity from the Shawinigan Water and Power Co. to run an aluminum smelter using processed bauxite shipped by rail from the United States. By the end of World War I, global industrial demand for aluminum had increased from less than 100 tons/year in 1900 to over 40,000 tons/year, and Alcoa had secured a monopoly over aluminum production in North America. By the early 1920s, however, Alcoa's smelting capacity

in the US had been reached. Shawinigan Water and Power, which was selling electric power to other industries and residential users in eastern Quebec, was also approaching full capacity.

At this point the prospect of a far larger power site on the Saguenay River, a major tributary to the St Lawrence, came to Alcoa's attention. A huge section of the best land for power development in the Saguenay region had been acquired shortly before World War I by James B. Duke, the American tobacco magnate who apparently hoped to develop a giant synthetic fertilizer complex there. Nothing much came of this scheme, and in the early 1920s a portion of the area was leased to the Canadian newsprint company, Price Brothers.

The town of Arvida was built in six months in 1926 to provide 250 homes for employees at Alcoa's smelter on the St Maurice River in Quebec. (Rio Tinto Alcan)

Duke's notion of using the rest of the site to develop his own aluminum enterprise brought Alcoa—alarmed at this prospective challenge to its monopoly—into the picture. In 1925 a merger of the three interests—Duke, Price Brothers, and Alcoa—was negotiated; Duke's death later that year led to an increased Alcoa commitment to what would become one of the largest aluminum operations on the continent and the foundation of the Aluminum Co. of Canada.

Even before the merger was officially completed, Alcoa had begun erecting a smelter near the Price Brothers mill at Kenogami, and in 1926 the company began to develop a model town, christened Arvida (in honour of Alcoa's president, Arthur Vining Davis). It was designed by architects from New York, who were advised to develop housing styles that would resemble French-Canadian homes, to accommodate both the workforce Alcoa wanted to attract from Quebec and the American managers and technicians. Catholic and Protestant churches, schools, a hospital, and various recreational facilities were rapidly built by the company, although the onset of the Depression delayed street paving until well into the 1930s; and the houses proved to be poorly insulated and too small for many of the families that moved into the town.

In both its virtues and defects, Arvida reflected the perceptions of labour relations typical of many larger multinational enterprises in Canada: although Aluminium Ltd (later renamed Alcan Aluminum Ltd) was created as a nominally separate Canadian firm in 1928, ownership links with Alcoa remained through the 1950s. The American managers were encouraged to learn French, or at least enough to communicate with workers in the plant, which for the time represented an enlightened approach. In 1937 the company signed collective bargaining agreements with two Catholic unions. But differences over wages and working conditions culminated in an angry, albeit short-lived, strike in 1941. During World War II the company began selling its houses to permanent workers on liberal terms, meanwhile extricating itself from full responsibility for the costs of running public facilities.

Sources: Duncan Campbell, *Global Mission: The Story of Alcan* (Toronto, 1985), 85–133; Jorge Igartua, 'Corporate Strategy and Locational Decision-Making: The Duke-Price-Alcoa Merger of 1925', *Journal of Canadian Studies* 20 (Autumn 1985): 82–101; David Massell, *Amassing Power: J.B. Duke and the Saguenay River, 1897–1927* (Montreal and Kingston, 2000); George D. Smith, *From Monopoly to Competition: The Transformations of Alcoa, 1885–1936* (Cambridge, Mass., 1988), 138–45.

for these councils was largely the handiwork of Canada's first Minister of Labour (and future Prime Minister), W.L. Mackenzie King, who devised an employee representation plan for the Rockefeller Foundation while in temporary exile from Canadian politics during World War I. He described his ideas in characteristically turgid fashion in a book entitled *Industry and Humanity*, published in 1918. Imperial Oil created an industrial council in 1919 similar to one established by its parent, Jersey Standard (a Rockefeller firm). Another innovator in this area was International Harvester, whose industrial relations chief,

Arthur Young, proselytized the industrial council concept in the US and Canada in this era. Several larger Canadian-owned companies followed suit, notably Massey-Harris, which may have simply been keeping pace with its rival, Harvester. A more elaborate system emerged in the Canadian National Railways maintenance shops in the mid-1920s, involving formal co-operation between management and the rail workers' unions—CNR president Sir Henry Thornton's endorsement of this arrangement derived in part from his experience with the British industry, where a similar system had been introduced in World War I.

Except for the CNR experiment, these committees functioned on an individual plant rather than company- or industry-wide basis, and trade union representatives were deliberately excluded. The independent unions castigated these councils as 'company unions', mere puppets of management intended to pre-empt any genuine collective bargaining. The charges were not ill-founded: most industrial councils were dominated by managers, and employee representatives were generally docile or loyal supporters of the 'company' position. Controversial issues such as wages, hours, or job security were rarely raised for serious discussion. Unwelcome proposals could be vetoed by top management, who could also unilaterally terminate the councils. At the same time, industrial councils did provide managers with an early-warning system on labour unrest, and some improvements in working conditions were achieved. During the 1920s, when the independent union movement was badly devastated and demoralized, the industrial councils provided a means through which workers could express their concerns even though they were usually powerless to do anything more effective unless management chose to act.[3]

Many business people throughout this era had little use for 'welfare' schemes or industrial councils, sharing the view of the American industrialist Samuel Insull that the most satisfactory labour relations policy was 'a long line of men waiting at the gate'. From their perspective, labour unions were, at best, parasites on the productive forces of capital and, at worst, led by dangerous radicals intent on destroying the free enterprise system. The rise of militant organizations such as the Industrial Workers of the World, which flourished briefly (and was opposed by the established craft unions as well as by business) in Canada and the US in the 1910–20 period, tended to confirm their worst fears. The hard-line approach was most entrenched among small- and medium-sized proprietary firms, such as those that banded together into the Citizens Council to defeat the Winnipeg General Strike in 1919. But this strategy of confrontation was not restricted to small business. Several of the most prolonged and bitter strikes of this era involved large corporations, notably the Grand Trunk Railway strike of 1910–11 and the Besco confrontations with coal and steelworkers in Nova Scotia in the mid-1920s.[4]

The notion that collective bargaining agreements with trade unions could help ensure stability in the workplace was a view few employers were willing to accept before World War II. Smaller businesses feared the power that well-organized independent unions might exercise over their industries. Many of the larger companies established in the early 1900s carried heavy debt loads incurred by expansion and consolidation, and regarded control of labour costs as essential for their long-term strategies. The cadres of managers emerging in these firms were equally unwilling to concede to workers any substantial role in setting the pace of production or rates of pay for which they, as managers, were held accountable by their superiors and by shareholders. The economic downturns that punctuated the period of general growth from 1900 to 1930 perpetuated in the business community attitudes of caution and pessimism prevalent in the depressed 1890s. Even the CPR, which introduced some of the most sweeping 'welfare' programs in Canada and developed a working relationship with the skilled craft unions, resisted radical unions that tried to establish industry-wide collective bargaining in 1902–3, and periodically advocated legislation to ban strikes on the railways.

Confrontation between labour and business and pressure from both sides, though for different purposes, brought more government attention and occasional intervention in industrial disputes after the 1880s. In 1886 the growth of the Knights of Labor, a movement originating in the US, induced the Macdonald government to appoint a Royal Commission to investigate labour relations in Canada. As is frequently the case, nothing much came of this exercise and the abrupt decline of the Knights diminished incentives for action. A new round of strikes on the railways and in the mines in the early 1900s led to the establishment of a federal Department of Labour; and in 1907, Mackenzie King, as Labour Minister, introduced the Industrial Disputes Investigation Act (IDIA), which provided for conciliation boards to attempt to resolve labour–management disputes in advance of strike action by workers or employer lockouts in the transportation, utilities, and resource industries. The IDIA was thus limited in its reach and could not, in any case, impose arbitration if conciliation failed (as in the case of the Grand Trunk strike of 1910–11). In its early years, however, King could boast of a 90 per cent success rate for conciliation. The IDIA was less effective in dealing with confrontations between militant industrial unions and employers in the aftermath of World War I, and in 1925 the Act was held by the Supreme Court to have exceeded federal jurisdictional authority. By this time, the federal government and most of the provinces had worked out agreements to keep the system going.

Government involvement in labour relations was not consistently oriented towards conciliation. Courts at all levels tended to be hostile to unions, and provincial governments joined employers in seeking injunctions against strikes, sometimes also using police power to quell labour unrest. During the Winnipeg General Strike in 1919, federal troops were deployed to maintain 'order' while local police and employers' groups suppressed demonstrations; strike leaders were subsequently arrested and deported. Provincial and federal forces were also used during the Cape Breton strikes of the 1920s, and the RCMP established a special unit to carry out surveillance of labour unions after World War I. In general, even the conciliation measures were intended primarily to stem labour militancy. While King and other political leaders characterized government's role as that of 'impartial umpire' in labour disputes, the basic objectives of government policies were to maintain social stability and minimize the economic disruptions that strikes entailed, an approach that benefited employers more than workers.[5]

THE ROOTS OF REGIONAL INEQUALITY

Business consolidation and vertical integration were accompanied by significant shifts in the types of economic activities and distribution of wealth among the regions of Canada between 1890 and 1920. Although the case can be made that these changes were underway before this time, economic integration accelerated the concentration of finance and industry in central Canada at the expense of the Maritimes and the west coast. The National Policy tariffs have been identified as a critical element in this transformation, but in the first decade of the National Policy the trend is less apparent. In 1890 British Columbia surpassed all other provinces in per-capita manufacturing output; and although the Maritimes lagged behind the rest of the country in per-capita manufacturing output, the region retained market shares in several industries commensurate with its proportion of the population—and its industrial growth rate in the 1880s had surpassed that of Ontario and Quebec. As late as 1901, two of the 10 leading chartered banks in Canada were located in Nova Scotia, which also had the two largest iron and steel producers and the largest sugar refinery in the country. By the time Canada entered World War I, however, virtually all of the major financial institutions had relocated to Montreal or Toronto; and both BC and the Maritimes fell well below the national average in per-capita manufacturing, while Ontario substantially exceeded this level.

Even within central Canada changes were apparent by this time. Although Quebec was the main beneficiary of Maritime decline, particularly in the cotton textile industry, and Montreal remained the financial heart of Canada through the 1930s, the province was losing ground in a range of traditional industries. Flour mills and railway equipment manufacturing shifted to the prairies and steelmaking capacity concentrated principally in Ontario. The 'new' industries, such as electrical equipment and automobiles, developed almost entirely in Ontario. By the 1920s Ontario had become the centre for producer-goods manufacturing while Quebec focused more on light industry, some consumer goods, and financial services.

Although explanations for these shifts are varied, at a very simplified level they tend to move in two different directions. One line of interpretation focuses on the natural advantages of central Canada over other regions, or at least those conditions that enabled Ontario and Quebec to become the main beneficiaries of industrial growth and consolidation in the early twentieth century. Even before Confederation these two provinces contained more than three-quarters of the population of British North America, and their territorial acquisitions between 1870 and 1914 provided a natural resource hinterland that attracted both domestic and foreign investment. Southern Ontario's proximity to the burgeoning industrial heartland of the American Midwest made it a logical site for industrial expansion through direct investment from the US. Railway development—generating financial crises in central Canada in the 1860s—in the longer term created a transportation network undergirding the growth of Montreal and Toronto as the centres of the emerging transcontinental rail system from the 1890s through World War I. Once the process of industrial growth took hold in central Canada, it became more or less self-generating, attracting capital and labour from other regions of the country as well as from abroad. The differentiation of industrial activities between Quebec and Ontario reflected variations in energy sources and in the distribution of skills in their workforces.

An alternative line of argument emphasizes the economic consequences of government policies, which were in turn influenced by business elites in central Canada and the votes of those who depended on them for capital and jobs. The National Policy tariffs created a captive market for industries centred in Ontario and Quebec, and reoriented production and trade flows in BC and the Maritimes from export markets to a continental system in which higher transportation costs put both regions at a disadvantage. Government-subsidized railways were similarly intended to redirect trade patterns on east–west lines, with Toronto and Montreal at the hub. Rail freight rates, set initially by the few large carriers and subsequently by government commission, discriminated in favour of central Canadian shippers. By the early 1900s, bankers and industrialists in the peripheral regions recognized the trend of these developments and either sold out to central Canadian financial interests or relocated there, accelerating the process of regional change. In this context, the consolidation of industry and financial institutions in Montreal and Toronto exploited competitive advantages conferred upon them by the federal government in the 1880s and 1890s, enhanced by provincial policies—most notably in Ontario—after the turn of the century.

The debate over uneven regional development, and the role of business groups and government policies in these processes, has been most advanced in the Maritimes. The controversy, in fact, can be traced back to the 1920s when the Maritime Rights Movement, backed by business interests in the region, protested allegedly discriminatory federal tariff and railway policies that benefited their competitors in central Canada. Although the Maritime Rights Movement disintegrated before the end of the decade, many of these arguments were resuscitated by regional historians in the 1970s and 1980s, and were elaborated by political economists who perceived the 'deindustrialization' of the Maritimes in the early twentieth century as presaging on a smaller scale the eventual fate of a Canada colonized by branch plants and financially integrated with the United States.[6]

During the 1880s merchants and shipbuilders in Nova Scotia and New Brunswick diversified into a range of industries, principally targeting the central Canadian market, to exploit opportunities presented by the National Policy and the Intercolonial Railway. Even before the depression of the 1890s, some of these industries, notably cotton textiles, had succumbed to competition and takeover by Quebec firms, and regional financial institutions were beginning to redirect their investment into central and western Canada or overseas. Meanwhile, the diversion of Maritime capital into industrial pursuits limited investment in rebuilding the region's merchant marine to compete effectively in the new era of steamship traffic. Although general conditions of economic prosperity masked the decline of the region in the early 1900s, in the years following World War I the major remaining industries of the Maritimes faced a series of insurmountable crises. By this time more than half the manufacturing capacity and virtually all the financial institutions in the region had passed into the hands of central Canadian firms. During the 1920s, over 1,000 Maritime companies disappeared, almost all of them locally owned enterprises.

Some of the problems of aspiring industrialists in the Maritimes were of their own making, others were the result of economic shifts beyond the control of anyone in Canada. Industrial promoters in the Maritimes in the 1880s had little experience in or technical knowledge of the fields they were entering. As with traditional merchant ventures, financing was done on a short-term basis and in amounts sufficient only to cover initial start-up and operating costs. In some cases, particularly in textiles, mills were built on a larger scale than the prospective market would justify. The Gibson mill near Fredericton, NB, for example, could have supplied the entire Canadian market if it had ever operated at full capacity. During the 1890s, local and outside entrepreneurs began to focus on developing the coal and iron industry. Although these ventures proved to be more successful and durable, their long-term competitiveness was limited by the poor quality of local coal and iron ore and the geographically scattered locations of various stages of production in the industry. Ironically, local preoccupation with developing iron and steel capacity may have diverted capital from areas where there was substantial growth in the 1890s, for example, in pulp and paper milling and tobacco processing.

Changing conditions of demand and supply in the transatlantic world, as well as in Canada, constricted the range of opportunities for Maritime businesses and stymied their best efforts at critical points in this era. Declining demand in Britain for Maritime lumber exports from the early 1880s eroded the region's capital base and induced local entrepreneurs to shift into production for the domestic market, where the long-term advantage lay with competitors in Ontario and Quebec. Sugar refining, in which the region held almost one-third of the market and 40 per cent of the country's exports through the early 1900s, thanks to its proximity and trade links with the Caribbean, suffered a serious setback with the entry of US and European competitors into Canada's domestic and export markets after World War I. In that same period, lumber shipped via the Panama Canal to the east coast from British Columbia compounded the problems of the Atlantic region's sawmilling industry. Throughout the period from 1880 through the 1920s out-migration, particularly of working-age males, depleted the Maritimes population, contributing not only to the region's productivity problems but also to the steady decline of its political leverage in Ottawa.

Federal government policies influenced the region's economy, although not always to the detriment of Maritime businesses. As noted earlier, the National Policy provided new investment opportunities for the region in the 1880s when exports were declining. At the same time, as critics of the National Policy argue, this reorientation worked to the long-term disadvantage of the region. Perhaps more seriously, the federal government took no interest in rebuilding Canada's merchant marine fleet while committing large subsidies to developing the country's railway system. In export-oriented countries such as Japan and Germany, governments vigorously promoted merchant marine development; and even in the US, the merchant fleet began to recover in the early 1900s after a generation of neglect. The failure of Maritime shipbuilders to make the transition from sail to steam has sometimes been cited as an example of entrepreneurial lack of vision, but the incentives, such as they were, encouraged diversion of their resources and energies into other fields.

Transportation costs, particularly railway freight rates, were a central element in determining the competitive position of Maritime vis-à-vis central Canadian firms. The history of freight rates in this era is complex and controversial. During the mid-1880s, John Stairs, the Halifax industrial promoter, successfully lobbied the Intercolonial Railway to charge lower rates on westbound (i.e., to central Canada) shipments than it charged on eastbound shipments of refined sugar. Other interests jumped on this bandwagon, and by 1899 the region's shippers enjoyed an average 12 per cent lower freight cost for their westbound goods over competitors from Ontario and Quebec. As a railway financed and operated by the federal government, the Intercolonial was highly susceptible to rate-setting based on political pressure, and whatever their deficiencies as business strategists, Maritimers like Stairs had well-honed skills as political horse traders.

Understandably, shippers in central Canada were less delighted over the differentials, and the establishment of the Board of Railway Commissioners provided them with a forum for airing their grievances before an 'objective' audience. Their protests before the Board became more effective as Maritime parliamentary representation declined. In 1915, sugar refiners in Montreal and Ontario, alarmed by the threat to their traditional markets posed by an aggressive new firm, Atlantic Sugar of Saint John, NB, renewed long-standing complaints over the sugar differential before the Board. The Board's authority over the government-owned railway was ambiguous; but following the merger of the Intercolonial and the CNR in 1918, the new Crown corporation's management took steps to eliminate differentials for all freight. Maritime efforts to exempt the Intercolonial rates from this new policy were defeated in Parliament, and the Board rejected appeals from regional shippers, applying what one Maritime historian calls 'misguided symmetry', by maintaining that rates

should be based on 'fairness' to all parties and commercial considerations. The increase in westbound freight rates combined with the post-war recession devastated the region's industries and contributed directly to the rise of the Maritime Rights Movement. Later in the 1920s the Liberal government of Mackenzie King partially restored the differential in order to defuse the movement, but by that time many of the region's factories had closed down. Those that remained soon would confront the harsh gales of the Great Depression.

Maritimers in the 1920s, and their more recent chroniclers, asserted that the Intercolonial Railway and its freight rate differentials were linked to the commitment of the central Canadian parties to Confederation, i.e., Quebec and Ontario, to support the Maritimes region. Laissez-faire-minded observers (and those from Ontario and Quebec) have regarded these claims with bemusement, as reflecting the self-interested wishes of Maritime businesses for special treatment not accorded other regions. It may be worth noting that the Maritime differential was not unique: the Crow's Nest Pass arrangement imposed by the federal government on the CPR and other western carriers established differential rates to benefit western shippers. At the same time, changes in freight rates at the end of World War I were not the sole cause of Maritime economic troubles; at worst they were the culminating development in a series of problems contributing to the region's decline that dated back to the 1890s.

The difficulties of Maritime business cannot be attributed entirely to the machinations of predatory capitalists on Saint James Street in Montreal or myopic politicians in Ottawa; nor, by the same token, were they simply the victims of their own failings as entrepreneurs. The problems were deep-seated and cumulative, and many of the region's business figures contributed to the situation by responding in appropriately businesslike fashion. The Halifax directors of the Bank of Nova Scotia and the Royal Bank began moving their investments and eventually their headquarters out of the region in the 1890s. Ambitious entrepreneurs like

Aitken and Dunn joined the tide of migrants to greener pastures. The local owners of NS Coal & Steel and Rhodes & Curry (later Canadian Car & Foundry) merged their enterprises with those of central Canadian capitalists. The federal government that eliminated the Intercolonial freight rate differential was led by a Halifax native, Sir Robert Borden; and the most vigorous foe of the Maritime Rights Movement in the 1920s was a transplanted New Brunswicker, R.B. Bennett. Their lack of regional 'patriotism' is hardly surprising. Few people thought of the Maritimes (or anywhere else in Canada, for that matter) as a 'region' before the 1920s. Aspiring industrialists and bankers sought footholds in the lucrative markets of central Canada, which naturally led them towards relocation there as circumstances dictated.[7]

Historians of other 'peripheral' regions of Canada have sometimes joined forces with the Maritimers in denouncing the CPR/Bank of Montreal clique or 'Empire Ontario' for their centralizing strategies. To some extent, however, the Maritime situation was unique. As noted earlier, British Columbia had experienced a modest industrial boom in the 1890s, losing ground thereafter in part because of the high transportation costs to reach markets in the prairies and in part because of relatively high wage rates that reflected the small BC population as well as labour militancy. But industrialization in British Columbia never developed on a scale equivalent to the late nineteenth-century Maritimes, nor did the region possess the financial houses that for a time graced the business centres of Halifax and Saint John. The Prairie provinces perceived themselves as virtual colonies of central Canadian business from the time the Hudson's Bay Company released its grip on that region. The largest private grain dealers, flour millers, mines, railway shops, and wholesale merchant houses were branches of corporate and family firms in Ontario and Quebec; farmers, ranchers, miners, and retailers operated on credit from the chartered banks of the East.

Perhaps the greatest misfortune for the Maritimes was that the region never was a prospective hinterland for central Canada: in the 1880s and 1890s that region was a source of competition in the protected industrial markets. Later, after these competitors were vanquished or submerged, the Maritimes became essentially a neglected appendage of the emerging industrial and commercial heartland, populated (so it appeared to other Canadians) by exotic fisherfolk, kilted bagpipers, discontented coal miners, and politicians perpetually seeking government handouts.[8]

THE PERSISTENCE OF SMALL BUSINESS

While the large corporations and family dynasties like Eaton and Massey commanded the greatest amount of attention of investors, politicians, and the public—not to mention future scholars—it should be kept in mind that most businesses in this era operated on a much smaller scale. As late as 1930, 89 per cent of all manufacturing firms in Canada had an annual average output of less than $200,000 and employed fewer than 50 people. Small independent retailers comprised more than 90 per cent of all enterprises and accounted for over 80 per cent of sales in this sector of the economy. More than one-quarter of the country's workforce was involved in farming or fishing, areas in which small-scale, decentralized operations predominated. In contrast to the US and Britain, where large integrated enterprises established themselves in consumer goods by the early twentieth century, in Canada these were principally found in the producer goods sector and in the processing of natural resources for export markets. Consequently, while most Canadians, particularly those outside major cities, may have read about big business in their newspapers, their usual everyday contacts were with peddlers and small shopkeepers, local realtors, insurance agents, and manufacturers.[9]

In some industries technological and market conditions made large-scale operations unfeasible or limited their ability to dominate markets: numerous small bakeries, clothiers, tanneries,

To counteract the spread of chain stores like Eaton's and Simpsons, general stores, like this one in Didsbury, Alberta, adopted 'modern' methods of accounting and marketing in the early 1900s. (Glenbow Archives NA-703-8)

sawmills, and furniture factories could be found across Canada despite the growth of large companies in these fields. In other areas, vigorous efforts to achieve economies of scale through vertical integration and consolidation were at best only partially met. The fisheries provide examples of this phenomenon.

Fishing itself remained a largely decentralized pursuit, at least until the introduction of sea-going freezer-trawler 'fish factories' by the Europeans and Japanese after World War II. But the development of new methods of preserving fish through refrigeration and canning in the late nineteenth century presented opportunities for larger-scale organization in processing and marketing fish products. This was particularly the case in

the salmon fishery of British Columbia where canneries thrived from the 1880s, exporting much of their output to Britain with relatively little competition—the American canneries on the Alaska coast were mainly oriented to the US market—until the Japanese entered the field after World War I. Canadian canneries, mostly locally financed and owned, were concentrated along the Fraser River and on Vancouver Island.

In 1900 Henry Doyle, who managed a Vancouver branch of his family's California-based cannery, launched a scheme to amalgamate the BC salmon industry, which had suffered recurrent cycles of overproduction punctuated by periods of salmon stock depletion due to overfishing. The BC Packers Association, combining 39 canneries that accounted for over half the province's output and financed with $2.5 million from US and central Canadian banks, was established in 1902. Doyle was ousted as general manager two years later following disputes with his backers, but BC Packers faced more serious difficulties. A loosely organized operation, the enterprise was unable to prevent its own members from engaging in independent selling of their output on the side; and the salmon boom that ran from 1905 to 1913 attracted new entrants, including Doyle himself, into the industry, setting up their canneries in the numerous bays and estuaries of the BC coast.

By the end of World War I, BC Packers controlled less than one-fifth of the province's industry, which was again experiencing falling prices as Americans and Japanese fought them for the British market and declining supplies of salmon. In 1928 a new effort at amalgamation produced BC Packers Ltd, a much more tightly structured enterprise that comprised (again) about half of the salmon canning output in the province. But several substantial operators remained outside the new organization, and other independent canners diversified into tuna and similar less expensive fish products. The Depression of the 1930s hurt BC Packers, but inadvertently improved its market position by eliminating many smaller rivals in remote sites. The success of BC Packers was thus more a result of general economic conditions than of its own strategic foresight.

A somewhat similar sequence occurred in the Great Lakes fishery. Although overshadowed by Canada's ocean-based industry, the Great Lakes fishery is one of the world's largest freshwater fisheries, supplying both Canadian and US markets. In the nineteenth century most fishing and processing were carried out by small operators on both sides of the border, although the Hudson's Bay Company controlled much of the packing and marketing of the catch from Lake Superior. The US imposition of protective duties on imported fish in 1890 transformed the situation as Canadian fishers formed linkages with American processing firms to circumvent the

tariff. The Chicago packer, A. Booth & Co., established a trust in 1898 that eventually controlled 80 per cent of the western Great Lakes output, absorbing Canadian producers into a subsidiary, Dominion Fish Co. New York-based merchants moved in a similar fashion to dominate the eastern Great Lakes.

This trend towards consolidation and integration began to unravel after World War I. Improvements in transportation and methods of preservation enabled smaller packers to increase direct sales to the metropolitan markets of the American east coast, and the attenuation of import duties in 1913 reduced the influence of American firms in the Great Lakes fishery. Co-operatives and fishermen's trade associations emerged in the early 1900s to compete with the big packers and lobbied with some effect on provincial governments for introduction of regulatory measures to restrict American entrants. Meanwhile, overfishing and industrial pollution had depleted the Great Lakes of many of the most desirable types of fish, so that the decline of larger firms may reflect as well the relative deterioration of profitability in the fishery—much as the decline of the west coast salmon stocks limited the dominant role of BC Packers in that region.

During this period shifts in markets and the technologies of fishing and processing were also transforming the east coast fishery. By the 1920s large firms had emerged that integrated fishing, using steam trawlers, with on-shore packing and marketing. At the same time, however, decentralization and small-scale operations persisted in the industry. Although the number of people engaged in fishing and the number of independent packing enterprises diminished steadily, in 1930 there were still over 500 such ventures: 60 per cent of them had an average annual output of less than $10,000. By contrast there were fewer than 100 such firms in BC, and more than two-thirds of these had an output in excess of $200,000 per year. Many of the larger-scale Maritime companies were family-owned or partnerships, notably the Zwicker family firm and W.C. Smith Co. of

Lunenburg, NS, and the Leonard Fishery Co. of Saint John, NB.

Declining demand for dried fish products in the Caribbean and American import duties after 1886 threatened this traditional sector of the industry, although it experienced a renaissance during the period before World War I, prior to its final eclipse in the 1920s. By this time the market for fresh fish was emerging, enhanced by the development of refrigeration. After 1913, US duties on boned and skinned fish were reduced and other fresh fish was admitted free, reflecting in part the decline of the New England fishing fleets. Meanwhile, Maritime fishers and packers diversified into higher-value fish such as haddock, supplementing the traditional cod.

By the 1920s, improvements in processing technology, including filleting and rapid freezing, had spread from the US into Canada. Before this time, the most significant developments had involved vessel design and fishing technology. Beginning in the 1880s, Maritime schooners became larger, sometimes with auxiliary steam power, permitting longer voyages and larger catches. Lunenburg in particular became the centre of the 'banker fleet' as well as the construction site for the racing schooners of the 1920s, of which the *Bluenose* was the most famous. During the early 1900s larger steam-driven trawlers made their appearance in east coast waters. By 1927 there were 10 trawlers operating in the Maritimes, each capable of bringing in between 150,000 and 300,000 pounds of fish per voyage.

The new technologies of fishing, processing, and preserving required substantial increases in capital investment. The average cost of outfitting vessels alone more than doubled between 1900 and World War I; a steam trawler cost close to $1 million. Some companies, such as Smith's, met these needs by enlarging their partnerships, integrating fishing and packing, and diversifying into fresh fish marketing. Others raised capital from central Canada, and American fish marketers also entered the Maritime industry. The largest operations in the early 1920s, based in Halifax, were the

Maritime Fish Corporation and the National Fish Co., both of which owned or chartered several trawlers and had a number of cold-storage and processing plants at various Maritime outports. Both of these firms were taken over in 1928-9 by a New York company, Atlantic Coast Fisheries. During the 1930s, however, the properties were reacquired by H.G. Connor, who had founded Maritime Fish Corp. in 1910. Meanwhile, the Smith family in Lunenburg had expanded its position by acquiring a chain of packing plants from Ralph Bell, a Halifax merchant who would administer the Canadian aircraft industry during World War II, and return to Nova Scotia to amalgamate the Smith and Connor companies into National Sea Products Ltd in 1945.

Although the trend towards large-scale consolidations in the east coast fishery was underway by the 1920s, certain factors slowed the pace of this process and limited its impact. From the early 1900s the traditional long-line fishers had assailed the introduction of steamer trawlers in their waters as a threat to their livelihood as well as an inherently wasteful practice, since trawler nets scooped up everything in their path, decimating the fish population. The W.C. Smith Co., which relied on schooner fishing until the 1930s, joined in this protest. In 1930 the Canadian government introduced a trawler licensing system with high differential fees for foreign-owned vessels. The combined effect of this measure and the Depression reduced the trawler fleet to three ships by the mid-1930s.

In addition, some sectors of the fishery remained beyond the reach of big integrated firms. The lobster fishery, for example, identified by a Canadian government report in 1927 as 'one of the most important and valuable branches' of the industry, was characterized by small-scale operators and regulated by the provincial governments. During the late 1920s the Antigonish Movement focused its efforts on developing co-operatives in the lobster fishery, with some financial support from the Nova Scotia government during the Depression.

In each of the fisheries, then, the growth of large integrated firms was offset to some extent by the physical and economic characteristics of the industry, by government measures in response to pressures from smaller producers, and by the emergence of co-operatives. These counter-trends were not sufficient to perpetuate or restore traditional patterns of small-scale individual enterprise, but they did set limits on empire-building in the industry. In general, the most successful ventures through the 1930s were medium-sized companies with some degree of vertical integration, predominantly proprietary or private limited-liability companies.[10]

A similar pattern might have been predicted for Canadian agriculture. Certainly in the US this was the case, particularly after World War I when the prolonged agricultural depression, aggravated by drought and insect invasions, decimated the ranks of marginal farmers. The survivors consolidated landholdings, introduced mechanization on a large scale, and organized powerful lobbies to secure government price supports for their products. In Canada, a somewhat different process unfolded. Farmers on the prairies banded together into producer co-operatives and used their political clout to procure provincial government support for large quasi-public grain elevator and marketing enterprises. Canada's western farmers suffered the ravages of a depression that began long before the stock market crash of 1929, and many smaller operators went under. But the big storage and marketing structures remained and expanded as prosperity returned during World War II. There is a certain irony here, since many of the ideas about producer co-operation and government-owned elevators were originally devised by American farmers during the Populist era of the 1890s. In the US these 'radical' challenges to big business disintegrated in the early twentieth century, but took root and institutional form in Canada.

As in the US, farmers' journals and almanacs from the early 1900s urged their readers to adopt 'businesslike' practices, not just improved methods of cultivation and crop rotation and the introduction of machinery, but also more standardized bookkeeping techniques and more efficient management of harvest workers. While the extent to which this advice was embraced is unclear, farmers, especially in the prairie West, were quite sensitive to the connections between their earnings and the prevailing commercial arrangements for storing, transporting, and marketing grain. Western ire focused initially on the CPR's freight rate policies and then on the large private elevator companies with their linkages to the Winnipeg Grain Exchange. Seeking redress for their grievances through political pressure on the western provincial governments, farmers also turned to more direct techniques of organization for marketing their products.

Ideas about co-operatives were percolating into Canada from the US and Britain in the 1890s. Farmers also had some immediate experience to draw upon: from the early days of prairie settlement, local communities had been making arrangements for shared use of equipment and labour at harvest time. In 1906 a British immigrant to Manitoba, Edward A. Partridge, proposed extending the idea of co-operation to grain marketing. Partridge's venture, the Grain Growers' Grain Co., was initially denied a seat on the Winnipeg Grain Exchange, but drew upon political support from farm pressure groups to secure its position on the Exchange in 1907. Meanwhile, farm groups were agitating for establishment of provincially owned line elevators to challenge the private elevator 'combine'.

While western political leaders were reluctant to enter directly into the business of running elevators, they were prepared to offer financial support to 'farmer-owned' companies. In 1911 the Saskatchewan Co-operative Elevator Co. was incorporated; and in the following year Manitoba, which had briefly experimented with a government-owned system, leased its 174 elevators to Partridge's Grain Growers' Grain Co., which, in turn, provided financial guarantees in 1913 to a Farmers' Co-operative Elevator Co. in Alberta. In

1917 the Alberta and Manitoba companies amalgamated to form United Grain Growers Ltd, with $2 million in capital raised from farmer members, under the leadership of Thomas A. Crerar, who had succeeded Partridge as president of the Grain Growers' Grain Co. in 1912 and later headed the short-lived federal Progressive Party in the 1920s. The Saskatchewan Co-operative remained separate, but by the mid-1920s both companies were almost equal in size, and together they controlled more line and terminal elevators than any of the private firms.

Grain marketing and pricing continued to be a source of contention among western farmers. During World War I the federal government established a Board of Grain Supervisors, which purchased wheat at fixed prices to supply domestic requirements as well as sales to Allied governments overseas. When the Winnipeg Grain Exchange resumed operations in 1919, the price of wheat promptly spiralled, leading the government to set up a Canadian Wheat Board that resumed fixed-price purchases of all grain. Farmers had initially been cool to the Wheat Board since its set price was below the current market price; when market prices collapsed after the termination of the Board in 1920, many of them became vigorous advocates of its restoration. But opinions on the issue within the farmers' organizations were divided: Crerar, in particular, opposed re-establishment of a compulsory system. The Liberal government of Mackenzie King, elected in 1921, took the position that a peacetime Wheat Board would exceed federal constitutional authority, and proposed to revive it only if the legislatures of all the Prairie provinces endorsed the plan. When Manitoba failed to do so (by a three-vote margin) the Wheat Board died—at least until the Great Depression.

Meanwhile, a movement spread across the West for creation of a system of controlled grain marketing through voluntary associations, called 'pools', modelled on the elevator co-operatives. Individual farmers would purchase shares (at $1 each) in the enterprise: when enough were signed on to account for 50 per cent of the acreage in a province, the provincial government would issue a charter authorizing the pool to purchase grain from the shareholders, at a contractually established price, and market it through a centralized sales agency with professional managers. Profits would be reinvested to strengthen the pool's asset base and enable it to maintain stable prices. Directors or 'trustees' would be elected by local shareholders on a proportional representation basis.

Prairie farm organizations supported the pool concept but it had some unusual advocates, notably Aaron Sapiro, a peripatetic lawyer from California (whose clients included the Hollywood producer Louis B. Mayer and the Chicago gangster Al Capone), who stage-managed a colourful campaign across the prairies in 1923–4 to persuade farmers to sign up for the pools. Another improbable supporter was the millionaire Calgary lawyer and future Tory Prime Minister, R.B. Bennett, who helped Sapiro draft the first wheat pool contract in Alberta in 1923. Saskatchewan and Manitoba followed Alberta's lead in 1924, each province creating a Co-operative Wheat Producers Co. The pools contracted with the co-operative elevator lines for handling the crop.

In 1926 the Saskatchewan Wheat Pool acquired the line elevators of the Saskatchewan Co-operative Elevator Co. for $11 million and commissioned a noted engineer, C.D. Howe, to design a new terminal elevator complex at the Lakehead. United Grain Growers declined a similar offer from the Alberta and Manitoba pools but continued to handle their output; these pools developed their own country elevator networks but avoided direct competition with United Grain Growers. By 1929 the three wheat pools owned more than 1,600 line and terminal elevators, held cumulative assets of $29 million, and were handling and marketing more than half the country's wheat crop through a single central sales agency, Canadian Co-operative Wheat Producers.Ltd. In the US, the newly elected President, Herbert Hoover, established a Federal Farm Board closely patterned after the Canadian pools.

The Great Depression wracked prairie wheat growers and nearly destroyed the pools. Faced with global overproduction, the US, followed by Britain, Germany, France, and Italy, imposed prohibitive duties on grain imports in 1930–1. The 'dust bowl' drought and wheat rust decimated grain output later in the 1930s, reducing overproduction but ruining hard-pressed western farmers in the process: per-capita income in the three Prairie provinces fell by more than 66 per cent from 1929 to 1935, with farmers bearing the brunt of the decline. The pools' central sales agency, which had vainly attempted to prop up prices at the outset of the crisis, collapsed in 1931. Prime Minister Bennett saved the co-operatives from bankruptcy by arranging for federal government guarantees of their liabilities, and in 1934 he proposed to re-establish the Canadian Wheat Board. The Liberals effectively blocked recreation of the Board with compulsory powers (which were finally conferred in 1943), but the co-operatives managed to stagger through the worst years of the Depression, marketing their wheat through the Voluntary Board and hanging on to their elevator networks. With the revival of export trade in World War II, the co-operatives recovered, with the Saskatchewan Wheat Pool emerging as the leading firm in the elevator and grain-handling field. The co-operatives also diversified, acting as purchasing agents and distributors of seed and fertilizer for their members.[11]

The wheat co-operatives overshadowed other ventures of this type in Canada, but they were not unique. The Depression stimulated the growth of the co-operative movement, although necessarily on a much smaller scale than in the wheat pools of the 1920s. In 1940, there were more than 1,000 co-operatives, with 450,000 members, in a range of agricultural fields, including dairy products, livestock and poultry, and fruits and vegetables, as well as the fisheries co-operatives.

Much of the rhetoric of the co-operative movement, then and now, emphasized co-operatives and their 'democratic' decentralized structure as an alternative to 'capitalist' corporate organization.

Some observers have questioned the extent to which these claims corresponded with the realities of co-operatives, especially in large organizations such as the wheat pools. The pools and elevator co-operatives necessarily relied on hierarchies of professional managers to run their operations effectively. Although the managers were accountable to directors or trustees elected by the co-operative membership, inevitably, the directors would be obliged to allow a fair degree of latitude to management, as in most joint-stock corporations. Although members of co-operatives could play a larger role in the selection of directors through proportional representation than the average shareholder in a large corporate enterprise, as in other organizations incumbents tended to be re-elected, creating a more or less self-perpetuating elite. One survey indicated that over one-third of directors in the large farm co-operatives served five terms or more. While the principles of organization of co-operatives differed from private corporations, in effect, co-operatives—particularly the prairie farm co-operatives—constituted a consortium of small profit-oriented proprietors. Although the wheat pools were sometimes denounced by their corporate competitors as 'bolshevik' experiments, impeccable conservatives like Bennett and Hoover saw them as alternatives to 'big government' and 'socialism'.

The disjunction between rhetoric and reality was also apparent in the history of Quebec's credit union co-operatives, the caisses populaires. Alphonse Desjardins, a journalist and French-Canadian proto-nationalist who established the first caisse populaire at Lévis, Quebec, in 1900 and tirelessly promoted the idea, envisioned these co-operatives as instruments for the preservation and advancement of the French-speaking communities of Canada. They provided mortgages to lower-income homeowners and loans to small businesses unable to secure credit from the large anglophone banks. There were 140 caisses in operation when Desjardins died in 1920. The movement slowed over the next two decades, but then grew rapidly during and after World War II, expanding from its rural and small-town base into the larger cities, with 15 per cent of the French population of Quebec as subscribers in 1945. Although caisses also appeared in French-Canadian communities in the Maritimes and the West, the movement centred in Quebec, where, by the early 1980s, one-third of all personal savings were deposited in credit unions.

Ties of religion as well as ethnicity combined to promote the caisses. The Catholic hierarchy of Quebec vigorously supported the movement, which was seen as a development that might stem the migration of French Canadians from Quebec; and the church drew on the resources of the caisses to finance its construction projects in the province. The caisses were perceived as one of the social bastions preserving traditional French-Canadian communities against the tides of secularism and industrialization.

While the movement stressed ethnic and religious solidarity, in practice the leaders of the caisses were predominantly French-Canadian small businessmen and professionals. Although Desjardins advocated credit policies that would ensure that low-income earners qualified for loans and that most of the money loaned would remain in the local communities, as the caisses evolved more 'businesslike' criteria became the norm for loans, and investment gravitated towards larger, more profitable ventures. By 1945 almost half of the total assets of the caisses consisted of bonds, including provincial and federal government notes as well as corporate securities. During the 1920s a trend towards centralization emerged as the caisses grouped into regional confederations that drew on a portion of the asset base of their local members for investment, culminating in the formation of the Fédération de Québec des unions régionales de caisses populaires Desjardins (FQUR) in 1932. Under its first president, Cyril Vaillancourt, the FQUR operated much like a chartered bank with the local caisses as branches, although a number of these, particularly in the Montreal area, resisted Vaillancourt's 'dictatorship'. This development, like the founding of the caisses in 1900, reflected in part the tensions accompanying changes in Quebec society and the French-Canadian middle class.[12]

Whatever their deficiencies as democratic institutions, co-operatives provided small business people with an instrument not only for gaining economic leverage against bigger competitors but also for enhancing their political influence. Other forms of direct political pressure were employed by small business groups throughout this era. At the federal level their power was limited and diluted, but in provincial politics small businesses could prove to be a formidable force, as the histories of Ontario Hydro and the prairie wheat pools demonstrate. Many of Canada's financial and corporate leaders were inclined to regard these small business pressure groups as retrograde forces, seeking to use government authority to perpetuate outmoded and inefficient practices. But institutions such as the co-operatives did represent an innovative effort by small businesses to accommodate the changing economic conditions while preserving their traditional independence.

PART II

THE AGE OF
THE ACTIVIST STATE,
1930–1988

CHAPTER 7

The Incomplete Leviathan

Government intervention in the market economy was hardly a twentieth-century novelty in Canada or in other industrializing countries. Long before Confederation, governments were involved in schemes to encourage the development of canals and railways, promote industry, and attract foreign investment through direct subsidies, public loans, tariff duties and drawbacks, and patent laws. Governments at all levels continue to play this promotional role today. Regulatory measures—to restrict exploitation of child labour, to prevent adulteration of food products and other commodities, and to establish safety requirements in mines and factories—were also in place by the late nineteenth century, although the means of enforcement often left something to be desired. There were even ventures into public enterprise, usually as a result of failures on the part of private companies to complete projects deemed to be essential to the economy: most of the canals wound up in government hands and the Intercolonial Railway linking the Maritimes to central Canada was undertaken by the federal government in the 1870s.

At the turn of the century, several new factors generated pressures for governments' more systematically activist role in the economy. The emergence of large-scale enterprises and the integration of local and regional markets into a national system presented novel and unanticipated problems for public authorities. Farmers, owners of small businesses, industrial workers, and urban consumers clamoured for measures to protect their interests against the perceived economic power of big business. In times of economic hardship, governments were pressed to assume greater responsibilities for alleviating distress. The demands of modern warfare, peaking around the middle of the century, required an unprecedented degree of economic co-ordination of the nation's resources. As the role of government expanded, public officials acquired increasing confidence in their ability to control the course of events, stimulating new interventionist initiatives. While business leaders continued to employ the rhetoric of laissez-faire liberalism, their enterprises were increasingly enmeshed in a web of governmental relationships, embracing public contracts, subsidy arrangements, regulatory agencies, and joint public/private undertakings.

The rise of the activist state was not a uniquely Canadian phenomenon, and in many respects governments in Canada were far less interventionist than those of other industrializing nations. In the realm of social welfare, for example, through the post-World War II era Canada lagged well behind continental European countries and even Britain and the United States. Formal structures of collaboration between government and domestic businesses that emerged in 'late industrializing' countries such as Sweden or Japan were not explicitly followed in Canada— although informal networks of this sort were at work in federal policy-making in the late nineteenth century and in Ontario in the early 1900s. While the proliferation of Canadian Crown corporations has projected an image of an intensely activist state, in other dimensions—particularly in the area of economic regulation—governments in Canada have been less obtrusive in the affairs of business than was the case even in that heartland of free enterprise, the United States.

For the most part, Canadian historians have focused on the promotional role of governments in the economy, with Crown corporations representing a variation on this theme. There is a general consensus that Canadian governments have been consistently interventionist, but views differ over the sources and purposes of this activism. Followers of Innis stressed the interconnection of government policies and the development of staple-exporting industries, but they were not in agreement over the role of business vis-à-vis government in these pursuits. Hugh Aitken maintained that these policies represented 'defensive expansionism' on the part of governments, to encourage economic growth and to protect the east–west linkages that defined the country from the southward pull generated by the American economy. The political economists, on the other hand, saw the initiative for governmental measures coming from the business community, particularly the staple-exporting merchants and their banking affiliates; in the more recent past these groups have had to share their influence on the state with representatives of the foreign (mostly American) multinationals in the extractive and manufacturing sectors.

Other scholars, deriving their ideas in part from proponents of the concept of 'corporate liberalism' in the US, emphasized the dominant role of big business in shaping Canadian governmental policies in the twentieth century. Not only overtly promotional measures but also government regulation of business were the result of pressures from the large industrial enterprises and banks anxious to create conditions of economic predictability and social stability through government action, to restrict markets and at least give the appearance of meeting the demands of farmers and industrial workers for a more socially equitable system. Far from being experiments in socialism (or instruments of nation-building), Crown corporations played a necessary role in moderating the forces of the market, on the one hand, and political radicalism, on the other.[1]

All of these views reflect perceptions of a vigorous and expanding governmental presence in the economy characteristic of the post-World War II era. Many of the groups and pressures for an activist state—big business elites seeking stability; small businesses and others seeking to constrain big business; promoters with their schemes; ambitious government bureaucrats and intellectuals—were at work long before that point. But governments had neither the will nor the resources to proceed very far along this course. Economic mobilization in World War I, as will be discussed in the next chapter, was limited in both its extent and impact. This chapter will focus on forays by the federal and provincial governments into regulation of big business in the early 1900s, and the haphazard responses of governments at all levels to the prolonged and devastating economic crisis of the Great Depression.

THE REGULATORY IMPULSE

As noted above, there was nothing unique about the movement for expansion of government regulation of business that emerged in Canada around the end of the nineteenth century: every industrialized or industrializing country was experiencing similar pressures, although the responses varied considerably. Canadian governments could look abroad for models to emulate as well as for practices to avoid. Bismarck's Germany introduced major social welfare programs in the 1880s. In

Britain, even in the heyday of laissez-faire, measures had been enacted to regulate health and safety conditions in factories and mines, and Canadian governments had followed suit in the 1870s and 1880s. Just across the border, in the years after the Civil War, American state governments had begun experimenting with railroad freight rate regulation through quasi-judicial agencies, experiments culminating in the federal Interstate Commerce Commission Act of 1887. Three years later the US Congress passed what appeared to be a sweeping measure against 'monopolistic' businesses, the Sherman Antitrust Act. Britain and continental European countries were less inclined to try to ban big business altogether, but they imposed certain constraints on 'unfair competition'[2]

At the same time, Canada had its own distinctive regulatory patterns, reflecting its particular circumstances and traditions. In electric utilities and in railways, government-owned enterprises coexisted with regulatory agencies, and a similar pattern was to emerge in the air transportation industry. The Canadian government, unlike the American, did not engage in 'trust-busting'. Instead, it followed the European practice of attempting to police corporate behaviour, despite persistent pressures from farmers and small businesses for more stringent measures against alleged monopolies.

Canadian constitutional arrangements had an impact on regulatory structures. A number of areas where regulatory initiatives occurred fell within provincial jurisdiction, and others were subject to concurrent federal and provincial authority. In the field of corporate securities, for example, both the Dominion and provincial governments had chartering (and implicit regulatory) powers: a shrewd businessman such as Charles Sise of Bell Canada could select the jurisdiction that would best serve his purposes. Provincial efforts to control the issuing of securities within their boundaries were held to be inapplicable to Dominion-chartered companies by the Judicial Committee of the Privy Council in Britain—effectively Canada's court of final appeals through the post-World War II era. But the federal government, in turn, was restricted in its control over the resale of securities by brokers or investment houses. One way around this problem was for governments at both levels to pass similar laws, as in the Security Frauds Prevention Acts of 1931–2, although not every province was prepared to participate.

Jurisdictional disputes also complicated regulation of the insurance industry. From the 1870s on, both Dominion and provincial (primarily Ontario and Quebec) governments sought to control this field. The courts and Britain's Privy Council consistently ruled in favour of provincial regulatory priority, even over companies that operated across provincial boundaries. But the federal government persisted in efforts to maintain a foothold in the field, asserting its right to regulate Dominion-chartered and foreign insurance firms, with backing from larger companies that wanted the imprimatur of federal endorsement of their solvency to help them secure business outside Canada. After much bickering, the Dominion and provincial governments negotiated a compromise in 1934 under which the federal government would issue certificates of solvency to federally chartered companies while leaving the balance of regulatory controls in provincial hands.

While federal–provincial divisions helped create a realm of legal ambiguity for businesses seeking to minimize regulatory constraints, the powers of the state at all levels over private property were far more extensive in Canada under the BNA Act than in the US, where businesses could seek protection of their rights through the courts, at least up to the 1930s. Appeals by businesses of decisions made by Canadian regulatory bodies were thus stringently limited, so that the main arena for debate over these matters was in Parliament and the provincial legislatures. On the other hand, as will be seen, regulatory commissions and tribunals were inclined to be cautious about exerting their powers, but, at the same time, they were attentive to political pressures that could be brought to bear on the ministers and cabinets to whom they were accountable.

In Canada, both regulatory measures and Crown corporations were sometimes initiated to advance overtly nationalist goals, particularly in the years after World War I when American economic and cultural influence was perceived to be expanding. From the late nineteenth century, some regulatory legislation was clearly designed to complement the National Policy by protecting Canadian producers against foreign competition: licensing arrangements in the fisheries were intended to restrict American entry; 'inspection' fees levied on petroleum imports in the 1880s and 1890s supplemented customs duties. In the 1930s, Crown enterprises such as Radio Canada and Trans-Canada Air Lines were created to head off the threat of large US entrants into these markets, and the regulatory bodies established in these fields used licensing and review powers to buttress the position of these national enterprises.[3]

The range of government regulation extended piecemeal between the 1880s and 1930s. Earlier chapters have touched on some of these activities, such as electric utility regulation, grain marketing, banking regulation, and labour disputes arbitration. The federal government also monitored the production and distribution of food products, fertilizers, and drugs to prevent adulteration and false labelling, and regulated hunting, timber-cutting, and mining on Dominion lands. The first national park was established at Banff in Alberta in 1887. Between 1909 and 1921, a national Conservation Commission reflected the influence of the American conservation movement, but acted principally as an information-gathering body. Provincial regulatory measures encompassed mining and factory health and safety, workers' compensation boards, and mining and forestry on provincial lands. Outside the Maritimes, provincial governments controlled all subsoil resources. Regulation of insurance, trust and loan companies, and joint-stock enterprises occurred at both federal and provincial levels. Jurisdictional disputes punctuated the history of water-power regulation, with the federal government steadily retreating from

assertions of control over navigable waterways after the 1920s.

Along with banking, the Dominion government initiated measures in the early 1900s in two areas that impinged on the operations of the largest corporate enterprises in the country: the establishment of the Board of Railway Commissioners in 1903, and the Combines Investigation Act of 1910. The history of these two laws and their enforcement indicates the complex character of regulatory politics and the limits of government intervention in the years before the Great Depression.

The federal government had, of course, been directly or indirectly involved in the development of the nation's railway system since Confederation. Regulation of railway operations, however, had been more haphazard in the late nineteenth century. In 1868 the federal Railway Act assigned such tasks to a cabinet committee, based essentially on pre-Confederation arrangements in the province of Canada. This Railway Committee was responsible for monitoring safety measures on rail lines, and, at least in theory, could review freight rates and establish limits on railway company profits.

In practice, there was relatively little governmental interference with the lines, even the publicly owned Intercolonial Railway. Rates were set by company freight officials on a largely ad hoc basis, varying widely among routes and among shippers. In general, rates tended to fall in the late nineteenth century, but companies sought to compensate themselves for lower rates on competitive routes by charging higher tolls in areas where they controlled the market. In the most heavily competitive areas, such as southern Ontario where railways faced water-borne carriers as well as each other, major shippers could extort partial or total rebates of the tolls paid to the railways.

By the 1880s, disgruntled shippers were demanding more vigorous action by government to eliminate discriminatory freight rates and rebating. Rural communities in Ontario and the prairies, which had initially welcomed the coming of railways, now saw themselves as victims of monopolistic pricing and inadequate service. Merchants in the Maritimes and eastern Quebec, whose fortunes were declining as railways abetted commercial centralization in Montreal and southern Ontario, joined the chorus of complainants, along with retailers and small-scale manufacturers who felt they had to bear the burden of rebates granted their larger competitors.

With pressure growing from within his own Conservative Party, Prime Minister Macdonald set up a Royal Commission in 1886. Two years later Parliament, following the Commission's recommendations, expanded the powers of the Railway Committee to resolve freight rate disputes, and also banned rebating. But shippers remained dissatisfied: few of them bothered to lodge complaints with the Railway Committee, whose enforcement capabilities were limited. Meanwhile, the railway companies, emulating American lines, sought to stem the decline in rates by private negotiations among themselves. Although their efforts were not notably successful, rates did begin to stabilize in the late 1890s, and shippers were suspicious of these potentially collusive arrangements. Their suspicions seemed to be confirmed in 1898 by rumours of a secret agreement between the Grand Trunk and CPR to grant rebates to the American behemoth, Standard Oil Co., which had recently taken over Imperial Oil.

The Liberal regime under Laurier had undertaken to exert indirect control over railway rate decisions by encouraging competition—an approach that contributed to the chartering of new transcontinental lines—and extracting concessions from the railways in return for subsidies, as in the Crow's Nest Pass Agreement with CPR. This was a time-honoured practice also followed by provincial governments: Manitoba, for example, imposed provisions for scheduled rate reductions and a ban on discriminatory rates in its 1901 contract with Canadian Northern Railway. But these methods were basically limited to situations where governments had some bargaining leverage over the companies. The Standard Oil episode helped convert Laurier's railway minister,

A.G. Blair—with the Prime Minister as a reluctant follower—to the cause of regulatory reform. In 1903 the Board of Railway Commissioners replaced the Railway Committee, with authority over most provincial as well as federally chartered lines, empowered to review and amend freight rates, and to prevent discriminatory rates and rebating. Three years later the Board's authority was enlarged to cover telegraph and telephone companies operating across provincial lines.

Although Blair became the first chairman of the three- (later six-) person board, the central figure throughout its early years was Simon J. McLean, who had carried out a review of the railway situation for the government in 1899, drafted much of the original legislation, and served on the Board from 1908 to 1938. McLean, like Mackenzie King, represented a new element in Canadian governance, the intellectual academic-cum-bureaucrat: university-educated, usually in the emerging social sciences, and intent on bringing the skills of the non-partisan 'expert' to the administration of public affairs. Although King quickly veered off into a conventional political career, McLean remained committed to the ideal of objective public service, providing an early example of the Ottawa 'mandarins' who flocked into the federal bureaucracy in growing numbers and with increasing influence on policy-making from the 1930s. McLean and King were also, in the words of the Board's major historian, Ken Cruikshank, examples of 'policy entrepreneurs', bridging academic, political, and business communities to develop effective structures of public administration to deal with complex social and economic issues—much as professional managers were contemporaneously erecting systems of communication and control within the large corporate enterprises.

McLean, like Progressive reformers in the US, believed that regulatory agencies could be effective if shielded from partisan political influences, but he also concluded that American ventures into regulation were crucially weakened by a judiciary that, in America at least, was dominated by doctrinaire exponents of laissez-faire ideas. The Act creating the Railway Board was thus carefully designed to limit appeals to the courts. At the same time, the Board was accountable to the cabinet, and its members had to be sensitive to the political as well as economic implications of their decisions. The Board's reviewing and discretionary powers were broad, but this characteristic was offset by the cautious instincts of the commissioners who sought to mediate, if possible, rather than pass judgement on disputes, an approach that led critics to see them as defenders of big business rather than architects of a reformed transportation system.

In the United States, many historians of government regulation subscribe to the 'capture theory', according to which regulatory commissions almost invariably have been transformed into creatures of the industries they were intended to regulate—with the Interstate Commerce Commission as a classic case. Dependent to a large extent on the information and technical expertise of the industrialists, often personally susceptible to blandishments offered by business (such as employment with large salaries after their terms end), government commissioners may end by sanctioning de facto cartels in the regulated industries rather than working on behalf of an ambiguously defined 'public interest'. Some historians have gone further, arguing that big businesses in the railroad and other industries promoted government regulation in the first instance in order to cartelize and eliminate smaller competitors.

Cruikshank and others who have examined the history of regulation in Canada are more cautious on these issues. The big railways did not vigorously oppose regulation, nor did they welcome it. Shaughnessy of the CPR, for example, lobbied unsuccessfully for the right of railways to appeal Board decisions to the courts on substantive as well as procedural grounds.

Board commissioners were generally (with some exceptions, such as McLean) politicians or jurists with no direct ties to the industry either before or after their terms of office. At the same time, as politicians they were well aware of the crucial role of railways in the Canadian economy and consequently were willing to permit 'reasonable' differentials between long- and short-haul freight rates to help prop up heavily debt-burdened lines. More frequently, the Board found itself adjudicating disputes among shippers from different regions of the country—and its efforts to achieve 'equitable' results were perceived by those in the Maritimes and the western provinces as basically serving the interests of central Canadian businesses. During World War I, the government undercut the Board by directly authorizing rate increases. By the mid-1920s the commissioners were badly divided over their appropriate role in resolving regional struggles, further undermining the Board's credibility.

By this time the federal government had taken over a substantial part of the railway industry, and all parties concerned with rates were turning to avenues of influence outside the Board to achieve their goals. The Board continued to function, however, reconstituted as the Board of Transport Commissioners in 1938 and reorganized again into the Canadian Transport Commission in 1967 with a broadened mandate—but still facing perplexing problems in determining its status vis-à-vis other instruments of government in the field: Parliament, the judiciary, and the Crown corporations.[4]

The telephone industry represents a curious variant to the regulatory environment of the railway field. During the 1880s–90s, Charles Sise had extended the reach of Bell Canada across Ontario and Quebec and ensured the company had a stake in other provincial telephone systems in the Maritimes and British Columbia. The Canadian telephone system might well have followed a route similar to the Bell system in the United States under Theodore N. Vail, who was able to orchestrate what became a virtual monopoly under government regulation that lasted up to the 1980s. Since it held a federal charter, Bell Canada was under the regulatory umbrella of the Board of Railway Commissioners for many years, and the

Board was generally sympathetic to the needs of the company.

A different pattern emerged, however, at the provincial level. The Maritime provinces had their own regulatory bodies for the telephone companies within their jurisdictions. In the Prairie provinces, dissatisfaction with Bell services mounted in the early 1900s: Sise had set up Bell companies there but they were largely restricted to a few urban areas, as the company was not prepared to invest in the kind of wiring required for rural areas. This animosity boiled over in 1907–8 with investigations of the inadequacy of telephone services, followed by the establishment of provincially owned phone systems, not unlike the public electric power companies in Ontario and elsewhere. Alberta led the way, buying up Bell properties in 1907 and setting up Alberta Government Telephones (AGT); in this case, another, municipally owned system already existed in Edmonton, and for many years these two public companies operated independently, until they were privatized in 1990, forming the base for Telus. Saskatchewan and Manitoba also established Crown-controlled telephone companies, in 1908. The Saskatchewan public system still operates today while the Manitoba company was privatized in 1996. In the telephone field, then, public ownership in effect was a substitute for regulation, although Bell managed to avoid any further inroads on its system in central Canada.[5]

If railway regulation provided at best a rather mixed record of effective government intervention, combines legislation represented an even more ambiguous example. Agitation against the 'trusts' spilled over from the US in the late 1880s and produced a measure against 'combinations' that acted 'to restrain or injure trade . . . lessen the manufacture of any article . . . [or] lessen competition'. The Liberal opposition in Parliament ridiculed the government's Act as meaningless, because it attached the qualifier 'unlawfully' to its description of banned practices, and of no real consequence even to those businesses that might be prosecuted. Once in power, the Liberals

proposed in 1897 to give the measure some teeth by threatening to remove tariff protection from 'trusts' engaged in uncompetitive practices, but added their own weasel-word, 'unduly', to limit the likely application of the law, for which, in any case, enforcement provisions remained vague. Between 1889 and 1910 only eight cases were brought forward, all but one of them after 1903; five were successfully prosecuted, resulting in modest fines against the perpetrators.

Events in the US helped revive the energies of big-business critics in Canada. The Sherman Act had been rendered largely irrelevant in the 1890s by US Supreme Court decisions, but the American merger movement of 1899–1903 set the stage for a more vigorous antitrust effort. Although then (and later) the American government lacked the resolve and resources to systematically uproot big business, it was successful in 1909–11 in 'busting' two of the largest 'trusts': the explosives cartel dominated by Du Pont, and John D. Rockefeller's much-hated Standard Oil Co. Ironically, antitrust in the US simply spawned big business in tighter corporate forms, but at the time these events seemed to portend a more effective exercise of governmental control over business consolidations.

By 1909–10 the merger movement had spread to Canada, and city dwellers experiencing inflation—which was attributed to the influence of these big consolidations on markets—added their voices to the agrarian chorus against 'monopoly'. In response, Laurier's ubiquitous Labour Minister, Mackenzie King, introduced the Combines Investigation Act in Parliament in 1910. King shared the view of many American as well as Canadian political leaders—including former US President Theodore Roosevelt—that antitrust was a blunt instrument that, if used rigorously, would destabilize the economy and penalize large enterprises that had acquired market power through technological and organizational innovations. It would be preferable to police 'abuses' of power rather than break up inherently efficient companies. In Britain at this time, there was a growing sentiment that their enterprises were, if anything, too small and inefficient, contributing to that country's declining industrial competitiveness. These arguments had a special resonance in Canada, where even the largest industrial agglomerations were dwarfed by their American competitors.

Choosing regulation over trust-busting, King proposed to establish a typically convoluted process in which complaints about abuses of market power would be investigated by ad hoc boards convened for the occasion by the Minister of Labour. The definition of these abuses remained vague, but companies or 'combinations' found to be engaging in them could be subject to various penalties, including possible reduction of tariff protection. Perhaps not surprisingly, this law was enforced with less vigour than its predecessors: only one case was pursued between 1911 and 1923, and no action was taken.

Renewed concern over inflation in World War I led to the replacement of King's Act in 1919 by a Combines and Fair Practices law that empowered the short-lived Board of Commerce to initiate investigations of uncompetitive practices. After the 1919 measure, along with the Board of Commerce, was held unconstitutional by Britain's Privy Council, Mackenzie King—now Prime Minister—introduced a new Combines Act in 1923. Under this law a permanent official was installed in the Labour Department with power to investigate mergers as well as collusive practices that might restrain trade 'against the interest of the public'. The continuing impotence of this regulatory venture is reflected in the fact that only 14 investigations were opened (in response to over 500 complaints) between 1924 and 1940, of which only one case involved a merger. Meanwhile, the country witnessed a merger movement in the late 1920s of far greater magnitude than the pre-war consolidations.

The logical conclusion from this history is that Canada's political leaders had no intention of policing big business (much less busting trusts), but simply wished to defuse public outcries against 'monopolies'. The equally checkered

history of antitrust in the US, and the experience of European countries and Japan with regulation of competition, suggests that the fundamental problem was not simply a lack of political will to enforce the law. Distinguishing 'good' from 'bad' trusts proved in practice to be a daunting task, and the public was at best ambivalent about the evils (and virtues) of big business. During the 1930s, public ire over economic hardships focused on large corporate enterprises, rekindling another outburst of antitrust enthusiasm, but World War II and the period of post-war prosperity muted much of this resentment. Canadians' sense of their vulnerability as a small, relatively open economy contributed to this ambivalence: in the 1970s a Royal Commission established in the wake of a new round of amalgamations concluded that the central problem for Canada was not the 'corporate concentration' it was set up to investigate, but rather the fragmented character of Canadian business, which required more centralization and integration to prepare the country for the new era of global competition.[6]

In practice, government regulation was far less sweeping than the range of its activities would suggest. This outcome was not solely the result of pro-business attitudes on the part of Canada's political leaders—although they were inclined to be as solicitous as possible of the interests of the large corporations their promotional policies had helped to create while still responding to the demands of other constituents. The capabilities and financial resources of governments in the early twentieth century were quite limited. Before the introduction of income taxes their revenue sources were not substantial, and deficit financing was anathema to both the electorate and the business elites.

Reliable statistical information about the economy was still rudimentary, focused principally on trade flows and government budgets: the Dominion Bureau of Statistics was not established until 1918, and employment levels were not measured until the Great Depression. Despite being less patronage-ridden than that in the US, government service in Canada remained a low-paid occupation of low esteem, and university-educated figures such as S.J. McLean were exceptional. Universities in Canada were only beginning to mould themselves into centres for research and training in the natural and social sciences, and could hardly have supplied the recruits even if governments had sought them. For the most part, neither political nor business leaders exhibited much interest in the academic world—with exceptions such as Joseph Flavelle, who played a major role in reorganizing the University of Toronto and other institutions in the early 1900s. At a time when business people were just starting to wrestle with the problems of running large complex organizations, it is perhaps not surprising that governments proved less than fully capable of dealing with the equally thorny tasks of adjudicating economic controversies among a multitude of businesses and other pressure groups.

CONFRONTING THE GREAT DEPRESSION

What made the depression of the 1930s 'great' was not just its severity but also its long duration and seeming imperviousness to any remedial action. Canada and other industrialized nations had experienced downturns in the past—the depression of the 1890s was, arguably, even worse, at least for those who were unemployed and without access to the meagre relief that was provided in the 1930s. The short but steep slump following World War I had lasting effects, particularly on the Maritimes, which never fully recovered from the collapse of their industrial base. But the Great Depression struck a Canadian economy that was already unstable, destroying the export markets and international capital sources upon which it was crucially dependent. Recovery from the catastrophic conditions of 1932–3, when over one-fifth of the country's labour force was out of work and gross national income was little more than half the 1929 level, was slow and incomplete

up to World War II. The prolonged and debilitating slump reinforced the habitual caution of the business community, constraining new domestic investment and similarly limiting the willingness of political leaders to experiment with novel techniques of economic intervention. Ultimately, however, the sources of both the decline and recovery were well beyond the control of anyone in Canada.

The Great Depression was global in scope and in large part was the result of events stemming from unstable conditions in international finance and trade in the 1920s. The New York stock market collapse in 1929 triggered a panic that spread to other capital markets worldwide, but it was not in itself the 'cause' of the Depression. By the late 1920s output of commodities—including wheat and newsprint, Canada's major exports—was exceeding demand; industrial investment, as well, was producing excess capacity in manufacturing, at least in terms of the existing consumer market, particularly in the United States. These circumstances set the stage for a global trade war, inaugurated by the highly protectionist Smoot-Hawley Tariff passed by the US Congress in 1930. Meanwhile, after the Wall Street crash, American bankers, whose credit had propped up the international economy in the late 1920s, began frantically recalling their loans. Other countries responded by imposing exchange controls and suspending the convertibility of their currencies: Britain and Canada left the gold standard in 1931, and the US did the same in 1933. By this point, world trade had collapsed to one-fifth of its 1929 level. Efforts to reconstruct the international system proved fruitless as countries scrambled to protect what was left of their domestic markets, dumping surpluses abroad. These developments fell particularly hard on the small, export-oriented Canadian economy.

Many of the actions taken by governments around the world proved inadequate or counterproductive. Protectionist measures and currency restrictions aggravated the rapid deterioration of international trade. As their revenue sources disappeared, governments retrenched, contributing to deflation and shrinking domestic consumer markets. Some social reformers saw a model in the Soviet Union, where Stalin was introducing extensive state controls over the economy through his Five-Year Plan. But none of the beleaguered capitalist nations chose this route, although the fascist states (and the US, briefly, in 1933–5) experimented with enforced cartelization of industries to try to stabilize wages and prices. The remedies advocated by the British economist J.M. Keynes—a revamped international monetary system and greatly expanded government spending to counter the decline in private-sector investment and production—were not embraced until after World War II. Some countries, notably Nazi Germany and the US in the New Deal era, increased public outlays, but not as a result of conversion to Keynesianism. Germany's economic recovery in the mid-1930s was largely an incidental by-product of Hitler's armaments program. In the US, President Franklin D. Roosevelt's New Deal was fashioned on an ad hoc basis, and his decision to cut spending in 1937 helped plunge the country back into depression until the outbreak of war in Europe restimulated the economy.

Canada's political leaders were no more, nor less, farsighted than their counterparts abroad. Mackenzie King and the Liberals were fortunate in that they were pitched from office in 1930 as the Depression's impact was just beginning to be felt, and returned to power in 1935 after the worst was past—earning an undeserved reputation for economic competence that helped stand them in good stead with the electorate for the next 20-plus years. They also benefited from the fact that the Conservative leader, R.B. Bennett, was a virtual caricature of the bloated plutocrat, from his pince-nez to his spats.

Bennett had been one of the country's leading corporate lawyers, general counsel to the CPR, and board member of assorted other major enterprises before embarking on a political career. His initial program of action was very much in keeping with Tory traditions, combining protectionism with vague promises to 'blast' Canada 'into world markets'. When these remedies failed to show any effects, Bennett turned with increasing desperation to a variety of expedients in 1933–5. Many of these measures were torpedoed by the British Privy Council as unconstitutional, but several of his innovations—the Bank of Canada, Radio Canada, and reciprocal trade negotiations with the US—were taken over, modified, and expanded by the Liberals after 1935.

Although Canada was badly battered by the Depression, some industries fared better than others and commenced recovery in advance of the economy as a whole. The staple-exporting sectors were particularly hard-hit and (except for minerals) slow to recover, acting as a brake on the rest of the economy throughout the decade. Wheat prices sagged from over $1/bushel in 1929 to little more than 50 cents/bushel in 1932. Drought and dust storms drove many farmers from the prairies in the mid-1930s and reduced overall output, but even with partial price stabilization through the Canadian Wheat Board after 1936, farm income was still only one-third what it had been in the late 1920s. Price declines in newsprint were not as dramatic, but in 1937 the industry was still operating at little more than half capacity: in this field, market decline was aggravated by the overexpansion of investment in the merger boom of 1926–8. Other industries, including the railways, were similarly burdened with excess debt and capacity, augmented by the collapse of the wheat economy.

On the other hand, some of the domestic tariff-protected industries, such as textiles, were showing signs of life by 1933. The auto industry, which sank like a stone in the early 1930s, experienced a modest if incomplete recovery later in the decade, thanks both to protectionism and to Bennett's push for imperial preference at the Commonwealth Conference in Ottawa in 1932—which also had the effect of temporarily redirecting Canadian exports towards Britain through World War II. The mining industries were also improving by mid-decade. The value of gold boomed in the deflationary conditions of the early 1930s, enriching speculators like Harry Oakes, and the arms race pushed up demand for nickel as the threat of war loomed in Europe and Asia. In striking contrast to the US situation, Canada's chartered banks survived the Depression without a single failure—reflecting the strength of the branch system, their orientation towards short-term commercial credit, and their emphasis on a rapid liquidation of other debt, to the distress of the securities market, at the outset of the Depression.[7]

Pressures for government intervention in Canada reflected, in part, the varied fortunes of these industries in the Depression. Manufacturers and bankers in central Canada favoured protectionism (and later imperial preference) and balanced budgets. From the West and the resource industries generally emanated demands for more interventionist measures, expansion of the money supply, and reciprocal trade with the US. The unwillingness or inability of federal politicians in either of the major parties to accommodate these demands (except for trade agreements) stimulated the growth of more radical movements and experiments with interventionism at the provincial level.

But government intervention, such as it was, reflected more than Depression-stimulated pressures. The Bank of Canada, established despite opposition from most of the chartered banks, did not (as some westerners had hoped) inflate the currency; the economists who supported the idea stressed the role of the Bank as a source of long-term stability and representative of Canada's position in international dealings with other central banks (see box, p. 122). Likewise, the Canadian Radio Broadcasting Commission, established in 1932, functioned as a complementary National Policy, protecting Canada's airwaves. Renewed agitation against big business that led to the Price Spreads Commission in 1934 focused on small retailers' hostility to chain stores, a hostility antedating the onset of the Depression.

Reform in the securities exchange field also reflected issues that predated the Depression, although the collapse of share values prompted more serious efforts at regulation than had previously been contemplated. Mining stocks had figured prominently in the activities of the markets in Ontario and Vancouver since the early 1900s, and inevitably spurred speculative booms that encouraged the entry of shady promoters who produced prospectuses filled with glittering promise based on salted claims or, as often as not, no assets at all. The bond drives of World War I introduced a much wider audience of gullible investors to the securities markets, and by the late 1920s even the more respectable brokerage houses were concerned about the lack of regulation in this field. In earlier times there had been several attempts, particularly in the Prairie provinces, to set up 'blue sky' laws that would impose some order in the public floating of securities. In 1928, Ontario introduced a more comprehensive Security Frauds Prevention Act, followed by Saskatchewan a year later, and British Columbia and Quebec in 1930. The onset of the Depression and an upsurge in public outrage over some dramatic examples of fraudulent promotions persuaded Ontario to set up a provincial Securities Commission to police the markets. Not every province adopted this degree of formality, but by the mid-1930s at least some form of regulation was in place elsewhere. There was some pressure for federal legislation to supersede provincial regulation, particularly as some companies (including a brokerage firm that was facing prosecution under the Ontario Act) held federal charters. A decision by the Judicial Committee of the British Privy Council (which effectively superseded the authority of the Canadian Supreme Court at that time) in 1932, however, upheld the primacy of provincial jurisdiction in this area, the effect of which continues to hold to the present.[8]

As in the case of the regulatory measures of the early 1900s, Depression-era interventionism was as much symbol as substance. In addition to hiking tariffs, when he first came to power

THE BANK OF CANADA

The establishment of the Bank of Canada was the most substantial and enduring government measure of the Depression era; and although most of the chartered banks initially opposed it, in the long term they were probably the main beneficiaries. As with most other forms of government intervention in Canada, the sweeping powers allocated to the Bank were exercised cautiously by those entrusted with its administration.

Proposals for the creation of a central bank had surfaced before World War I, with support from at least some members of the banking community. During the brief but sharp panic of 1907, many of the chartered banks had reached the limits of their capacity to issue bank notes as authorized under the 1871 Banking Act, stimulating demands for a more flexible system. When the outbreak of war in 1914 led to a run on the banks by alarmed depositors, the government passed a Finance Act that allowed banks to cover deposits with Dominion notes, issued as loans by the Minister of Finance, supplementing the banks' hard currency reserves.

Towards the end of the war there were proposals for a government bank that would have exclusive powers to issue currency: this idea was particularly attractive to western Canadians, who regarded the chartered banks as agents of 'eastern' business interests restricting their access to credit. Most bankers resisted the proposal, arguing that a government-controlled bank would be susceptible to political pressures to inflate the money supply; and, of course, they opposed the loss of their right to issue notes. A few, notably E.L. Pease of the Royal Bank, however, endorsed the concept of a central bank similar to the American Federal Reserve system, in which bankers exercised a substantial degree of influence over policies. But the Canadian Bankers' Association rejected a proposal along these lines in 1919 and successfully lobbied for continuation of the Finance Act arrangements through the 1920s.

The chartered banks weathered the worst of the Great Depression, but the methods employed to do so—foreclosing rapidly on delinquent debtors and maintaining high interest rates—rekindled western demands for government action to restrict their powers and expand the supply of credit. By 1933 several provinces were proposing to pass debt adjustment laws, and even Bennett recognized the need to take some action. As usual, a Royal Commission was set up, under a prominent British banker, Lord MacMillan, to review the alternatives. Meanwhile, one of Bennett's key advisers, Clifford Clark—like S.J. McLean, an economist and 'policy entrepreneur'—vigorously pushed for a central bank on the grounds that it would provide a stable money supply, represent Canadian interests in the international banking community, and head off more radical demands for currency inflation. Despite continued resistance from the chartered banks, the MacMillan Commission found these arguments persuasive and Bennett's Finance Minister, E.N. Rhodes, introduced proposals for a Bank of Canada in early 1934.

By this time the bankers were isolated in their opposition. The Liberals under King, seeking to undercut the rising Co-operative Commonwealth Federation (CCF) on their left, criticized the Bennett proposal as insufficient in that it would establish the Bank of Canada as a private rather than government-controlled institution. The most contentious issue during the parliamentary debates focused on whether the Bank's notes would be issued in French as well as English. Although the Rhodes bill went through as originally drafted, after the Liberals returned

Prime Minister Mackenzie King and Graham Towers, first Governor of the Bank of Canada, at the laying of the cornerstone of the Bank building in August 1937. (Photographer: Canadian Government Motion Picture Bureau PC 550.15-10 Bank of Canada Archives)

to power, King proceeded to revise the Bank's charter in 1936 (and again in 1938), transforming it into a public institution issuing bilingual notes.

Meanwhile, the Bank of Canada opened its doors in 1935 under Graham Towers, a former official of the Royal Bank, whose training as an economist buttressed his credentials as an apolitical 'expert' with ties to the emerging public-service mandarinate. As Governor of the Bank from 1935 to 1954, Towers walked a fine line, seeking to preserve the institution from political influence and reassure the banking establishment of the essential 'soundness' of the Bank's policies while responding to pressures for action to deal with the economic crisis. With British Columbia, Alberta, Saskatchewan, and Manitoba all sliding into bankruptcy in 1935–6, these pressures focused on demands that the Bank bail out the provinces through loans to cover their outstanding bonds. Towers feared that any such action would set a dangerous precedent for the Bank, carrying out tasks more appropriate for the elected federal government. After much manoeuvring, he persuaded King on this point, and also prodded the Prime Minister to initiate a Royal Commission to review the whole field of federal–provincial financial arrangements.

During World War II the Bank's role expanded beyond its initial mandate to cover seasonal fluctuations in the money supply to encompass exchange controls and wartime financing. Under Towers in the early post-war years the Bank used its powers to modulate the pace of economic growth, to the general satisfaction of both bankers and the government. Later, the Bank's position vis-à-vis the government would become more controversial as it sought to constrain inflationary pressures, leading to at least one occasion during the Diefenbaker era when the cabinet exerted its authority to remove an overly independent Governor, James Coyne. By the 1970s the Bank of Canada was perceived by the banking community, ironically, as a bastion of financial prudence besieged by spendthrift politicians rather than as a dangerous experiment in government economic intervention.

Sources: J.L. Granatstein, *The Ottawa Men: The Civil Service Mandarins, 1935-51* (Toronto, 1982), 49–61; J.L. Granatstein and Doug Owram, *The Government Generation* (Toronto, 1986), 210–15; Linda M. Grayson, 'The Formation of the Bank of Canada, 1913-38', Ph.D. thesis (University of Toronto, 1974), E.P. Neufeld, *Bank of Canada Operations and Policy* (Toronto, 1958); George S. Watts, *The Bank of Canada: Origins and Early History* (Ottawa, 1993).

Bennett initiated public works projects and relief aid to the provinces—a pointed contrast to King's miserliness. Imperial preference, as in the days of Sir John A. Macdonald, was draped in the garb of Anglo-Canadian patriotism, even though the British were reluctant participants and the trade agreements had little immediate impact on the economy of either country. The real intent of Bennett's abortive 'New Deal' proposals of 1935 is a matter of some controversy. By this point an election loomed and few of his earlier initiatives had produced much economic improvement. Bennett's brother-in-law, W.C. Herridge, stationed in the Canadian embassy in Washington, took note of the political benefits reaped by Roosevelt from his New Deal programs of 1933–4 and urged Bennett to follow suit. In January 1935 the Canadian Prime Minister, in a series of radio broadcasts, unveiled a variety of measures, including unemployment insurance, old-age pensions, a new combines law, and government marketing programs for wheat and other natural products. The proposals, when they came before Parliament, were rather less sweeping in substance, and in the next few years most of them were ruled by the courts to be unconstitutional invasions of provincial jurisdiction.

Many historians have dismissed Bennett's New Deal as largely a public relations ploy. But Bennett did not simply pull his proposals out of a hat. Many of the 'New Deal' and associated measures had been matters of considerable public debate before 1935 and had at least some support in the business community. The Wheat Board, which was reconstituted in 1935, had been set up originally by the Borden government at the end of World War I; Bennett had been involved in initiating the wheat pools in the early 1920s after the Liberal regime allowed the Wheat Board to lapse. Despite the virtual collapse of the pools in 1930, Bennett was at first cool towards re-establishing the federal Wheat Board, although he agreed to intervention in the form of government purchases of wheat surpluses in the futures market to try to stabilize prices.

In 1933 the Canadian government participated in an international wheat agreement negotiated in London, which established export quotas and committed participants to try to impose production controls at home. Within a year, however, this agreement was unravelling, and western Canadian restiveness finally pushed Bennett to move towards direct controls. Still hoping to preserve the market system in some form, Bennett set up the Wheat Board as a purchaser of last resort rather than a government marketing monopoly. Even this limited venture encountered stiff Liberal opposition, although King subsequently was obliged to retain the Wheat Board to keep his western political supporters on side.

Similarly, the Natural Products Marketing Board established in 1934 was the culmination of a series of efforts by producers to stabilize commodity prices, first through voluntary agreements and then through provincial ventures into compulsory cartelization. In 1927, British Columbia fruit growers successfully lobbied for a provincial law empowering what was essentially a producers' co-operative to establish production controls and price floors for the industry; the arrangement was extended to dairy products in 1929. Two years later, however, these measures, along with a similar Saskatchewan law controlling grain production, were held unconstitutional by the courts since interprovincial sales were affected by them.

In this context the federal law was devised, under which local marketing boards would be authorized by a Dominion Board to control prices and output of various commodities entering interprovincial markets. To circumvent constitutional complications, similar provincial laws were passed to cover intra-provincial marketing. These arrangements, however, were insufficient to protect the Board from the British Privy Council, which ordered its dissolution in 1937. Meanwhile, provincial governments in Nova Scotia, Ontario, and Quebec developed legally acceptable alternative measures for stabilizing prices in the dairy industry through the traditional exercise of licensing powers.

The theme running through all these complicated structures was the effort of the Bennett government to implement economic policies to combat the Depression while preserving the private property system. While Bennett was no more consistent in his philosophy than most politicians, there are continuities linking his support for the wheat pools in the 1920s to his Depression-era programs. As a big-business lawyer,

Bennett was not doctrinaire about the sanctity of unrestrained competition and free markets: cartels and government intervention were acceptable in the interests of greater economic efficiency, or if necessary to head off more radical alternatives. Bennett was not unique in adopting this position: in the US, both Presidents Hoover and Roosevelt (at least in the early phases of the New Deal) were prepared to sanction restrictions on the market system, preferably through 'voluntary' agreements in the private sector, with government providing appropriate incentives for their co-operation.

In Canada the Liberals were less inclined to tamper with markets, although perhaps more willing to engage in direct intervention through Crown corporations, which maintained the distinction between public and private sectors of the economy. Even within the Conservative ranks, however, Bennett's views were contested, most notably by Harry H. Stevens. A Vancouver MP, first elected in 1911, Stevens was a long-time champion of BC business interests, which brought him into conflict with the CPR and other elements of the 'eastern' business establishment. In 1930, Bennett installed him in the cabinet as Minister of Trade and Commerce, a position of somewhat limited importance since Bennett tended to run the government as a one-man show. In 1934, Stevens took charge of a parliamentary committee (later reconstituted as a Royal Commission) to investigate charges that large retailers like Eaton's and the chain stores were using their market position to extort low purchase prices from small manufacturers while maintaining high markups on prices to consumers. This 'Price Spreads' inquiry stirred up much interest and rankled a number of prominent (Tory) retailers. Before the end of the year Stevens and Bennett were at odds over the investigation, and Stevens resigned from the cabinet.

One of Bennett's 'New Deal' proposals was the Dominion Trade and Industry Act, which was intended to supersede the Combines Investigation Act. Although the new measure would prohibit discriminatory pricing, thus addressing the target of the Price Spreads investigation, the means of enforcement were (as usual) very weak. Essentially, the Dominion Tariff Board—an agency set up in 1932 to monitor importers' appeals for relief from customs duties—was assigned the task of enforcement, removing the issue from the Labour Department, where at least there were some knowledgeable officials on hand. In addition, the Board was authorized to allow collusive price agreements where it determined competition was 'wasteful'. Outraged, Stevens left the Conservatives altogether, forming his own Reconstruction party in the 1935 election. Although receiving only 9 per cent of the popular vote, the renegade 'party' cut into Tory support in Ontario and the West, which helped ensure Bennett's defeat.

Insofar as they were aware of these nuances of policy, members of the business community were not of one mind, except perhaps on the dangers posed by the CCF and other radical movements. Alvin Finkel, in *Business and Social Reform in the Thirties*, has argued that the big-business elite were far more receptive to government intervention in the economy (at least on their terms) than many of the conventional political leaders in Canada. Not only government-sanctioned cartels but even social welfare measures found favour with at least some of these figures: in 1934 Sir Charles Gordon, president of the Bank of Montreal and Dominion Textiles, urged Bennett, unsuccessfully, to have the federal government take over the burden of unemployment relief from the near-bankrupt municipal and provincial governments. Arthur Purvis, president of the Anglo-American chemical company, CIL, chaired the National Unemployment Commission, set up by the Liberal government in 1938, whose recommendations for national unemployment insurance, vocational education, and public housing programs went far beyond anything contemplated at the time by Prime Minister King. For these businessmen, the need for social stability in the face of a prolonged depression took priority over fiscal caution and constitutional niceties.

If Purvis reflected a 'corporate liberal' viewpoint, this approach was rejected by others such

as Joseph Flavelle, for whom government intervention permissible in wartime was unacceptable for a mere economic slump. In general, it is fair to say that most businesses supported government measures that would help them survive the rigours of the Depression without necessarily endorsing interventionism in principle. As Finkel notes, Sir Herbert Holt promoted compulsory cartels in the newsprint industry to salvage his foundering venture, Canada Power and Paper, while denouncing a more conventional form of government promotion of the Beauharnois Power Co., whose project to harness the hydro power of the St Lawrence threatened Holt's control of the Montreal utility market. Small retailers who endorsed Harry Stevens's campaign against chain stores wanted the right to make their own price-fixing arrangements. Western business interests joined forces with farmers to urge the establishment of the Bank of Canada as preferable to the inflationary experiments advocated by prairie political spellbinders like Alberta's 'Bible Bill' Aberhart.

Bennett's last effort to salvage his political fortunes, the negotiation of a reciprocal trade agreement with the Americans, was expropriated by the Liberals (possibly with the connivance of sympathizers in the US government) and became for King the main instrument for pulling Canada out of the Depression. In 1934 the US Congress had opened a small gap in America's 'Chinese Wall' of tariff protection, authorizing the President to negotiate bilateral trade agreements that would reduce duties on imports from specific countries in return for appropriate reciprocal concessions. Despite his earlier advocacy of imperial preference, Bennett began testing the trade-negotiating waters in Washington as early as 1933. But talks moved sluggishly and remained incomplete when Bennett went down to defeat in October 1935. Within less than a month the new government of Mackenzie King had a reciprocity agreement in hand, the first major trade agreement between the two countries since 1866.

Reciprocity in 1935 involved only agricultural and other natural resource products, thus avoiding the wrath of the manufacturers' lobby that had blocked Laurier's more ambitious initiative in 1911. Maritime fish processors were disappointed because the agreement excluded cod, in deference to New England interests, but by and large Canadian businesses were satisfied. US restrictions on Canadian whisky imports were alleviated; in the 1920s they had been banned outright by American Prohibition laws—which had not prevented enterprising distillers such as the Bronfmans and Harry Hatch, owner of Hiram Walker and Gooderham's, from participating in a thriving smuggling business. The repeal of Prohibition in 1933 opened prospects of a much larger trade.

In 1937–8, Canada negotiated a revised reciprocity agreement with the US, in the context of broader Anglo-American trade arrangements. The result of these convoluted negotiations—which involved talks with other Dominions as well as with the US and Britain—was that Canada lost preferential treatment in the British market for some (mostly agricultural) products, and removed some restrictions on US imports, including some industrial goods—thus arousing opposition from the Canadian Manufacturers' Association. On the other hand, Canada gained greater access to the US market for a range of products, including codfish, and the 1938 agreement removed or raised American quotas on other imports the 1935 reciprocity deal had left intact. King could also point to the 47 per cent increase in US–Canada trade and a 27 per cent rise in gross national income in 1935–7 as results of reductions in continental trade barriers.

Although the renewed slump in the US economy in 1938 eroded these gains, the Liberals remained committed to trade policy as the main route to recovery. In 1938, King set up a Royal Commission to look into ways of streamlining government financing and services in the federal system. By the time the Commission's report came out in 1940, wartime mobilization and prosperity had replaced Depression-era concerns. But its proposals, which included a federal takeover

of unemployment compensation and old-age pensions, laid the groundwork for Dominion–provincial revenue-sharing programs that flourished in the years after World War II.[9]

The disruption of trade between Canada and the US in the early 1930s did not destroy other business relationships that had been growing since the turn of the century. The tariff wars of the Bennett era stimulated an increase in the number of US manufacturing firms entering Canada from 534 in 1929 to over 800 by 1936, although the level of total investment declined. Reciprocity led to the departure of a few of these companies, but improving economic conditions in the later 1930s brought an increase in investment as US companies in the auto and mining industries began to expand capacity in Canada. In 1939 the book value of US direct investment was back to pre-Depression levels, at close to $2 billion (US), with manufacturing accounting for about 60 per cent of the total.

Although the badly battered newsprint industry remained in the doldrums throughout the decade, its continental character produced an unusual experiment in transnational cartelization, involving governments on both sides of the border. Even before the onset of the Depression, the Quebec and Ontario governments had been backing efforts by pulp and paper companies to establish voluntary price and production agreements. With one of the largest firms, the American-owned International Paper, refusing to co-operate, the cartel disintegrated by 1930. When the US government in 1933 embarked on its own venture into compulsory cartelization—the National Recovery Administration—Canadian newsprint companies hastened to join their American counterparts in a 'code of fair competition'. American newspaper publishers, however, campaigned vigorously against the Canadian participants, who were summarily excluded in 1934 shortly before the NRA was itself dissolved by US court order. At this point, the premiers of Quebec and Ontario joined forces with the Newsprint Association of America to reconstruct the

TABLE 7.1

IMPACT OF THE GREAT DEPRESSION ON CANADA'S LEADING
NON-FINANCIAL CORPORATIONS* (RANKED BY ASSETS, 1929)

Rank 1929	Assets 1929**	Net Revenue 1929**	Assets 1935**	Net Revenue 1935**
CPR	1,225	52.0	1,373	24.0
International Paper	393	5.1	270	n/a
Imperial Oil	223	23.0	199	25.7
Abitibi	178	7.9	121	***
Minn. & St Paul RR	177	9.9	172	-5.0
Bell Telephone Canada	151	9.3	212	8.5
MacKay Co.	122	5.4	125	-1.6
Canada Paper	117	5.3	83	***
Dominion Steel	106	6.4	42	-0.6
Montreal Light	103	3.0	175	0.5
International Nickel	96	14.5	198	18.5
Price Bros.	85	3.4	64	***
Duluth & South Shore RR	66	-0.8	70	-21.0
Twin City Transit	65	2.0	64	0.3
Duke-Price	64	3.9	62	4.3
Imperial Tobacco	63	4.8	70	5.8
Massey-Harris	59	2.7	31	0.2
Hudson's Bay Co.	57	2.4	36	0.2
Steel Co. of Canada	56	5.3	62	3.7

*Excludes Crown corporations (e.g., CNR), private firms (no public stock offerings; e.g., Eaton's), and companies with principal assets abroad (e.g., Brazilian Traction Co.).

**All figures in $ million (Cdn) at current values. 'Earnings' = net earnings before taxes.

***Companies in receivership in 1934–5.

Source: *Canadian Annual Financial Review* (Toronto, 1929, 1935).

cartel, using their control over forestry leasing permits to bring recalcitrant (and for the most part financially vulnerable) producers in line.

Direct investment did not flow only in one direction, although the American tide was inevitably more significant. Five Canadian banks, numerous insurance and trust companies, and over 70 manu-facturers had branch operations in the US by the mid-1930s, representing about $250 million (US) in direct investment. Most of these had been estab-lished before the Depression, but Canadian whisky distillers and brewers set up shop in the United States during the hiatus between the repeal of Prohibition and reciprocity. Hiram Walker built the largest distillery in the world in Illinois. The Bronf-mans followed this lead, acquiring full control over Distillers Co./Seagram's from their British part-ners in the process, eclipsing Hiram Walker as the largest whisky producer in Canada by the 1940s and becoming the world's premier distiller in the post-World War II era. Although the US was the main area of Canadian foreign investment from the 1920s, some of the largest individual firms continued to be found in the utilities field in Latin America up to World War II. With combined assets of over $500 million (Cdn) in 1935, the three Canadian 'utility multinationals' in Brazil, Mexico, and the Caribbean comprised one-quarter of the country's total overseas investment.

Despite its devastating effect on particular firms and industries, the Depression did not funda-mentally alter the structure of business consoli-dation that had emerged in Canada between 1909 and 1929. The impact of the economic crisis was particularly hard on the newsprint and steel industries: by 1933, three of the largest pulp and paper companies and two of the three leading iron and steel firms were in receivership. Companies whose fortunes were tied to agri-culture, such as Massey-Harris, or to consumer goods also suffered huge losses. At the same time, the utilities and mining companies, despite rela-tively sluggish earnings compared to the 1920s, continued to dominate the economic landscape, and several, most notably Bell Canada and Inter-national Nickel, grew substantially during the Depression decade (see Table 7.1). Even in the most beleaguered industries, well-managed firms such as the Steel Co. of Canada and Ontario Paper fared reasonably well.

Nonetheless, in contrast to the US in particular, the 1930s did not witness in Canada the emer-gence of new, technologically innovative enter-prises: there were no counterparts to Tom Watson of IBM or Juan Trippe of Pan Am Airlines on the scene. The successful Canadian entrepreneurs of the era, like K.C. Irving and Sam Bronfman, tended to move into established markets. As was the case with government policies, in the Canadian business community the Depression reinforced traditions of caution rather than experimenta-tion, a return to the tried-and-true on the part of the investing public rather than pioneering into unknown markets with novel technologies.

CHAPTER 8

The Arsenal Economy

War forced the pace of government intervention in the economies of industrialized nations in the twentieth century; not coincidentally, the requirements of industrial mobilization for war established close and continuing relations between governments and significant elements of the business community. Traditional methods of blockading trade were supplemented in the twentieth century by new instruments of economic warfare: the 'blacklisting' of merchants suspected of trading with the enemy, the 'freezing' of bank accounts and other forms of liquid capital held by citizens of an enemy state, and the confiscation of their fixed assets. The financial requirements of total war led to the imposition of income taxes, initially covering the wealthy and business corporations and eventually embracing virtually the entire population. Shortages of labour and materials created by the diversion of resources for war production prompted the introduction of wage and price controls to check inflationary pressures, as well as direct state involvement in labour–management relations. Ultimately, most governments established centralized controls over their economies to give priority to production for military needs, and state-owned enterprises sprouted in specific war-related industries.

Although these ventures into a command economy were usually dismantled when the emergency conditions of war abated, they provided government and business leaders alike with evidence of the potential capabilities of centralized economic organization. At the same time, those who had to deal with wartime bureaucracies became aware of the limitations of state power—although for many contemporaries the euphoria of victory may have masked these deficiencies. Finally, the mobilization of economies for war generated government subsidies to certain defence-related industries, which by the 1950s had fashioned a system of special relationships popularly designated the 'military-industrial complex'.

The extent of war-stimulated government interventionism varied among industrial countries. During World War I, state controls were probably most advanced in Germany, France, and Britain: by 1915–16, these governments had imposed comprehensive wage and price controls and established centralized state agencies to allocate labour and resources for war production. The United States, which did not enter the war until 1917, moved with less alacrity towards a command economy; its major agency for economic mobilization, the War Industries Board, functioned primarily through 'co-operative' committees of private business leaders. Virtually the entire apparatus of direct government controls was dismantled after the war, although income taxes endured as a permanent feature of the economic landscape.

During World War II, European governments resorted again to direct controls, and even in the US various centralized agencies (sometimes competing with each other) were in place by 1942. But perhaps the most enduring legacy of that war for Americans was the establishment of a system of indirect incentives—'cost-plus' contracts, tax write-offs, and government loans— to encourage private-sector conversion to war production. This system was resurrected as the primary mechanism for government economic mobilization during the prolonged arms race of the Cold War era, reaching its apogee in the early 1960s, and resurging in the 1980s, entailing major changes in the structure and location of American industrial activities.

The Canadian experience of wartime mobilization parallels that of the US, albeit on a much smaller scale and with some peculiarly 'Canadian' features, notably the extensive reliance on Crown corporations to carry out tasks that private enterprise was deemed unable, or unwilling, to undertake. During World War I, after a fair amount of confusion and hesitation, the government moved to establish various economic control measures, although the major instrument of industrial mobilization, the Imperial Munitions Board, was linked to the British rather than the Canadian government. World War II featured a far more activist government effort, including a plethora of Crown corporations, some of which continued to operate beyond the wartime emergency, particularly in the field of atomic energy. During the Cold War era, peaking in the mid-1950s, the government briefly ventured into erecting a mini-military-industrial complex centred on the aircraft industry, only to abandon the effort amid great (and continuing) controversy.

One notable by-product of the century's war mobilization was a strengthening of links between US and Canadian industrial economies. During both world wars, but especially in 1941–5, continental economic integration was vigorously pursued by governments on both sides of the border. In the Cold War years, a more piecemeal integration of defence-related industries took shape, accompanied by development of Canada's 'strategic' raw materials, principally for US military procurement agencies.

Business leaders played a major role in government programs to mobilize the Canadian economy for war. While the government gave lip service to the notion that war preparedness was 'everybody's business', and the Ottawa 'mandarins' retrospectively highlighted their own significance in these undertakings, the upper echelons of wartime agencies were dominated by 'dollar-a-year' men from private industry—not too surprisingly, given the close ties between big business and federal political parties in Canada since the age of Macdonald and the CPR, if not indeed throughout Canadian history.[1]

WORLD WAR I

In 1914, Canadians were no more prepared for war in industrial terms than they were militarily. After the Boer War—Canada's only significant military involvement since the Northwest Rebellion of 1885—the government had contracted with a Scottish promoter, Sir Charles Ross, to manufacture a rifle for the Canadian militia; his factory in Quebec had yet to produce any volume of weapons when Canada followed Britain into the European war. Aside from a Dominion arsenal in Quebec, Ross was the only military manufacturer in Canada. Following Laurier's Naval Bill of 1910—which had contributed to his political demise—the British arms maker, Vickers, had been lured into setting up a shipyard in Montreal; but as of the summer of 1914, delays in bringing the bill into force dissuaded Vickers from any major investment.

Not surprisingly, arrangements for military procurement took shape in a haphazard fashion. Shortly after the outbreak of war, Britain's War Minister, Lord Kitchener, contacted the Canadian Militia Minister, Sam Hughes, with an order for shell components for the British Army. Hughes sought, unsuccessfully, to interest the US Steel Corporation in the contract. American manufacturers were technically barred from such activities by US neutrality—although, curiously, Vickers was able to negotiate a deal with an American firm, Electric Boat Co., for assistance in the production of submarines in Canada. In any case, Hughes then turned to some 'reliable' associates, setting up a Shell Production Committee under Alexander Bertram, a Montreal steelmaker. An assortment of contract brokers also turned up in London and New York, bearing letters from Hughes identifying them as 'agents' of the Canadian government soliciting war orders; the most notorious of these characters was J. Wesley Allison, whose alleged profiteering and shady dealing would contribute to Hughes's eventual downfall.

Rumours of profiteering, patronage, and mismanagement of military orders under Hughes's aegis prompted Prime Minister Borden to set up a War Purchasing Commission, excluding Hughes, in the spring of 1915. But procurement for British war orders remained in the hands of the Shell Committee despite increasing dissatisfaction with that agency's operations. Aside from complaints from Canadian businesses that Bertram and other cronies of Hughes were monopolizing contracts, the Shell Committee seemed demonstrably incompetent. Ten months after the outbreak of the war, the Canadians had only managed to deliver 3 per cent of British orders, totalling $170 million. Problems of production were partly a consequence of Bertram's lack of organization— he tried to run the entire operation out of his own office, assisted only by an agent in London—but also reflected underlying weaknesses in Canada's industrial capabilities, particularly in quality control. Canadian manufacturers lacked the precision equipment and skilled workers necessary to produce munitions meeting the requirements of the British military.

Similar problems plagued the suppliers of Canadian arms. Ross proved unable to deliver on orders to supply rifles to the Canadian Army: as late as 1916 only two-thirds of a 1914 contract for 100,000 rifles had been met. Troops in the field found the weapons faulty and unreliable. Despite Hughes's fulminations, in 1916 Borden cancelled the 'Ross rifle' and Canadian forces were resupplied with British-made Lee-Enfield weapons.

Meanwhile, in Britain similar episodes of mismanagement and political favouritism in arms production had led to the establishment of a centralized Ministry of Munitions under David Lloyd-George in early 1915. The Canadian Shell Committee's failures generated pressure from London to place all arms production for British needs in Canada under the control of the new ministry, or at least to remove Hughes and his cronies from the process. In November 1915 Borden agreed to replace the Shell Committee with a new agency, the Imperial Munitions Board (IMB), which would be directly responsible to the British Ministry of Munitions rather than to the Canadian government. Borden's choice as chairman of the IMB was Joseph Flavelle, head of the Toronto meat-packing firm, William Davies Co., who had a reputation for disinterested public service and, of course, impeccably Conservative political credentials. Shortly thereafter, in the wake of scandals over the Ross rifle and Allison's activities, Hughes was forced out of the government altogether.

The IMB's achievements, in contrast to the sorry performance of the Shell Committee, contributed to Flavelle's reputation as an organizational genius. Defenders of Hughes have argued that, despite its failings, the Shell Committee laid the groundwork for Canadian industrial mobilization; in any case, the period 1914–15 was a time of ad hoc experimenting and on-the-job learning for all the warring industrial states. In some areas, such as steel ship construction, the IMB performed with little more distinction than its predecessor. Furthermore, Flavelle's approach to organization was not too different from Bertram's or, for that matter, most of Canada's industrialists: in running both the IMB and his private enterprises, Flavelle consistently emphasized personal leadership, decentralization, and teamwork among 'reliable' associates rather than the development of complex systems of organization. In contrast to the American situation, where the War Industries Board stimulated visions of close relations between government and business to promote national economic objectives, Flavelle and his fellow Canadian war mobilizers emerged with their views of a 'traditional' business–government relationship relatively intact.

At the same time, that 'traditional' relationship in Canada was not based on purely laissez-faire principles, and Flavelle was quite willing to extend government economic intervention when circumstances required. As early as 1904, Flavelle had endorsed Borden's proposal for a single government-owned western railway; and during the debates over railways in 1916–18, he continued to press for amalgamation and nationalization of the country's rail lines.

The IMB operated primarily through contracts with private companies, parcelling out over $1.23 billion in orders from Britain between 1916 and 1920. Nevertheless, Flavelle did not hesitate to set up government-controlled concerns to produce materiel unavailable from private suppliers, or to take over private companies (Ross's factory was 'nationalized' in 1917) that consistently failed to produce the quantity and quality of production required. Seven 'National Factories' were created during the war, producing such items as acetone for explosives, detonation fuses, and aircraft frames. These ventures were placed under managers recruited from the private sector and were all closed down or returned to private ownership after the war.

Flavelle also saw to it that orders were spread reasonably widely throughout Canadian industry, although (as in World War II) the major beneficiaries were in Ontario and Quebec, which received over three-quarters of the contracts. Flavelle's efforts to avoid the charges of favouritism and corruption that had swirled around the Shell Committee were not always successful: in 1917, the Davies company was alleged to have profiteered on its sales of bacon to Canadian troops. Although the IMB had nothing to do with these transactions, Flavelle's presumed political influence and his reputation for unctuous self-righteousness fuelled the controversy. Notions about conflict of interest were at best rudimentary in Canadian business and political circles; indeed, the emergence of this issue as a matter of public debate was largely the result of wartime scandals.

Although the IMB was independent of the Canadian government, its operations helped impel that government to further forms of intervention in the economy. By diverting industrial resources to war production, the IMB contributed to shortages and inflationary pressures in the domestic civilian economy that ultimately required the government to play a role in controlling wages and prices—although these measures fell considerably short of centralized planning. At the same time, the IMB's links with US industrial suppliers, particularly in 1917–18, contributed to the country's balance-of-payments difficulties and led to at least a partial integration of the two economies to deal with the allocation of continental resources for war production.

In late 1916 a combination of factors—the IMB's activities, an unexpectedly poor wheat harvest, and abrupt increases in demand for Canadian newsprint—produced a rapid rise in consumer prices, precipitating strikes in some industries and general complaints against hoarders and profiteers. Facing the prospect of an election the following year, the Borden government moved gingerly towards establishment of economic controls. W.G. O'Connor, a Halifax lawyer and associate of Borden, was appointed Commissioner of the Cost of Living in the Department of Labour to investigate charges of hoarding and price gouging. While limited, the Commissioner's powers were not inconsequential: O'Connor's report on meat packers, leaked to the press, led to the public outcry against the Davies company and Flavelle.

By 1917, controllers had been appointed to allocate food, paper, and fuel supplies. In 1918, a War Trade Board was in place to co-ordinate with a corresponding agency of the US government, with licensing authority over imports and exports to ensure the flow of essential materials to war industries. Government conciliation boards sprouted to deal with labour disputes on the railways and in the war plants. These various agencies engaged in unprecedented efforts to gather systematic statistical information on production output, the labour supply, wages, prices, and related matters.

The Armistice of November 1918 brought a halt to most of these experiments in state activism, but the immediate post-war period witnessed a brief resurgence of intervention in certain areas. A Canadian Wheat Board operated in 1920–2 as a successor to the wartime Board of Grain Supervisors. A more ambitious though even more short-lived undertaking was the Board of Commerce, created in 1919 to cope with steeply rising prices in a range of consumer goods. Its controversial career was terminated in less than a year, shortly before the courts ruled that it represented an unconstitutional extension of federal power.

Although the Board was meant to try to hold down prices, control profiteering, and, incidentally, block potentially monopolistic cartels, it was initially supported by some business groups, most notably sugar refiners, who hoped the agency would impose price stability that the industry was unable to secure through voluntary agreements. In its early actions the Board did indeed prop up prices for sugar and other commodities, seeking to ensure a steady flow of goods by guaranteeing producers reasonable profits. But it was subject to cross-pressures from consumers and wholesalers demanding lower prices and other industrialists opposed to any regulation. Newsprint producers, in particular, resented the Board's efforts to restrict their exports in order to ensure adequate paper supplies to Canadians. By early 1920 the Board's inconsistent policies had alienated virtually all interested parties. Ultimately, the government refused to sanction the Board's decisions, the commissioners resigned, and the agency disintegrated even before the British Privy Council demolished it as a legal entity. If nothing more,

the Board's unhappy history starkly revealed the limited nature of state power except in the extremities of wartime.

A more enduring legacy of World War I was the strengthening of economic links between Canada and the US, reflecting both the decline of British financial power and the emerging continental nature of Canada's business relations. Here, also, the IMB played a significant, albeit less than enthusiastic, role, a consequence of Canada's increasing technological as well as financial dependence on the Americans during the war.

In the early stages of the war the Canadian government turned to its traditional source, the British money market, to finance anticipated increased costs. But by the middle of 1915 it was apparent that British financial resources could not be tapped further for Canadian needs. The Minister of Finance, Thomas White, skeptical of Canada's ability to mobilize domestic capital, turned—for the first time in Canadian history—to the New York market, floating a $45 million loan. White also issued $50 million in 'Victory bonds' in Canada, which, to his surprise, raised more than $100 million. By 1919 almost $2 billion had been raised from the Canadian public. In 1916 the government introduced a business profits tax, with an income tax in the following year, purportedly only for the duration of the war. Although domestic revenue sources thus became an important component of war finance, the government continued to rely heavily on borrowing in the United States. By 1917, Canada's balance-of-payments deficit with the US was approaching $400 million.

In theory, IMB contracts were financed by the British government, but in fact all but a small proportion of this total was covered by advances from the Canadian government to Britain at a rate of $25 million per month from July 1916 to the end of the war. The Canadian government, in turn, had to depend on a steady flow of US money to sustain these operations.

Beyond these circuitous financial connections, the IMB had more direct links to American businesses. As the example of Vickers and Electric Boat indicates, Canadian manufacturers relied on the Americans for a variety of needs. Coal, oil, and copper for industrial processes flowed in from the US, and the war plants also imported machine tools, gauges, chemicals for explosives, and aircraft engines. The war had substantially increased Canada's dependence on US imports at the expense of Britain, achieving in practice the goal the rejected Reciprocity Agreement of 1911 had sought to accomplish. The British never regained the share of the Canadian market they had occupied prior to the war.

While welcome from a military standpoint, American entry into the war in 1917 created a dilemma for the IMB and the Canadian government. The US military would now have first call on American producers, although in the short run Canadian war industries were better prepared to make use of these supplies. Of more immediate concern was the problem of financing. By 1917, Britain was largely dependent on American loans, and the Americans were in a position to demand preferential treatment for their suppliers. Even before the US officially declared war, American companies were filling British (and French) contracts; neutrality, as the Germans bitterly pointed out, was little more than a word. A full-scale shift of British orders to the US—which the British threatened unless the Canadian government took on the full burden of financing their IMB orders—would imperil the Canadian war economy. Compounding these difficulties was an American government ban on further foreign borrowing, which raised Canada's balance-of-payments deficit with the US to a crisis situation. During the summer of 1917 some Canadian manufacturers began moving their operations across the border or selling their assets to Americans.

Flavelle, who had been a vigorous opponent of the Reciprocity Agreement in 1911, was a reluctant convert to continentalism. Nevertheless, in the fall of 1917 he dispatched emissaries to Washington to try to secure a place for the IMB in American economic mobilization arrangements. Fortunately

for the Canadians, the US military faced a crisis of its own: it was having to compete for supplies with America's allies and the industrial mobilization effort was in chaos. An agreement was worked out under which the US Army Ordnance Department would place orders with the IMB, although the Canadians would have to accept a 7 per cent differential, on the grounds that labour costs were lower in Canada (which was not, in fact, the case) and that the US government would forgo collecting war taxes on this production.

The IMB–Ordnance Agreement did not in itself significantly transform the IMB's operations. By the end of the war only $178 million, or about 16 per cent, of IMB contracts came from the US. This amount was offset by $130 million in orders that the IMB was obliged to parcel out to American manufacturers since the Canadians had also agreed to accept competitive bidding on British contracts. The agreement did, however, smooth the way for negotiations ensuring that a portion of US loans to Britain would be earmarked for financing British contracts with the IMB in Canada. In 1918, when the US War Industries Board (WIB) was empowered to allocate all raw materials and industrial supplies for American war production, the Canadians were able to secure a portion of these supplies to keep their own industries running—thanks in large measure to vigorous lobbying by Lloyd Harris, scion of the Ontario farm machinery family and president of his own auto firm, who headed the Canadian War Mission in Washington. The sudden end of the war blocked further movement towards continental economic integration for the time being, and Canadian manufacturers were the first to suffer when the WIB began cancelling war orders. During 1919–20, enterprising Americans came to Canada to buy surplus Canadian industrial assets and inventory at bargain prices.

Did World War I have a lasting impact on Canada? By 1920 the IMB and most of the other wartime agencies had closed shop, and the government's forays into economic planning were brief and not very successful. After the post-war recession, manufacturing output was somewhat larger than at the peak of the Laurier boom, but there were no significant shifts in the size of the workforce in most industries, and pre-war trends towards regional centralization of manufacturing and the growth of clerical occupations were, if anything, reinforced by the war. There had been dramatic growth of a more militant trade union movement between 1916 and 1919, stimulated in part by wartime shortages and rising prices, but also by the apparent failure of the conservative Trades and Labour Congress to win concessions from government agencies such as the IMB. This militancy spilled over into the post-war era, cresting in 1919 with more than 200 strikes across the country, particularly in mining and manufacturing. But apart from some lingering conflicts in areas such as the Nova Scotia coal and steel industry, internal divisions within the labour movement and a vigorous counteroffensive by business and public authorities—culminating with the suppression of the Winnipeg General Strike—overcame these challenges to businesses by the early 1920s.

There were, however, some enduring changes in the business community as well as in particular industries. Largely because of special wartime circumstances, Cominco acquired a zinc process and Ontario a nickel refinery. Prairie farmers acquired at least a vision of the potential capabilities of centralized processing and marketing through wheat co-operatives. Corporate and income taxes, despite the promises of Finance Minister White, were here to stay. The War Measures Act, with its provisions for government economic controls, remained on the books for future emergencies. While continental economic integration flourished only partially and briefly, the war hastened trends that carried Canada away from its traditional orientation towards Britain as the major source of capital and the primary market for its products. Although the Great Depression temporarily interrupted this process, it could be said that for Canada the 'American century' commenced at the very moment that Canadians

were acquiring a sense of their national identity on the battlefields of World War I.[2]

WORLD WAR II

Although the outbreak of war in Europe in 1939 came with considerable forewarning, Canada was not much better prepared than it had been in 1914. This situation was due in part to the resolutely isolationist position of the Prime Minister, Mackenzie King, but other factors played a role. The Depression had eroded the morale as well as the assets of Canadian businesses, and a sharp slump in 1937–8 after the modest recovery of mid-decade left industrial production well below 1929 levels. Federal government efforts to develop national economic policies were stubbornly resisted by the premiers of the two largest provinces, Ontario and Quebec. Following the Munich crisis in autumn 1938, King increased government expenditures on military needs from $36 million to $65 million, and both the naval and air forces (such as they were) had begun upgrading after 1936; but King was deterred from more substantial measures by his sensitivity towards anti-war sentiments in Quebec that, as he could well recall, had helped topple Laurier from office in 1911.

In 1937 the British government, beginning its own belated military buildup, had arranged to underwrite the costs of production of Bren guns by a Toronto firm, John Inglis Co., generating an acrimonious debate in the Canadian Parliament over allegations of political favouritism by the Liberal government. This episode, with its overtones of World War I controversies over contracting, put yet another damper on King's enthusiasm for war preparedness. Aside from the Inglis contract, only National Steel Car Co. of Hamilton was engaged in munitions production on the eve of war in September 1939. The Bren gun affair did, however, persuade the government to establish a Defence Purchasing Board (later the War Supply Board) with guidelines in place for competitive bidding and a 5 per cent profit rate on contracts.

Meanwhile, National Steel Car had joined forces with other Canadian manufacturers in a project that laid the groundwork for what was to be one of the country's most successful ventures in war production. In the spring of 1938 the British Air Ministry dispatched a mission to North America to secure contracts for production of British-designed planes. Interested companies agreed to establish a joint venture, Canadian Associated Aircraft Ltd, to take on some of this work. Although King's response to the venture was initially cool, once the war began his views shifted. Canadian airframe manufacturing would fit in with the proposed British Commonwealth Air Training Plan (BCATP) to use Canada and other Dominions as training grounds for pilots and crews, a scheme that offered the advantage of limiting Canada's military contribution to the war effort while maximizing economic benefits at home. Although the Associated Aircraft operation was short-lived, a number of firms took over contracts to build trainer planes while King used the BCATP to secure re-election of his government in early 1940, confounding his provincial and pacifist rivals.

Spring 1940 also witnessed the fall of France and aroused fears that Britain faced invasion by the Axis powers. These events strengthened public support for the war effort and galvanized the Canadian government to mobilize the nation's resources. Military spending for 1940–1 increased tenfold over 1939 levels. A Department of Munitions and Supply, with sweeping powers over industrial production and raw materials, was established, absorbing the War Supply Board. To head this new department, King turned to Clarence D. Howe, his Minister of Transportation, who had already established a reputation for effective, if abrasive, administrative leadership. An American-born engineer, Howe had run a successful firm designing and building grain elevators and terminals at the Lakehead before embarking on a political career in the mid-1930s. In King's cabinet from his first term, Howe had overhauled the Board of Railway Commissioners and the CNR,

reorganized the government's administration of harbour facilities, sponsored the bill creating the Canadian Broadcasting Company, and established Trans-Canada Air Lines, the first of many of what Howe regarded as 'his' Crown corporations.

Like Flavelle in World War I, Howe was to earn a reputation at the Department of Munitions and Supply as a master organizer, and went on after the war to run, directly or indirectly, so many departments and agencies that by the 1950s he was hailed (or denounced) as the 'Minister of Everything'. To his admirers, who included a number of businessmen he recruited to run war agencies, Howe was a Napoleonic figure: decisive, efficient, a master of details. Despite his image as a 'businesslike' minister, however, Howe functioned best in situations where volume of production rather than cost or quality control was the major measure of achievement. Like Flavelle, Howe's approach to organization involved selecting 'reliable' people to head his agencies and then leaving them to run things. But his criteria for choosing leaders was sometimes idiosyncratic—Ralph Bell, the Nova Scotia fish-packing magnate, was asked to run the Aircraft Division, for example, because he had experience flying a plane—and their effectiveness was linked, at least partly, to their personal relations with him. Howe feuded with other strong-willed figures, notably H.R. MacMillan, the BC timberman, who dared to question his methods of running the Munitions Department in 1942; and he was openly contemptuous of critics in Parliament, displaying an arrogance that became even more apparent in the post-war era.

Whatever his failings may have been, Howe was an energetic and versatile figure who, through the force of his own personality, provided a sense of overall direction to the war mobilization effort. Business confidence was inspired not only by Howe's reliance on 'practical' businessmen to run the wartime bureaucracies but also by generous contracting policies, similar to those eventually introduced in the US to arouse corporate enthusiasm for the war effort. Government loans and subsidies to contractors were supplemented by provisions for accelerated depreciation of the valuation of war plants and other assets for tax purposes.

At the same time, Howe endeavoured to avoid episodes such as the Shell Committee scandal, adhering to the War Supply Board guidelines of 5 per cent profit rates, with efforts to recover excess profits. War production demands were sufficiently large that charges of favouritism, as in the Bren gun affair, were generally avoided though not absent. In 1941, for example, CCF critics in Parliament raised questions about the large number of war contracts awarded Canadian Industries Ltd, a joint subsidiary of the American company Du Pont, and Britain's Imperial Chemical Industries, whose president, Arthur Purvis, was on leave to serve as head of the British Purchasing Mission in New York.

Maritime businesses complained of regional discrimination in the disposition of contracts and government investment in manufacturing. Dosco's president, Arthur Cross, asserted in 1941 that the Munitions Department had poured $4 million into steel companies in central Canada when his own firm had idle capacity. He attributed this situation to Howe's preoccupation with the post-war industrial interests of his home province, Ontario; others called attention to the close ties cultivated with Howe since the mid-1930s by Algoma Steel's chief, Sir James Dunn. Maritime shipyards protested the government's construction of new facilities on the Great Lakes and the reluctance of the Munitions Department to expand ship repair capacity on the Atlantic coast in favour of Montreal, contributing to the problems of naval convoys during the critical period of the Battle of the Atlantic in 1941–2. While shipbuilding and repair work represented the largest proportion of war contracts awarded to the region, only 6 per cent of all wartime ship construction was done in the Maritimes, while British Columbia accounted for almost half the total—perhaps not surprisingly, in the view of critics, since Howe's Director-General for Shipbuilding was H.R. MacMillan.

Howe had little patience with the CCF (or with Maritime manufacturers for that matter), but he also—again like Flavelle—had few qualms about using the full powers of the state, seizing private factories (National Steel Car among them), and creating a wide range of Crown corporations. Forty-six such entities were established to produce aircraft, ships, chemicals, optical equipment, and targeting devices as well as munitions; to build houses for workers in the new war plants; and to allocate raw materials to contractors. Most of these Crown corporations were intended only for wartime requirements, but Howe also deployed them to develop Canadian industrial capabilities for the post-war period in fields such as machine tools, metal fabrication, and aircraft engines.

One prominent example of this kind of venture was the Polymer Corporation. In the wake of Japanese conquests in Southeast Asia in early 1942, North America faced serious shortages of natural rubber. Even before this point, Canada was experiencing problems: in 1940, Howe set up Fairmont Co. to stockpile rubber and other scarce materials through foreign purchases and acquisition of scrap materials for recycling. After Pearl Harbor, however, it was recognized that these sources would be inadequate, particularly since the Americans had mounted their own rubber stockpiling operation. In the 1930s, petroleum and chemical companies in the US, Britain, and Germany had been experimenting with processes to develop synthetic rubber from fossil fuel by-products, but little had been done in this field in Canada. To develop synthetic rubber capacity, Howe set up Polymer Corporation in 1942 and contracted with the Michigan firm, Dow Chemical, and a subsidiary of Imperial Oil (whose parent, Jersey Standard, had carried out the most advanced research in the field before the war) to provide technical and managerial assistance. Raw materials were acquired from the Rubber Reserve Co., a US government enterprise that was also engaged in a crash program to develop synthetic rubber. By early 1944 a plant was in operation in Sarnia, Ontario, at a cost of about $50 million.

By the end of the war Polymer had produced over 785,000 tons of tires, tire cording, and other rubber products.

After the war most of the Crown enterprises were closed down or sold to private companies. Polymer, however, was retained in government hands—in part because no interested buyers could be found willing to pay the asking price, but also because Howe regarded it as one of his great success stories and was reluctant to part with it. Polymer continued to operate at a profit through the 1950s, eventually diversifying into plastics and other petrochemical products. In 1972, as Polysar Ltd, it was folded into the Canada Development Corporation. Another wartime Crown enterprise, Eldorado Mining, also remained under government control, initially for national security purposes, and was subsequently linked with Atomic Energy of Canada Ltd to form the base of the country's ambitious venture into the nuclear power field (see box, p. 140).

Howe and his disciples asserted, with some justification, that these wartime measures—in contrast to the World War I experience—ensured that Canada emerged in 1945 with a strong and diversified industrial base. The comparison is not entirely clear-cut, however, since the post-World War II era was one of generally sustained economic growth, unlike the unstable and uneven record of the 1920s. Altogether, $1.6 billion went into new capital investment in industry during the war; the Munitions Department disposed of about half these assets to private enterprise when the war ended. The transportation network, the merchant marine, and the construction industry also benefited from this wartime investment, enhancing the infrastructure as well as manufacturing capabilities.[3]

Without markets, the creation of this enlarged capacity would have been a formula for disaster, as indeed had been the case in the aftermath of World War I. Howe and other government officials were naturally preoccupied with the development of Canada's export trade as the war economy wound down in 1945–6. But exports were not the major ingredient in Canada's economic growth in the immediate post-war period. Wartime employment, a rising birth rate, and forced savings laid the groundwork for an enlarged domestic consumer market, augmented by an unprecedented net inflow of immigrants in the early 1950s.

As in World War I, the massive diversion of resources into war production contributed to shortages and inflationary pressures in the civilian market, pushing the characteristically hesitant Prime Minister towards imposition of economic controls. Shortly after the declaration of war in 1939, a Wartime Prices and Trade Board (WPTB) was set up in the Labour Department; import and foreign exchange controls were introduced; and trade in some 'luxury' items was curtailed (whisky was not so designated; even economic controllers needed their Scotch). In 1940, wage ceilings were imposed and a range of new business profits and excise taxes introduced. By mid-1941, however, as the cost of living rose to 7 per cent, the Canadian Manufacturers' Association began supporting demands from the Bank of Canada for more substantial measures. In September of that year, the WPTB was transferred to the more politically formidable Department of Finance and placed under an energetic official from the Bank of Canada, Donald Gordon. The government then imposed a full-scale wage and price freeze.

Like Howe, Gordon recruited bankers and other businessmen to administer the WPTB system, which helped smother complaints from the private sector, and mounted a vigorous publicity campaign to secure public support for controls. Producers and distributors were offered subsidies to offset cost pressures, in order to prevent them from trying to pass costs along to the consumer. They were also tacitly encouraged to reduce the quality of goods and services if necessary to hold the price line. Rationing of gasoline, tires, some food products, clothing, and other items was introduced. Labour relations in war-related industries were brought under federal jurisdiction to keep wages in line with prices.

CANADA AND ATOMIC ENERGY

During World War II both the US and Britain initiated programs to develop an atomic bomb, assuming—incorrectly, as it turned out—that Germany was ahead of them in nuclear research. Canada's role in this effort came about inadvertently: during the 1930s the LaBine brothers had established one of the few existing uranium mining operations, Eldorado Mines, refining the ore into radium for medical uses. In 1944, Howe's Munitions Department took over Eldorado to provide uranium for the Manhattan Project. Meanwhile, a British research team under an Austrian scientist, Hans von Halban, working on a nuclear reaction process using 'heavy water' (deuterium) as a moderator, transferred operations to Canada in 1942, partly on the assumption that the needed material could be procured from Cominco's smelting. Most of the heavy water was ultimately provided by the Americans, but a successful nuclear reactor was tested at Chalk River, Ontario, in 1945 shortly after the end of the war. Upon these foundations, the Canadian government erected its post-war program to develop nuclear power through another Crown corporation, Atomic Energy of Canada Ltd (AECL).

The Chalk River project had been carried out in co-operation with the British (although the Canadian government footed most of the $4 million bill), and Canada wanted to maintain that connection after the war. By the late 1940s, however, it was clear that the US would be a more reliable market for Canadian uranium; and C.J. Mackenzie, who as head of the National Research Council also presided over the country's nuclear power research, was confident that Canada could develop its own reactors for 'peaceful purposes', primarily electrical power generation—a view shared by Howe. Eldorado Mines remained under government control,

ZEEP—Zero Energy Experimental Pile—the first nuclear reactor built outside the US, at Chalk River, Ontario, September 1945. (Copyright Atomic Energy of Canada Limited)

selling uranium to the US Atomic Energy Commission. In 1952, the Chalk River operation was reconstituted as AECL, which negotiated an agreement with Ontario Hydro in the following year to develop a larger-scale reactor at an estimated cost of $26 million. Less publicized were arrangements to sell plutonium produced by the reactors to the Americans for use in their accelerated nuclear weapons program. Although Eldorado and AECL remained legally separate, from 1953 to 1958 they were both under a Howe protege, William J. Bennett; AECL took over Eldorado's commercial marketing of radioactive isotopes for industrial as well as medical purposes.

Bennett proposed a strategy of development by stages for AECL: a demonstration reactor was initiated with technical assistance from Canadian General Electric (CGE) for completion in 1962. Meanwhile, however, pressure grew for a more rapid move to commercial development as the international nuclear power industry gained momentum. As in the case of the Avro Arrow, costs of prototype development were exceeding early estimates, adding to pressures for a faster return on government investment, particularly after Howe and the Liberals were removed from the scene in Ottawa in 1957. Howe's successor as Minister of Trade and Commerce, Gordon Churchill, pushed Bennett's successor, Lorne Gray, to announce in 1959 that AECL would move on immediately to a major project, the CANDU reactor at Douglas Point, Ontario, at a cost of over $100 million. To position Canada for the increasingly competitive export market, AECL would also take over most of the technical work rather than subcontracting to private enterprise, CGE having been assigned blame for many of the cost overruns on the demonstration project. The Douglas Point reactor went into operation in 1966, two years behind schedule and the subject of much controversy over design and construction problems.

Initially, the CANDU was to be marketed abroad by private firms, with AECL providing technical backup. CGE made several forays in this field in the mid-1960s but decided to abandon the effort in 1968, having made only one sale, to Pakistan, as it faced formidable competition from larger US, German, and other companies, often with government-backed financing in hand. Technical problems involved in the Douglas Point project may also have been a factor. After 1968, AECL took over marketing as well, with similarly limited success until the 1970s. By that time, however, sales to Argentina and South Korea embroiled the Crown corporation in scandals over bribery.

AECL transferred heavy-water technology to India in the 1960s (with the Canadian government assisting in financing), but Canadians and Americans were alarmed to discover that, despite safeguards, India had used plutonium from its nuclear plants to develop an atomic bomb in 1974. Public concern over nuclear reactor safety after the Three Mile Island accident near Harrisburg, Pennsylvania, in 1978 (and the far graver Chernobyl disaster of 1986) contributed to changing attitudes towards an industry that had once been seen as the most advanced of 'high technologies'—for many Canadians, the nation's adventure into atomic energy seemed from the perspective of the 1990s to have been costly and ill-advised, the result of scientists' infatuation and bureaucratic empire-building. But as the new century dawned with renewed concerns over future oil shortages and global warming, the case for power from the 'peaceful atom' was heard again in the land.

Sources: Robert Bothwell, *Eldorado: Canada's National Uranium Company* (Toronto, 1984); Bothwell, *Nucleus: The History of Atomic Energy of Canada* (Toronto, 1988); G. Bruce Doern, *Government Intervention in the Canadian Nuclear Industry* (Montreal, 1981).

How effective were wage and price controls in Canada in World War II? The cost of living rose by less than 3 per cent and, whatever its faults, the Canadian controls were probably more successful than similar exercises in other countries; but the WPTB allowed a wide range of exemptions and exceptions, and public support, always somewhat precarious, dwindled rapidly as the end of the war approached. Farmers, with Jimmy Gardiner a vigorous spokesman in King's cabinet, fought a rearguard battle against controls, and meat rationing was lifted temporarily in 1944–5 under pressure from this quarter. Other primary producers were able to get increases on the grounds that their prices were artificially low when the freeze was imposed. Contemporary critics argued that the subsidy arrangements benefited well-organized manufacturing groups and retail chains while smaller merchants were ignored. On the whole, however, it seems fair to say that controls were more effectively applied during World War II, and phased out in a more orderly fashion in 1945–6, than had been the case during and after World War I—due in part at least to the administrative and public relations skills deployed by Gordon and his 5,000-plus controllers. Gordon's success led to his later recruitment to run the Canadian National Railways from 1949 to 1965. The effectiveness of controls and rationing helped create a pent-up consumer demand that buoyed the Canadian economy after the war.

Organized labour made gains during the war, in contrast to its experience in World War I. In part, this reflected the cautious support of Mackenzie King, erstwhile champion of labour–management conciliation in the Laurier era. In 1940, an Order-in-Council (PC 2685) appeared to acknowledge the right of workers to join unions and to expect 'fair and reasonable standards of wages and working conditions'—although, as in the case of the Industrial Disputes Investigation Act, government had limited enforcement powers. Subsequently, relations deteriorated as Howe opposed work stoppages in what were deemed to be strategically important industries and pushed for intervention to block strikes at Arvida and GM's St Catharines plant in 1941. King also remained (characteristically) inactive when Ontario's Premier Mitch Hepburn sided openly with management in breaking a bitter strike in the nickel industry at Sudbury. Continuing divisions between the craft-centred Trades and Labour Congress and the US-spawned Congress of Industrial Organizations also weakened the strength of the labour movement in the early years of the war.

By 1943–4, however, unions such as the International Association of Machinists and International Brotherhood of Electrical Workers had established themselves in the emerging war-related industries such as shipbuilding and aircraft production, and the United Auto Workers consolidated its position in the Canadian as well as the US auto industry. Sensing the leftward drift of Canadian political sentiment highlighted by CCF gains in the Prairie provinces and Ontario, the King government issued a new Order-in-Council (PC 1003) in 1944 (optimistically dubbed a 'Magna Carta for Labour') that imposed rules for the formal recognition of unions' rights to collective bargaining and certification procedures based in part on the model of the Wagner Act of 1936 in the United States.

As had occurred at the end of World War I, the dismantling of wage and price controls in 1946 stimulated a wave of strikes; but in this case the unions were able to withstand counter-attacks, even when employers exploited nascent Cold War fears by charging that many of these strikes were provoked by 'Communist' unions—sometimes rightly, as in the case of the seamen's strike in Ontario and the textile workers' strike in Quebec. Bolstered by the legitimacy conferred by PC 1003, the emerging industrial unions in the steel, rubber, and meat-packing industries won significant victories in 1946–7, although asbestos workers in Quebec lost a bitter contest, in which the Duplessis government vigorously supported companies such Johns Manville against strikers.

Union strength was particularly augmented by a decision imposed by Canadian Justice Ivan Rand as part of a binding arbitration procedure to end a UAW strike against Ford in 1946: the 'Rand formula' (which was subsequently applied more broadly across Canadian industries) rejected demands for a 'union shop' but obliged employers to establish an automatic 'check-off' to collect union dues—a measure that effectively ensured the financial viability of unions, at least for the next generation.

In addition to the increased power of labour unions in the business–labour nexus, probably the most significant development of World War II was the strengthening of economic links between

Canada and the United States, accompanied by the continuing decline of British political as well as economic influence in Canada. The circumstances that produced this outcome were similar to those that prevailed in 1916–18, but in World War II they took effect more rapidly and with more enduring consequences.

The British government had begun scouting the prospects for Canadian munitions procurement in 1938, and dispatched a British Purchasing Mission to Ottawa shortly after the outbreak of war with the Commonwealth Air Training Plan in hand. The British proposed that Canada should bear about 40 per cent of the costs (the other Dominions would absorb a smaller amount) and Britain would cover its share through purchases of Canadian wheat and other raw materials, and, if necessary, the sale of British assets in Canada. The Canadians insisted on a smaller financial commitment, which was achieved by reducing the estimated costs of BCATP. All this dickering shortly proved to be beside the point since all estimates were unrealistic and Britain's incapacity to pay was apparent even before the end of 1940. By this time most British investments in Canada had been liquidated and gold transfers were drying up. As in 1916, Britain wanted the Canadian government to effectively take over the financing of war production in Canada.

The Canadian government had been able to substantially increase its revenues by boosting income tax levels and expanding them to cover more than one-fifth of the population. Rising employment due to war production helped raise revenues from $467 million in 1939 to over $1 billion by the end of 1941, with corporate and business taxes contributing about one-quarter of this total. Additional revenues were raised through government bond and Treasury certificate sales, totalling $745 million in 1940 and $1.3 billion in 1941. By this time, however, expenditures were running well over $1 billion a year, with the end of the war nowhere in sight.

More critical was the problem of balance of payments. Even before the war, Canada had run deficits in trade and payments with the US, offset by exports to Britain. Wartime demand had boosted exports to Britain, particularly in value-added manufactured products, but the expansion of Canadian war production aggravated deficits in the American account. One-third of parts and materials for Canadian industrial operations had to come from US sources. By the spring of 1941 Canada faced a $478 million balance-of-payments deficit with the US, with every indication that this would increase, and Britain made it clear that it could no longer cover the costs of imports from Canada.

The United States was (again) officially neutral, but President Franklin Roosevelt was openly sympathetic towards Britain and had circumvented congressional restrictions by arranging for sales of US goods to Britain (and Canada) on a 'cash and carry' basis since 1939, subsequently transferring surplus warships to Britain in 1940. With British financial resources depleted by March 1941, Roosevelt sponsored a 'Lend-Lease' bill in Congress that would permit large-scale exports of war material to Britain without requiring immediate compensation—although Americans would later use this aid as a lever in post-war trade negotiations. The dilemma for Canada was that, as in 1916, Lend-Lease would incline the British to redirect all war production orders to the US, except those the Canadian government was willing to finance. The Canadians were also reluctant to request direct aid through Lend-Lease, as this might create pressures from the American side for liquidation of all Canadian assets in the United States.

Two factors were working in Canada's favour: first, thanks to Howe's Munitions Department, Canadian industrial plants were geared up for war production while US economic mobilization was floundering. Second, Mackenzie King had directed much effort to cultivate ties with Roosevelt—who in any case was inclined to see Canada's welfare as vital to America's long-term interests: in 1940, the two leaders had established a Permanent Joint Board of Defence to co-ordinate continental military measures. In April 1941, shortly after passage of the Lend-Lease bill, King and Roosevelt negotiated the 'Hyde Park Agreement' under which the US would place up to $300 million in military contracts in Canada for 1941, and a portion of the $7 billion authorized under Lend-Lease for British war orders would be earmarked for the Canadians. Canada was not obliged to sell off American assets, and even the foreign exchange controls imposed by Canada in 1939 were left undisturbed.

Howe wasted no time exploiting the new situation, creating War Supplies Ltd to sell Canadian products in the US, and dispatching one of his prized proteges, E.R Taylor, to wheel and deal for contracts among the chaotically disorganized procurement bureaucracies in Washington. Between May 1941 and 1945, War Supplies Ltd netted over $1 billion in US orders. Taylor went on to succeed CIL's Arthur Purvis as head of the British Purchasing Mission in the US, and after the war created Argus Corporation, which by the 1950s made him one of Canada's wealthiest figures, a mid-century Max Aitken. Meanwhile, US Lend-Lease aid to Britain rose to $30 billion before the end of the war, with Canada procuring orders that topped $1.4 billion. Altogether, Canada spent about $9 billion on military production in World War II, exporting more than one-third of this total.

The Hyde Park Agreement opened the way for more far-reaching economic links between the two countries, particularly after the US entered the war in December 1941. In contrast to World War I, a Canadian representative sat on the Combined (Anglo-American) Resources and Production Board established in 1942; and after some dickering, Canada also gained a seat on the Combined Food Board. Meanwhile, by the end of the war Canada–US trade exceeded $2 billion a year, a figure larger than Canada's total trade average in the years just before the war. Almost three-quarters of Canada's imports came from the US, reflecting a trend underway since the negotiation of reciprocity in 1935.

Under the umbrella of continental defence measures, the US government also constructed a variety of military installations and infrastructure, particularly in the Canadian West, including air fields, radar stations, and a highway to link Washington state with Alaska at a cost of $130 million. Among the most controversial of these undertakings was construction of an oil pipeline from Norman Wells in the Northwest Territories to Fairbanks, Alaska. This Canol Project was poorly planned and eventually abandoned, but it drew the attention of both Canadian and some American businesses to the potential resources of this wilderness region. During the 1920s, Imperial Oil had discovered oil and set up a modest refinery at Norman Wells on the Mackenzie River. In 1942 the US War Department decided to build a pipeline to link Norman Wells to planned air bases in the Yukon and Alaska. Despite advice from Imperial that the oil supplies were limited and of poor quality, the US military hastily embarked on the project at a cost of over $130 million over two years—by which time the strategic value of the pipeline had largely vanished. Excoriated by a US congressional investigation, the War Department decided to abandon the pipeline less than a year after it went into operation. Although Imperial had increased its estimates of the Norman Wells field's potential, neither the company nor the Canadian government was interested in acquiring the pipeline. At the same time, however, the Canadian government—irked by the arbitrary way that US authorities had gone about this project—decided to buy the Alaska Highway, in part to avoid further incursions. Meanwhile, Imperial Oil found the results of its role (subsidized by US government funds), modest though they were, sufficiently encouraging to step up exploration and drilling in the less remote hinterlands of Alberta.[4]

Canada emerged from World War II with a greatly enlarged manufacturing base, including some industries that had not previously existed, and a potentially strong domestic consumer market. The federal government had extended its position in the national economy, and its leaders felt confident of their capabilities to play a major role in reshaping post-war Canada. Although the impetus for expanded social welfare programs introduced towards the end of the war was largely a political response to the growing popularity of the CCF, such measures as family allowances, old-age pensions, and an enlarged federal role in economic planning also reflected the ambitions and visions of Ottawa's bureaucratic mandarins.

The war also accentuated economic ties between Canada and the United States. While the Hyde Park arrangements lapsed as the economies reconverted to peacetime, close trade relations were maintained. American mining and petroleum companies took a renewed interest in Canadian resources. The Canadian political environment was hospitable to such investment, which spilled over readily into manufacturing and services. For a period of time after the war, Canada was in the happy position of having both strong domestic and healthy export markets, enabling the country's businesses to solidify wartime gains, while new inflows of capital helped buoy the economy, especially after 1950. The roller-coaster conditions of the 1920s were thus avoided as the country enjoyed its most sustained growth since the Laurier era. The onset of the Cold War would extend that record of prosperity while accelerating the trend towards continental integration.

MOBILIZATION FOR COLD WAR, 1949–59

Even before the end of World War II, the 'Grand Alliance' of Britain, the US, and the Soviet Union was coming asunder as the victors debated the future of Germany and Eastern Europe. By 1947 the USSR and the Western powers were on a collision course, and both sides prepared for a protracted era of tension. During the early stages of the Cold War, the US relied primarily on various forms of foreign economic and military aid to contain what was perceived as Soviet expansion. By 1950, in the wake of Soviet atomic bomb testing and the Communist revolution in

China, America began to rearm, and the outbreak of a shooting war in Korea hastened the pace of remilitarization. For the Canadian government, and for Canadian business, these developments presented both problems and opportunities.

While the most immediate issues in 1945 involved reconversion of the economy to peacetime levels, government officials were particularly anxious to sustain Canada's export trade. In 1944 at Bretton Woods, New Hampshire, the Americans had proposed to use their financial power to reconstitute the international monetary system and to pressure or cajole other countries into a multilateral reduction of trade barriers. While significant aspects of the Bretton Woods system, such as the International Monetary Fund, the World Bank, and the General Agreement on Tariffs and Trade, have continued in altered forms into the present, the keystone of Bretton Woods— national currencies fixed to the American dollar, and the American dollar based on the gold standard—broke apart in the early 1970s, first in 1971 when the US ceased its backing of the dollar with gold reserves, and finally, in 1973, when international bankers could not stop the move away from war-inflated US dollars to other currencies. At the outset of the Bretton Woods arrangement, although Britain's 'sterling bloc' was one of the main targets of this effort, the Canadian government was in favour of measures that would also prevent a resurgence of US trade protectionism. To help resurrect British markets, Canada in 1945 offered a post-war loan of $1.25 billion.

Britain, however, was far worse off than anyone had imagined, and after the Canadian government dismantled economic controls and restored its currency to parity with the US dollar in 1946, American goods poured into Canada. By early 1947 Canada again faced balance-of-trade deficits with the US reminiscent of 1941, which the floundering economies of Britain and Western Europe could not offset. Between 1945 and 1946, Canada's balance of payments with the US was transformed from a $30 million surplus to a deficit of $600 million.

At this point the US unveiled the Marshall Plan, which would channel billions of dollars in aid to Western Europe to help rebuild these economies, bolster the region against 'social unrest' (described to the US Congress as Soviet subversion), and incidentally revitalize these markets for American exports. Again, as in 1917 and 1941, Canada faced a dilemma since American aid would not guarantee markets for Canadian goods. In the fall of 1947, Canadian officials once again trekked south, while King threatened to impose import quotas to demonstrate the gravity of the situation.

The Americans proved remarkably accommodating. As in the case of Lend-Lease, Canada was allowed to take over a portion of the Marshall Plan orders from Europe—which ultimately came to over $1 billion between 1948 and 1950. Howe, who had been Minister of Reconstruction since 1944, added Trade and Commerce to his portfolio to spearhead the export drive. American trade officials also introduced a more dramatic proposal, to establish a US–Canada customs union. Although Howe and other members of King's cabinet supported the proposal, the Prime Minister—who could still recall the fate of his mentor, Laurier, in 1911—ultimately demurred. Canada did, however, participate in the General Agreement on Tariffs and Trade (GATT), committing the country to dismantle its protective tariff system, although this process was to take 30 years.

Canada's participation in the Marshall Plan marked the beginning of a steady course of continental economic and military collaboration. The mining industry was an initial beneficiary of this trend. During World War II, Canada had been a major supplier not only of uranium to the Manhattan Project but also of nickel, lead, and zinc for America's military needs. Even before the onset of the Cold War, the US Congress had authorized development of stockpiles of 'strategic materials'.

Unfortunately for Canada, this law gave preference to US suppliers and was buttressed by prohibitive duties on a range of minerals, measures that fell particularly hard on Alcan, which had substantially increased its aluminum capacity in World War II. By 1948, however, American stockpiling authorities were increasing their purchases of Canadian minerals. After the outbreak of war in Korea, Congress quadrupled stockpile targets. In the following year a Materials Policy Commission chaired by William Paley projected an even greater increase in US stockpile requirements. The prospect of this bonanza had already attracted US mining companies into Canada: $1.4 billion in new investment in mining and smelting facilities poured in between 1945 and 1955, most of it coming after 1950.

Growth in mining investment and exports was not restricted to stockpiled materials. World War II almost exhausted the iron ore reserves of Minnesota's Mesabi Range; and as early as 1942 the M.A. Hanna iron company of Cleveland was scouting the prospects for new iron sources in northern Quebec and Labrador. Seven years later, five American steel firms joined Hanna to form the Iron Ore Co. of Canada, investing over $250 million in the region between 1949 and 1954. The development of Labrador's iron reserves had an additional spinoff: American steelmakers began to lobby vigorously for construction of the St Lawrence Seaway, a project dear to Canadian (or at least central Canadian) hearts since the 1920s, but which had been thwarted by opposition from American railroaders and eastern seaboard business interests. Despite their continued resistance, the measure was pushed through the US Congress as necessary for national security in 1954; the Seaway opened for business five years later.

The Korean War also resurrected continental economic mobilization. After World War II the Permanent Joint Board on Defence engaged in desultory discussions of this issue and a Joint Industrial Mobilization Committee was set up in 1949. Canadian officials lobbied with modest success for a share in US military procurement provided under the Mutual Defense Assistance Act, that country's first step towards rearmament in that same year. Even after the outbreak of war in June 1950, however, the Americans, anticipating a swift victory, were only prepared to accept the principle of reciprocal arms purchases with Canada without attaching a dollar figure. Chinese intervention in the war in November of that year precipitated more vigorous activity on both sides of the border.

The Canadian government, with the Liberals still in power, announced a $5 billion rearmament program in 1951 and established a Department of Defence Production (DDP) with Howe, naturally, at its helm. As usual, Howe used tax concessions and other incentives to stimulate arms production, although there was little reliance on Crown corporations; and Howe relied on informal negotiations with his US counterparts to flesh out the reciprocal arms trade agreement made in October 1950. Although the Canadians continued to bicker with the Americans over aluminum exports—an issue of diminishing importance as the Canadian aircraft industry began to absorb more domestic output after 1951—there were relatively few major controversies. In 1951–2 there was some cause for alarm as the DDP spent $500 million more in purchases from the US than it earned from arms sales; but by 1953 the trade balance was evening out, abetted by US stockpiling as well as more US procurement of military equipment in Canada. Conventional military spending began to tail off after the Korean armistice in 1953, but stockpiling continued to grow and the US began to develop a system of radar installations across Canada to protect the US against Soviet long-range bombers. These projects created some construction jobs, although there was limited use of Canadian industrial suppliers.

There was one further by-product of the Korean War: what could be called an industrial development strategy that had been gestating in an ad hoc way since World War II. The basic premise of this strategy was that Canada had reached a level of competence sufficient to support development of a limited number of technologically advanced industries—drawing, as in the past, on foreign sources of capital and knowledge, but intended to establish the base for an innovative and diversified industrial economy. Atomic energy was one strand

of this approach, but Howe, at least, focused on two interrelated pet projects—a Canadian airline and a domestic aircraft industry—although the centrepiece of the latter, Avro, proved to be more of a 'tar baby'.

Howe's interest in aviation went back to his pre-World War II days as Minister of Transport. In the 1930s Canada had no cross-country air service, although the Winnipeg grain merchant, James Richardson, was trying to construct one, enlisting support from the two major railways. Howe, however, decided early on to develop a government-owned line, initially luring the presidents of CPR and CNR to serve on its board, and recruiting Philip Johnson, a former executive with Boeing Aircraft and United Airlines in the US, to head the Crown enterprise, Trans-Canada Air Lines (TCAL), launched in 1937. Beatty of the CPR pulled out when it became clear that Howe would exercise real control over TCAL. In 1939 he acquired Richardson's network and created a subsidiary, CP Airlines, which established a strong foothold in the West. Canadian airlines thus duplicated the mixed public/private configuration of Canadian railways and utilities. Another potential rival emerged briefly in World War II when Lord Beaverbrook contemplated developing a British Commonwealth airline system—which, fortunately from Howe's viewpoint, never got off the ground.

Howe resisted efforts to privatize TCAL, and showered it with largesse whenever the opportunity arose, beginning with air mail contracts in 1938. The Air Transport Board, established in 1944 to regulate airlines, was under the authority of the Transport Minister and up to 1967 was in effect required to give TCAL any routes it applied for; CP Air, on the other hand, did not acquire a transcontinental route until 1959, after Howe and the Liberals had been thrust from power. The rationale for this apparent favouritism was that TCAL provided service to commercially unprofitable areas of the country. Through the 1950s, CP Airlines focused on the international market while lobbying against the domestic routing structure.

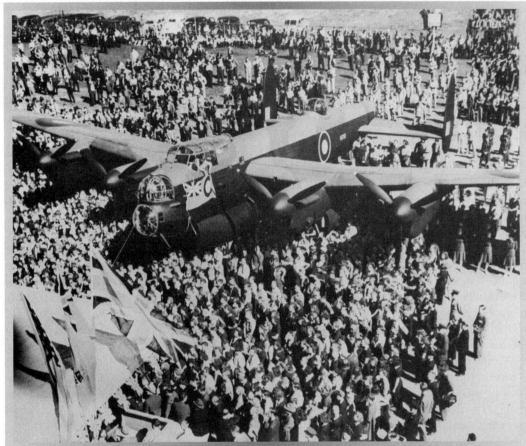

The first Avro Lancaster bomber emerges from Victory Aircraft's Malton plant in Toronto on 1 August 1943. In the 1950s Avro became, for a time, Canada's 'chosen instrument' in aircraft manufacturing, culminating with the Arrow fighter/interceptor. (Courtesy of the Canadian Aviation Museum, Ottawa)

Although it acquired a firmer foothold in the domestic market in the following decade—by which time even the resurgent Liberals were persuaded of the virtues of 'competition', strengthening the independent regulatory powers of the Air Transport Board in 1967—both major carriers faced pressures from US airlines and from smaller companies seeking to establish regional commuter lines. Nevertheless, CP Air and Air Canada (as TCAL was renamed in 1964) maintained a dominant position in the Canadian market, swallowing up regional competitors

through the 1980s, while the regulatory agency restrained American incursions.[5]

The aircraft manufacturing industry was largely a by-product of World War II. During the 1920s a few companies, mostly British, notably Vickers and De Havilland, had set up Canadian operations, lured by the prospects of providing small bush planes for mining and forestry companies as well as aircraft for the embryonic Royal Canadian Air Force (RCAF). Except for Vickers, briefly in the mid-1920s, none of them established plants to design as well as assemble planes, and there were no domestic engine manufacturers in 1938—by which time many of the existing airframe companies, battered by the Depression, were barely functioning.

As noted earlier, wartime demand not only stimulated production but brought technical and design experts to Canada, again mostly from Britain. Altogether, Canadian manufacturers produced over 16,000 planes, half of them for export, and overhauled another 6,500. Two of the largest plants were set up (or taken over) by the government during the war: a Vickers-run operation near Montreal became Canadair Ltd, producing (American) Douglas DC-4s; the National Steel Car plant at Malton, outside Toronto, was reorganized as Victory Aircraft, one of the largest airplane makers, producing Lancaster bombers. In addition, the Munitions Department joined forces with the National Research Council to form Turbo Research Ltd, which worked with the British developing jet propulsion engines.

While Ralph Bell and others involved in the wartime aircraft program were vigorous proponents of a continued post-war government role in the industry, Howe was initially hostile. By 1945 he had become a partial convert, but believed the preferred route would be to encourage foreign aircraft firms with well-developed design capabilities to establish operations in Canada. To that end, the Canadair plant was leased to a US firm, Electric Boat (later General Dynamics); and Victory Aircraft's assets were turned over to Hawker-Siddeley Group, the British company that had developed the Lancaster, which set up a subsidiary, A.V. Roe (Avro) Canada in 1945. As inducements, the Canadian government offered generous rental-purchase terms and the prospect of contracts to build planes for the RCAF and TCAL. In 1946, Avro was allocated Turbo Research Ltd, with the understanding that it would continue work to develop an 'all-Canadian' jet engine; Avro's British chief, Sir Roy Dobson, brought a number of airframe designers and engineers across the Atlantic to demonstrate Hawker-Siddeley's commitment.[6]

In effect, Howe set up Canadair and Avro as competitors for military and civilian contracts, envisioning a symbiotic relationship between Canada's public air carriers and the aircraft manufacturers that would put Canada in the forefront of developing jet airplanes, perhaps even ahead of the British and the Americans. These hopes proved premature: Avro developed a commercial jet transport, the Jetliner, in 1948–9, but had to use a British-made engine, and was unable to satisfy TCAL's requirements. The airline ordered less advanced modified DC-4s from Canadair, and Howe's Reconstruction Department wound up absorbing the costs of the Jetliner, which was never brought into commercial production.

Avro was successful in developing a jet engine, the Orenda, in 1949, to be introduced in a military fighter plane, the CF-100, for the RCAF. With the coming of the Korean War, pressure mounted on Avro and other aircraft builders to step up production. Defects and production-line problems led Howe to push Hawker-Siddeley to bring in one of his proteges, Crawford Gordon, to take over running the Canadian operation. A hard-driving, abrasive figure in the Howe mould, Gordon strong-armed production increases and even managed to export some CF-100s to Belgium, although the total costs of development and production, over $700 million, significantly exceeded initial estimates (a difference ranging from $200 to $350 million, depending on accounting methods). This was hardly a unique situation in the history of military aircraft, but it was one the government was hard-pressed to defend as the atmosphere of crisis cooled following the end of the Korean War.

The Korean conflict had stimulated a mini-boom in the Canadian aircraft industry as other companies, still mostly British, flocked to Canada, concentrating largely in southern Ontario. The largest of these operations, after Avro and Canadair, was De Havilland, which expanded its Canadian production and transferred research and design capabilities as well, wisely choosing to focus on smaller planes such as the Beaver and the Otter, suitable for short-range flights and wilderness conditions that required takeoff and landing on water or small airstrips.

Even before the CF-100s were rolling off the line, the RCAF was laying plans for a more advanced fighter-interceptor, intended to counter the threat of Soviet long-range bombers. Despite the Jetliner fiasco and Howe's skepticism about the managerial capabilities of Avro, the company received favoured treatment as Canada's 'chosen instrument' for developing this new aircraft. In 1954 Avro submitted a proposal for the CF-105 (the Arrow), with an 'all-Canadian' engine, the Iroquois, at a projected cost of $118 million for 40 planes. From the outset, however, the Arrow was plagued with problems. Alarmed by rising costs, the DDP cut back on its initial production commitments, which raised the unit costs. The RCAF was dissatisfied with the initial weapons control system, and Avro had to redesign the plane to accommodate a more advanced alternative. When the US Navy cancelled a missile program that Avro planned to use, the Canadian government decided to have the company take over development of this element as well. By 1957 the Arrow project had cost $146 million but Avro was still working on a prototype. To offset costs, both the company and the government looked abroad for buyers, but in vain.

At this point the Liberal government was defeated after more than 20 years in power. The new regime of John Diefenbaker was confronted with new cost estimates by DDP indicating that the Arrow would cost over $800 million to bring to full production. On the other hand, cancellation would devastate the economy of southern Ontario, where thousands of subcontractors depended on a continued flow of public funds to Avro. Meanwhile, the Soviet Sputnik seemed to signal the end of the era of manned bombers, which the Arrow was supposed to counteract. After some dithering, Diefenbaker cancelled the project early in 1959.

Defenders of the Arrow, then and later, denounced this decision, arguing that it effectively destroyed the nascent Canadian aircraft industry, demonstrating a lack of faith in Canada's technological potential. The Arrow was a state-of-the-art plane, and its escalating costs were the result of government vacillation and interference with the program. Critics have maintained that the Arrow project was simply too big and expensive for a country of Canada's size to handle. Conclusions about Avro vary: the most charitable view is that it was a victim of circumstance, its reach exceeding its grasp; alternatively, the company is portrayed as a gathering of buccaneering opportunists, squandering public funds on technological white elephants. In many respects the Arrow controversy resembles the debate over Canadian Northern Railway, another project whose unhappy fate was shaped by changes in political as well as economic conditions.

The main beneficiaries of the Arrow debacle were foreigners. Many of the technical personnel from Avro migrated to the US to work in their aerospace industry. In 1961 the RCAF replaced the CF-100s with aircraft produced by General Dynamics; ironically, this arrangement paved the way for a US–Canadian Defense Purchase Sharing Agreement in 1963, which helped pry open the US military procurement market for Canadian manufacturers on a long-term basis. Meanwhile, Avro's British parent, Hawker-Siddeley, survived the Arrow cancellation reasonably well. Beginning in 1955, Dobson and Gordon had embarked on a diversification strategy, exploiting investor enthusiasm over Avro's high profile as Canada's major military contractor. Within two years Avro acquired Canadian Car & Foundry and a significant share in Algoma Steel and, in 1957, swallowed up Dosco, making it for a brief period the third largest company in Canada. By this time almost half the earnings of Hawker-Siddeley came from its Canadian subsidiary. Diversification cushioned the shock of the Arrow and other cancellations of military aircraft by the British government at the same time. Dosco eventually proved to be a burden on the company (renamed Hawker-Siddeley in Canada in 1962), which dumped it in the laps of the Canadian and Nova Scotian governments in 1967.[7]

While the Avro drama was unfolding, another less-heralded but equally significant initiative wound its way through the corridors of military and business bureaucracies in the 1950s. During World War II, scientists in the US and UK had developed cumbersome but effective electronic computing devices to help deal with complex calculations involved in using increasingly technical weaponry: the British had broken elaborate German military codes, and in the US, the first electronic computer, ENIAC, was used to handle ballistics measurements for the US Army. After the war the inventors of ENIAC set up a commercial enterprise to market their computer, christened UNIVAC. Within a short period of time, a number of other companies emerged on both sides of the Atlantic, marketing large main-frame computers, principally to government agencies, but also to big firms in fields such as railways and insurance that had to manage vast quantities of data.

In Canada, early interest in computers centred in the Defence Research Board (DRB), an inter-service agency set up in 1947 and intended at least in part to circumvent the competition for technology and resources that characterized the US military. Although the issue of computer capability was not the highest priority for the DRB, Canada's lack of access to computers in the late 1940s led to an effort to develop a 'made-in-Canada' machine at the University of Toronto under the leadership of Josef Kates, an Austrian refugee like Hans von Halban, who was involved in Canada's early nuclear testing at Chalk River, Ontario (see box, p. 139). Kates, however, was considerably younger—he was still a graduate student when the project began.

Meanwhile, the Royal Canadian Navy had been pursuing a separate project (called DATAR—Digital Automated Tracking and Resolving), based on its experience with transatlantic convoys in World War II, that sought to employ computer technology to assist in future anti-submarine warfare. In 1948 the DRB awarded the contract

for development to Ferranti-Canada, subsidiary of the British electrical equipment firm, Ferranti, which had decided to move into electronics after World War II.

The Ferranti-Canada contract soon had an impact on the University of Toronto (UTEC) project after the head of Ferranti UK, Sir Vivian Bowden, persuaded W.B. Lewis, the Director of Research of Canada's atomic energy program at Chalk River, to consider adopting a Ferranti machine. Lewis was backed by C.J. Mackenzie, the powerful head of the National Research Council, and in 1952 UTEC was cancelled. After the cancellation of UTEC, Kates and others who had worked on the project became the first generation of Canada's computer technologists: in 1953, Kates designed a computerized seat-selection program for TCAL, and subsequently set up systems for traffic monitoring and scheduling for public transit in a number of cities in Canada and the United States.

For a few years in the mid-1950s the Ferranti-developed DATAR system provided Canada with a lead over other countries in the field of automated electronic naval warfare, paralleling in certain respects Avro's bid for technological leadership in the aircraft industry. But, like Avro, Ferranti-Canada needed a wider client base, and by 1955 both the US and British navies were looking to their own suppliers; and—another similarity—both the Canadian government and Ferranti were finding the transition from prototype to full-scale production of DATAR to be technically and financially challenging. In 1956, when the government cut plans to increase its fleet of destroyers, the DATAR project also died. As its historian, John Vardalas, concluded: 'Unlike the Avro Arrow, which went out with a bang, DATAR died with not even a whimper, and along with it went the RCN's flirtation with military self-reliance.'[8]

Despite their breezy self-confidence, Canada's political elite and their business allies left behind a rather mixed legacy. Their ventures into high technology benefited a small cadre of scientists and engineers and enriched foreigners—even the feckless British—at public expense. The stockpiling bonanza resulted in what some critics have characterized as rapacious exploitation of the nation's resources and environment. Even before the end of the 1950s, Canadian nationalists were expressing concern over the extent to which defence, trade, and investment policies were carrying the country into America's political and economic orbit—and these complaints grew in volume over the next decade as the US became mired in an unpopular war in Southeast Asia. At the same time, the Cold War era was a period of unprecedented prosperity for Canada, produced a new crop of millionaires (some of whom linked their fortunes to government largesse), and encouraged provincial governments to emulate what seemed to be effective techniques for promoting economic development, combining government 'planning' with foreign investment.

CHAPTER 9

Province Builders

The Depression, World War II, and the Cold War not only extended the role of government in the Canadian economy but also enhanced the power of the central state. In the 1930s the virtual bankruptcy of many provinces in Canada pushed a somewhat reluctant federal government into areas hitherto regarded as largely or exclusively provincial responsibilities; financial arrangements made during and after the war confirmed this shift. By the 1960s and 1970s, however, the centralizing trend was beginning to be challenged, reflecting changes in economic circumstances as well as political perceptions.

The post-war era's resource boom in the oil and gas industry, mining, and forestry provided provincial leaders, especially in the West, with a renewed confidence in the future, and rekindled traditional resentments against a federal government perceived as dominated by central Canadian interests. In the business community, regionally based entrepreneurs and branches of foreign-owned multinational resource companies—neither of which had close ties with central Canada's established financial and manufacturing elites—felt similar antagonism. Both regional entrepreneurs and multinationals were prepared to turn to provincial governments for various forms of promotional assistance as well as defensive actions against regulatory initiatives emanating from Ottawa. At the same time, they were equally willing to take advantage of federal programs that worked to their benefit. Federal–provincial disputes over revenue-sharing and resource control that came to a head in the 1970s and early 1980s reflected these various divisions and cross-currents.

Provincial governments' actions on behalf of their business constituents were entrenched in the Canadian political environment. Since the 1890s, Ontario and, to a lesser extent, Quebec had built railways, offered subsidies, and used regulatory powers to boost local economic growth; the western provinces had also followed this path, albeit on a smaller scale. What was new in the post-World War II era was the extent to which provincial governments went about these activities in a deliberate and conscious fashion. At the federal level the C.D. Howe approach to economic development, blending traditional promotional techniques and Crown corporations, provided a model of sorts, although this was not the only source of inspiration for aspiring province-builders. In its prairie stronghold the Co-operative Commonwealth Federation (CCF) experimented with social planning, eventually moderating its more ambitious visions and adopting a more conventional mix of government activism and incentives for private enterprise. In Quebec after 1960, French-Canadian nationalists followed a unique course,

TABLE 9.1
CANADA'S 20 LEADING NON-FINANCIAL CORPORATIONS, 1955 AND 1980

Rank by Assets 1955	Rank by Sales 1955	Rank by Assets 1980	Rank by Sales 1980
1. Canadian Pacific	6	1. Canadian Pacific	2
2. Bell Canada	15	2. Bell Canada	6
3. Alcan	11	3. Alcan	7
4. Imperial Oil	3	4. Inco	12
5. Inco	7	5. Imperial Oil	4
6. Seagram's	2	6. Noranda	17
7. BC Power	n/a	7. Gulf of Canada	11
8. Shawinigan Power	n/a	8. Massey-Ferguson	8
9. British-American Oil	13	9. Alberta Gas Trunk Line	n/a
10. Interprov. Pipeline	n/a	10. Dome Petroleum	n/a
11. Massey-Harris	12	11. Shell Canada	9
12. Hiram Walker	10	12. Seagram's	n/a
13. Stelco	18	13. Hudson's Bay	10
14. General Motors	1	14. Trans-Canada Pipe Line	16
15. Cominco	n/a	15. Stelco	n/a
16. International Paper	16	16. Genstar	n/a
17. Ford Motor Co.	9	17. Anglo-Canadian Telephone	n/a
18. Imperial Tobacco	n/a	18. Ford Motor Co.	3
19. Abitibi Paper	n/a	19. Texaco Canada	13
20. MacMillan-Bloedel	n/a	20. General Motors	1

Note: Excludes Crown corporations.

deploying government policies to strengthen and diversify the provincial economy, but with the specific objective to promote the growth of a francophone business elite.

Deliberate province-building through government action had many of the same pitfalls as government-directed economic development at the national level. Targeted industries that flourished under government largesse withered when forced to face the rigours of the market. Ambitious megaprojects proved to be ill-conceived or poorly timed, conveying only their debts to future

TABLE 9.2
CANADA'S 30 LEADING NON-FINANCIAL CORPORATIONS,
BY SALES AND SECTOR

Sector	% of Total 1955	% of Total 1980
Utilities*	6	10
Manufacturing	46	27
Mining & Forestry	16	10
Oil & Gas	13	16
Other	19	37

*Includes railways. By 1980, two of the companies in this category (CPR, Bell Canada) could be classified as 'diversified' companies rather than simply utilities, which would raise the 'other' category to 44 per cent.

Sources: Elizabeth Trott, 'The Top 30 Canadian Corporations', *Monetary Times* 125 (Apr. 1957): 34–6; *Canadian Business Magazine* 53, 27 (July 1980): 63–4.

generations of taxpayers. Opportunistic business promoters and patronage-seeking politicians distorted the direction of government projects.

Underlying these problems was the circumstance that few provinces had the necessary resources or degree of control over their economic environment to carry out consistent and effective long-term development programs. These weaknesses were particularly apparent in the economically disadvantaged provinces of Atlantic Canada, where one government project after another foundered, even when reinforced with aid from a procession of federally financed regional development programs. Even the stronger provinces (and, for that matter, the federal government) had their share of white elephants and disasters, and while governments became more actively involved in creating and shoring up business ventures in the years following World War II, many companies in the private sector continued to thrive and new large players appeared, particularly in the petroleum sector after the oil crisis of the early 1970s (see Tables 9.1 and 9.2). By the 1980s there was a growing appreciation—by no means restricted to the business community or to Canada—of the difficulty governments at any level face when seeking to direct or control events in an unpredictable and changing market system.

THE RISE OF THE WEST

'The West must pay tribute to the East', the aspiring young financier, James Dunn, told his erstwhile New Brunswick colleague, Max Aitken, while the two of them were briefly domiciled in Calgary around 1900, 'and I'm off to the East to collect tribute.' This probably apocryphal remark neatly summarized the tensions many westerners perceived between their region and the emerging business elite of central Canada. Western antagonism towards the chartered banks, the CPR, and their political henchmen in Ottawa spawned not only political protest movements but also regionally supported ventures such as the Canadian Northern Railway and the elevator and grain-marketing co-operatives.

The early history of Confederation had left a curiously mixed legacy. A perpetual sense of regional grievance, never far below the surface, combined with recognition by the West's political and business leaders of their ultimate economic dependence, was never more apparent than in the disastrous decade of the Great Depression. Traditions of labour militancy and agrarian unrest that produced the Progressives and the CCF existed alongside (and not infrequently at odds with) a strong regional entrepreneurial bent and 'open-door' attitudes towards foreign, especially American, investment. All of these patterns shaped western Canadians' response to the opportunities presented by a renewed demand for the region's resources after World War II.

The post-war resource boom encompassed the established forestry and mining sectors as well as such new fields as uranium in the West and iron ore in Labrador and northern Quebec, but certainly the most dramatic developments occurred in the oil and gas industry centred in Alberta. In the nineteenth century, Canada's only producing oil fields were in southwestern Ontario, although as early as 1719 explorers had noted the presence of petroleum deposits in the West, and in 1788 Peter Pond of the North West Company had come across the massive tar sands of the Athabasca River region. A century later the Geological Survey of Canada began mapping the resource potential of what was to become Alberta.

In its early years, however, southern Alberta witnessed the growth of the ranching industry, with significant input from south of the border. Even before the establishment of the province, an American-born entrepreneur, Isaac G. Baker, had entered the region, diversifying from trading in buffalo hides into cattle ranching, later setting up a general store in the burgeoning town of Calgary and investing in real estate and local banks. Baker's success attracted other aspiring ranchers to the region, including British (mostly absentee) investors and Canadians such as Matthew Cochrane of Montreal, a political associate of John A. Macdonald. The Macdonald government encouraged ranching by providing generous long-term leases of public lands for grazing, and the industry thrived, despite setbacks such as the brutal winter of 1886–7 that killed much livestock. Ranching

was to have a lasting impact on the business culture of the region, exemplified by the Calgary Stampede, first held in 1912.

Shortly before World War I, rumours of oil stimulated a mini-boom in Alberta after a local rancher, William S. Herron, discovered natural gas and light oil in the Turner Valley south of Calgary. Prospectors and promoters flocked to the region in 1913–14, but the Turner Valley proved to be more productive of stock swindles than commercial petroleum and the boom collapsed fairly quickly. Herron's enterprise, Calgary Petroleum Products, with the backing of prominent local business figures such as Senator James Lougheed and R.B. Bennett, prospered for a time but after a refinery fire in 1920 the company passed into the hands of Imperial Oil, whose subsidiary, Royalite, was the major producer in the area through the ensuing decade.

The pre-war debacle did not, however, deter other entrepreneurs from prospecting in the region. In 1926, 'Major' Jim Lowery, a peripatetic Calgary businessman and sometime politician, cobbled together Home Oil Co. with financial support from Vancouver investors, benefiting from the buoyant stock market of the late 1920s. The Depression, dry wells, and a global oil glut in the early 1930s dampened Home Oil's future but the company diversified into gold mining in British Columbia to keep afloat. Another Calgarian, R.A. Brown, who ran the city's tramway and lighting systems, also entered the oil business, supporting his activities in the Depression by borrowing from Imperial and from British–American Oil Co., and introducing a scheme known as 'royalties financing' in which investors purchased direct shares in the revenues of producing wells. Brown's venture, Turner Valley Royalties, began full-scale production in 1936, which lured Home Oil back to the region. A third entrepreneur, Frank McMahon from BC, entered the Alberta fields in the mid-1930s, establishing Pacific Petroleums Ltd, which made a modest strike near Brown's wells in 1938.

Although by the end of the 1930s Royalite and independent production made Alberta self-

Waiting for Leduc No. 1 to blow in, 13 February 1947—the beginning of a new 'oil era' in western Canada. (Provincial Archives of Alberta/P.2733)

sufficient in oil and gas, the big strike anticipated since 1914 proved elusive. As World War II ended both Imperial and Shell Canada stepped up exploratory work in the West, and Imperial's Leduc and Redwater finds near Edmonton in 1947–8 ushered in Alberta's 'age of oil'. Imperial's success brought other major companies into the region and rekindled investor enthusiasm in the smaller ventures as well. The Pembina field, discovered in the early 1950s, had proved resources of oil 10 times the size of Leduc, which had in turn dwarfed the Turner Valley. By the mid-1950s the recoverable reserves of Alberta oil were reckoned to exceed 3.6 billion barrels, with the more remote fields of the north and the tar sands as yet untapped. Natural gas reserves were estimated at over 11 trillion cubic feet, equivalent to about 2 billion barrels of oil.

As in the turn-of-the-century mining industry in Ontario, the Alberta oil patch included both large-scale multinational firms and smaller independents of both Canadian and American vintage. Inevitably, the 'majors' dominated the field. The most significant new finds of the 1940s and 1950s were developed by these big companies, so that by the end of the following decade almost half of the province's crude oil production was accounted for by five firms: Imperial, Shell, Texaco, Gulf, and British Petroleum. All were linked into global corporate networks that integrated production, transportation, refining, and marketing. Most of the independents operated at the production end of the industry, although several branched further afield. The Hudson's Bay Company resurrected its interest in its joint oil and gas venture with the US firm, Continental Oil, in the 1940s, and earnings from this source helped carry the firm through its transition into retailing. In 1949, Pacific Petroleums set up a subsidiary, Westcoast Transmission, to pipe natural gas from northern Alberta to Vancouver and—after years of lobbying with US regulatory authorities—to tap into the American west coast market. In 1952, Home Oil passed into the hands of the Brown family of Calgary; under R.A. 'Bobby' Brown Jr, the company expanded rapidly into

pipelines, natural gas ventures overseas in Europe, and an ill-timed move into the Alaska oil fields in the 1960s. A Colorado-based family, the Nielsons, established a mid-sized integrated venture, Husky Oil, which developed its own western Canadian distribution network in the 1970s.

The complex structure of the oil industry helped preserve the role of both the larger independents and the numerous small ventures that sprang up in the wake of Leduc. The Big Five controlled more than one-third of the potentially oil-bearing lands (most of which were on Crown property, leased from the Alberta government), but were willing to farm out their leases to small operators—at a stiff price, to be sure—both to spread the risks involved in exploratory work and to stem political difficulties by fostering the image of an open and competitive industry. Most of the larger firms also subcontracted drilling and supply operations to local companies, encouraging competition to keep costs down. Although relations between the majors and independents were hardly free of strife, an atmosphere of peaceful coexistence rather than Darwinian struggle generally prevailed.

While the subsidiaries of the multinationals were headquartered in Toronto or Montreal, the independents congregated in Calgary, where their shared values and experiences imparted a special regional flavour to the oil and gas industry. Many of these independents saw themselves as self-made men, imbued with a faith in entrepreneurial capitalism despite their dependence on and interconnections with the oil majors; taking a proprietary view of their companies even when these were joint-stock ventures; and sharing the region's anti-eastern, anti-Ottawa sentiments even though they were far removed from both the small-farmer populists and the mercantile-ranching elite who had flourished in Alberta early in the twentieth century. Twenty years after Leduc, the oil industry had spawned a new generation of professional managers and technicians in the service of the multinationals and the larger regional independents, but replicating the 'free enterprise' ideas of their forebears, even as they turned to the provincial government to protect and advance their interests.

The complex and contradictory nature of the oilmen's community was reflected in the politics and policies of Alberta's government. During the 1930s the Social Credit Party had come to power, reflecting western grievances and expounding quasi-populist ideas. But even as he inveighed against the bankers of Bay Street, Premier Aberhart affirmed his party's commitment to support private property rights and business interests, especially in the oil fields. His successor, Ernest Manning, pursued this course through the 1940s and 1950s, welcoming the oil multinationals, balancing the province's need for revenues against the industry's desire for profits, and seeking to smooth over potential conflicts between the majors and the independents. The main areas of government intervention involved the 'pro-rationing' of oil production in Alberta and the issue of natural gas pipelines to markets outside the province.

In 1930, Ottawa transferred control of subsoil resources to the Prairie provinces; and during the mid-1930s intense exploitation of the Turner Valley fields—and competition between Imperial and the independents—aroused fears that these resources would soon be depleted, leaving the Depression-wracked province in perpetual poverty. The result was the creation of Alberta's Oil and Gas Conservation Board in 1938. During its early years the Conservation Board had little impact on the industry, particularly since Imperial Oil refused to adhere to its rulings and the government was reluctant to antagonize the one big company actively engaged in exploration. After Leduc and Redwater, Imperial Oil and the other majors entering the field became more receptive to government regulation, believing that it could stem a threatened production glut and keep small producers from siphoning off potential reserves from lands adjacent to their own leases— a practice that had worked very well for Pacific Petroleums in its early years. The independents, too, were supportive of an allocation system that would ensure them of a share in the field and

protect them from unrestrained competition with the oil giants. In practice, the enforced cartelization of oil production was of most benefit to the majors, particularly in the 1960s when changes in the original allocation formula encouraged production from higher-cost reservoirs. Nevertheless, a majority of oil producers, large and small, continued to endorse the Conservation Board as a mediator of disputes within the industry.

In the early 1950s the subject of natural gas exports, the most explosive political issue facing the Alberta government, encouraged another step towards intervention in the industry. Ottawa (meaning C.D. Howe) was now anxious to promote gas exports abroad to boost the country's trade position; meanwhile private companies, including McMahon's Pacific Petroleums, were lobbying for permits to move gas to the west coast or southward to the American Midwest. Alberta voters, however, treasured this cheap and abundant energy source, and proponents of local industry argued that it must be preserved for economic diversification. In 1949 the provincial government gave the Conservation Board control over natural gas exports with the requirement that long-term supplies for Alberta should be protected. By 1954, Howe was pushing development of the Trans-Canada Pipeline, threatening Alberta with the potential loss of markets in central Canada and the US if it persisted in hoarding its reserves. The province responded by creating Alberta Gas Trunk Line, which would carry all natural gas produced for export. The company was not a Crown corporation, although the province as well as representatives of Alberta's gas producers and utilities held shares in it. Voting shares could not be transferred to investors from outside the province.

Social Credit's interventionist forays had been primarily responses to particular situations. Conservatives who came to power under Peter Lougheed in 1971 pursued a more deliberate course of action, although they, too, preferred to proceed indirectly, relying on incentives to private enterprise to achieve provincial economic goals. Lougheed, grandson of the Calgary capitalist who had helped found Alberta's earliest oil venture, had close ties to the province's oil and mining leaders, most notably the Mannix family whose wealth from construction activities early in the century had created a diversified utilities and mining empire. During the 1960s Lougheed resuscitated the Tories as the political wing of indigenous business and managerial groups anxious to sustain Alberta's prosperity beyond the oil era. Providentially, the energy crisis of the early 1970s provided the new regime with leverage and opportunities to fulfill these ambitions.

Lougheed undertook to reset provincial royalties from oil production on Crown lands above the ceilings established in 1951, and to push domestic oil and gas prices, which were regulated by the National Energy Board, towards rising world price levels. These efforts encountered stiff resistance from the oil majors, some of which threatened to move their operations abroad, and from the federal government, which continually squabbled with Alberta over pricing as well as tax and royalty-sharing arrangements. Despite their frustration over federal–provincial bickering and a forced withdrawal from the more ambitious designs to boost oil revenues, the Alberta government benefited from rising oil prices throughout the decade.

In 1976, Lougheed announced the creation of the Alberta Heritage Fund, which was intended to finance provincial economic diversification; within five years the Fund held over $8.5 billion. An Alberta Energy Company, with the province holding 50 per cent of the shares, was set up to invest in such areas as petrochemicals and tar sands development. Alberta Gas Trunk Line was allowed to move beyond its original role as a common carrier for natural gas. Under the leadership of Bob Blair it emerged as a major player on the western energy scene, outmanoeuvring the major oil companies in the early 1970s in bidding on the Alaska Highway Pipeline, acquiring control of Husky Oil in 1979, and diversifying into petrochemicals and production equipment for the oil and gas industry.

Provincial development was not without pitfalls, most notably in the oil sands. Despite the potential oil wealth, estimated in the hundreds of billions of barrels, buried in bituminous muskeg, the cost of extraction and processing deterred development before the oil price hikes of the 1970s. A decade before, the American independent, Sun Oil, had begun pouring $130 million into a small project, Great Canadian Oil Sands near Fort McMurray; it operated with continuous deficits until 1975 and kept going only through the steadfast commitment of Sun's owner, J. Howard Pew, to 'North American energy independence'. Despite this ominous precedent, in 1973 the Alberta government joined a consortium of four US major oil companies, including Imperial, to develop the Syncrude Project, which anticipated an ultimate output four or five times that of Great Canadian Oil Sands, at a cost of $1 billion. Within a year, Syncrude was floundering as projected costs soared to twice the original estimate, and one of the partners pulled out. To avert disaster, Alberta brought the Canadian and Ontario governments on board and made substantial royalty concessions to the remaining corporate participants. Syncrude lurched on, but the collapse of oil prices in the 1980s reinforced doubts about its long-term commercial viability.

The end of the oil boom ended much of Alberta's enthusiasm for province-building. To keep the oil industry from shutting down, the government renegotiated royalty arrangements and issued new incentives. The disposition of the Heritage Fund was increasingly controversial. Whether industrial diversification, even into an area such as petrochemicals, was a realistic policy began to be questioned, given the province's isolation from prospective markets. Although Alberta remained a resource-rich and comparatively wealthy province, the 1980s marked the apparent end of more than 30 years of oil-stimulated growth and the confidence it fostered in Alberta's business and political leaders.

The post-World War II oil boom spilled over into neighbouring Saskatchewan, which also benefited from discoveries of potash, a major raw material in chemical fertilizers, in the 1940s. The Great Depression and the dust storms of the 1930s had hit Saskatchewan even harder than Alberta, and that experience, combined with a strong agrarian populist heritage, brought the CCF to power in 1944. The party was to remain in government for 20 years. Saskatchewan harboured virtually no mining or oil entrepreneurial elements, and so the socialist government might have been expected to adopt a resolutely interventionist approach towards these industries. The failure of early experiments with Crown enterprises in other fields tempered the enthusiasm of provincial leaders for pursuing this course. Instead, the CCF focused its attention on social policies while encouraging private development of its resource industries.

In the potash industry a major investor was the American-based International Minerals & Chemicals Co., which established the world's largest potash mine near Esterhazy, Saskatchewan, in the early 1960s. Other multinationals, British and German as well as American, held the major share of this market; Noranda entered the field through a joint venture with an Ontario co-operative, Central Canada Potash. Imperial Oil was initially cool towards development in socialist Saskatchewan. Independents such as Husky Oil, which began exploratory work there in the 1940s, were joined eventually by Imperial's former satellite, Royalite Oil (which was sold to Canadian investors in 1949), and Saskatchewan became a base for Royalite's western distribution network.

The CCF government was overturned in 1964 by a rejuvenated, business-oriented Liberal Party under Ross Thatcher, who essentially continued the pattern of encouraging foreign investment in the resource sector while seeking to dismantle other elements of the CCF program. The sudden collapse of the potash boom at the end of the decade—reflecting a slump in agriculture that also struck the farm implement firm, Massey-Ferguson, in the midst of a major international expansionary thrust—brought the CCF, now

recycled as the New Democratic Party, back to power. The new regime under Allan Blakeney adopted a far more interventionist policy towards the resource industries, reflecting in part a growing anti-American, anti-foreign investment sentiment in Canada as well as a modest resurgence of populism in the beleaguered farming community.

In 1975, after several years of bickering with the multinationals in the fertilizer field over royalties and taxes, the NDP government created the Potash Corporation of Saskatchewan (PCS) and proceeded to acquire a 40 per cent share of the industry in the province. The PCS integrated forward into marketing, setting up sales branches in the US and pursuing markets overseas, relying on its base as a producer of almost one-quarter of the world's potash output in the early 1980s. Meanwhile, in the oil and gas industry, Saskatchewan formed a somewhat incongruous alliance with Alberta to resist federal incursions in the 1970s. As in the case of Alberta, the Saskatchewan government, despite gestures towards economic diversification and the establishment of a Heritage Fund, became increasingly tied to the fortunes of the province's resource sector and vulnerable to the downswing in raw material prices in the 1980s. In 1989 the Progressive Conservative provincial government privatized the Potash Corporation.

An exception to this generalization, however, was the history of Ipsco. In 1956, in the Tommy Douglas years, the Saskatchewan government provided support for the Prairie Pipe Manufacturing Co., a private company founded by a Texan, Bill Sharp, which proposed to supply steel casings and pipes for the province's publicly owned power corporation. In the 1960s Prairie Pipe expanded by taking over a 'mini-mill' using electric arc technology in place of the traditional open-hearth processes used by the major steel companies. Within 20 years the Interprovincial Pipe & Steel Co. (Ipsco) emerged as one of the foremost steel producers in Canada at a time when established companies such as Stelco and Algoma were facing technological obsolescence and declining markets. In the 1990s Ipsco expanded into the United States. By this time, the provincial investment in the company had been phased out, but Ipsco was long regarded by prairie populists as an example of successful public–private partnership. In 2007, Ipsco was acquired by a Swedish steel company, Svenskt Stal AB.[1]

A resource-based strategy of province-building characterized the development of both leftward-leaning Saskatchewan and conservative Alberta during this era. In British Columbia, a similar pattern emerged: the Social Credit dynasty of the Bennetts, which controlled the province's political affairs with only one brief interruption between 1952 and the end of the 1980s, vigorously pursued pro-business (and particularly pro-foreign investment) policies, punctuated by forays into interventionism. The BC government was somewhat more successful than those of the Prairie provinces in promoting diversification, particularly in the financial and service sectors, although the heart of the province's economy continued to be in the forestry and mining industries.

Even before World War II, the province's mines and lumber producers were beginning to recover from the worst ravages of the Depression, and the post-war era witnessed a dramatic expansion of capacity and technological change in both industries. New uses for pulpwood in synthetic fibres, film, plastics, and other products—and a revitalized construction industry—widened the market for wood products, while chainsaws, automated chippers, and waste recovery techniques improved productivity. In 1947 the province introduced a system of forestry management licensing intended to encourage sustained yield production through controlled harvesting and tree farming, and opened up the large reserves of the northwest coast and the interior. American multinationals such as Weyerhaeuser, Celanese Corporation, and Crown Zellerbach entered the province to exploit these new opportunities. At the same time, domestic producers expanded and consolidated. H.R. MacMillan merged his company with another large lumber firm,

Bloedel, Stuart & Welsh, in 1951, and then took over the Powell River Co., the largest newsprint producer in the region. MacMillan also joined the Ontario conglomerate, E.P. Taylor, in setting up BC Forest Products Ltd, which scattered company mill towns across the hinterlands of the province. From its BC base, MacMillan-Bloedel transformed itself in the 1960s into a multinational with investments in US lumber mills, paper and box manufacturing in Europe, and similar ventures in Latin America and the Pacific archipelagos.

In the mining field, Alcan established a smelter at Kitimat while Cominco continued to exploit its holdings at Trail. Cominco also diversified into steel and chemicals, and went the multinational route in the 1960s, principally through joint ventures in India, Australia, and Japan. Japan in particular became a major market for BC minerals. Output of all minerals (plus, by the 1960s, some oil and gas) increased 10 times over by value between 1950 and 1975, and more than doubled again in the following decade.

In its early stages the post-war resource boom in BC centred on the developed areas of the southwest coast. Transportation links into the northern coast and interior were few, and near-frontier conditions prevailed. The opening of the interior was largely the result of measures taken by the government of W.A.C. 'Wacky' Bennett. The New Brunswick-born hardware store owner in the Okanagan Valley led an insurgent Social Credit Party, which drew its strength from hinterland farmers, migrants from the prairies during the Depression and World War II. In the 1950s and 1960s Bennett made development of the neglected backcountry the heart of his economic policies. His rhetorical populism, like that of Aberhart and Manning in Alberta, was joined with vigorously pro-business attitudes apparent in his promotion of consolidation and foreign investment in the resource industries and his strident hostility towards labour unions, which by the 1960s formed the nucleus of his main political opposition, the NDP. But Bennett's version of free enterprise embraced a willingness to resort to government activism, displayed particularly in the takeover of the province's ferry system in 1958 and of the utility industry three years later.

The 'provincialization' of the electric power system was an outgrowth of Bennett's desire to open up the interior for development. In 1957, Axel Wenner-Gren, a Swedish promoter whose international business empire included the Electrolux vacuum-cleaner company and a variety of banking and industrial projects in Latin America, unveiled before the receptive Premier a scheme to develop a massive hydroelectric dam on the Peace River in northeastern BC. This undertaking clashed, however, with a federal government initiative to reach an agreement with the Americans on the border-straddling Columbia River. Under the 1961 Columbia River Treaty, Canada would build storage dams in BC, with the US guaranteeing that 50 per cent of the electric power generated in Washington state from the Columbia would be returned to Canada. Since Wenner-Gren's (and Bennett's) scheme was based on supplying BC's power needs from the Peace, Bennett opposed the treaty, proposing instead that electric power should be developed on the Canadian side of the Columbia River for export to the United States.

In the 1960 provincial election the CCF/NDP had advocated a government takeover of BC Electric. Bennett skirted the issue, focusing on alleged 'communist' influences in the trade unions and the opposition party. But soon after his party's re-election, he proceeded to follow precisely this course, taking over both BC Electric and BC Power, and establishing the BC Hydro & Power Authority. Bennett's venture into socialism related directly to the convoluted Columbia/Peace River situation. BC Electric had refused to agree to purchase power from the Peace River project (which was set up as a 'mixed' enterprise, with the Wenner-Gren group in a minority position), leading Bennett to conclude that the utility planned to draw its power needs from the US under the proposed Columbia River Treaty. Once the private utilities were in his control, Bennett focused his wrath on the federal

government, summoning up ancient regional grievances against Ottawa. Faced with American threats that the entire treaty might be scrapped, the federal government gave in to Bennett. In 1963 it agreed to revisions under which the Columbia River power developed in BC would be exported to the US, and the proceeds would be used by BC Hydro & Power to finance the Peace River project, completed in 1967 as—of course—the Bennett Dam. Canadian nationalists fumed over this 'giveaway' of the nation's resources, but Bennett solidified his political position at home and relied on Peace River power to attract industries (mostly pulp processors) into the province's hinterland.

Despite the sustained post-war boom, BC's economy remained dependent on raw materials extraction for export markets, and sluggish demand in the early 1970s, combined with growing dissatisfaction in Vancouver over Bennett's hinterland preoccupations, brought the NDP temporarily to power. Political misjudgements by the NDP and rising inflation after the energy crisis of 1973, however, helped Social Credit rebound under W.A.C.'s son, Bill Bennett. Although renewed growth in the resource industry markets enabled the Socred regime to stay in power for more than a decade and a half, exploiting bitter labour–business and urban–rural divisions at election time, the problem of long-term economic diversification began to loom larger in the 1980s.

During this period trade links with the Far East, especially Japan, were extended, augmented by an influx of both people and money from Hong Kong, which faced absorption into mainland China at the end of the century. The benefits of this migration centred primarily in the financial and service sectors of Vancouver, although Japanese companies such as Mitsubishi invested in BC mines and fisheries. Fluctuations in resource export markets—forestry products in particular, which were also affected by American protectionist measures both before and after the Canada–US Free Trade Agreement, which came into effect in 1989—eroded many of the economic gains from earlier decades in the province's hinterland. The diverging paths of business in metropolitan Vancouver and the interior, punctuated by debates over environmental controls in the resource industries, perpetuated a tradition of political and economic division in the province that had been muted during the decades of growth and prosperity after World War II.[2]

'MAÎTRES CHEZ NOUS'

French-Canadian nationalism was a staple element in nineteenth-century Quebec politics, and the province's political leaders of all persuasions had been emulating Ontario's promotional policies since the early 1900s. After World War II these two traditions began to converge, and from 1960 on a formidable array of ambitious francophone business people, politicians, and policy-oriented intellectuals set out to use the power of the state to advance their position in the provincial economy and to strengthen and diversify its industrial base. While the French-Canadian business community was divided over the question of Quebec separatism, there was a broad consensus on the benefits accruing from government intervention on behalf of their economic and cultural interests.

Although there is a lingering popular notion that French Canadians traditionally avoided or were excluded from commercial pursuits, numerous francophone businesses did operate throughout the nineteenth and early twentieth centuries. As noted in earlier chapters, French private banks established networks across Quebec and the Maritimes and financiers such as Louis J. Forget and F.L. Beique emerged as millionaires in the early 1900s. Louis-Adélard Senécal built a diversified industrial empire by reinvesting profits from railway speculation, and entrepreneurs such as the Montreal book publisher Jean Baptiste Rolland and the banker J.E.A. Dubuc ventured into the pulp and paper industry in the late nineteenth century. Despite its reputation for hostility towards industrial and commercial development,

the Catholic hierarchy in Quebec endorsed the efforts of the caisses populaires to promote manufacturing enterprises in rural communities in the early 1900s.

Historians of Quebec such as Paul-André Linteau have argued that for the most part these francophone businesses functioned on a relatively small scale: usually proprietary in nature, they served local markets and lacked the capital necessary to embark on larger, technologically advanced operations. During the merger era of 1909–29 many of these enterprises were absorbed into consolidations dominated by Anglo-Canadian capitalists in Montreal or were isolated in hinterland markets. The Great Depression hurt large and small firms alike but struck the smaller proprietary enterprises with particular force and reinforced the pattern of anglophone domination of the province's major industries: textiles, newsprint, metal mining, and banking.

Maurice Duplessis, who dominated the political scene and was Premier of Quebec through much of the period from the mid-1930s to 1959, seemingly did little to reverse this process. Duplessis and his party, the Union Nationale, cultivated French-Canadian voters and espoused Quebec's autonomy in its relations with Ottawa; his critics maintained that his policies encouraged a massive expansion of foreign direct investment in the province after World War II, generating economic growth but ignoring indigenous francophone business interests. Among the largest of the new investors was the Iron Ore Co. of Canada, a consortium of American steel producers and Ontario-based mining firms brought together by M.A. Hanna of Cleveland, Ohio, in 1949 to exploit the iron reserves of the Ungava region on the Quebec–Labrador border. Duplessis, his opponents charged, had negotiated a generous royalty arrangement with the Iron Ore Co. in return for under-the-table contributions to the Union Nationale. Equally controversial were Duplessis's repressive labour policies, highlighted by government action to break a strike in 1949 against American-owned asbestos companies.

TABLE 9.3

US DIRECT INVESTMENT IN CANADIAN INDUSTRY, 1929–77
(US-OWNED ASSETS AS % OF TOTAL ASSETS)

Industry	1929 (%)	1954 (%)	1967 (%)	1977 (%)
Manufacturing	30	41	45	42
Mining	32	49	56	40
Oil & Gas	n/a	67	60	51
Utilities*	23	9	7	5
All Industries	15	24	28	24

*Includes railway investments.

Sources: *Foreign Direct Investment in Canada* (Ottawa, 1972), 20–1; Jorge Niosi, *Canadian Multinationals*, trans. Robert Chodos (Toronto, 1985), 37.

Table 9.3 shows the extent of US direct investment in Canada from 1929 to 1977.

Conrad Black (in his capacity as biographer of Duplessis rather than as financier-conglomerator) has argued that criticism of Duplessis, in these matters at least, is overstated. There was substantial growth not only in the resource sectors of the economy but also in manufacturing, with output more than doubling between 1944 and 1959. Per-capita income increased by this same magnitude and standards of living improved in general, most notably in Montreal and the new industrial towns. Despite his reputation as a fiscal conservative, social benefits also improved under Duplessis, reducing the traditional role of the Catholic Church. Furthermore, it is fair to say that Duplessis's efforts to attract foreign investors and promote rapid resource development were not noticeably different from those of his predecessors in Quebec or, for that matter, in Ontario earlier in the century.

French-Canadian businesses were by no means quiescent in this period. Although most were found in the fields of financial services and retailing, some ranged further. The Simard family, with earnings from dredging contracts procured through the federal Liberal government in the 1930s, built a diversified shipbuilding and steel-fabricating duchy at their home base of Sorel, carefully keeping on good terms with Duplessis. Another family dynasty, the Vachons, developed a province-wide and then national market for their baked goods between the 1930s and 1960s; their firm eventually passed into the hands of a Quebec Crown corporation, reorganized as Culinar Inc. At the same time the Vachons were beginning to sell their 'Jos. Louis' cakes, a talented mechanic in Valcourt, Armand Bombardier, was developing the snowmobile, originally intended as a kind of all-weather, all-terrain vehicle for rural households in Quebec. Its racier successor, the Ski-Doo, found a larger market as a recreational toy in the 1960s. Another enterprising French Canadian of this era was Charles Trudeau, who began supplementing his earnings as a lawyer in the 1920s by developing a small network of auto rental agencies and gas stations in the Montreal area. When he sold them to Imperial Oil in 1932, he used the profits to amass a fortune on the securities markets. His son Pierre, later Prime Minister of Canada, first entered politics in the 1950s as a vigorous critic of the Duplessis regime.

The example of Pierre Trudeau indicates one of the unintended legacies of Duplessis's development policies. As Quebec's economy grew and diversified in the post-war era, the rural power base of the Union Nationale was undermined. French Canadians moved into the industrial cities, joined by a rising tide of immigrants. Better-educated francophones aspired to move into professional and managerial positions, and they translated their frustrations over the dominance of the Anglo-Canadian and foreign business elite into demands for political change. The Liberal Party in Quebec, moribund since World War II, was resuscitated by leaders like Jean Lesage to become the vehicle for this transformation, and came to power a year after the death of 'Le Chef' in 1959.

The Quebec Liberals were a composite of ambitious French-Canadian professionals, intellectuals, trade unionists, and business people, an inherently unstable alliance. Eventually, they split into factions over issues such as social reform and Quebec separatism, but in the early 1960s the Lesage regime was able to push through the 'Quiet Revolution', a sweeping program of economic as well as social and cultural reforms. Many of the measures of the Quiet Revolution were intended, directly or indirectly, to enhance the position of French-Canadian businesses and thus welded their interests to the fortunes of the Liberal Party in Quebec. Divisions in the Liberal Party led to a Union Nationale return to power in 1966–70; the exodus of left-wing Liberals to the Parti Québécois left the business element as the linchpin of the Liberals when they re-emerged after 1970 under Robert Bourassa.

To a much greater extent than any of the other provincial governments of this era (including the CCF in Saskatchewan), the Lesage regime was prepared to resort to state intervention to achieve its ends. While C.D. Howe's development strategy had some influence, a more significant model was France after World War II with its panoply of nationalized industries and technocratic planning structures. At the same time, there were limits to this ambitious interventionism. As in the case of the western provinces, Quebec ultimately had to confront the natural limits of its financial resources, as well as the province's ties to Ottawa and the national economy. In addition, francophone business leaders aspired to operate in national and international markets, and the Quebec government had to balance its provincial development orientation against these aspirations. The presence of large foreign-owned corporations in both the resource and manufacturing sectors also inhibited the manoeuvres of Quebec's government planners; although reduction of foreign control was an objective of the Quiet Revolution, it was necessary to balance this goal against the need to stimulate employment and maintain tax revenues. Government policies in the 1960s and 1970s strengthened the position of francophone businesses, particularly in the construction industry and financial services. Nevertheless, the foreign presence in mining increased significantly in this period, and in 1978 almost half the province's largest manufacturing firms were linked to multinationals.

Crown corporations or mixed public–private enterprises provided one mechanism for province-building in Quebec, although (as in other provinces) results often fell short of expectations. In 1962 the province set up the Société Générale de Financement (SGF) as a provider of seed capital for new industrial ventures. The SGF included private financial institutions as well as the government and, notably, the caisses populaires; private-sector investors held half the seats on the board of directors, although the government and caisses populaires group generally worked together. The SGF's particular mandate was to develop heavy industry in the province while also promoting French-Canadian enterprises.

Initially, the Société hoped to achieve these goals through joint ventures, but over time the role of the government became predominant—the SGF itself became a wholly government-controlled affair after 1972. An early effort to set up an auto industry in partnership with the French firms Peugeot and Renault had disappointing results. An investment in the Simard family's Marine Industries in 1962 quickly took on the appearance of a bail-out rather than a development project, with SGF purchasing majority control of the floundering enterprise for $12 million. Somewhat more successful was Soquem, which undertook mineral exploration and development, but its general financial performance was poor and its role in the industry was limited until the 1980s, when the Quebec government expanded its capital base.

The Lesage government regarded the creation of a steel industry in Quebec as essential to its development program. Here again, however, the search for private partners, considered essential by SGF to guarantee commercial success, proved fruitless. In 1964 the government created a steel enterprise, Sidbec, without resolving the public-versus-private debate. In 1967 Sidbec began operations as a Crown corporation, cobbled together from an assortment of unhealthy enterprises, including Marine Industries and a Quebec mill set up by Dosco, whose British owners—Hawker-Siddeley, Avro's parent company—were anxious to divest themselves of their now-decrepit steel investment. Sidbec limped along, running chronic deficits through 1986, and embarking on an ultimately disastrous iron mining venture, undertaken at least in part as a result of political pressures to create jobs in the north St Lawrence shore region of Quebec. Although the company was able to provide a reliable supply of steel for provincial industries, it did not become the base for heavy industry envisioned by its proponents in the 1960s.

The best-known interventionist measure of the Quiet Revolution was the development of Hydro-Québec as a government-owned utility monopoly, spearheaded by Lesage's Minister of Natural Resources, René Lévesque. French-Canadian spokesmen had long advocated 'nationalization' of the province's utilities, and the Liberal Party during its brief ascendency in Quebec in World War II had taken over the much-hated Montreal Light, Heat & Power, creating Hydro-Québec in 1944. For Lévesque, however, it was essential to 'repatriate' the much larger system operated by Shawinigan Water & Power, which was owned by Power Corporation, a holding company established in 1925 by the investment house of Nesbitt-Thomson.

While other Liberals, including Premier Lesage, initially resisted his idea, quailing at the prospective cost of financing the takeover, Lévesque argued that a publicly owned utility would be shielded from federal taxation—a consideration that had also weighed heavily with BC's Premier W.A.C. Bennett as he embarked on utility provincialization. In addition to making electric service more efficient by reducing duplication and thus controlling power rates, Hydro-Québec could be an instrument for industrial diversification and expansion of service into remote areas of the province. Lesage was eventually persuaded and staged the 1962 re-election campaign on the issue, invoking the slogan, '*maîtres chez nous*'—a battle cry that would resonate for Quebec separatists in later years.

Like Sidbec and other such ventures, Hydro-Québec did not fulfill all the extravagant expectations of its proponents. Despite substantial expansion of capacity, the utility could not cover all the growing energy demands in the province in the 1960s and early 1970s. Nevertheless, it did provide many new technical and managerial opportunities for francophones, and was able to hold the line on rates after the energy crunch of 1973 because it was less dependent than other utilities on oil. Well-managed, with indirect financial support from the Quebec government, Hydro-Québec's bonds achieved consistently high ratings. In the early 1970s a reconstructed Liberal regime under Bourassa embarked on the huge James Bay hydroelectric development project, which provided Quebec with surplus power for export when it was completed a decade later, although resistance by Native Canadians in the James Bay region and a sagging US energy market in the early 1990s curtailed Bourassa's plans for an even larger project. Of all the Crown enterprises spawned by the Quiet Revolution, Hydro-Québec has had the most enduring success.

René Lévesque also played a role in one further nationalizing foray, this time as Premier of the Parti

Québécois government in the province from 1976 to 1985. Despite his welfare-state rhetoric and the leftist base of the PQ, Lévesque as Premier generally soft-pedalled interventionism: with independence as his main goal, he sought to avoid signals that Quebec would not be hospitable to private investment. Shortly after coming to power, Lévesque went to New York to reassure a skeptical audience of US bankers and industrialists that Quebec had not become a northern Cuba.

Nevertheless, the PQ government did move towards nationalizing the asbestos industry in 1978–80, with the declared intention of establishing an integrated processing and refining operation that the largely foreign-owned private firms refused to undertake. Although the initiative seemed plausible since Quebec's output accounted for almost one-third of the world's asbestos production at the time, serious problems soon emerged. The government was only able to acquire control of one of the four major producers, and General Dynamics, the American parent of that company, the Asbestos Corporation, chose to contest the takeover in the courts, delaying the process. Meanwhile, the industry itself slid into crisis, in part because of the health hazards of asbestos for workers in the industry: litigation over this issue drove the largest US producer, Johns Manville, into bankruptcy in the early 1980s. As the market remained sluggish even after the general economic recovery of the mid-1980s, the asbestos venture appeared to be yet another costly white elephant for Quebec.

While Quebec's experience with Crown enterprises produced, at best, mixed results, other more indirect forms of intervention proved to be more significant. Along with Hydro-Québec, the most notable initiative of the Quiet Revolution was the creation of the Caisse de dépôt et de placement in 1965, which became a major instrument for expanding francophone businesses in Quebec and Canada. Initially set up to hold Quebec's pension fund—which provided the occasion for an early confrontation between Quebec and Ottawa as the federal government had its own plan for a Canada

pension fund—the Caisse de dépôt also became the portfolio manager of revenues from a variety of government bodies, with assets of over \$14 billion by the early 1980s.

In its early years the Caisse de dépôt invested primarily in provincial and Hydro-Québec bonds, thus assisting in the expansion of the Crown venture and freeing the provincial government from reliance on anglophone financiers. But it also helped fund francophone enterprises such as Provigo, a provincial grocery chain set up by Antoine Turmel in 1969; by the 1980s Provigo owned a wide range of supermarkets, convenience store chains, and mail-order houses across eastern Canada. The PQ government had broader ambitions for the Caisse de dépôt, pressing it to become more of a venture capital source for expanding francophone businesses such as Bombardier and the National Bank of Canada (the erstwhile Banque Nationale). The Caisse also bought into traditionally anglophone firms such as Dominion Textiles, and used its financial power to protect French-Canadian firms from 'foreign' takeovers: in 1977 it blocked the Nova Scotia-based Sobey family from acquiring Provigo, although later the Caisse allied with the Sobeys to oust Turmel as chief executive of the retail company.

The Caisse de dépôt did not restrict itself to supporting French-Canadian entrepreneurs in Quebec. In the 1970s the Ontario-born conglomerator, Paul Desmarais, who had acquired and reorganized Power Corporation, drew on the Caisse for assistance in his empire-building, to the point where in 1982 the federal Parliament restricted provincial companies from acquiring more than 10 per cent of a federally chartered enterprise, in order to defend the CPR against a Desmarais/Caisse de dépôt invasion. This episode naturally was seen by Quebec nationalists as confirming the tradition of anglophone bias in Ottawa.

Whatever their feelings on this issue, most francophone business people were not enthusiastic about Quebec separatism. Desmarais played a prominent role in opposing the PQ during the referendum on sovereignty in 1980, and the business community generally endorsed the return of the Liberals under Bourassa to power in 1986. Prosperity in the latter part of the decade induced some francophone business people to express more confidence about Quebec's ability to survive on its own during the debates following the collapse of the Meech Lake agreement. Recession in the early 1990s that hit Montreal particularly hard dampened much of this enthusiasm, and leading business figures such as Desmarais continued to argue that, in economic terms, French Canadians benefited more from decentralized federalism.

Despite the preoccupation of Quebec governments since the 1960s with creating a diversified industrial economy, manufacturing in the province declined, especially during and after the recession of the early 1980s, and despite examples such as Bombardier, most francophone businesses were concentrated in the financial and service sectors of the economy. These areas of course experienced substantial growth in this period, and reflected general shifts in the North American economy as manufacturers tended to migrate overseas. Overproduction and foreign competition also damaged the resource-based industries; multinationals such as the Iron Ore Co. phased out or scaled down their operations in Quebec, leaving pockets of high unemployment in the hinterlands even while Montreal prospered. The inability of the provincial government to achieve its diversification goals in the 1960s and 1970s or to do more than delay or cushion the impact of broader economic changes in the 1980s revealed the limits imposed on even relatively well-endowed provinces led by vigorous and talented technocrats. These problems were even more painfully apparent for Quebec's eastern neighbours in Atlantic Canada.[3]

THE PERILS OF PROVINCE-BUILDING

For the Maritimes the Great Depression descended in 1921 and its most enduring impact was on manufacturing. Federal government action to restore freight rate subsidies in the late 1920s and protectionism in the era of R.B. Bennett helped boost coal shipments to central Canada, and restrictions on trawlers enabled the local fish processors to regroup, as exemplified by the formation of National Sea Products by Ralph Bell in 1945. After World War II, financial aid from federal and provincial sources contributed to the expansion of the longliner fleet and the beginnings of a conversion by National Sea and other firms to trawler operations. While the traditional lumber producers faced growing competition from west coast suppliers after World War I, the pulp and paper industry expanded, particularly in New Brunswick where companies such as Consolidated Bathurst set up integrated mills and where K.C. Irving (see box, p. 170) built an extensive empire based on paper, lumber, gas stations, and newspapers, among other holdings.

Gains in the resource sector were offset by continuing problems in heavy industry, and federal policies in this area probably contributed to long-term decline. Although defence-related production in World War II helped Dosco, under pressure from Howe's ministry the company was obliged to close down its refurbished steel plate mill in 1946; the declining market for coal, as railways and manufacturers shifted to oil-based power, eroded its earnings from this source. The merchant marine, which had expanded rapidly in World War II, was equally rapidly dismantled: 74 deep-sea vessels were sold off to foreign shipping companies and the proceeds used by the federal government to help underwrite the expansion of the Great Lakes barge fleet. Rising freight rates after 1949 resurrected the old regional competitive problem for Maritime manufacturers. New capital investment in the region's industrial base lagged at half the national level in the early 1950s. Although the Maritimes experienced overall growth in the decade following World War II, the rate of growth was only two-thirds the national average. Migration out of the region, which had reached catastrophic levels in the 1920s, slowed over the next two decades, but Maritimers worriedly observed a renewal of this

K.C. IRVING, 1899–1992

Despite the persistence of economic troubles in Atlantic Canada and the apparent inability of governments at any level to surmount these problems, in the post-World War II era the region produced a variety of entrepreneurs who erected family dynasties: the Sobeys and Jodreys in Nova Scotia, the McCains in New Brunswick, the Crosbies in Newfoundland, among others. The most prominent of these regional empire builders was K.C. Irving. His networks of gas stations, lumber mills, newspapers, shipyards, and shipping lines extended from his native New Brunswick through the Maritimes and into Quebec and the New England states. By the 1980s the Irvings' closely guarded fortune, estimated at over $7 billion, made them one of the 10 wealthiest families in North America if not the world—far wealthier than the more flamboyant and transitory millionaires of the era like Donald Trump or Robert Campeau. The founding father, still keeping watch over his enterprises in his eighties from a modest headquarters in Saint John, NB, up to his death in 1992, seemed to embody the traditional values of proprietary capitalism that had flourished in the Maritimes a century earlier.

Kenneth Colin Irving was born in 1899, son of a prominent local merchant in the small town of Buctouche in eastern New Brunswick, a vigorous exponent of the Presbyterian virtues of relentless work, thrift, and paternalism. After serving with the Royal Flying Corps in World War I, K.C. became a local dealer for Ford Motor Co. and Imperial Oil. Like Charlie Trudeau in neighbouring Quebec, by the end of the 1920s Irving had set himself up as an independent agent, developing a network of auto service and repair garages across New Brunswick supplied with gas and oil by his own retail company, Irving Oil. During the Depression, Irving's enterprises fared well, benefiting from the fact that car owners chose to hang on to their aging vehicles (inevitably requiring repairs), and from local resentment, shared by Irving, of Imperial Oil's 'monopolistic' pricing. Also during the 1930s, K.C. inherited a paper mill from his father and used earnings from his auto repair business to acquire large timber holdings in anticipation of a resurging market for paper products. Among his acquisitions—which included a bankrupt bus line in Saint John, several local newspapers, and the New Brunswick Power Co.—Irving picked up a small plywood manufacturer, Canada Veneers, in 1938. When the British Air Ministry (under Lord Beaverbrook) came shopping in World War II, Canada Veneers secured the contract for wood frames for over 6,000 De Havilland Mosquito aircraft for the RAF and RCAF.

After the war, K.C. parlayed his earnings from this enterprise into a much-expanded oil and gas operation, moving into refining in the 1950s; purchased corvettes from the Navy to establish a cargo line that ranged across the western hemisphere; continued to expand his service stations and paper mills; diversified into home construction materials; and in 1959 took over the Saint John Dry Dock—where business had slumped when government contracts dried up after the Korean War—and substantially expanded its capacity just in time for a renewed naval buildup in the 1970s.

K.C. Irving's approach to business generally and to diversification resembled that of one of the heroes of his youth, Henry Ford. Dedicated to vertical integration, Irving acquired enterprises that would either supply or provide markets for his main businesses: petroleum and paper products. Earnings were ploughed back into the business; external debt was held to a minimum. Irving sought to keep his companies

Maritime millionaires—K.C. Irving (left) and Lord Beaverbrook (right)—vacationing in the Bahamas. (Provincial Archives of New Brunswick p 194/205)

under personal or family control. Irving Oil, for example, founded in 1929 as a joint-stock venture, quickly passed back into K.C.'s hands as he used its profits to purchase most of the common shares—although later he was obliged to share ownership with the US firm, Socal, in order to finance his refinery. He reared his sons to take over running the businesses, but continued to spend as much time as possible overseeing affairs even after he established residence in Bermuda as a tax haven.

As the major figure on the local economic scene, Irving enjoyed public and political support in New Brunswick for many years. Even the noxious effluent from his Saint John paper mill was greeted as evidence of Irving's prosperity and jobs for New Brunswickers, although in the 1980s the Irvings did make efforts to control these emissions. By the 1960s, however, the extent of Irving's economic influence became a matter of political debate: K.C. feuded with the Liberal Premier, Louis Robichaud, over the latter's efforts to roll back tax concessions granted in earlier years to Irving companies. Partly as an offshoot of this dispute, Irving came under fire in the 1970s from the federal Liberal government for allegedly creating a media monopoly in the province—a charge that was ultimately dismissed by the Canadian Supreme Court. Although the arrival of Conservative regimes on the federal and provincial scene in the 1980s abated political tensions, the Irvings continued to encounter criticism from trade unionists and environmentalists.

The public image of this proverbially publicity-shy dynasty is ambivalent. On the one hand, the Irvings can be seen as representing qualities that, in the conventional wisdom, are far too rarely found among not just Maritime but Canadian businesses: entrepreneurship, efficient organization, financial prudence, and dedication to quality in products and service. On the other hand, critics portray them as secretive, ruthless, confrontational with labour, indifferent (at least until recently) to the environmental consequences of their operations, a dynasty whose far-flung enterprises have, paradoxically, blocked the growth of other regional entrepreneurs and have at best only marginally alleviated the population decline and high unemployment rates in their home province.

Sources: John DeMont, *Citizens Irving: K.C. Irving and His Legacy* (Toronto, 1991); Russell Hunt and Robert Campbell, *K.C. Irving: The Art of the Industrialist* (Toronto, 1973).

movement by the early 1950s, particularly among younger people.

Maritime political and business leaders agreed that the decline of manufacturing was the region's fundamental problem, setting the stage for a series of government initiatives to attract new industry, undertaken at first by the provinces and supplemented by federal regional development programs in the 1960s–80s period. At the provincial level, Nova Scotia engaged in the most systematic and sustained effort, involving collaboration between the government and local business notables. In 1956 the Progressive Conservative Party, after more than 20 years in opposition, returned to power under the leadership of Robert Stanfield, whose family had operated a successful textile firm in Truro since the 1850s. Stanfield's vehicle for reindustrialization was Industrial Estates Ltd (IEL), derived from a British experiment with regional development in the 1940s, and a forerunner of Quebec's SGF and the Bank of Canada's Industrial Development Bank. Although IEL was a Crown enterprise with capital provided by the Nova Scotia government, it was run by business people; Frank Sobey, who had developed a regional supermarket chain from his base in Pictou, presided over IEL (along with his growing family enterprises) from 1957 to 1970. Stanfield vowed to ensure that IEL's decisions would be free of political influence. Its task was to provide seed capital and other inducements to industrial firms to locate in the province.

Between 1958 and 1971 IEL provided over $150 million in total to 77 enterprises, many of them locating in rural and small-town communities in the province and over two-thirds of them employing fewer than 100 people. As a vehicle for hinterland industrial diversification, the operation was a success: its most significant catch was the French company Michelin Tire, which set up two plants in the early 1970s, attracted in part by the competitive wage rates advertised by IEL (and supplemented by a controversial provincial law passed in the 1980s to impede union organization of the plants). On the other hand, critics maintained that as a venture capital instrument IEL was unsound: even its successful investments represented a drain on a financially strapped province—Michelin, for example, was provided $50 million in loans at interest rates well below those Nova Scotia was obliged to pay for borrowing the money. In addition, many of these manufacturers were chosen by IEL principally on the basis of 'creating jobs', perpetuating the labour-intensive aspect of the region's industries.

Two of IEL's largest undertakings proved disasters. In 1963 an American scientist-promoter, Jerome Spevack, persuaded IEL to help underwrite his enterprise, Deuterium Ltd, which was bidding on a contract to produce heavy water for Atomic Energy of Canada. Although Spevack seemed to possess strong technical credentials, the cost of the plant that was constructed at Glace Bay in

Cape Breton was badly underestimated and there were serious design flaws. By the time the plant was completed an initial IEL commitment of $12 million had spiralled into a $140 million direct investment by the province. In 1971 the federal government took over the plant and poured another $225 million into its rehabilitation. By this time AECL had more heavy water than it was likely to ever use. The plant was closed down in 1985, never having achieved full production.

While this fiasco was still in its initial phase, IEL lured an Ontario company, Clairtone, to relocate to Nova Scotia. A small but rapidly growing manufacturer of high-fidelity phonograph sets, Clairtone needed funds to expand production and responded with alacrity to IEL's offer of $8 million. Partly under pressure from IEL to create more jobs and partly because its owners decided to diversify into a new market, the plant erected at Stellarton, NS, in 1966 was set up to produce colour television sets. The bad timing of this move, and problems in quality control, rapidly undermined the venture. After several years of sustained losses totalling $20 million, Clairtone finally closed down in 1972.

The Clairtone debacle, however, had an interesting aftermath. The two hapless Ontario entrepreneurs involved, David Gilmour and Hungarian-born Peter Munk, moved on to invest in luxury hotels in the South Pacific, and then acquired a small oil and gas company, Barrick Petroleum. When oil prices began to collapse in the 1980s, Munk used Barrick as a base for moving into the gold-mining field, culminating in a dramatic find by one of its holdings, Goldstrike Mine in Nevada in 1987. From this point on, Munk became a major player in the mining industry, with operations in Australia, Latin America, Russia, and South Africa. In 2006, Barrick acquired Placer Dome, making it the largest gold-mining company in the world.

Nova Scotia was hardly unique in the field of publicly financed disasters. The New Brunswick government in 1972 backed a promoter named Malcolm Bricklin who proposed to produce a sports car of novel design. By 1975 the Bricklin venture had gone under, along with the province's commitment of $23 million. During the 1960s Prince Edward Island poured over $9 million into a shipyard and fish-processing plant, a project that collapsed when anticipated foreign funding failed to materialize. Maritimers were not the only producers of white elephants: Quebec, Alberta, and Saskatchewan had their share, although their relative wealth cushioned the impact of these mistakes. During this period the government of Manitoba, seeking like Premier Bennett in BC to open up its northern regions, found itself with a money-losing forestry products complex at The Pas, which had an asset value of less than half the $150 million in loans extended to the project's foreign promoters.

By the 1960s the federal government was moving into the field, creating a series of acronymically euphonic regional development programs: ARDA, FRED, DREE, DRLE, ERDA, and ACOA. These agencies produced fewer dramatic disasters—although federal energy megaprojects foundered spectacularly in the 1980s—and could boast some modest successes. But overall, the federal programs did not substantially alter the prevailing pattern of industrial location and development in central Canada. Provincial recipients chafed under the restraints imposed by Ottawa and levels of funding that failed to match the rhetoric that accompanied the unveiling of these programs. Federal bureaucrats and politicos, in turn, felt that the programs did not have the visibility desired to demonstrate Ottawa's commitment to reducing regional disparities in Canada.

While most chroniclers of provincial development schemes concur on their general lack of success, explanations for these failures vary. Some argue that all such undertakings were fundamentally flawed: governments cannot be entrepreneurial, and when they attempt to do so they fall prey to shady promoters and political interest groups. Other critics have been less categorical, emphasizing specific, if recurring, problems: those who made investment decisions, even experienced business people, often proceeded on the basis of hunches and guesswork. Details about development projects were shrouded in secrecy, excluding even the government officials ultimately accountable for the investment of public funds. The objectives of these province-building agencies were often ambiguous; the underlying goal was to create jobs (and thus grateful voters) in the short run, limiting the range of investment options and bypassing capital-intensive industries that could provide the base for a more diversified, growth-oriented economy in the long run. Finally, the concept of 'targeting' industries channelled government money away from areas where it could have been most productively used: as economist Roy George observed apropos of IEL, the $150 million expended by Nova Scotia to attract specific firms might better have been used to improve the province's infrastructure, education, and social services—which could have provided a stronger incentive for industrial relocation and private-sector investment.[4]

Few communities had a longer or more frustrating experience with the hazards of province-building than Canada's 'youngest' province, Newfoundland. During the nineteenth century, St John's merchants had wrested control of the local fishery from English companies and mobilized opposition to Confederation in 1867. Attuned to European markets for saltfish and in charge of the import trade, which was mostly from Britain and the US, the merchant elite controlled politics in the precariously situated island colony and dominated the economy of the outports. A sharp break in fish prices in the mid-1890s precipitated a commercial crisis in St John's, aggravated political tensions in what was essentially a two-class society, and stimulated efforts on the part of the island's government to diversify the economy.

While St John's had produced entrepreneurial families such as the Bowrings, who began in the 1850s to develop a transatlantic shipping and trading empire, most of the merchant community operated on a smaller, local scale. The collapse of the local banks in 1895 reinforced their inherent

conservatism. Newfoundland's political leaders looked to foreign capital for diversification and growth, proffering land grants and tariff concessions to British, American, and Canadian enterprises that chose to invest there, principally in Newfoundland's mineral and forest resources. In the 1890s Henry Whitney developed iron mines at Bell Island to serve his Nova Scotia-based steel industry and in the early 1900s American and British promoters—including International Power & Paper—set up pulp and paper mills at Grand Falls and Corner Brook. The British Marconi company obtained a telegraph monopoly. Most controversially, a Montreal-based promoter-engineer, Robert Reid, undertook completion of a railway across the island in the 1890s, financed largely with public funds although Reid was assigned title to Crown lands and a rail and steamship monopoly for his commitment. In 1921 the Newfoundland government was obliged to take over the bankrupt line, re-enacting on a smaller scale Canada's pageant of railway development.

Worse was to follow. Even before the Great Depression the island's newsprint operations were in financial straits, and the cod fishery, which had boomed through World War I and the 1920s, slid into crisis in 1931–3. By this point more than one-quarter of Newfoundland's population was on relief. The government, unable to cover the interest on its debts, voluntarily surrendered Dominion status, which had been achieved in 1907, to a British-appointed Commission of Government that ruled Newfoundland until 1949.

Military spending during World War II, particularly by the Americans, who erected an air base at Gander and also maintained a presence in St John's, on the east coast, and at Stephenville, on the west coast, resuscitated the economy. The Commission of Government promoted establishment of a co-operative fish enterprise, Newfoundland and Associated Fish Exporters Ltd (NAFEL), which could trace its roots to the fishermen's unions earlier in the century. But the prospects for the fishery were not promising: NAFEL faced competition from Iceland and Norway, the salt cod market was declining as demand grew for fresh-frozen fish, and European trawler fleets were soon to invade the Grand Banks. In 1949, prodded by an energetic political leader, Joey Smallwood, Newfoundland joined Canada. He was to be provincial Premier for more than 20 years.

Like his predecessors in the 1890s, Smallwood sought to salvage Newfoundland's economy through diversification. He pinned his hopes particularly on development of Labrador, which had been divided between Quebec and Newfoundland (largely to the latter's advantage) by the British Privy Council in 1927. Anxious to attract manufacturing enterprises to the island portion of his domain, he recruited a self-styled economic expert from Latvia named Alfred Valdmanis to spearhead the effort. Valdmanis seemed to be a good choice, luring German and Swiss investors apparently apprehensive of the unsettled state of affairs in Europe in the early 1950s. Discovered to have been extorting bribes from his clients and submitting fraudulent accounts, Valdmanis was dismissed in 1954 and jailed. In short order, many of the enterprises set up under his aegis collapsed and the Newfoundland government found that financing these ill-advised ventures had dissipated the surplus cash reserves built up in the 1940s.

Fortunately, Smallwood had other, grander irons in the fire. After Valdmanis's fall, he backed another promoter, John Doyle, who proposed to develop iron ore resources at Wabush Lake in Labrador; the establishment of the Iron Ore Co. astride the Quebec/Labrador border lent credence to his ideas. In this case, Smallwood's instincts proved more sound. In 1957 an international consortium that included both Dosco and Stelco, as well as American and European investors, bought the project from Doyle and seven years later opened a $235 million iron mine at Wabush. Critics, however, argued that the direct benefits of this development to Newfoundland were considerably smaller than those accruing to the corporate participants.

The centrepiece of Smallwood's program was development of the electric power potential of Labrador's Hamilton River. In 1952 he travelled to London, procuring (through Lord Beaverbrook) an audience with Prime Minister Winston Churchill, who in turn introduced him to the merchant banking Rothschilds. The Rothschilds organized the British Newfoundland Development Corporation (Brinco), a consortium of British firms upon which was bestowed—in lieu of cash from Newfoundland—control over virtually all of the Hamilton River watershed with exclusive rights to develop hydro, mining, and forestry resources. Smallwood's expectations for rapid development of power at what was renamed Churchill Falls, however, were to be stymied for 20 years. To justify a project that would ultimately cost over $1 billion, Brinco wanted to secure power markets in the US and central Canada; the power would have to be transmitted through Quebec, where political leaders of all persuasions continued to contest the 1927 Labrador boundary settlement. For a time, Smallwood promoted an alternative power transmission cable line through the Maritimes to New England, but by the mid-1960s it was clear that Brinco would have to negotiate with Hydro-Québec. After further bickering, in 1969 the two parties reached an agreement under which Quebec would purchase most of the power from Churchill Falls for 65 years at a fixed price (averaging around 2.5 mills per kilowatt hour); in addition, Hydro-Québec took on $115 million in Brinco stocks and bonds. By 1974, the Churchill Falls damsite, the largest such project undertaken in Canada to that date, was in operation. Smallwood, who had been ousted from office two years earlier, was not on hand to take the credit.

In any case, Newfoundlanders were increasingly persuaded that there was little credit to be given. In 1974, the province acquired Brinco's shares in Churchill Falls for $160 million and integrated it into the government-owned Newfoundland & Labrador Hydro Corporation, partly in response to public dissatisfaction over rising electric power rates and resentment that Brinco and Hydro-Québec were reaping most of the benefits. Subsequently, the Newfoundland government challenged the validity of the 1969 contract between Brinco and Hydro-Québec, noting the vast discrepancy between the price paid Newfoundland for its power and the rates charged Quebec and US customers (which ranged up to 30 mills per kilowatt hour), but in 1984 the Supreme Court of Canada upheld the contract. Rather than stimulating a new era of economic growth for Newfoundland, Churchill Falls left a legacy of bitterness and frustration.

There were other setbacks. During the early 1980s the province's leaders looked to the development of offshore oil and gas as their source of renewal; another Supreme Court decision placed the Hibernia field under federal jurisdiction, the oil boom collapsed, and further offshore development came to at least a temporary halt. The expansion of the fishery under Canadian jurisdiction to 200 miles in 1977 seemed to portend better times for the province's oldest industry, but the cycle of boom and bust continued in the fisheries, aggravated by the increasing numbers of European 'factory trawlers' on the Grand Banks. By the early 1990s the rapid decline of the codfish stock led the North Atlantic Fisheries Organization and the Canadian government to place a moratorium on activity in the offshore cod fishery; meanwhile, fish processing companies such as National Sea Products, which had expanded into multinational production in the US, were obliged to retrench. Even the traditional staple of Atlantic Canada's economy seemed to be in peril.[5]

CHAPTER 10

Mandarins and Multinationals

The quarter-century following World War II was an era of unprecedented economic growth for Canada. The average growth rate of the gross national product between 1950 and 1970, even taking into account inflationary pressures, rose 5.7 per cent per year, outpacing the Laurier boom of the early 1900s. While the benefits of prosperity were not spread equally across all regions, even in Atlantic Canada employment and income levels were rising, and by the end of the period the country could boast the second highest standard of living in the world.

During the ensuing 15 years, however, matters took a turn for the worse. Through the late 1970s inflation eroded real gains in income. National unemployment rates, which fell below 4 per cent of the workforce in the late 1960s, hovered around 8 per cent through the next decade and rose to 12 per cent in 1981–3, marking the worst economic slump since the Great Depression. Chronic imbalances in Canada's balance of payments and rising government deficits, which had been a matter of relatively modest concern in the 1950s and 1960s—when they were offset by booming commodity exports, new capital investment, and employment growth—now became major issues for the public generally as well as for the business community.

Despite these dramatic shifts in the economy, certain features of Canada's business landscape remained constant between 1950 and 1980, although there were pressures for change that would become more apparent in the 1980s. The large corporations that had emerged in the years before World War II continued to dominate the national scene. Even though C.D. Howe's acolytes lauded gains in secondary manufacturing, the major industrial producers throughout the period were in resource extraction and processing, notably petroleum and paper products. The export staples remained the linchpins of the economy, but there was substantial growth occurring in the financial, retailing, and service sectors.

Federal government policies, whether in the form of indirect macroeconomic planning or through direct intervention in the marketplace via regulatory measures, Crown corporations, or subsidies, played a greater role in the economy in the years 1945–84 than ever before. Fortified by their experience in World War II and by an enlarged revenue base derived from income taxes, Ottawa's bureaucratic mandarins set out to introduce the techniques of Keynesian economics to smooth out business cycles—although their aspirations in this regard were hampered by the vagaries and resistance of politicians and business leaders. By the 1970s their task was supplemented by a variety of other missions, sought or unsought: revitalizing the industrial sector; protecting Canada's energy resources; reducing regional economic inequalities; promoting indigenous technological research; and, not infrequently, bailing out disasters in the private sector in order to limit the economic (and political) repercussions of industrial failures. Despite some successes, notably in trade negotiations with the United States and other nations, by the end of this era the Ottawa planners had become scapegoats for the manifold troubles of the economy.

None of these trends were unique to Canada. One of the most important features of the post-World War II era was the growing interdependence of the major industrial economies of Western Europe and North America, fostered by monetary and trade agreements initiated by the US—with Canadian support—in the late 1940s and 1950s. These arrangements were intended to reduce economic barriers among nations and avoid a return to the trade wars of the Depression era. At the same time, they encouraged the growth of multinational enterprises: in the first instance, these companies were largely of American parentage, and Canada was a recipient of a renewed surge of US direct investment in its manufacturing and resource sectors. By the early 1970s the degree of American economic influence had re-emerged as a major issue in Canadian politics and policy, its saliency reinforced by the energy crises of 1973–4 and 1979–81. By this time, however, American multinationals faced vigorous competition from European and East Asian firms, and Canadian enterprises were expanding abroad as well. Although Canada remained linked to the US through ties of investment and trade, the central issue, increasingly, became the long-term ability of both countries to compete effectively in the globalized economy.

THE CARETAKER STATE

The years between the end of World War II and the 1970s have sometimes been designated 'the age of Keynes' in the industrialized capitalist nations. By this account, these countries embraced many of the policies advocated by the British economist

during the Depression: the reduction of trade barriers among nations and the deployment by governments of fiscal policies at home that would, through indirect means, cushion the impact of fluctuations in business cycles. Focusing on the demand side of the market, governments fashioned taxing and spending measures to prop up consumer demand and encourage capital investment in periods of economic distress, and (in theory) to dampen inflationary pressures when economies were running at close to full capacity.

In actuality, this era was short-lived and Keynesian ideas were never fully embraced. Members of the business community, especially bankers, were less than whole-hearted in accepting government policies that produced regular budget deficits; politicians generally endorsed tax cuts and government spending to fight recessions but were reluctant to openly support tax increases and spending cuts to combat inflation. Even during the 1960s, when political and business leaders achieved a certain level of consensus on the viability of Keynesian techniques, factors other than the pursuit of economic equilibrium were influencing policy-making, and that consensus eroded steadily during the 'Great Inflation' of the 1970s.[1]

In Canada, a relatively early commitment to Keynesianism was achieved, thanks to the influence of the mandarin successors to Clifford Clark at the Finance Department, through the years of Liberal hegemony in Ottawa. Even C.D. Howe's Reconstruction Ministry endorsed the counter-cyclical measures proposed in the White Paper on Employment and Income in 1945. Although emphasis was also placed on the traditional goal of boosting exports, in fact, the main engine of growth in the immediate post-war years was the domestic market. At the same time, political considerations—federal bureaucrats' desire to expand into areas of provincial jurisdiction and the Liberal Party's need to counteract CCF appeals by co-opting their social welfare proposals—underlay the commitment to government spending programs.

During the 1950s 'macroeconomic management' showed signs of disarray. The successor to Graham Towers at the Bank of Canada, James Coyne, began to tighten controls on the money supply in order to address what he perceived as the menace of inflation (which was growing at about 2 per cent per year at mid-decade). Friction between the masters of fiscal and monetary policies reached a head in the early 1960s when the Diefenbaker government sought to expand spending to cope with a recession beginning in 1958. Coyne's resistance led to his resignation-cum-dismissal in 1962, an event that met with a mixed response from the business community but one sufficiently negative to deter future prime ministers from taking similar actions.

Back in power in 1963, the Liberals introduced a new panoply of spending programs intended to do more than simply counteract a business slump: measures to aid 'have-not' regions, a national health insurance program, and creation of an Industrial Development Bank. The decade of the sixties witnessed a major change in the scope and degree of government intervention in the economy, and not just in Canada. In Britain, the Labour government unveiled plans to resuscitate that country's ailing industrial system. In the US, President Lyndon Johnson declared a 'war on poverty', which, unhappily for him, coincided with an escalating military conflict in Southeast Asia. In Canada, Prime Minister Trudeau proclaimed his intention to create a 'just society'.

All these heady visions disintegrated in the years that followed, but governments did not abandon their hopes of managing economic affairs. In the 1960s the underlying aim was to redistribute the benefits of sustained economic growth; in the next decade, governments sought to contain inflation through wage and price controls. By the middle of the 1970s, economists and government planners perceived inflation to be only one of a range of interconnected problems: declining productivity rates in manufacturing, particularly troubling in the face of new competition from the industrializing nations of the East Asia rim;

apparent scarcities in energy resources, which were exploited by the oil-producing countries' cartel, the Organization of Petroleum Exporting Countries (OPEC); and, finally, constraints on the ability of governments to deal effectively with these issues. Conservatives in Canada (and elsewhere) attributed this last problem to public deficit financing and the growth of long-term debt; resurgent nationalists in Canada focused on the alleged practices of multinational corporations—transferring jobs and investment away from North America and circumventing the regulatory and taxing powers of national states.

Between 1973 and 1983 much of the attention of federal policy-makers was devoted to the subject of foreign direct investment in Canada and the development of the nation's energy resources—issues that were increasingly perceived as interlinked. The government embarked on a series of what were essentially ad hoc arrangements but which, in effect, represented yet another interventionist thrust: propping up or taking over faltering large firms in troubled industries. Bailouts were by no means new to the Canadian economic scene; the Welland Canal and Canadian Northern Railway, for example, had been kept afloat by government loans for years before finally becoming public enterprises, and even the mighty CPR had relied on injections of government funds in its early years. But the regularity with which public monies were used to salvage foundering firms in the 1970s inspired the New Democratic Party (NDP) leader David Lewis to ridicule the private-sector recipients as 'corporate welfare bums'—even as his party supported Crown takeovers to preserve jobs.

Bailouts were rarely justified simply as measures to save jobs. In 1967, when the British company Hawker-Siddeley (previously Avro Canada) decided to jettison its ailing coal and steel subsidiary, Dosco, government intervention was presented as a facet of regional development policy for the Maritimes. In fact, the Cape Breton industry had been nursed along with freight subsidies and rail and defence contracts since the 1940s, although not in sufficient amounts to persuade Dosco's owners to undertake major improvements in the region's mills and mines. In the wake of Hawker-Siddeley's departure, the federal government and Nova Scotia worked out an arrangement under which the province would take over the steel mills while the mines were placed under a federal Crown enterprise, Cape Breton Development Corporation (Devco), its mandate being to phase out coal mining and try to develop a more diversified industrial base for Cape Breton. Then the energy crisis of the early 1970s appeared to resuscitate prospects for coal markets, and diversification languished. Meanwhile, the steel operation (Sysco) limped along, propped up by provincial subsidies and continuing federal rail contracts. By the 1980s the region's coal industry, too, was largely dependent on government purchases as Nova Scotia converted its electric power system to coal-based generation. As instruments of economic development, neither Devco nor Sysco had been particularly successful, and both remained vulnerable to shifts in government policies that could reduce or remove their financial support.

During the early 1970s the federal government intervened in central Canada's aircraft manufacturing industry. Again, this move was portrayed not as a bailout but rather as a measure to support Canadian technological innovation and reduce foreign ownership; and again, intervention followed years of government subsidization and took place in the context of a severe slump in the industry. Liberal leaders in Ottawa may have also have been mindful of their party's harsh criticism of Diefenbaker during the Avro Arrow debacle in 1959. In 1974, the Canadian government purchased De Havilland Aircraft, another Hawker-Siddeley subsidiary (acquired at the tail end of Avro Canada's merger binge), and two years later, bought Canadair from its American parent, General Dynamics. Both companies were in financial difficulties but both were also developing new aircraft that the Canadian government touted as state-of-the-art technology. De Havilland's Dash-7 had the capability of landing

and taking off from short airstrips; Canadair was developing the Challenger, a small-scale jet suitable for the 'executive travel' market.

In addition to the $76 million paid to acquire the companies, over the next decade the federal government poured another $160 million into the Dash-7 and more than $1 billion in subsidies and loan guarantees into the Challenger. Unfortunately, both Crown enterprises moved to full-scale commercial production of their aircraft during the hard recession of the early 1980s, and their consequent losses made them targets for critics as costly and allegedly mismanaged government enterprises. Both were subsequently reprivatized: Bombardier took over Canadair after the federal government agreed to write off much of the debt incurred for the Challenger. De Havilland, ironically, passed into the hands of an American firm, Boeing Aircraft, en route to its eventual absorption into Bombardier's empire.

The recession of 1981–3 left its mark on more than the Canadian aircraft industry. In large measure the recession was a by-product of tough monetary policies imposed by the US Federal Reserve that drove interest rates up to 20 per cent and higher in order to break the inflation gripping the international economy in the late 1970s. The Bank of Canada pursued a similar course, perhaps more out of necessity than preference, given that Canada's balance-of-payment difficulties more than offset increases in exports after 1975. Inflation was brought down from 12 per cent per year in 1979 to under 5 per cent by 1984 by the 'old-time religion' of credit restraint rather than Keynesian measures; national unemployment rates rose above 10 per cent of the workforce for the first time since 1939. Manufacturers, whose fortunes had been mixed at best in the 1970s, were badly hit by the monetary squeeze. Even the energy sector faced an uncertain future as the combined impact of recession, fissures in OPEC, and the development of new oil sources began to affect international markets.

At the same time a crisis loomed in Atlantic Canada. During the 1970s the beleaguered region had experienced a renewal, at least of hope for better times ahead, based in part on offshore oil and gas discoveries and also on the proclamation in 1977 of a 200-mile 'economic zone' off the coast that excluded foreign trawlers from much of the Grand Banks area. By the end of the decade Canada had become the largest exporter of fish in the world, and processing companies were expanding their fleets and plants: in Nova Scotia, National Sea Products was swallowed by a Cape Breton rival, H.B. Nickerson, in 1977. Expansion was costly, however, and the credit crunch of 1981–2 caught fishery companies heavily leveraged, particularly with the Bank of Nova Scotia.

By 1982, Ottawa, aware of the magnitude of the industry's debt troubles, established a Royal Commission under Michael Kirby, one of Trudeau's closest advisers, to search for solutions. The solution unveiled in the Atlantic Fisheries Restructuring Act in the following year entailed a substantial consolidation of enterprises in the region with an infusion of federal money accompanied by a significant degree of government ownership, to be shared with the banks. After much bickering with the Bank of Nova Scotia over the level of government financing required to make the enterprise viable and with the province over the social costs of closing down small plants in the outports, Fisheries Products International (FPI) was set up in Newfoundland, with the federal government as a substantial investor.

In Nova Scotia, negotiations were equally complicated: local processors, backed by a consortium that included the Jodrey and Sobey families, and the provincial government resisted Kirby's plan for what was essentially to be a Crown enterprise. They succeeded in reorganizing National Sea Products in 1984 as a private firm with minority government participation. National Sea then set out to become a multinational, establishing processing plants and marketing agencies in the US. Rapid depletion of the northern cod and other fish stocks later in the decade—which Canadian processors blamed on foreign fleets violating the 200-mile limit, and environmentalists blamed on general overfishing of the Grand Banks—precipitated a new crisis in the fisheries in the early 1990s, forcing National Sea to sell off much of its newly erected empire and to retreat to its original home base in Lunenburg, NS.

Yet even at this low point, there were signs of life in the industry: during the 1980s, John Risley, a Halifax entrepreneur with no previous experience in the fisheries business and no connections with the traditional companies, took over a small lobster pound that became the base for Clearwater Fisheries. Focusing on airlifted exports to new markets in Europe and East Asia, Clearwater diversified by taking over a number of defunct family enterprises. By the 1990s, Risley set out to do what had eluded governmental agencies at all levels: bring about a consolidation of the Atlantic fishing industry. Exploiting divisions at FPI, Risley acquired a foothold on the board of the Newfoundland company and ousted Victor Young, who had carried the company through the worst of the northern cod crisis. But his plans for further downsizing of smaller fish processing plants in the province's outports aroused the patriotic opposition of Newfoundlanders against outsiders. Stymied in this venture, Risley was successful in consolidation at home, taking over National Sea Products in 2003.[2]

THE MULTINATIONAL STORM

While economic policy-makers in Ottawa, Washington, and elsewhere were primarily concerned with trade issues, the arrangements they negotiated with one another in the late 1940s and 1950s would have significant implications for international capital flows. Increase in world trade, combined with the growth of international direct investment, laid the groundwork for what by the 1980s was called the 'globalized economy'. The Bretton Woods system had provided a stable base for currency exchanges for more than 25 years; US aid programs pumped billions of dollars into Western Europe and East Asia, resurrecting markets and stimulating new industrial growth. Paradoxically, multilateral tariff reductions encouraged companies in the US, and then in other industrialized countries, to develop sales and production facilities abroad. This was in part to ensure themselves of a foothold in emerging regional markets such as the European Economic Community (EEC), and later to circumvent non-tariff barriers that many countries, including the US itself and Canada, resorted to in the unstable economic climate of the 1970s. New technologies in communications, computers, and air travel provided the sinews of more closely knit multinational structures and brought hitherto remote areas into the global marketing networks—much as railways, steamships, and the telegraph spawned corporate integration at the national level in the nineteenth century.

While business leaders might hail the multinational enterprise as a symbol of progress and global prosperity, other observers were less sanguine. Critics in the Third World denounced the multinationals as instruments of a new 'Western imperialism', corrupting governments and consigning their countries perpetually to the role of 'hewers of wood and drawers of water' for the industrialized centres of Western Europe and North America. At the same time, trade unionists and social reformers in those industrialized centres warned that multinationals were exporting manufacturing jobs to low-wage nations in the Third World, concealing their profits in foreign tax havens such as Switzerland or Bermuda, and using their mobility and political influence to avoid regulatory measures imposed by national states. Perhaps not surprisingly, Canada, as a country traditionally dependent on exports of natural and semi-processed goods for foreign earnings but also with a small (though vulnerable) manufacturing base, produced critics of multinationals who offered both lines of argument simultaneously. During the Cold War era with its steady economic growth, these views had at best a limited audience. As economic conditions worsened in the ensuing decades, however, distrust of big business resurfaced, focused now on multinationals

and reinforced by the continuing ambivalence of Canadians towards the United States.[3]

As early as 1921, American investment in Canada had surpassed that of Britain, with direct investment comprising almost half the total. Although the Depression curtailed the flow of new capital into Canada from the US, by 1940 growth had resumed, primarily in the form of branch plants in manufacturing. By 1950, Americans had over $6.5 billion invested in Canada (52 per cent in direct investment), and the rapid development of the country's mining and petroleum resources quickened the pace of growth in that decade. By 1960, US investment in Canada exceeded $16 billion, and that figure more than doubled over the next 10 years, by which time direct investment comprised over 60 per cent of the total. Canada was the largest single-country recipient of US private capital throughout this period, and although inflows were beginning to pick up from other sources in the 1960s, at the end of that decade American investment still comprised 80 per cent of the total figure of $44 billion.

This massive influx of American capital after World War II had a dramatic impact on patterns of ownership in Canada's industries, most notably in mining and petroleum, where US firms controlled well over half the assets by 1967. American ownership in manufacturing also grew steadily, if less dramatically: in specific industries, including automotive products, chemicals, rubber, and tobacco, foreign firms controlled between 80 per cent and 100 per cent of the assets. At the same time, the American and other foreign positions in railways and other utilities declined significantly, reflecting both the growth in Crown ownership in these areas and shifts in investor interest as the Canadian domestic market expanded and its resource hinterlands were opened up for exploitation.

By the 1960s other trends were becoming apparent. In the immediate aftermath of World War II, Ontario was the major recipient of US direct investment. By the end of the 1950s, however, the rate of new foreign investment, particularly in manufacturing, was levelling off there while western Canada was experiencing substantial new inflows—a circumstance that may have influenced the varying attitudes in the regions towards the benefits of foreign investment. In addition, American investors and companies were finding new opportunities, particularly in Western Europe following the creation of the Common Market in 1957 and in the burgeoning, capital-hungry economies in the East Asia Pacific rim. Canada's share declined from more than one-third of total US foreign investment in 1960 to about one-quarter by the mid-1970s, although American ownership remained substantial, particularly in the oil and gas industry. A similar pattern can be discerned in the distribution of control over Canada's largest private companies. In 1955 one-third of the country's 30 top non-financial corporations were partially or wholly foreign-owned; that proportion had declined to 25 per cent by 1980. Ironically, the debate over US economic control in Canadian industry took place at a time when that control was beginning to diminish.

Up to the mid-1950s the only debatable issue about foreign investment in Canada was how to get more of it. C.D. Howe's post-war reconstruction plans were predicated on fresh inflows of foreign capital, and the federal government offered numerous incentives to encourage such growth. Accelerated depreciation of assets for tax purposes, introduced in World War II, was extended to foreign direct investments (except in banking and trade) after the war. When Canada imposed exchange controls in 1947–8, repatriation of earnings by foreign investors was exempted in order not to deter new capital imports. The government also extended direct aid for specific projects that would develop Canada's natural resources and infrastructure. One such undertaking precipitated the first serious public controversy over the consequences of this open-door policy towards foreign investment: significantly, in light of the preoccupations of later years, this episode involved the oil and gas industry.

In the early 1950s a consortium of US and Canadian investors, led by the Texas oilman Clint Murchison, undertook to build a gas pipeline from Alberta to the American Midwest via Ontario. Like many such ventures, the Trans-Canada Pipe Line Co. experienced numerous delays and unanticipated costs, but Howe, who was wedded to the scheme (which, among other things, offered jobs to his constituents in northern Ontario), kept the faith. In 1956 he agreed to set up a Crown enterprise to build part of the line and to extend $80 million in new loans to Trans-Canada. With the Arrow debacle looming in the background, the opposition in Parliament denounced the Liberal regime for its generous aid to foreigners seeking to deplete the nation's resources.

Howe forced his measure through, but the 'Pipeline Debate' brought the issue of American economic influence to the fore and contributed to the government's electoral defeat in the following year. By this time, even the Liberals were badly divided on the issue: Walter Gordon, a Toronto businessman (and Liberal) who chaired a Royal Commission on Canada's Economic Prospects—created over Howe's protests—brought forth a report in 1957, shortly before the election, that focused on the dangers of foreign direct investment. Gordon emphasized in particular its impact on Canada's balance-of-payments problems; and, in terms reminiscent of Sir John A. Macdonald, Gordon warned that Canada faced possible economic if not political 'integration' with the United States.

Diefenbaker's squabbles with the US government over defence and trade issues—including a dispute over efforts by Washington to prevent US-owned subsidiaries in Canada from trading with Communist China—strained Canadian–American relations, but they did not disrupt the inflow of US direct investment, and Gordon's views represented a minority sentiment, especially in the Canadian business community. During the reshuffling among the Liberals after 1958, Gordon acquired influence with the new leader, Lester Pearson, and emerged as the Finance Minister when the Liberals returned to power in 1963. Gordon's initial budget, which included

Scourge of the multinationals: Walter Gordon lecturing at an 'Americanization of Canada Teach-In', University of Toronto, March 1970. (D. Griffin, *Toronto Star*)

provisions for a 30 per cent tax rate on foreign takeovers of Canadian companies, aroused such an outcry in Canada's financial quarters that it was hastily withdrawn, and Gordon himself departed from the cabinet shortly thereafter.

Although Canada's exports had rebounded from the recession, deficits in its trade balance with the US persisted through 1962–3. Automotive imports accounted for over half of the total, reflecting the predominance of a handful of American firms in Canada and the fact that most of their branch operations in Canada were assembly plants, importing vehicle parts from US suppliers of their parent companies. These plants also produced only a limited range of vehicle models, and Canadian consumers were demonstrating a preference for imports, particularly those that were less expensive or were equipped

with new technology such as automatic steering. A Royal Commission set up under Diefenbaker had proposed measures to persuade the American companies to enlarge their Canadian operations to achieve economies of scale in production by encouraging exports. Ironically, companies such as Ford had set up Canadian affiliates earlier in the century in part to enable them to export their products into other parts of the British Empire. Since World War II, however, this export market had diminished and US auto companies had gone into direct production overseas; Canada was simply another, relatively small market.

When the Liberals returned to power in 1963, further complications ensued. Walter Gordon and his fellow nationalists sought to increase the 'Canadian content' in automobiles, and some further to the left advocated creation of a semi-nationalized auto industry, citing the examples of Brazil and Mexico. Another group within the new government, however, wanted measures that would encourage a 'continental' market in automobiles in which the Canadian plants could expand production. Their aim was not 'free trade' per se, in which the US automakers might simply abandon production in Canada, but a form of 'managed trade' in which trade barriers would be reduced or eliminated, but with safeguards to ensure that there would continue to be substantial Canadian content in the final product.

After prolonged and intense negotiation, which involved not only US and Canadian government trade officials but also the executives of the major US auto companies and their Canadian affiliates, the 'Auto Pact' was signed in January 1965. Under this arrangement, Canadian affiliates of US automakers would be able to export vehicles to the American market duty-free up to an amount equal to Canada's imports of parts, with the added provision that 60 per cent of the material and parts of those vehicles should be produced in Canada. The Pact experienced a rocky few years at the outset, as US parts makers and other opponents of the arrangement mounted a campaign against it, and the Nixon administration in Washington contemplated cancelling the Pact as part of the measures taken to restrict foreign imports in 1971; but in this instance heads of the US auto companies intervened on its behalf.

The Auto Pact encouraged expansion of US and Canadian auto production with a concurrent increase in parts manufacturing in Canada, mostly in Ontario. Canada's trade deficit with the US was eased and the Canadian share of the North American auto market doubled from 7 per cent in 1963 to over 14 per cent in the early 1980s. In the short term, the Auto Pact could be lauded as a demonstration of the benefits accruing to Canada from the continental integration of the industry and the diplomatic friendship that followed economic connections. Later, as American auto manufacturers were facing rising competition, particularly from Japan, Canadian nationalists could lament that the Auto Pact had solidified Canada's dependence on the declining American industry. Canada's response was to provide incentives for Japanese and Korean automakers to set up branch plants in Canada, moves that aggravated trade relations with the US, and indirectly led to the negotiation of the Free Trade Agreement in 1986–7.[4]

By the late 1960s public concern over the purported dangers of American economic influence was increasing. Several factors were at work: US involvement in Vietnam rekindled anti-American sentiments largely dormant since World War II. More material considerations were also involved: as US balance-of-payments problems emerged in the 1960s, Washington began imposing restraints on capital outflows, disregarding pleas from the Canadian government for special treatment that had been accorded in the past. In 1971, when the US faced deficits in both its trade and payments balances—for the first time since World War I—American President Richard Nixon introduced import ceilings and surcharges, setting the stage for devaluation of the dollar (effectively ending the Bretton Woods currency arrangements) later in the year. Although Canada was not the main target of these protectionist measures, as America's largest trading partner it would inevitably be affected. Canadian officials sought to negotiate exemptions from the trade restrictions, exemptions that were eventually provided, but the episode demonstrated Canada's economic vulnerability. The Trudeau government announced its intention to promote trade outside North America, which proved to be a rather quixotic quest: in 1982, more than two-thirds of Canada's exports and imports were with the US, a proportion essentially unchanged since 1971.

Meanwhile, Canadian nationalists had fleshed out their critique of the impact of foreign direct investment on the country. Branch plants in manufacturing, it was argued, were inefficient since their parent firms restricted them to short production runs for the small domestic market (as in the auto industry case), rendering them unable to achieve economies of scale. The benefits of foreign technology, which supposedly would flow into Canada along with direct investment, were not apparent: the multinationals for the most part did not equip their subsidiaries with research capabilities or state-of-the-art products and processes. Although foreign-owned firms were recruiting and training more Canadians for technical and managerial positions than in the past, this trend, too, was seen as debilitating: the best and brightest Canadians were being inducted into multinational corporate organizations while indigenous entrepreneurship languished.

By the early 1970s significant elements of the federal Liberal Party and most of the NDP embraced this critique and lobbied for measures to restrict further foreign direct investment. Although Prime Minister Pearson and his successor, Trudeau, were not stalwart economic nationalists, they recognized the potential political strength of the nationalists' appeals, particularly in Ontario's troubled industrial heartland. Pearson brought Gordon back into the government in 1967 and allowed him to set up a new Task Force on Canadian Industry that elaborated on the sins of the multinationals.

In 1971 the Canada Development Corporation, originally conceived by Walter Gordon, was created. The CDC was to be a 'mixed enterprise'—the government held a majority of shares but would presumably dilute its holdings to 10 per cent over the years. In practice, this dilution was never wholly achieved. The CDC was mandated to 'help develop Canadian-controlled . . . corporations in the private sector' but also took over several Crown enterprises, including Polymer and Eldorado Mines. In effect, it was a kind of government-sponsored conglomerate. In 1973, CDC acquired a strong position in the US-owned mining and chemical firm, Texasgulf, and later it did the same with the French gas company, Aquitaine. Although the CDC did not become the main instrument for 're-Canadianization' of the economy, as its proponents hoped, by the end of the decade it had acquired a substantial asset base of about $2 billion—roughly equivalent to

Brascan—and successfully resisted efforts by governments at various levels to turn it into a dumping ground for bailouts.

In 1973 the Trudeau government, temporarily dependent on NDP support to stay in power, took a further step down the nationalist road with the establishment of the Foreign Investment Review Agency (FIRA). This agency, the brainchild of yet another federal task force chaired by Ontario MP Herb Gray, was proposed as a moderate alternative to the expansion of government ownership advocated by the NDP. FIRA would screen new foreign direct investments—with exemptions for small foreign firms (with assets under $250,000) and, more significantly, new investments by companies already operating in Canada. Although the introduction of FIRA generated much adverse publicity in the American business community (and it was 'defanged' in 1984 as part of the Mulroney government's effort to demonstrate that Canada was no longer 'hostile' to foreign investment), many Canadian nationalists regarded it as a half-hearted affair. In practice, more than three-quarters of all applicants had their investment proposals approved; more applicants simply withdrew their applications than were rejected outright by FIRA. In retrospect, it seems fair to say that, despite the plethora of commissions and task forces and the rhetoric of parliamentarians, the actual policies introduced by the federal government in this area were cautious, designed to placate public alarm without significantly jeopardizing the inflow of foreign capital that most Canadian political and business leaders saw as essential for continued economic development.[5]

While much of the Canadian business community was skeptical, if not critical, of these measures, a curious form of nationalism, or at least protectionism, flourished in Canada's banking and financial services industry, and it is perhaps worth noting that Walter Gordon's career had begun on Bay Street. There was no formal restriction on foreign banks, but there was also relatively little activity on this front until 1963, when the small Dutch-owned Mercantile Bank was sold to Citibank of

New York. The transaction quickly became entangled with the growing controversy over American investment in Canada, and the Bank Act of 1967 imposed significant limits on foreign ownership in this particular sector. Similarly, the acquisition of Royal Securities by the large US brokerage house, Merrill-Lynch, in 1969 triggered alarm bells in the cozy Bay Street underwriters' community. Two years later the Ontario provincial government imposed a 25 per cent restriction on foreign ownership of any investment company authorized to operate on the Toronto Stock Exchange, a measure that reflected recommendations from several committees of the dealers. Not only did this law discourage further forays, but it led to the withdrawal of several US-owned brokers from the TSE over the next 15 years.[6]

In only one area (besides banking) did Canadian government policies approximate the nationalist rhetoric. Before 1973 most attention was focused on the foreign presence in manufacturing; from that point, the issue of American direct investment was increasingly linked to the development and control of Canada's energy resources. Developments on the international scene in the early 1970s set the stage for dramatic intervention by the federal government in the oil and gas industry and culminated with the National Energy Program of 1980–1—which in turn fell victim to abrupt shifts in global oil markets.

As had most of the other industrialized nations, in the 1950s Canada added oil and gas to coal as a source of energy for both industrial and residential uses, with a modest increase in hydroelectric power. Canada also had large reserves of petroleum, and the National Energy Board (NEB), established in 1960 to regulate the market, consistently encouraged exports through the decade. Although western Canadian oil and gas looped through Ontario en route to the US market, Quebec and the Atlantic provinces depended on imports, principally from South America. In 1959, Home Oil had proposed construction of a pipeline from Alberta to Montreal, but Imperial Oil and Shell, the major suppliers for the eastern region, lobbied

successfully against it. These elements comprised the 'National Oil Policy', such as it was, through the early 1970s.

But circumstances were changing. The United States—whose domestic producers had limited supplies from Canada and elsewhere through the 1960s—became a net importer of oil, and oil-producing countries, principally in the Middle East and Latin America, had set up a cartel, the Organization of Petroleum Exporting Countries (which did not include Canada or Mexico), to try to limit production and thus boost prices. The events of October 1973, when the Arab countries embargoed oil exports to countries that supported Israel and OPEC effectively jacked up the price of crude oil from $2 (US) per barrel to over $8 (US) per barrel, demonstrated the consequences of these changes. While Canada's immediate energy needs were not imperilled, two episodes in the 1973 crisis highlighted the role of foreign ownership in the energy sector. At the height of the crisis, tankers carrying oil to eastern Canadian ports were reportedly diverted to the US; moreover, the Canadian government learned that the country's potential oil reserves, based primarily on information from the industry, had been significantly overestimated.

In the wake of the 1973 crisis the Trudeau government, prodded by the NDP and by bureaucrats in the federal Department of Energy, Mines and Resources (who regarded the NEB as too closely tied to the industry), imposed controls and new taxes on oil and gas exports, froze domestic prices, announced its intention to build a pipeline linking Montreal to western supplies, and in 1975 established a Crown corporation, Petro-Canada. The export controls and tax measures naturally infuriated Alberta and triggered a decade of federal–provincial bickering. For producers in the private sector, domestic and foreign-owned, the development of Petro-Canada generated an equally bitter controversy; when the Crown corporation set up its headquarters in downtown Calgary, local oilmen promptly dubbed the spot 'Red Square'.

In fact, Petro-Canada was initially a rather modest undertaking, intended primarily to explore for oil on Canada's northern frontier and to carry out research and development in synthetic fuels and other 'unconventional' energy areas. For these projects there would be little immediate commercial return and, hence, limited private investor interest. Very much in keeping with the Howe tradition, the federal government transferred to Petro-Canada its share in Alberta's Syncrude project and also in a northern exploratory venture, Panarctic Oils. This strategy shifted, however, when Wilbert Hopper, a former energy consultant with the US firm Arthur D. Little and deputy minister of the Department of Energy, took over Petro-Canada in 1977. The original legislation required that Petro-Canada eventually become 'self-financing', and Hopper reasoned that this objective could not be met if the company restricted itself to unprofitable activities. Under Hopper, Petro-Canada began acquiring private companies involved in petroleum refining and distribution with the aim of creating an integrated system that (among other things) would be hard for a future government to dismantle. The earnings from these 'downstream' operations would be used to finance frontier development.

In Petro-Canada's initial expansionist foray, Hopper was outmanoeuvred by another quasi-public entrepreneur, Bob Blair of Alberta Gas Trunk Line, in a bidding war for Husky Oil. Subsequently, Petro-Canada acquired Pacific Petroleums Ltd, a large western gas producer, from its American parent, Phillips Petroleum. After avoiding a privatization effort by the short-lived Conservative government of Joe Clark, Petro-Can took over the Belgian-owned Petrofina and then British Petroleum's Canadian holdings, which provided it with a network of refineries and service stations across the country. By 1985, when it acquired Gulf Canada's refining and marketing operations, Petro-Canada was the second largest oil company in Canada, with over $8 billion in assets and one-fifth of the country's petroleum retail market.

Most of these acquisitions were made after 1980; prior to that point, government policy and financing had emphasized Petro-Canada's

frontier role. The $1.25 billion used to purchase Pacific Petroleums had been secured from Canadian banks in exchange for shares in a subsidiary, Petro-Canada Explorations. Developments in the international oil market and in domestic politics in 1979–80, however, loosened government restraints on financing Petro-Canada's expansion and also laid the groundwork for the National Energy Program (NEP). The overthrow of the Shah of Iran by Islamic fundamentalists in 1979 and the outbreak of war in the Persian Gulf between Iraq and Iran a year later created an atmosphere of uncertainty about future oil supplies from that region. Once again, OPEC exploited the situation, driving the price of oil to unprecedented levels—$26 (US) per barrel and higher.

The sudden inflation in world oil prices and continued fear among Canadians over the long-term security of their supplies tilted public opinion towards a more nationalist and interventionist approach to energy issues—which helped protect Petro-Canada from the Clark government's privatization initiative in 1979 and contributed to the abrupt resurrection of the Liberals in the 1980 federal election. Reinstalled in power, the Trudeau government introduced a wide-ranging set of measures intended to expand Canada's energy resources, augment federal control over domestic prices and exports, and reduce foreign ownership in the nation's oil and gas industry.

The National Energy Program was a complex and controversial piece of legislation. The oil-producing provinces, particularly Alberta, were antagonistic. Even though the price of their oil and gas for the domestic market was allowed to rise towards world market levels, the NEP tax and royalty arrangements reduced their share of revenues. The Reagan administration in Washington was outraged by Canada's affront to free-market principles and, more specifically, by the export restrictions and provisions of the NEP that discriminated against US companies. Within the industry, the reaction was generally critical, but the NEP had been designed to provide incentives to the smaller, Canadian-owned firms as well as Petro-Canada.

The Petroleum Incentives Program (PIP) provided subsidies and tax benefits specifically for companies with more than 50 per cent Canadian ownership that embarked on exploratory ventures. It reserved for them, as well, access to oil and gas deposits on federally controlled Crown lands—which encompassed most of the untapped regions of the northern interior and Beaufort Sea as well as the offshore areas. The government reserved the right to expropriate up to 25 per cent of any new oil and gas discoveries on these lands, with Petro-Canada as the logical beneficiary. At the same time, Petro-Canada's capital budget was increased to almost $1 billion with the clear mandate to increase 'Canadianization' of the industry, and, of course, it qualified for the PIP grants.

Not surprisingly, Petro-Canada favoured the NEP while the multinationals, particularly Imperial Oil and Texaco Canada, were hostile. Somewhat surprisingly (to the government), many Canadian-owned companies were also opposed; their responses reflected a mixture of considerations. The Calgary-based oilmen were generally resistant to government intervention (at least in terms of regulation) on principle, and they shared the Alberta government's resentment at the NEP's tax and export control measures that offset price increases. In addition, many of them were not involved in frontier exploration and lacked the capability to mount major ventures in this area, and not a few preferred to move their exploratory activities to the US, which was busy deregulating its oil and gas industry. On the other hand, a few, most notably the American-controlled Dome Petroleum, were prepared to work with the new energy regime; but Dome's fate provided what seemed to be a salutary lesson to other potential collaborators (see box, p. 190).

Through 1981 and 1982, the NEP was assailed from without by the US government while multinationals began reducing their Canadian operations. The federal government, however, with its base of support in the petroleum-consuming provinces of central Canada (and its renewed promise to extend pipelines to Quebec and the Atlantic region), remained committed to the program. Once again, international developments were crucial to the course of events in Canada. By 1982 the recession and development of new energy resources weakened OPEC's ability to control prices, and the cartel itself began to crumble. Since the NEP had been predicated on the assumption that oil prices would continue to rise, the steady decline in prices after 1982 undermined the program and eroded public support. By the time the Conservatives under Brian Mulroney came to power in 1984, vowing to dismantle the NEP, the energy issue had lost its saliency. The oil sands and offshore megaprojects were scaled down or virtually abandoned. The major legacy of the era of energy crises was Petro-Canada—which, as Hopper had anticipated, was so large and so embedded in the country's petroleum production and distribution system that even a government committed to privatization was unwilling to try to uproot it until the 1990s.[7]

The issue of foreign control of the Canadian economy had also lost much of its impetus, for a variety of reasons. As noted earlier, by the early 1980s the rate of American direct investment was falling: from an average growth of 11 per cent per year in the mid-1970s it dropped to less than 5 per cent per year. The Canada–US Free Trade Agreement at the end of the decade would lead to the departure of some firms that had long operated in Canada. During the 1970s, some European and Japanese multinationals established beachheads in Canada. Ironically, nationalist policies, combined with the recession, induced several of them, including the French gas company Aquitaine, Belgian Petrofina, and British Petroleum to sell their holdings to Canadian Crown corporations. At the end of the 1980s American-owned companies continued to dominate the branch-plant scene, particularly among the largest firms: Exxon's Imperial Oil was one of the top five firms by all rankings, and General Motors held its long-time position as the largest Canadian company ranked by sales up to the recession of the early

THE RISE AND FALL OF DOME PETROLEUM

Next to Petro-Canada, the company most closely associated in the public mind with frontier oil exploration and Canada's energy security in the early 1980s was Dome Petroleum. Ironically, this self-styled 'chosen instrument' of national energy policy was an American-owned enterprise. This was hardly a novelty in Canadian history: earlier 'chosen instruments'—Avro in the 1950s, the Grand Trunk Pacific in the Laurier era—had also been foreign entities. As in those earlier episodes, Dome was to soar spectacularly in the fevered days of the second energy crisis only to plummet into an abyss of debt and political controversy.

Dome Petroleum was a by-product of Dome Mines, an enterprise founded in 1918 by the New York investment banker Julius Bache. By the 1950s Dome Mines was one of the largest gold-mining ventures in Canada; its subsidiaries included Sigma Mines in Quebec and Campbell Red Lake Mines in Ontario. The post-Leduc boom aroused the interest of Bache's son-in-law (and partner) Clifford Michel in the Alberta oil fields, and in 1950 Michel set up a small venture, Dome Exploration, which in 1958 became a public joint-stock company, Dome Petroleum. While Michel chaired the board of the firm until 1976, its chief of operations was Jack Gallagher, a Manitoban who had worked as a field geologist for Shell Oil in the US, Exxon in South America, and Imperial Oil. Initially, Dome Petroleum's activities were primarily in the natural gas fields in southern Alberta, but Gallagher showed an early interest in the potential oil wealth of Canada's northern frontier. Dome joined a consortium, Panarctic Oils, that had substantial federal government support (it was later taken over by the Crown) in the early 1960s—an experience that brought Gallagher into contact with Ottawa's energy bureaucrats.

By the end of that decade Dome was one of the largest natural gas producers in the country, and this remained its major source of earnings. Meanwhile, Gallagher pursued his 'northern vision', centred now on the Beaufort Sea and reinforced by American oil discoveries at nearby Prudhoe Bay in Alaska. As a small player on the northern frontier, without the massive financial reserves of companies like Imperial, Dome depended on tax deductions for its Beaufort drilling ventures, and Gallagher cultivated his Ottawa connections, even joining the board of the Canada Development Corporation as a private-sector representative. These efforts paid off in 1977 when the federal government authorized a Frontier Exploration Allowance under which companies incurring exploration costs in excess of $5 million per well (Dome was the only candidate at the time) could write off two-thirds of their taxable expenses. This measure, along with growing public interest in energy development, made Dome an attractive investment, abetted by 'Smilin' Jack' Gallagher's persuasive personality.

By this time Gallagher had become chairman of the board, and had passed on operating management of Dome to his long-time associate, William Richards, in order to devote his energies to the Beaufort development. Richards's strategy for growth, however, was shaped more by the concurrent enthusiasm in the investment community for mergers and conglomerates. Under Richards, Dome embarked on an acquisition spree, taking over Trans-Canada Pipe Lines in 1978–9, Kaiser Resources in 1980, and Hudson's Bay Oil & Gas (HBOG) in 1981–2, making it briefly, in terms of assets, one of the 10 largest companies in Canada.

The unveiling of the National Energy Program initially posed some problems for Dome. The

Dome Petroleum drilling ships in the Beaufort Sea wintering close to the more traditional form of Arctic transportation. (The Canadian Press)

tax measures would affect its major cash source, gas exports; more ominously, the Canadian ownership provisions would restrict the company's access to grants and further drilling opportunities on Crown lands. Dome and other producers lobbied successfully to reduce the tax on gas exports, and Richards worked out a stratagem for circumventing the 'Canadianization' obstacle by creating a subsidiary, Dome Canada, with more than half of its shares offered exclusively to Canadian investors. Dome Canada was launched with much fanfare in March 1981, raising $434 million in equity capital. The new company promptly applied for PIP subsidies to pursue its Beaufort project.

But Dome Petroleum's success in its dealings with the government could not long conceal its troubles on another front. Richards's acquisition strategy was proving expensive: prying

HBOG from its largest shareholder, Conoco, cost over $2 billion, and Dome was already heavily leveraged with loans from a multitude of foreign and Canadian banks. Even to cover its interest payments, Dome had to increase revenues, and Richards concluded that this required a complete takeover of HBOG, buying out the remaining shareholders for another $1.8 billion. By early 1982 the company had incurred debts of more than $6 billion.

At this point world oil prices began to slip and Dome's creditors took alarm. As in the case of Massey-Ferguson a year earlier, several major Canadian banks, particularly the Toronto-Dominion Bank and the Imperial Bank of Commerce, had large sums advanced to Dome; the company's possible bankruptcy would reverberate through the country's financial community. Through the summer of 1982 bankers and government officials scrambled to work out a debt rescheduling arrangement for Dome, with the banks and the government putting up $1 billion for debentures convertible to stock. The bailout was the occasion for much acrimony. Existing shareholders complained about the dilution of their equity; Prime Minister Trudeau derided the banks for their lack of good judgement in leveraging Dome's expansionary binge; business commentators assailed the government for contributing to an environment of inflated expectations that influenced the behaviour of Dome's managers, the banks, and the investing public.

In the months that followed, Gallagher and Richards were forced out of Dome and its empire was dismantled: Trans-Canada Pipe Lines and other chunks of Dome's domain were picked up by Bell Canada Enterprises. Dome Canada, renamed Encor Energy, limped along as a much-diminished player in northern exploration; Dome Petroleum also continued to operate, but oil prices fell steadily through the 1980s and there was little investor interest in frontier development. In 1988, Dome Petroleum was swallowed by Amoco Canada, subsidiary of a Chicago-based oil major, for $5.2 billion, the most expensive takeover in the country's history; Amoco in turn was to experience

difficulties digesting its new acquisition in the recession that ensued, and eventually it was taken over by an even larger oil giant, British Petroleum (BP).

To some extent Dome Petroleum, like the NEP, was a victim of circumstances. Had oil prices continued to rise in the 1980s its designs might have been judged as far-sighted and bold. But Dome also contributed to its fate. Richards's acquisition strategy was mistimed and driven, at least in part, by a desire to make Dome the largest oil company in Canada: the HBOG takeover in particular duplicated rather than complemented Dome's areas of strength in the industry and put Dome out on a financial limb. Dome's expansionary thrust was affected less by developments in the energy sector than by the merger fever that swept the business community in the late 1970s, fuelled by inflation and easy credit. As a final irony, that easy credit was provided in large measure by Canadian banks, eager to slough off their image as stodgy and conservative and to demonstrate their competitive vigour in the emerging global financial marketplace.

Sources: Peter Foster, *Other People's Money: The Banks, The Government and Dome* (Toronto, 1984); Jim Lyon, *Dome: The Rise and Fall of the House That Jack Built* (Toronto, 1983).

1990s. Nevertheless, public fears of an American economic takeover, at least through direct investment, had diminished.

Pressures of global competition were also producing structural changes in American multinationals. In earlier times, industrial firms entering Canada had erected branch plants that were, in effect, miniature replicas of their home-based plants, producing primarily for the Canadian domestic market: this had been one of the criticisms nationalists had focused on. In the 1970s and 1980s some of these companies

began to overhaul their international production arrangements, reorganizing foreign subsidiaries to specialize in a few product lines for global or hemispheric markets and providing them with the technical capabilities needed to efficiently fulfill these 'missions' or 'mandates'.

IBM, for example, had set up a Canadian subsidiary before World War II, but it had largely been a sales agency for products made in the US, with modest local manufacturing capabilities. In the 1970s, however, IBM Canada acquired from the parent firm a western hemispheric 'mandate' in the microcircuits field, significantly expanding its manufacturing activities and exports. General Electric provided a similar mandate to its Canadian subsidiary for production of airfoils for jet engines. Westinghouse Canada and Litton Systems also developed specialized export operations for their parent firms' markets. Although relatively few foreign-owned companies were affected by these developments, many of them were in 'high-tech' fields whose expansion Canadian business and political leaders of all persuasions saw as essential for Canada's long-term industrial renewal. Overall, US-owned subsidiaries in Canada more than doubled their export sales, from $11 billion to over $28 billion, over the years 1976–84, with exports beyond the US averaging about one-sixth of the total.

Meanwhile, changing conditions in global competitiveness had a particularly dramatic effect on the traditional 'smokestack' industries such as iron and steel, textiles, autos and auto parts, and machine tools on both sides of the border. Technological changes and emerging competition from Japan and other East Asian countries as well as the European Economic Community undermined North American leadership in these areas, aggravated by the decisions of US (and some Canadian) multinationals to relocate factory operations to regions with lower wages and fewer regulations. The 'deindustrialization' of New England and the US Midwest was becoming apparent by the early 1970s and peaked a decade later, and these regions became known as the 'Rust Belt', characterized by closed plants, high unemployment, and declining populations.

These trends spilled over the border into Canada, where the union movement responded with nationalist rhetoric that tied factory closures to foreign multinational domination of the economy. Governments were pressured to try to stem the loss of jobs or at least take measures to alleviate the hardships experienced by long-term workers suddenly faced with a permanent loss of their livelihoods. By the late 1970s militant unions such as the Canadian wing of the United Auto Workers (UAW) were staging factory 'occupations' to physically block companies from transferring machinery and other hard assets from plants scheduled for closure. The federal government responded with proposals to require advance notice of large-scale factory shutdowns, and the Conservative government of Ontario amended its Employment Standards Act to tighten rules covering severance pay and preferential hiring rights for displaced workers. Although these measures provided Canadian workers with better treatment than their counterparts in US industries encountered from departing corporations, government action could at best only slow the pace of deindustrialization in many areas. By the end of the 1980s the role of manufacturing workers in the Canadian labour movement was declining, with leadership passing to unions in the public sector.[8]

Globalization of financial, commercial, and industrial markets undermined the regulatory and interventionist thrust of national governments that had been fostered by depression and war earlier in the twentieth century. While the National Energy Program marked the apogee of Canadian government activism (except in wartime), it seemed in retrospect to be a kind of last gasp rather than the logical culmination of a half-century of interventionism. By the early 1980s new regimes had come to power in the US, Britain, and elsewhere, espousing a reinvigorated credo of free enterprise, open markets, and a diminished role for the state in the economy. By the end of the decade the command economies of the Communist world were crumbling. In Canada, the Conservative electoral victory of 1984 marked the eclipse of the age of the activist state. For some Canadians, the events that followed portended the prospective disintegration of the country or, perhaps, its ultimate 'integration' into a continental economic empire that had long been displacing the older transatlantic empire within which Canada had first emerged.

PART III

CANADA IN THE NEW ERA OF GLOBALIZATION,

1980 TO THE PRESENT

CHAPTER 11

Canadians Abroad

'I think Canada lacks international savvy. It's too provincial', observed Dick Evans, chief executive of Alcan in a *Globe and Mail* interview in October 2006. 'Canada tends to be more inward looking as opposed to engaging in the international community. It's only opening up now to what is really going on in China and elsewhere.' His comments could be dismissed as the off-the-cuff remarks of an American-born manager. But Evans has not been the only critic of Canadian business on this point. Michael Porter of Harvard Business School, in his 1991 analysis, *Canada at the Crossroads*, highlighted the country's 'limited international competitiveness outside of the resource sector', which in turn was described as 'inward looking' and 'risk averse'. Others have lamented the absence of globally recognized Canadian companies and branded products such as Switzerland's Nestlé, Siemens in the Netherlands, Sweden's Ikea, and Finland's Nokia. Aside from Alcan itself, the now defunct Seagram, and possibly Research In Motion's BlackBerry, Canada has produced few famous global performers.[1]

Yet this portrayal of the 'inwardness' of Canadian businesses may be overstated. In the years following Porter's critique, Canadian exports more than doubled, from $150 billion in 1991 (US) to $316 billion (US) in 2006, accounting for 5.2 per cent of exports of all OECD countries (with a population share of only 2.6 per cent). Resource exports continued to be the largest category in 2006, thanks in particular to the spike in oil and gas development after 2001, with motor vehicles and engine parts as the largest industrial exports. Both of these areas were tied particularly to the North American market. Perhaps more interesting, however, were shifts in Canada's foreign investment position in this same era. Outward foreign direct investment (FDI) more than tripled, from $98 billion (Cdn) in 1990 to $450 billion (Cdn) in 2005. In 1990, 60 per cent of this FDI went to the United States, but by 2005 this share was down to 43 per cent; Mexico's share had risen from 6 per cent to 14 per cent, reflecting in part the impact of NAFTA, but there were significant shifts to Europe (from 22 per cent to 28 per cent) and other parts of Latin America, although Asia's share (as Evans noted) was virtually unchanged. In 1996, Canada became a net capital exporter, reflecting in part the shift in US investments to Asia (although US companies continued to hold over two-thirds of the FDI in Canada), but also the substantial growth of Canadian operations abroad. An OECD study in 2003 noted that Canada's outward FDI accounted for a larger percentage of its GDP than was the case for the OECD as a whole, substantially more (not surprisingly) than was the case for the US and Germany, and close to the levels of France and Spain.[2]

Historically, Canada has always been an export-oriented country, but Canadian businesses have also been more active abroad than is commonly recognized. At the beginning of the twentieth century Canadian financiers and engineers were major players in the expansion of electrical utilities in the Caribbean and Latin America, and they were followed by Canadian banks, which continue to play a significant role in the economies of the region. Despite Evans's skepticism, Canadian mining, petroleum, and forestry companies ventured far afield (albeit sometimes as part of the corporate strategy of foreign owners), particularly in the middle decades of the twentieth century. Manufacturing was one area where 'inwardness' was most prevalent, reflecting the protectionism afforded by the National Policy but also the orientation of British- and US-controlled firms with branch plants in Canada, at least up to the 1980s. But even in this area, there were notable exceptions, such as the Seagram, Bata, Bombardier, and Thomson companies (all family-controlled companies), and Nortel in the latter part of the twentieth century. Table 11.1 shows how Canadian firms ranked globally in 2007.

BANKERS IN WARMER CLIMATES

In 1960 the five leading Canadian banks were among the largest in the world in terms of their international operations: the Royal Bank and CIBC were ranked among the 12 largest banks, and Canadian banks overall held 15 per cent of the world's market in foreign currencies. As the Eurocurrency market grew and larger banks, particularly in Japan and the United States, expanded their international activities, Canada's relative share diminished, while changes in domestic banking laws opened up wider opportunities at home for Canada's Big Five. Even in 2005, however, four of Canada's largest banks were ranked among the top 30 financial institutions worldwide by *Forbes Magazine*.

Not surprisingly, the United States has been a favoured destination for Canadian banking investment. In 2001 the Royal Bank (now RBC) acquired Centura, a North Carolina bank, as a base for expanding into the southeastern states. Four years later Toronto-Dominion (TD) Bank (TD Canada Trust after 1999, with its banking operations designated as TD Bank Financial Group) bought 51 per cent of Banknorth Group, an assemblage of savings banks in the New England states, extending its operations into the mid-Atlantic region. But the first Canadian bank to take these steps was the Bank of Montreal (BMO), which in 1984 acquired the Harris Bankcorp of Chicago, a move undertaken under William Mulholland, whose experience with Morgan Stanley in New York provided a familiarity with developments in the US financial scene. Predating the Canada–US Free Trade Agreement, the Harris takeover provided the BMO with a position in the American Midwest that other foreign banks had overlooked, as they focused on the financial centres of the east coast and California.

Connections with the United States were close throughout the history of the Bank of Montreal. When the bank was first set up in 1817, almost half of its initial stock issue was held by Americans, and one of its early presidents was Horatio Gates, a New England merchant. To help facilitate cross-border trade, the bank set up contacts with local banks in Boston and New York, as well as in London. A more ambitious strategy emerged in the years of the Reciprocity Agreement: in 1858 the Bank of Montreal set up its own agency in New York, followed in 1861 by one in Chicago, to participate in the booming grain exchange. According to an American banking historian, it was at this point the largest bank in North America, and even as late as 1914 the Bank of Montreal was the largest bank in Chicago, closely followed by the Bank of Nova Scotia.

Other Canadian banks followed the trek southward, although each pursued a somewhat different course. The Canadian Bank of Commerce, established in 1866 by a group of Toronto merchants

TABLE 11.1
CANADIAN COMPANIES IN GLOBAL CONTEXT, 2007

Company	Industry	Rank on *Global 2000*
Royal Bank of Canada	Banking	77
Manulife Financial	Insurance	91
TD Canada Trust	Banking	116
Bank of Nova Scotia	Banking	127
CIBC	Banking	170
Bank of Montreal	Banking	177
Sun Life	Insurance	196
En Cana	Oil & gas	206
Alcan	Mining	286
Bell Canada	Telecommunications	297
Power Corporation	Diversified	300
Canadian Natural Resources	Oil & gas	340
Petro-Canada	Oil & gas	364
Canadian National	Transportation	444
Thomson Corporation	Media	483
Barrick Gold	Mining	485
Trans Canada	Oil & gas pipelines	537
National Bank of Canada	Banking	568
Onex	Diversified	760
Fairfax Financial	Insurance	1135

Note: Rankings in the *Global 2000* are based on a combination of assets, sales, profits, and market values.

Source: Based on *Forbes Global 2000*, 27 Mar. 2007, at: <www.forbes.com>.

under William McMaster to contest the Bank of Montreal, set up agencies in New York and Chicago in the 1870s that focused on facilitating foreign banking transactions for more localized American banks, including major transfers of dollars with sterling. McMaster, who had begun his career in Manchester, also set up a branch in London in partnership with the Bank of Scotland. The Bank of Nova Scotia (BNS) went into Minneapolis in 1885 to exploit the opportunities in financing flour marketing, when expansion into Manitoba proved premature; the wheat boom in Canada did not come until a decade later. The BNS also turned up in Chicago shortly thereafter, to benefit from foreign exchange expertise that had developed there.

But the Bank of Nova Scotia was also lured to more exotic tropical climes. In 2006 the BNS still maintained a foothold in the Caribbean, with branches in the Bahamas, Jamaica, Trinidad, and Puerto Rico, as well as subsidiaries in Mexico, Costa Rica, and Chile. For the most part these ventures date back to the early 1900s and were connected to the activities of the Canadian 'utility multinationals' set up by William Mackenzie, W.C. Van Horne, and Frank Pearson in that era. The Bank of Montreal, for example, followed directly in the wake of the Canadian-financed Mexican Light, Heat & Power Company in 1906. By the 1920s it was the largest bank in Mexico, although it began to seriously retrench operations in the Great Depression.

The Bank of Nova Scotia was probably the most vigorous in the region. In 1899 it acquired the accounts of United Fruit, the largest American company operating in Central America and the Caribbean, and shortly thereafter it took the accounts of the Jamaican government out of the hands of the venerable British-owned Colonial Bank. In 1911 the Colonial Bank, in turn, fell into the hands of the Canadian financier Max Aitken, who retrofitted it with a new charter enabling it to do business anywhere in the British Empire, and proceeded to set up branches in Britain and West Africa. In 1925, Aitken sold it to the British merchant bank, Barclays. Seventy years later another Canadian, Matthew Barrett, moved from the Bank of Montreal to Barclays and then, in the spirit of Aitken, set out to make it one of the world's largest multinational banks.

Another entrant into the Latin American scene at this time was the Merchants' Bank of Halifax, soon to change its name to the Royal Bank of Canada. Spearheaded by its ambitious general manager (in effect the chief executive officer), Edson Pease, who had already carried the bank into the burgeoning mining country of British Columbia, the Royal opened a branch in Havana in 1899, tied in with Van Horne's railway venture in eastern Cuba, but quickly developed a strong position in financing the Cuban sugar trade, holding the accounts of large US companies as well as local mills. The Canadian experience with handling the seasonal cycles of timber and wheat production was readily applied to the sugar business. Although Cuba continued as the hub of the Royal's operations, it soon had branches throughout the Caribbean and Central America. Although British banks were also active in the region, and US banks began to move in aggressively after World War I, the Canadian banks retained a strong position there through the 1970s.

The Latin American ventures provided a sometimes lucrative supplement to their Canadian operations—and balmy training grounds for aspiring young managers like the Royal Bank's Graham Towers, future head of the Bank of Canada. But there were hazards as well. When sugar prices collapsed in the 1920s, the Royal found itself saddled with plantations and mills, which the bank undertook to manage through the vicissitudes of the Great Depression. As with the Canadian-owned electric utilities, banks in Latin America came under increased scrutiny and pressure from local nationalists after World War II. Although their eviction from Cuba after Castro's revolution was carried out with less animosity than the nationalization of American-owned mines and plantations, the loss of Cuba was significant for the Royal and BNS. When Guyana nationalized the Royal's subsidiary in 1985, the bank decided to alter its overall strategy, selling off most of its Caribbean branches over the next few years. Between 1960 and 1980 there was a decline in the 'traditional' Caribbean and Central American share of Canadian banks' lending, from 15 per cent to about 11 per cent of total assets, a trend that would only be partially reversed by the North American Free Trade Agreement (NAFTA).

In the years after World War II, Seagram dominated the world's liquor industry: 1948 advertisement by Dean Cornwell. Source: (www.americanartarchives.com.cornwell.htm; copyright American Art Archives)

Historically, the banks followed Canadian commerce across the continent and overseas— the rum and sugar trade from the Maritimes into the Caribbean, the grain trade from Quebec and Ontario into the American Midwest. Until the aftermath of World War II, Canada's capacity for internal capital mobilization was limited, and so the Canadian banks linked up with partners in the large money markets of London and New York. At the same time, Canadian banking laws contributed to these trends, perhaps inadvertently creating incentives for the banks to go abroad, but also promoting institutional practices that strengthened the banks in international markets up through the middle years of the twentieth century.

Usury laws dating back to the eighteenth century limited the interest rates banks could charge on short-term loans to 6 per cent, and although modified and provided with exemptions from time to time, it was reconfirmed in federal Bank Acts through 1968. Banks were also restricted in the types of property acceptable as collateral, effectively keeping them out of the home mortgage and personal loan markets, territory occupied by trust companies and caisses populaires until the 1950s. Thus limited, to some degree by their own acquiescence, to commercial loans to 'trustworthy' clients, the banks sought expansion through services to businesses beyond Canada's borders, not necessarily restricted to Canadian enterprises, and in places where local regulations permitted a wider range of activities. The Bank Acts, however, also allowed for the establishment of bank branches across provincial boundaries, and those that emerged successfully in the merger wars of the early 1900s had gained experience from running far-flung operations that stood them in good stead when venturing abroad:

Pease's Caribbean exploits for the Royal Bank, for example, built on capabilities acquired in the course of setting up a branch system in British Columbia. Experience with branch banking could also provide an advantage for Canadian banks in competition with Americans whose banking laws were localized and more restrictive.

While Canadian banks felt free to operate in the US, a very different attitude emerged when American banks sought to enter the Canadian market, as the Mercantile Bank Affair of 1963 demonstrated. In that situation, Citibank of New York proposed to acquire the small Dutch-owned Mercantile Bank of Canada. The Canadian banking community exhibited alarm over this prospective invasion of their hitherto undisturbed domestic market, lobbying hard, and successfully, to block the takeover. But the 1967 Bank Act revision went much further than limiting foreign investment in Canadian banks. In addition, the 6 per cent interest rate limit was removed, and banks were now allowed to enter the mortgage and personal loan markets.

This marked the beginning of dramatic changes in the banking environment in Canada. The Bank Act of 1980 appeared to reverse the 1967 rule, allowing the entry of foreign banks into Canada, although limiting them to less than 10 per cent of the now enlarged market. In 1987 deregulation of financial services removed the barriers between banks, trusts, investment firms, and insurance companies. Although presumably creating a 'level playing field', in reality the banks were in the best position to exploit the new circumstances. Over the following decade most of the major trusts and securities dealers were swallowed up by the Big Five: TD acquired Waterhouse Investors and Canada Trust; the Bank of Montreal took over Nesbitt Burns; BNS absorbed both Montreal Trust and National Trust; CIBC got Wood Gundy; and the Royal Bank acquired Royal Trust and Dominion Securities.

In many respects, the outcome of this new era of mergers replicated the state of Canadian financial industry at the beginning of the twentieth century, except now the linkages were formal and institutional rather than the by-product of syndicate manoeuvres and interlocking directorates. The leaders of this revolution in banking did not, of course, present themselves as barons of a renascent capitalist order, but rather as providers of a full range of financial services to their clients, large and small.

On the international scene, however, developments were more complex. Paradoxically, the Canadian banks significantly increased their portfolios of foreign holdings, yet by the end of the 1990s they played a much lesser global role than had been the case a half-century earlier. One reason that Canadian bankers became less hostile towards foreigners by the 1980s was that they had encountered the challenges of the emerging structures of global finance. Some of their largest and most stalwart traditional business clients were finding that better deals were available, and only a long-distance phone call or transatlantic fax away. The Eurocurrency market and related vehicles were changing the concept of geographically distinct capital markets, and large companies like General Electric were transforming themselves into providers of new forms of financing. Given this situation, the protection of a national financial service market was of decreasing value. The same reasoning lay behind Canadian acquisitions of full-line banks in the United States.

At the same time, there appeared to be new opportunities in this environment, particularly if Canadian banks were prepared to join international partnerships or syndicates. In 1972, for example, Royal Bank entered into a partnership with the American behemoth, Citibank, along with Dutch, German, Italian, and Japanese members to form Orion Bank Ltd, which provided loans to large industrial companies, governments, and other financial syndicates. CIBC entered a similar partnership with Gordon Capital Corporation, a merchant bank. Many of the international loans (especially to governments in the heady days of 'petrodollar recycling' in the 1970s) were not always as 'sound' as a more conservative generation of Canadian bankers would have liked, although at least the risk was spread when the crises came—as they did. CIBC lost $63 million when Brazil suspended its interest payments in 1987; in 1991 the Royal pulled out of Orion, having written off millions in bad debts.

At a less ambitious level, Canadian banks focused on the 'wholesale' (business to business) market outside of their home base: TD, for example, set out in the 1980s to establish itself as a provider of services and advice to Japanese investors seeking opportunities in Canada, rather than competing with Japanese banks on their home ground. By the early 1990s Canadian (and other) bankers had become more familiar with the perils of globalization—ironically, at a time when politicians and the media had just begun to embrace the idea. Some banks, such as BMO, began to retrench to familiar North American if not Canadian venues, and even those that continued to pursue international strategies adopted cautious approaches on the TD model. There were ample opportunities at home, exploiting the enlarged 'retail' market.

Meanwhile, foreign competitors encroached on the Canadian market. Some were familiar faces, such as Citibank and American Express, which carefully limited their operations, mindful of potential Canadian partnerships. Others, such as ING, a direct marketing organization operating through the Internet, posed problems as they essentially piggybacked their services on the infrastructure of existing banks. By far the most significant challenge was posed by HSBC Canada, the Canadian subsidiary of the giant Hong Kong Bank, which by 2005 was ranked by *Forbes* as the fifth largest company in the world, with assets of $1.7 trillion. HSBC entered Canada in the 1980s, establishing retail branches to serve Asian immigrants to Vancouver, but within a decade it had acquired the branch system of Lloyd's Bank of Canada, Barclays Bank in Canada, and the Canadian operations of the American firm, Wells Fargo, among others. By this time it had become the seventh largest bank in the country and, like its Canadian brethren, had acquired a trust company and set up an American organization on the west coast, merged with HSBC's holdings in the US in 2004, with combined assets of over $120 billion.

Critics have taken particular note of the example of the Hong Kong Bank as a model for global expansion that somnolent (and well-nourished) Canadian bankers have failed to emulate. Canadian banks have countered that the essential issue with global competitiveness relates to scale of operations: twice in the last decade major bank mergers were brought forward, most recently in 1998 with the proposed amalgamation of the Royal Bank and Bank of Montreal (which would likely have led to the merging of CIBC and TD). The federal government ultimately vetoed these proposals, and to the public their objective was perceived to be the further centralization of control over the domestic banking scene rather than a strategy to create internationally competitive banks.[3]

THE GLOBALIZATION OF THE INSURANCE BUSINESS

Although the big banks were able to encroach on the territory of insurance companies in the years after deregulation, the largest companies in this field (whose assets matched those of the banks) successfully resisted them and countered with their own array of financial services, particularly to business clients. The big life insurance firms, especially Sun Life Insurance Co. and Manufacturers Life Insurance Co. (renamed Manulife Financial in 1990), also had a long history of international operations, driven in part by the same need to acquire larger markets, and thus a larger asset base, for their services than Canada could provide. Like the Royal Bank's Edwin Pease, Sun Life's Thomas B. Macaulay was a vigorous exponent of international expansion, and the company set up agencies in the West Indies and Central America in the 1880s, expanding into Japan, China, Malaya, India, and Egypt in the following decade. The company also opened agencies in the US and Britain. By World War I, Sun was one of the largest insurance companies in the world. Sun also made substantial investments abroad as well, particularly in the US utility holding company, Illinois Traction, which it sold in the 1920s for over $30 million. Manufacturers Life, at this time about one-third the size of Sun in terms of assets, established an agency in Michigan in 1903 and over the next decade followed Sun's lead into East Asia, South Africa, and the West Indies as well as the United States. Confederation Life of Toronto, which at the time of its founding in 1871 claimed to be one of the first Canadian-owned life insurance companies, also expanded into the Caribbean and Southeast Asia in the early 1900s, and later into the US and Britain.

World War II and revolutions in East Asia had an impact on Canadian insurance operations: many of the agencies in the region were forced to close, although efforts were made after the war to locate former policy-holders. By the 1970s, however, there was a renewed interest in foreign markets. Both Sun and Manufacturers Life reorganized their operations in this period to reflect this orientation: Sun set up a separate US head office in Boston in 1973, while Manufacturers Life, renamed Manulife in 1971, was restructured into three 'geographic' areas in place of its traditional functional organization, with divisions for Canada, the United States, and 'Fields Abroad', which was refined to separate units for operations in Britain (and the EEC) and Southeast Asia in the 1980s. During the following decade both companies expanded back into Asia through joint ventures, Sun in Indonesia, and Manufacturers Life in China and Japan, later picking up business in Indonesia from the Principal Financial Group.

Deregulation of financial services in 1987 was as much a boon to life insurance firms as to banks, despite the risks of competition in the merged fields. The market for whole life insurance had been in decline for decades, offset by the growth of public and private pension plans and the mutual fund industry. Many of the major Canadian companies moved into banking and investor services in the 1990s, adding the term 'Financial'

to their corporate names to indicate their wider scope of operations. Not all of these conversions proved successful: in 1992, Les Cooperants in Quebec was taken over by the Canadian Life and Health Insurance Compensation Corporation, an industry-sponsored organization set up two years earlier to provide for consumer protection against losses from company closures. In 1994, Confederation Life of Toronto, the fourth-largest insurance company in Canada with assets of $19 billion, went under, marking the most significant collapse in the country's financial sector since the Great Depression.

For survivors of this industry shakeout, however, circumstances improved by the end of the decade. In 1999, Canada's major insurance firms, with encouragement from the federal government, had also converted from policyholder companies to joint-stock enterprises, enabling them to tap larger capital markets. Thus fortified, the major insurance companies used their resources for further consolidation. In 2002, Sun merged its Canadian operations with Clarica (formerly Mutual Life), the fourth largest company in the industry. Two years later Manulife Financial took over the venerable US insurance company, John Hancock, vaulting to first place in the industry and second only to the Royal Bank of Canada in financial services, in terms of both assets and profits in 2005. Although dwarfed by global giants like American International Group and AXA Group of France, the two leading Canadian insurance companies, Sun and Manulife, were among the 10 leading firms worldwide in 2005 according to *Forbes*. In some respects, the Canadian insurance companies have adapted more readily to an environment of global competition than the banks.[4]

THE RESOURCE MULTINATIONALS

It was Canada's 'storehouse of resources' that had lured foreign investors since the early twentieth century, and even in 2006 over 17 per cent of foreign investment was directed towards minerals, oil and gas, and forestry products. Some of the largest of these foreign-owned companies, established in the first phase of resource development, survived the boom-and-bust cycles of their industries and emerged as vertically integrated operations that became global players. The factors that led them into overseas expansion obviously included the search for new fields for exploitation as the productivity of the original sites declined, but labour costs, restrictions on exports, and the need to achieve economies of scale in processing raw materials from various sources also played a role, as did the pressure of competition from giant European and Asian companies in increasingly global markets.

Alcan is probably one of the best examples of this process. Established in 1902 as Northern Aluminum, a wholly-owned subsidiary of the Aluminum Company of America (Alcoa), it was transferred to another Alcoa-controlled entity, Aluminium Ltd, in 1928. In this capacity, it became the centre for a wide expanse of bauxite mining and aluminum refining operations from Guyana to India, with partnerships with French, British, German, Swiss, Norwegian, and Japanese companies in the interwar era. During the 1940s US antitrust authorities charged that Aluminium Ltd was a vehicle through which Alcoa maintained an international cartel with foreign enterprises to control the industry, and this view was upheld by an American appellate court in a groundbreaking case in 1950. In the wake of this decision Alcoa severed all nominal ownership ties with Aluminium Ltd and Alcan, although critics noted that the Mellon and Davis families of Pittsburgh continued to hold substantial blocks of shares in both companies.

By this time Alcan had become a fully integrated company with its own refining capacity and access to cheap electricity in Canada, so that it was effectively the second largest aluminum company in the world, a status it was able to maintain through aggressive expansion in Canada and abroad. Although the Guyana mines were nationalized in 1971, followed by Jamaica six years later, Alcan acquired other sites in Brazil, India, and Malaysia while expanding fabricating facilities in Australia, Norway, Germany, and Japan. By the 1990s Alcan was ahead of its former parent, Alcoa, in terms of sales, but like other companies in the industry it faced a serious challenge when Russia moved into the market, requiring significant cutbacks in production, particularly in Canada and the United States, and the sale of many 'downstream' subsidiaries in Latin America and Asia. Although the two companies continued to exercise a leading role in the aluminum industry, they faced increasing rivalry from Russian and Swiss enterprises. Meanwhile, the industry experienced a new round of international consolidations: Alcan fended off a bid by Alcoa to reacquire its former subsidiary, but then it was taken over by the even larger British multinational, Rio Tinto, in August 2007.

Another scion of foreign parentage, International Nickel (Inco), had a more checkered career in international expansion. From 1929, when it took over the British Mond Nickel Co., through the 1950s, Inco, through its control of most of the nickel reserves of the Sudbury Basin in northern Ontario and Mond's refineries and European distribution network, maintained close to 90 per cent of the world market for the mineral, and its revenues were boosted substantially in that decade by US stockpiling of nickel supplies for military needs. But high demand attracted new suppliers, and by the end of the 1960s Inco's share had shrunk to less than 50 per cent of the market; furthermore, the area of growing industrial demand for nickel, the steel mills of Japan and East Asia, could be better served by overseas rivals, including its traditional competitor, the French company, Société Le Nickel, with its mines in New Caledonia in the South Pacific, joined by Australian and Japanese companies.

Inco had begun prospecting abroad for new mines in Central America in the 1950s, including a joint venture with the Cleveland-based Hanna Mining Co. in Guatemala, which eventually was taken over completely by Inco. But the project was plagued with high costs, squabbles with the local government over royalties, and a downturn in market demand that eventually led Inco to shut down its operation in 1982, with write-off costs of over $219 million. A more ambitious and more successful project was undertaken in Indonesia in 1976, and was accompanied by an attempt to enter the New Caledonia area, which encountered resistance from Le Nickel and was delayed many years as a result. Meanwhile, Inco continued to lose ground: by the end of the 1970s it held only one-third of the world market. Diminishing earnings and the declining value of Sudbury ores, along with the debt-financed costs of developing new ventures overseas, forced Inco to cut its Canadian workforce by two-thirds, which aroused massive labour protests and criticism in the national media, highlighting the irony of a Canadian company whose foreign expansion was accompanied by loss of jobs at home. In the 1990s, Inco turned its attention homeward once again, acquiring rights to a major new nickel (along with copper and cobalt) discovery at Voisey's Bay in Labrador. This project, in turn, embroiled Inco in controversies over Innu land claims and environmentalist concerns, and took almost 10 years to get underway in 2005, at a cost estimated at more than $4 billion.

Inco's major Canadian rival, Falconbridge, was also an international player. In 1929, shortly after it began operations in the Sudbury region, Falconbridge acquired a refinery in Norway, relying on the electrolytic refining process of N.V. Hybinette to offset Inco's powerful market position, and it continued to emphasize technological innovation: in the 1970s Falconbridge developed a process to produce sulphuric acid with reduced emissions of pollutants as part of an effort to improve the Sudbury environment. By the end of the 1960s Falconbridge was the second largest producer of nickel, with a 15 per cent share of the world market. It expanded overseas ahead of Inco, opening a nickel mine in the Dominican Republic in 1968. Falconbridge also diversified into other minerals, setting up aluminum plants in the US supplied from its Dominican Republic and Jamaican mines, and developing copper mines in

Chile and Peru, although it was never more than a small producer in these fields.

Through much of the latter part of the twentieth century, Inco and Falconbridge coexisted uneasily in Sudbury: even their workers were affiliated with rival unions. Meanwhile, control of the companies underwent significant shifts. By 1976, Canadian ownership of Inco had increased to 48 per cent, although Americans continued to play a role on the board and in senior management. After the death of its founder, Thayer Lindsay, in 1957, Falconbridge was taken over by McIntyre Porcupine, the gold-mining company established by J.P. Bickell. In 1988, one-fifth of the shares of Falconbridge were acquired by the Quebec-based mining company, Noranda, which in turn was controlled by the conglomerate Brascan, and the Noranda stake increased to 58 per cent in 2002.

This set the stage for a final bout of mergers in the aftermath of the opening of the Voisey's Bay mine, in the context of another cyclical rise in nickel prices. In 2005, Noranda bought the rest of Falconbridge, but retained the name for the merged companies. Inco then made a bid to acquire Falconbridge, which would reduce duplication as well as strengthen the market position of the new company. But the deal fell through, and over the next few months both Inco and Falconbridge were assailed by international bidders, including the US firm Phelps Dodge and China's Minmetals, seeking hostile takeovers. In the end, Falconbridge fell into the hands of the Swiss company XStrata, while Inco succumbed to the Brazilian Companhia Vale do Rio Doce—an ironic twist to a saga that went back to the early twentieth century when Canadian electric power entrepreneurs had set up Brazilian Traction.

While the behemoths struggled for global domination, smaller Canadian mining firms continued to build their business. One company that acquired both financial success and international notoriety was Sherritt Gordon Mines. It was established in 1923 by the prospector Carlton Sherritt and mining engineer John P. Gordon to exploit discoveries of copper (and later, nickel) deposits at Lynn Lake in Manitoba. Like Falconbridge, the Sherritt company resorted to technology to offset limitations imposed by the remote location of the mine, developing an ammonia leaching process that later became a major technique for nickel refining. A refinery was built at Fort Saskatchewan in Alberta to take advantage of local natural gas resources, and this eventually became its major site for development, expanding into nitrogen fertilizer production in the 1970s and 1980s. Subsequently, Sherritt bought Imperial Oil's fertilizer operation to become the largest producer in Canada. But in its initial line of business, mining, Sherritt was still a small player with limited access to resources for its refinery.

In 1991 Ian Delaney, a financial expert who had headed Merrill-Lynch Canada, led a shareholders' revolt and acquired control of Sherritt. Delaney diversified the company into oil and gas as well as enlarging the fertilizer investment, but became far better known for his exploits in Cuba. With the collapse of the Soviet Union, the Castro regime became (at least temporarily) hospitable to foreign capitalists, and made a deal with Delaney for nickel supplies. This move brought angry protests from the US government—the Helms-Burton Act of 1996, which encouraged lawsuits against companies that acquired 'confiscated' Cuban property, was directed particularly at Sherritt, and Delaney was placed on a US Treasury Department blacklist. Nevertheless, he planned more ambitious activities in Cuba through the renamed Sherritt International, whose operations were kept separate from the fertilizer side, which exported to the US market. In another 'contrarian' move, Sherritt joined the Ontario Teachers' Pension Fund in 1999 to acquire Luscar Energy, one of Canada's largest coal producers, anticipating a renewed concern over energy by several years.[5]

Companies in Canada's oil and gas industry have been somewhat less venturesome abroad until fairly recently. In part, this was because the Alberta oil patch proved more than sufficient for smaller producers, while the largest operators

were themselves subsidiaries of foreign companies, such as Shell and Exxon. The United States usually became the logical place for those who were expansionist-minded. K.C. Irving in New Brunswick, for example, built a chain of gas stations and service outlets in neighbouring New England in the 1970s, and some Alberta wildcatters shifted their activities to the western US when oil prices were in the doldrums in the 1980s.

Imperial Oil acquired a foothold in Latin America in the early years of the twentieth century under somewhat unusual circumstances. In 1913, Imperial's parent, Standard Oil of New Jersey, set out to buy rights to oil fields in Peru from a British firm, London and Pacific Petroleum Company. To circumvent the reluctance of the British owners to sell to the American behemoth, the transaction was carried out through Imperial, which was then presided over by Walter Teagle, destined soon to become chief executive of Jersey Standard. Imperial established a subsidiary, the International Petroleum Company, to exploit the Peruvian fields. Although eclipsed by the much larger Venezuelan production from the 1930s, IPC provided a steady supply of crude to Standard through the 1960s. In 1969 the Peruvian fields were nationalized, but with little impact on Imperial, which by this time was focused on developments in Alberta. Curiously, in 1998 the Canadian Petroleum Institute was asked by the Canadian International Development Agency to help locate new oil fields for Peru.[6]

Another oil multinational, British Petroleum (BP), sired a Canadian company with global ambitions. In the 1950s Anglo-Iranian Oil Co. established a network of service stations in eastern Canada, supplemented by the acquisition of Cities Service operations in 1964. These retail stations were eventually acquired by Petro-Canada. In the 1970s the renamed British Petroleum joined the race for Arctic oil, acquiring acreage in northern Canada through a new subsidiary, BP Canada Ltd, which also undertook exploration offshore of Newfoundland. Production from Canada helped offset the losses experienced by the parent company as a result of the Iran–Iraq war in the 1980s, but falling oil prices in the latter part of that decade led BP to sell the majority of its shares in the Canadian subsidiary in 1992.

The new company, Talisman Energy, was led by Jim Buckee, a British-born 'rocket scientist' (with an astrophysics degree from Oxford) who had headed BP's explorations in Alaska and Norway, and whose admirers regarded him as a visionary able to see beyond the limits of the Alberta oil fields. Under Buckee, Talisman focused on becoming an international exploration company. In 1993 it bought Encor Inc., an energy company that had been part of Bell Canada's empire during its era of conglomeration and had exploratory operations in Indonesia and Algeria, followed by Bow Valley Energy a year later. The Bow Valley acquisition made Talisman one of Canada's largest independent oil and gas companies while extending its overseas presence into the North Sea oil fields. Other Alberta-based companies such as Nexen (formerly Canadian Occidental Petroleum) also invested in the North Sea in this era.

In 1998 Talisman acquired a Vancouver-based company, Arakis Energy, that was to transform it from a rising star to an international pariah. Arakis had a stake in oil fields and pipelines in Sudan, plagued by civil war. Although Talisman shared ownership in the venture with Chinese and Malaysian companies, it became the central target of critics of the repressive Islamic regime in Sudan, and was sued by the Presbyterian Church of Sudan for supporting genocidal policies; in the aftermath of 9/11, there were threats from the US Congress to have Talisman ousted from its listing on the New York Stock Exchange. Although the lawsuit was eventually dismissed, Talisman sold off its Sudanese operations in 2002 and turned its attention to expanding activities in the North Sea and exploiting new discoveries in Trinidad. Under pressure from some investors for a 'scattershot' approach to international expansion and diversification, Buckee retrenched in 2006, reducing Talisman's involvement in the North Sea and Alberta tar sands.[7]

As in mining and petroleum, the Canadian forestry products industry was dominated through much of the twentieth century by foreign multinationals, such as the American company, International Paper, in Ontario and the British firm Bowater, which held massive forest reserves in Atlantic Canada; Bowater passed into US ownership in 1984 when its British and American assets were divided. Although timber is a renewable resource, it was initially treated as virtually another extractive industry; not until well past the middle of the century did some of the companies begin practising sustainable-yield forestry, and this approach was not necessarily embraced across the board. Declining reserves, governmental conservation regulation, and protectionist trade measures imposed by countries such as the United States that were target markets for wood and paper exports all had an impact on emerging Canadian forestry companies, and persuaded some of them to undertake international operations.

Perhaps the most aggressive Canadian forestry multinational in the late twentieth century was MacMillan-Bloedel of British Columbia. 'MacBlo' was created in 1951 through the merger of two family enterprises, with H.R. MacMillan as a major driving force. In 1959, a third large BC forestry company, Powell River, was added to the mix. While most Canadian companies, both in wood and paper products, were oriented towards the US market, MacMillan had always looked further afield, going back to 1923 when his company exported wood to Japan to help in the rebuilding of Tokyo after an earthquake. Japan continued to be an important market through the 1990s. During the 1960s, MacBlo integrated forward into the production of corrugated boxes for the British market, as the demand for sawn timber declined. The company also made investments in the southern United States, Brazil, and the Philippines to diversify its resource base. The following decade was difficult for all forestry producers as inflation affected both production and the housing market, and MacBlo retrenched from its more ambitious overseas operations. In 1981 the mining company, Noranda, acquired control of MacBlo, slashed its workforce, and forced it to divest its foreign packaging operations. By the end of that decade the company was once again in a strong position, based in part on exchange rates, exporting to both the US and Japanese markets.

Although in this era MacMillan-Bloedel was one of the largest industrial companies in Canada, with a reputation for technological innovation in wood products, and wielded significant economic and political power in its home province, it also became a focal point for environmentalist protests over its clear-cut policies, culminating in confrontations in the 1990s over plans to exploit the Clayoquot Sound rain forest. Ironically, MacBlo decided to abandon its controversial approach to logging at the same time that the Japanese market all but collapsed, and in 1999 it was taken over by the US multinational, Weyerhaeuser, which also acquired one of MacBlo's rivals, the Quebec-based paper company, Domtar, shortly thereafter.[8]

As in the mining industry, smaller Canadian forestry companies have also undertaken foreign investment in recent years as a hedge against market shifts (and in the case of the United States, a prolonged dispute over softwood lumber exports) and because of the need for secure supplies. Two of the BC forestry companies that emerged in the wake of MacBlo—Canfor and West Fraser Timber—established subsidiaries in the southern United States and distribution networks with East Asia.

Canada's largest pulp and paper company, Abitibi Consolidated, also ventured abroad from time to time, principally to the US, in efforts to offset its continuing dependence on the highly cyclical newsprint market, only to return to its core business and its Canadian resource base. After its collapse in the Great Depression, Abitibi Power & Paper remained in receivership for a remarkable 14 years, only emerging in the aftermath of World War II. Riding the post-war boom, Abitibi extended into the US, acquiring a Georgia-based newsprint company in 1968, and then took over another large Ontario firm, Price Brothers,

in 1974. Shortly thereafter the newsprint market crashed, and Abitibi-Price ended up in the grasp of the Reichmann family's real estate empire, Olympia & York, in 1978.

Servitude to the Reichmanns (or, rather, to the managers they brought in to run the firm) seems to have benefited Abitibi, as it diversified into office supplies in Canada and established a building materials operation in the United States, which together accounted for about half of the company's earnings by the end of the decade. But the return of hard times in the newsprint industry in the 1990s, combined with the bankruptcy of Olympia & York, dragged Abitibi back into receivership in 1992, having in the meantime sold off its building products divisions. By mid-decade it was back on its feet, however, and in 1997 merged with Stone Consolidated Inc. to become the largest newsprint producer in North America and the eleventh largest newsprint company in the world. Stone itself had been a Chicago-based company that produced containers and in 1989 had taken over Consolidated Bathurst, a long-time competitor with Abitibi in the paper market. As part of a return (again) to its 'core' strategy, Abitibi sold off its office-supply operations in the US and Mexico, including a company that specialized in bar-code scanning and a direct marketing venture, while retaining forest reserves and mills in the southern United States.[9]

The history of overseas expansion by Canadian resource companies has featured some bold (even 'risk-taking') ventures, but also a number of ignominious failures and the disappearance of some of the largest companies into the empires of foreign multinationals. In part, as in the case of banks, this fate simply reflects the size of Canadian firms vis-à-vis international competitors. When Weyerhaeuser acquired MacMillan-Bloedel, for example, it was more than nine times larger than the Canadian firm, and five times the size of Abitibi Consolidated in terms of assets. As one observer put it, 'Canadian companies don't have the habit of eating their way to the top of the food chain' even in their own country. On the other hand, even in the current era of global consolidation in many industries, smaller Canadian companies like Sherritt and Talisman have been able to manoeuvre their way effectively in the international economy and even survive (at least so far) the hazards of international politics. Similar patterns may also be seen in the more diverse manufacturing and service sectors.

MANUFACTURING (AND OTHER) MULTINATIONALS

Canada had become an industrial nation by the early twentieth century, but most of its manufacturers, whether Canadian- or foreign-owned, were focused on the domestic market, secure (they believed) behind the walls of the National Policy, at least up to the 1960s. As in the case of the banks and resource companies, few of them were large enough to contemplate entering global markets and few had special technological or other characteristics that endowed competitive advantages abroad. Serendipity and clever management, however, could help a company to become a world leader, as was the case of Bombardier (see box, p. 211). Also, proximity to the much larger US market offered opportunities for companies that could exploit regional trade and transportation connections or differences in exchange rates, and for a few companies, expansion south of the border could be a springboard to more far-flung international operations. Not surprisingly, investment in the US accounted for most Canadian external activities from the 1950s, and many of the participants were small and medium-sized firms, clustered near the border but increasingly finding niches in the growth areas of the American South and Southwest, and in other countries as well.

At the time of the country's Centennial celebration in 1967, one Canadian company appeared to have both the scale of operations and management capabilities to compete effectively on a global level. Massey-Harris, the farm implement firm, had been involved in export markets since the late nineteenth century, and during the 1920s it began setting up foreign manufacturing and sales operations in Europe, Latin America, and Australia as well as the United States, while fending off an invasion of its home territory by the US giant, International Harvester. In 1953, the Canadian company merged with the British manufacturer, Harry Ferguson, whose firm held important patents in the field and a strong position in markets outside North America. Meanwhile, the Massey family had ceased to play a role in management, and in 1947 the proto-conglomerate Argus Corporation had acquired a significant equity position in what was to become Massey-Ferguson. In the 1950s, with Eric Phillips of Argus as board chairman and a Ferguson veteran, Albert Thornbrough, as president, the company overhauled its management structure and expanded its operations; within a decade it boasted 36 plants in 10 countries, with sales operations across the globe, almost equally distributed across North America, Europe, and other regions. It was the third largest manufacturer of farm implements in the world. Massey-Ferguson was celebrated as the model multinational in a 1969 publication by Canadian economist E.P. Neufeld entitled *A Global Corporation*.

Within little more than decade, however, Massey-Ferguson became a model of a very different sort, a corporate basket case. Expansion in the 1970s, financed in large part by debt, was derailed by recession and high interest rates. To stave off disaster, the company began selling off many of its foreign properties and concentrating North American production at Brantford, Ontario. Conrad Black, as the new head of Argus, sought government assistance for a bailout (an event he would seldom boast of in his later career) and the refinancing of the much-shorn enterprise, now rechristened Varity Corporation. Varity, in turn, eventually sold its farm equipment business to an American company, AGCO Corporation, before disappearing itself into the jaws of another US firm, TRW. Perhaps a small consolation for Canadians, Massey-Ferguson's main rival, International Harvester, experienced similar woes

BOMBARDIER

'*Car mon pays, c'est hiver*' (In my country it is always winter) J. Armand Bombardier once remarked. In rural Quebec in the early 1900s, the long winters left remote villages and farms isolated for months by snow and ice on poor roads. It was to overcome this isolation that Bombardier, a talented mechanic in the mould of Henry Ford, set out to build an '*auto neige*'—motorized sled—in the 1930s, his earliest models featuring a vehicle with metal sprocket wheels mounted on rubber tracks that could carry up to seven passengers. Also like Ford, Bombardier focused on improving efficiency in production in the plant he set up in his home town of Valcourt, Quebec. During World War II, Bombardier produced 12-passenger snowmobiles for the Canadian military and similar equipment for forestry and oil exploration companies. In the 1950s explorers of the Antarctic wastes were relying on Bombardier's 'Muskeg' snow cruisers.

After the war, the introduction of paved roads in Quebec attenuated the conditions that led to the development of his snowmobile, but also posed a threat to Bombardier's core business. In 1959, Armand developed a smaller version of the snowmobile outfitted with skis, intended for use by trappers and surveyors. But his son-in-law, Laurent Beaudoin, an accountant who had recently joined the company, saw a much larger potential market for the 'Ski-Doo', as it was dubbed, for recreational users in an increasingly affluent society. Beaudoin's aggressive marketing paid off, and by the mid-1960s Bombardier was the leading producer of recreational snowmobiles in North America.

The energy crisis of the 1970s posed a threat to the gas-guzzling Ski-Doo market and Bombardier production and stock prices plummeted. By this time, Beaudoin had emerged as the dominant figure in the company (Armand died in 1964

at the age of 56, and his direct heirs were mostly content to leave matters in Beaudoin's hands). Responding to approaches from the Quebec government, which saw Bombardier as a symbol of emerging French-Canadian entrepreneurship, Beaudoin took the company into a completely new field, submitting a winning bid to build rail cars for the Montreal subway system in preparation for the 1976 Olympic Games. Within the next decade Bombardier had established itself as a major supplier to the resurgent mass transit market, with contracts in Chicago, Dublin, and Mexico City, and, most significantly, for the New York City subway system in 1982. To augment its technological and production capabilities, Bombardier acquired established companies in the field such as Budd and Pullman, and set up factories in Ireland, Finland, and the United States.

In 1986 another government overture—this time from Ottawa—led Bombardier into yet another industry. Anxious to advance its privatization policy, the Mulroney regime sold the Montreal-based aerospace Crown corporation, Canadair, to Bombardier at a substantial discount. Although plagued with problems, Canadair was on the verge of launching a jet commuter plane, the Challenger, and Beaudoin set off into this market, acquiring another (British) publicly owned aerospace manufacturer, Short Brothers, and the US company Learjet, which had pioneered in providing small jets for private businesses. In 1992 Bombardier also took over De Havilland, the other Canadian Crown company in the aerospace industry, so that in effect it had consolidated all of the country's aerospace enterprises under its wing.

Critics of Bombardier attributed its growth less to the entrepreneurial talents of Laurent Beaudoin than to his skills at making special

Joseph-Armand Bombardier (on left) with his *auto-neige, circa* 1943. (LAC WRM 2764)

deals and prying largesse out of both the Quebec and Canadian governments. The breakthrough subway contract with New York City, for example, was aided by Canadian subsidies, and the purchase of the aerospace Crowns involved write-offs of major debts incurred by those companies. More recently, Bombardier experienced attacks on its vaunted technical quality, as high-speed rail car systems for Las Vegas and Amtrak in the US encountered delays and problems. In 2006, Beaudoin, who had stepped down as chief executive of Bombardier three years earlier, returned to head up efforts to sustain the company through a new round of crises.

Sources: Peter Hadekel, *Silent Partners: Taxpayers and the Bankrolling of Bombardier* (Toronto, 2004); Larry MacDonald, *The Bombardier Story: Trains, Planes and Snowmobiles* (Etobicoke, Ont., 2001).

and restructuring in the 1980s, selling off its farm equipment divisions and renaming itself Navistar, which limped into the twenty-first century with massive pension obligations.[10]

Aside from Massey-Ferguson, probably the Canadian companies with the highest global profile were in the alcoholic beverage field, Seagram and Hiram Walker. Both companies laid claim to pedigrees stretching back to the nineteenth century, but were much more the by-products of Prohibition in the US in the 1920s, when they established markets that were exploited more systematically (and legally) after the repeal of Prohibition in 1933; and both were associated with rival entrepreneurial personalities, Samuel Bronfman of Seagram and Harry Hatch of Hiram Walker. During the 1930s, both companies moved into the US directly through the acquisition of local companies and the construction of new distilleries, mostly for the production of whisky but also gin and other spirits. Both were effective in developing brand loyalties for their products: during the early postwar years Walker's Canadian Club and Seagram's 7 Crown whiskies were among the most popular in the United States. The two companies pursued one another across the Atlantic as well, acquiring rum plantations in the Caribbean and scotch distilleries in the Scotland in the 1950s.

Over the next two decades, the companies had to face new challenges as consumer tastes shifted more to 'white goods', including vodka and light wines, and competitors emerged even in their 'home' market, the United States. By the 1970s Seagram emerged as the world's largest alcoholic beverages company, with strong positions in a wide range of products and a global marketing organization. Hiram Walker's major brands continued to hold their markets, but the company disappeared in the 1980s, selling its liquor business to Allied Lyons PLC, a British company, which later passed into the hands of the French firm Pernod Ricard.

Curiously, both Seagram and Hiram Walker also had investments in the oil business. In 1979, Hiram Walker took over Consumers Gas Co. of Toronto and a few years later acquired a Colorado-based firm, Davis Oil. But these proved to be poor investments, and in 1986 the oil and gas divisions of Hiram Walker fell into the hands of the Reichmanns, who also attempted, unsuccessfully, to acquire the liquor properties. Seagram's history in the oil business was much longer, dating back to the 1950s when Sam Bronfman purchased a Texas oil company to take advantage of the US oil depletion tax allowance, which could offset Seagram's profits in the liquor business. Sam's sons later sold much enlarged oil subsidiaries at the peak of the market and used the proceeds to acquire a significant position in the US chemical giant, Du Pont,

in 1982. The Du Pont earnings helped sustain Seagram's position in the alcoholic beverage field through the 1990s, and Seagram might remain today as a major Canadian company but for the idiosyncratic (and ultimately disastrous) decision of the family to try to transform it into a multimedia entertainment conglomerate.[11]

As in the case of resource industries, some of the most successful Canadian manufacturing and service companies operating abroad were drawn from the 'second tier'—firms that looked for opportunities in underserved markets or developed special niches based on particular technical or commercial capabilities. Two examples, drawn from opposite ends of the country, may provide a perspective that could be applied more broadly.

In 1975 Craig Dobbin, an underwater salvage operator and real estate developer in Newfoundland, began leasing a helicopter he had bought for personal use to the province's air ambulance service. He purchased additional craft and established Sealand Helicopters, which also contracted with Mobil Oil for service to offshore oil rigs. Subsequently, Dobbin took over other small helicopter companies that provided similar services in Toronto and Vancouver, combining them in 1987 into Canadian Helicopter Corporation (CHC). In the early 1990s CHC provided service to UN peacekeeping operations in Kuwait, Thailand, and Cambodia; more crucially, it acquired a controlling interest in British International Helicopters, which made CHC the world's second largest provider of helicopter services. CHC also branched into the repair side of the helicopter business, setting up in 1999 a new subsidiary, Vector Aerospace, for that purpose. By this time, CHC had 200 aircraft in 69 bases around the world, and it acquired its main rival, Helikopter Services Group of Norway, to become the global leader in this field. Honoured as 'Newfoundland's Businessman of the Millennium', in 2000, Dobbin moved the company's headquarters to Vancouver shortly before his death in 2006.[12]

In Calgary in the years just after World War II, Donald Southern set up Alberta Trailer Hire

Company (later the Alberta Trailer Company or ATCO), providing mobile homes for workers in the Leduc oil fields. Joined by his son Ronald in the 1950s, Southern's company built industrial mobile housing for construction projects from Alaska to Pakistan and Saudi Arabia as well as in the US, and built a plant at Adelaide to serve the Australian and East Asian markets. Not surprisingly, ATCO eventually invested directly in the oil and gas business in Alberta, acquiring exploration companies and distributors, including Canadian Utilities of Edmonton in 1980. To accommodate its diversification strategy, ATCO decentralized its organization along product lines in the mid-1980s. Although its petroleum business was set back by recession in the industry, ATCO's manufacturing operations maintained it, producing modular housing units for China and Eastern Europe in the 1990s. As prospects for the oil patch improved, ATCO began to emphasize its energy-related businesses, setting up a Canadian Utilities affiliate in Britain, a cogeneration plant in Australia, and pipeline projects at home. By the early twenty-first century, ATCO was a strong regional company in the energy field and continued to be a major supplier of industrial housing overseas. The company also was one of the few Canadian firms with a woman in a senior position, when Nancy Southern succeeded her father, Ronald, as chief executive of ATCO.[13]

CHAPTER 12

Fortune's Favourites

In the annals of Canadian history, pride of place in the world of business—for better or worse—is usually accorded to the large, bureaucratic institutions: the Hudson's Bay Company, the Canadian Pacific Railway, the Big Five chartered banks, some multinationals (Imperial Oil), and some Crown corporations (CBC, Air Canada). This perspective is also found in popular notions about Canadian entrepreneurship, as in the comment from a business school professor in 1988 that 'We don't make folk heroes out of our entrepreneurs. In Canada, everyone wants to be a civil servant'—or at least the employee of a large, well-established corporation.[1]

Just as the view that Canadian business has been parochial and inward-looking may need qualification, the notion that Canadian business is populated largely by corporate behemoths has also been receiving a second look. In 2006, for example, the Business Family Centre of the Sauder School of Business at the University of British Columbia reported that there were more than one million 'family businesses' in Canada, accounting for over 80 per cent of all business activity in the country, and these businesses produced 45 per cent of Canada's gross domestic product (GDP) and half of the country's private-sector employment. A comparative study conducted by the Family Firm Institute in Boston, Massachusetts, offered similar figures in 2005, and indicated that the proportion of proprietary family firms in the private sector in Canada was among the highest among industrialized countries, comparable to the 'entrepreneurial' United States and greater than the UK, Italy, Germany, and Australia, among others.[2]

Individual proprietorships and family firms constitute a majority of small and medium-sized enterprises in many countries. Of perhaps greater import is the position of family firms in the 'big business' sector. In 2006, four of the 10 largest companies ranked by revenues by the *Globe and Mail* were family-owned or family-controlled: Power Corporation (Desmarais family); Magna International (Frank Stronach); Loblaws (Weston family); and Thomson Corporation (Thomson family). Three of these four, along with the McCain family, were also identified as among the 100 largest family-owned businesses in the world by *Family Business* magazine in 2005. Others listed in the top 100 companies in Canada included Bombardier, Empire Corporation (Sobey family), Rogers Communications, CanWest Global Communications (Asper family), and Cogeco (Audet family). There are also Canadian family enterprises whose ownership is so closely held that estimates of their assets and the full extent of their organizations are not easily accessible, such as the Irving family of New

Brunswick and the Burnett family of Toronto. Again, Canada is not unique in the world in this regard, but the role of families in controlling large enterprises is a significant feature of the country's business landscape.[3] Table 12.1 indicates the top 10 family firms in Canada in 2006, listing their revenues and numbers of employees.

The term 'family firms' encompasses a variety of different forms, ranging from tightly controlled enterprises wholly owned by an individual or family to public companies where family members may exercise control over a minority of outstanding shares, sometimes through intricate arrangements allowing some categories multiple voting rights, as in the case of Frank Stronach, who could dominate Magna International with less than 5 per cent of the equity in the company he started in the 1970s. A variation on this theme is the 'closed end trust' in which a small group of investors, not necessarily related, could acquire strategic control over a range of large public companies by becoming the largest bloc of shareholders, even if they held only 20 per cent of the shares. This is a practice that goes back to the days of Max Aitken and George Cox, but it continued to be a feature of the Canadian business scene throughout the twentieth century, sprouting conglomerations of a bewildering array of unrelated companies and industries.

The 1980s and 1990s experienced a resurgence of the idea of entrepreneurship in North America, stimulated in part by the success of start-up companies in emerging fields such as biotechnology and computer software and the seeming inability of large, established companies such as IBM and GM to cope effectively with new competitive forces. Advocates of the new entrepreneurialism such as George Gilder maintained that the advent of globalization and the 'knowledge economy' rendered traditional forms of business organization, based on industrialization, obsolete. Business schools in the US and Canada began to teach courses on 'entrepreneurship', and even corporate managers like Lee Iacocca of Chrysler and Jack Welch of GE were portrayed as 'intrapreneurs', transforming their entrenched bureaucratic divisions into competitive 'profit centres'.

In this context, the large, multi-unit, professionally managed business could be seen as a corporate 'dinosaur', and the era featured much downsizing and streamlining of big enterprises. The family firm or 'closely held business', by contrast, could be seen as more 'entrepreneurial', more capable of reacting quickly to changing market conditions, more versatile.

Family firms, proprietary enterprises, 'closely held businesses' could exhibit many of these features. Where managers of large public companies were obliged to focus on short-term earnings targets, family firms could take a longer perspective. Strategic decisions and major changes in direction could be taken more readily. Loyalty based on kinship could reinforce business discipline. On the other hand, entrepreneurs could grow old, out of touch with changing markets, rigidly devoted to past dogmas. Family enterprises could disintegrate in squabbling over their inheritance following the departure of the founder, or an incompetent scion could be put in charge. In companies where the family was a minority—albeit significant—owner, decisions could be made that were neither in the interest nor subject to the scrutiny of other shareholders. All of these elements—the virtues and the drawbacks—were present in the pageant of entrepreneurial and family fortunes in Canada.[4]

ALL IN THE FAMILY

There is no particular historical pattern to the distribution of family firms across the spectrum of businesses in Canada. They are found in the resource sector (e.g., MacMillan, Price Brothers), producer goods manufacturing (e.g., Massey), consumer goods manufacturing (e.g., Bombardier, Bata), construction/development (e.g., Reichmann), retailing (e.g., Simpson, Eaton), and communications (e.g., Rogers, Asper). None of the larger banks are family-controlled, but there are proprietary companies in the financial services

TABLE 12.1
CANADA'S LARGEST FAMILY FIRMS, 2006

Family	Company	Revenues 2006 ($ billions)	Employees 2006
Weston	G. Weston/Loblaws	32	134,000
Desmarais	Power Corporation	26	25,000
Sobey	Empire Corporation	25	35,000
Stronach	Magna International	23	82,000
Schwartz	Onex	18	138,000
Bombardier	Bombardier	15	56,000
Thomson	Thomson Corporation	9	40,000
Rogers	Rogers Communications	8	21,000
McCain	Maple Leaf Foods	7	18,000
Pattison	Pattison Group	7	n/a

Note: 'Family firm' includes companies where individual or family shareholders have a significant minority position as well as those where a single family owns a majority of shares.

Sources: *Family Business Magazine* at <www.familybusinessmagazine.com>; 'The Top 1000', *Globe and Mail Report on Business* (July–Aug. 2006).

sector (e.g., Fairfax Insurance, ONE Financial). The larger clusters are found in the areas of consumer goods and retailing. One common feature of the largest of these enterprises is that relatively few have lasted more than three generations, at least not in their original form. But even here there are some exceptions.

Certainly the most long-lived of these companies in Canada was Molson Brewers, tracing its heritage back to 1786, which merged with the US company, Coors, in 2005 after a bitter controversy within the Molson family. The Molson Coors Brewing Company was the fifth largest beer maker in the world after the merger, and Molson's held almost half the market in Canada and a 20 per cent share in the ownership of the Montreal Canadiens.

Brewing was only one of many enterprises established by the founding father, John Molson, and his successors in the nineteenth century, and much like the Hudson's Bay Company, Molson's was a name associated with the growth of the Canadian economy in that era. In addition to the Montreal brewery, John Molson built the first steamship in Canada in 1809, later developing it into a shipping line. His son, William, participated in the building of Canada's first railway in the 1830s, and with his brother, Thomas, established the Molsons Bank, which operated from 1853 until 1925, when it was absorbed by the Bank of Montreal. The Molson family also had investments in distilleries, mills, hotels, wharves, mines, and foundries in Quebec. John Molson Sr and his sons, John Jr and William, were active in politics, serving in the province's legislative assembly. As in many other family businesses, relationships did not always run smoothly: Thomas Molson feuded with his brothers over his plans to set up a distillery, and he moved to

Kingston for a time, but then joined William, who was at odds with John Jr about setting up a bank. But the scale and diversity of the family's business activities was so large that even this internal bickering could be accommodated.[5]

The brewery business, however, provided a steady income as the province's population grew. Until the advent of refrigeration in the 1880s, breweries primarily served local or regional markets, and most were family enterprises like Molson's. In Halifax, Alexander Keith established an ale-making enterprise in the 1820s that prospered when the cost of rum production rose after the abolition of slavery in the Caribbean, and his success attracted others into the field, including John Oland in 1867. In Ontario, a number of brewers emerged in the period before Confederation, including John Labatt, Thomas Carling, and John Sleeman in the 1840s, and Eugene O'Keefe in 1862, who subsequently went into competition with Molson in Quebec in partnership with John Atkin. These names, familiar to Canadian beer drinkers today, were only the most durable of more than 100 brewing enterprises that arose (and many of which fell) in the nineteenth century.

The advent of refrigeration, mechanized packaging, and more intense competition in advertising demanded increased capitalization in the industry, and as in other fields, there was a period of growth and consolidation in brewing in the early 1900s. There were regional amalgamations in British Columbia and the Prairies, and two central Canadian ventures sought to absorb the national market, the Canadian Brewing Corporation based in Ontario and National Breweries Ltd emanating from Quebec. Both of these undertakings were to eventually be folded into E.P. Taylor's beer empire. The larger family companies, including Molson, resisted pressures to join these confederations and undertook to survive through new investment and expansion of the market, introducing 'light' beers in the 1930s.

In addition to competitive pressures, all of the breweries had to cope with various experiments in Prohibition in the early 1900s, although Molson

benefited from the fact that Quebec remained 'wet' throughout this era. By the late 1920s most provinces were abandoning full-scale prohibition, but in its place government-controlled package stores in many cases took over distribution, and there were provincial bans on the sale of beer manufactured outside their borders. In these circumstances, brewers seeking to develop a national market had to build plants in every province they chose to enter. For amalgamators like Taylor, this involved the acquisition of breweries across the country, including Carling and O'Keefe. Molson also made some acquisitions, but its main strategy in the 1950s and 1960s was to build new breweries outside Quebec, focusing particularly on Ontario and Atlantic Canada. The company also entered the US market, and by the end of the 1980s had become the second largest distributor of foreign beer there (after Heineken), although this distinguished position only provided it with 1 per cent of that market.

The Molsons also followed the fashion of the day, that is, 'diversification' or, more accurately, conglomeration, acquiring companies like Anthes Imperial, an office furniture firm, Aikenheads hardware chain, and Beaver Lumber in the 1970s, followed by expansion into the chemical industry through investment in Diversey, a US manufacturer of cleaning solvents, and the acquisition of an American subsidiary of the German company, BASF. Although in some respects this was similar to the diverse activities of the family in the previous century, the circumstances were very different. By the end of the 1980s the company, whose board was now chaired by Eric Molson, a seventh-generation family member, recognized that many of these efforts at diversification were underperforming and that the moves by larger producers abroad were driving the industry towards global competition and consolidation: Carling-O'Keefe, for example, had by this time passed into the hands of an Australian company, Elders IXL Ltd. One of the few positive results of this strategy appeared to be the acquisition of the Canadiens, which was useful in marketing beer; although, curiously, in 1988 the company stopped sponsoring *Hockey Night in Canada*. Its rival, Labatt's Breweries, acquired the Toronto Blue Jays in 1976 for much the same reason.

The first response to this challenge could be seen as 'more of the same'. Molson hired Mickey Cohen, a former Ottawa bureaucratic whiz kid, who orchestrated a merger with an Australian conglomerate. This move did have the virtue of giving Molson a share in control of the Australian brewery Foster, as well as its former rival, Carling-O'Keefe. But earnings continued to stagnate. Cohen departed, and through the 1990s the company sloughed off the fruits of its conglomeration era, often at a loss. Increasing emphasis was placed on developing the national market for beer, following the removal of interprovincial barriers to trade in this field in 1995, as well as consolidating a stronger position in the US market, which involved, among other things, allowing the American company, Miller, to acquire a 20 per cent interest in Molson.

But Molson faced strong competition from Labatt. That company had long before ceased to be a 'family firm' in any sense; both Molson and Labatt had become public companies in 1945, but the Molsons retained a significant bloc of voting shares and a role in management. In the 1960s Labatt had briefly fallen into the clutches of one of the largest American brewers, Joseph Schlitz of Milwaukee, but was liberated by a US antitrust suit and ended up under the control of the Canadian conglomerate Brascan. Like Molson, the company then set out to expand across Canada by building new plants and through acquisitions, including the venerable Maritime family firm, Olands—an Oland was to rise to the presidency of Labatt in the 1980s while another Oland scion set about building up a new Atlantic Canadian challenger, Moosehead Breweries. By that time, however, there were only eight breweries in the country not under control of Molson, Labatt, or Carling-O'Keefe, and the liberation of the trade from provincial restrictions set in motion another move towards consolidation after 1995. After a

complicated merger struggle with Gerry Schwartz, Labatt ended up in the hands of the Belgian giant Interbrew, which was looking for ways to enter the North American market.

These activities set the scene for a contest between Labatt and Molson for the mass market in beer in Canada, although both also faced new challenges from newly emerging 'mini-breweries' like Sleeman in Ontario and Granville Island in British Columbia, which were also seeking to take advantage of the free market and changing consumer tastes. Even as the two Canadian majors launched advertising campaigns against each other, the external scene continued to shift. In the 1980s Labatt had made a marketing deal with the US company, Anheuser-Busch, to market its leading brand, Budweiser, in Canada; and Molson had made a similar arrangement with Coors, the Denver-based beer company that was itself still a largely family-controlled firm. Molson's arrangement with Miller led Coors to cancel that deal, but after a new arrangement was negotiated, Coors began probing further for a merger. Eric Molson supported the idea, but at this point the family connection resurfaced. Eric's younger cousin, Ian Molson, who had earlier been designated the heir apparent to chairman of the board, raised objections and began accumulating voting shares while also soliciting support from Schwartz to bid against Coors. Eric Molson proceeded to mobilize the shares of other family members and the normally private affairs of the family became a matter of intense media attention. In 2006 the merger finally went through, presented as essentially an alliance of equals, and indeed the new company was named Molson Coors Brewing Co. But for observers in Canada, the merger represented the end of a family firm that had been founded more than 200 years earlier, and, ironically, a company whose recent advertising campaign had featured the slogan, 'I am . . . Canadian!'[6]

Although not as long-lived as the Molson dynasty, the Weston family achieved a kind of quasi-regal status in the middle of the twentieth century, replete with landed estates in Britain and Ireland, and hobnobbing with the British royal family—an ironic status for a family whose founding father, George Weston, was the son of a Cockney-born immigrant to North America who set up a bakery in Toronto in 1882, relying on mechanization and integration into flour milling to become one of the largest distributors of baked goods in the city by the early 1900s. The real empire builder, however, was his son Garfield Weston who, after serving in the Canadian Army in World War I, moved the company into production of tinned biscuits and embarked on expansion across Canada and into the United States. While the Depression temporarily checked his ambitions, Garfield redirected his efforts to acquiring and retrofitting bakeries in Britain for mass production. In the years following World War II, he pursued a strategy of vertical integration in the food business, acquiring mills, packaging factories, and grocery stores in the US, Australia, and South Africa as well as Britain. Among his acquisitions was the venerable Fortnum & Mason, grocers to the royal family, in 1951; four years later Weston took over an Ontario supermarket chain, Loblaw Companies Ltd, that had been established in 1919 specializing in small neighborhood 'groceterias'.

Garfield Weston was a great empire builder, but he was less interested in organizational matters, which were left in the hands of relatively autonomous regional managers. In Canada, the Weston and Loblaw operations were run by a long-time British associate, George Metcalf, who continued Garfield's expansionist policies through the 1960s, including what proved to be the unwise acquisition of a US chain, National Tea, whose stores were largely located in deteriorating downtown neighbourhoods, and some anomalous entities such as the E.B. Eddy paper mill and the salmon processor, British Columbia Packers. Despite its formidable size, which periodically invited investigations by antitrust authorities in the US and Canada's Royal Commission on Corporate Concentration in the 1970s, the Weston/Loblaw business was increasingly vulnerable with its debt burden

from expansion as profit margins, always tight in the food distribution business, diminished.

In 1978 Garfield died, and his empire was divided among the heirs. The North American component passed on to his youngest son, Galen Weston, who had been educated in Canada and demonstrated his business acumen by establishing a chain of supermarkets and department stores in Ireland, virtually from the ground up. Even before Garfield's death, Galen had become involved in the Canadian operation, becoming chief executive of Loblaw. He reorganized the sprawling Weston enterprises into three functional areas: food products; Loblaw (the supermarket division); and a 'resource' division for the assorted other operations, most of which were jettisoned by the 1990s. He recruited two talented managers, both veterans of the US consulting firm McKiney & Co., to help resuscitate the floundering Loblaw company, the largest part of the Weston business. David Nichol focused on marketing, including the introduction of what became the popular specialty brand of goods, 'President's Choice'; Richard Currie developed an overall strategy for debt reduction and store consolidation, including disposal of the US venture. By the 1990s, Loblaw's profit position was strengthened, and the company had not only recovered its position as the largest food retailer in Ontario, but controlled more than one-third of the Canadian market, expanding into Atlantic Canada and the West.

Loblaw's success was due in large measure to the strength of its management, but the Westons also benefited from the misfortunes suffered by key competitors in the retail food industry, many of which were also family firms. In Quebec, which always proved a tough market for Loblaw, one of the largest of these was Steinberg's, a supermarket chain that traced its origins back to a grocery store established in 1913 by Ida Steinberg, an immigrant from Hungary. Her five sons, dominated by Sam Steinberg, expanded across Quebec and into New Brunswick and the Ottawa area, also setting up a discount department store chain, Miracle Mart, and a real estate venture,

Ivanhoe Investments. After Sam's death in 1978, however, the company's fortunes slipped amid squabbling between his daughter Mitzi, who ran the Miracle Mart operation, and her two sisters. In the early 1990s Weston tried to buy the Steinberg chain, but encountered resistance—as a 'foreign' company—from the Quebec government, which undertook instead to arrange for the acquisition of the foundering enterprise by the Caisse de dépôt et de placement, which in turn sold it to two other Quebec-based chains, Provigo and Metro-Richelieu. By the end of the decade, however, Loblaw was in a position to absorb the enlarged Provigo company.

Another dynastic challenger to Loblaw was the Oshawa Group, founded by two brothers, Max and Maurice Wolfe. Beginning as produce wholesalers in Toronto in the early 1900s, in the years after World War II the Wolfes found that the emerging supermarket chains were bypassing them to purchase directly from suppliers. One of Maurice's sons, Ray Wolfe, came up with the idea of moving into the supermarket field, based on the franchise model developed by a Chicago group, the Independent Grocers Alliance (IGA). In 1951, Ray formed the Oshawa Group, which acquired the Canadian rights to IGA and rode the post-war boom across Ontario and into Atlantic Canada and the West; the franchise system enabled growth through new equity issues, while the Wolfes retained control of the voting shares. Ray's death in 1990, however, triggered intra-family feuding: his son, Jonathan, chosen to take over management of the Group, encountered resistance from other family members. A reorganization effort, superintended by a Boston consulting firm, Conflict Management Group, temporarily settled conflicts with a professional manager, Alistair Graham, running the operation. By 1998, however, when Graham retired, tensions resurfaced, and the Oshawa Group became the focus of a bidding war between Loblaw and a Maritime rival, Empire Company Ltd.

The victorious bidder, Empire, was in turn a family enterprise controlled by the Sobey family of Stellarton, Nova Scotia, which within a few years emerged as the main rival to Loblaw in central Canada. Around the time that the Wolfe brothers began selling produce in Toronto, John W. Sobey was peddling meat and building a butcher's store in Stellarton. His son Frank extended the business into a small chain of supermarkets in central Nova Scotia in the 1940s and 1950s, eventually moving into development of shopping malls and acquiring a pharmaceutical chain, Lawton's Drugs. The third generation of three Sobey brothers pushed further afield, looking particularly at the Quebec market. In the 1980s the Sobeys acquired a significant foothold in Provigo, as well as in a New England supermarket chain. The takeover of Oshawa Group, however, proved to be the largest step beyond the Atlantic regional market. By 2006, Empire held 16 per cent of the retail food market in Canada, second only to Loblaw.[7]

Even as they jousted for position in the Canadian market, the major supermarket chains were also girding themselves for the invasion of the US giant (and family firm) Wal-Mart, with its 'supercentres' that included burgeoning retail food areas. As of 2006, Wal-Mart had a relatively small foothold in this sector in Canada, but its sheer size and demonstrated success in the general retail market posed a significant challenge. Even the most-entrenched of family enterprises in Canadian retailing would have to tread carefully in these circumstances, remembering the recent fate of that most quintessential Canadian dynasty, the Eatons, whose collapse reflected both the impact of new competition and fundamental weaknesses in the structure of family firms.

For more than three generations the Eaton family controlled the company founded by Timothy Eaton, and its chain of department stores, mail-order catalogues, and annual Santa Claus parade became part of the fabric of the nation's cultural life. The year 1978 marked an apogee of sorts, with the opening of the massive Eaton Centre in Toronto, encompassing eight square blocks of prime downtown real estate. But even at this point there were symptoms of incipient decline. A year before, the company had discontinued its catalogue, which in some respects could be seen as an adjustment to the realities of an increasingly urban retail market. Four years later the company dropped its sponsorship of the Christmas parade, citing high costs. By this time Eaton's was encountering competitive problems, not only from its traditional rival, the Hudson's Bay Company, but from discount chains and more specialized retailers. During the 1970s Eaton's had focused on the development of malls in downtown core areas in Ontario, benefiting from support from the Ontario Downtown Renewal program; but this move left it with an unprofitable real estate inventory and malls with high vacancy rates, while the population was shifting to the suburbs. By the 1990s Eaton's had slumped to little more than a 10 per cent share of the retail market in Canada, where it had held more than half of that market in the years following World War II. In this context the arrival of Wal-Mart and other 'big box' stores spelled disaster.

Critical observers attributed many of these mistakes to the incompetence or at least the inattention of the family's fourth generation, who were more interested in horse breeding, auto racing, or charitable giving than in minding the store, while failing to bring in professional managers at the top to make up for their shortcomings. In 1997, George Ross Eaton, who had presided over the company since 1988, recruited George Kosich, who had overhauled The Bay, hoping he would duplicate that feat for Eaton's; but this move led to threats of litigation from the rival retailer. A year later the family announced that Eaton's was bankrupt, and after a year of efforts to reorganize the store into an upscale-oriented operation (the store had abandoned efforts to compete with discounters in the early 1990s) it went public and was taken over by Sears Canada in 1999. Within a few years not only had the family been separated from ownership of its chain, but the Eaton name itself had virtually disappeared from public view. Much like Massey-Ferguson a decade earlier, one of Canada's most famous commercial dynasties disappeared rapidly from the scene.[8]

CONGLOMERATORS

Company growth through mergers and acquisitions has been a continuing feature on the business scene throughout the twentieth century, so much so that the legal and accounting professions spawned an entire subcategory of specialization. But the rationale for mergers has shifted over the years: in the early 1900s in Canada, as in the US and in the European industrialized economies, mergers proved to be a central vehicle for consolidation of national markets, supplemented by what the American business historian Alfred Chandler Jr designated strategies 'of scale and scope', the latter involving the integration under one umbrella of companies engaged in related activities, depending, for example, on similar raw material inputs or common industrial processes. In the post-World War II era, however, a new phenomenon began to emerge: companies that exercised control over a wide range of essentially unrelated lines of business. In the United States, in particular, a vogue for 'conglomerates' thrived. Entrepreneurs such as Royal Little, James Ling, and Charles Bluhdorn cobbled together empires that combined electrical equipment and aerospace manufacturers, auto parts makers and film companies; venerable firms such as International Telephone & Telegraph under Harold Geneen vigorously pursued conglomeration on a scale that invited scrutiny by the US Congress in the early 1970s. By that time, however, conglomerates were losing their appeal; claims that these configurations would produce unusual 'synergies' were met with increasing skepticism as the stock market boom of the 1960s subsided.[9]

In Canada, on the other hand, the creation of 'conglomerates', even though the term was not yet invented, began long before they became a fad in the US, and outlasted them, culminating with an orgy of expansion in the 1980s. In some respects there was nothing entirely new going on: turn of the century financiers like George Cox and Max Aitken had fashioned diversified manufacturing and utility empires. But the conglomerators of the 1970s and 1980s came from a wider business community, including newspaper publishers, building contractors, and real estate speculators, joined eventually by old-line companies like Canadian Pacific and Bell Telephone. The environment of the time helped encourage visions of glory. As in the US, the growth of pension funds and mutual funds enlarged the domestic capital pool and spawned a subculture of fund managers prepared to move large blocks of money to maximize short-term earnings, and bankers now facing potential competition from overseas lenders were more attentive to the needs of large clients. At the same time, the relatively small size of the Canadian economy may have pushed ambitious empire builders towards conglomeration, along with investment abroad, as ways of enlarging their corporate ventures.

One of the earliest proto-conglomerators of the post-war era was E.P. Taylor. Even before service with C.D. Howe's Ministry of Munitions in World War II helped assure him of entry into the country's leading boardrooms and clubs, Taylor had erected a mini-empire in the Canadian brewing industry. He formed an alliance with a British group that provided him with the capital to assemble the Brewing Corporation of Canada by buying up small brewers at Depression-era prices. By the end of the 1930s, Taylor's company held one-third of the Ontario beer market and had branched into soft drinks (Orange Crush) and acquired hotels and restaurants.

Taylor's wartime activities brought him in contact with Floyd Odlum, an American financier who specialized in acquiring and cultivating stocks in undervalued companies. From Odlum, Taylor derived the idea of forming a 'closed' investment trust, essentially a partnership with a very small circle of shareholders that would buy blocks of voting shares in a few companies, sufficient to influence management decisions. The main criterion for selection was the growth potential of the target company irrespective of its particular line of business. In this sense Argus Corporation, the investment firm set up by Taylor

with several Toronto associates in 1945, represented a pioneering form of conglomeration. Over the next decade, Argus acquired shares and board representation on a range of medium to large Canadian companies, including Dominion Stores, Domtar, BC Forest Products (in association with another wartime crony, H.R. MacMillan, who also sat on the Argus board), Hollinger Mines, Norcen Energy, and Massey-Harris.[10]

In 1969, Taylor, who had become much more interested in horse breeding, stepped down as chief executive of Argus, leaving it in the hands of his erstwhile partner, Bud McDougald, who ran the company until his death in 1978. At this point, a new and colourful character entered the scene. Not since the days of R.B. Bennett in the Great Depression has anyone so personified the idea of 'capitalist' in the public mind as Conrad Black, who deliberately cultivated and celebrated this image, indulging in a lavish lifestyle, inveighing against the 'socialist' excesses of Canada, quarrelling with prime ministers, and melodramatically confronting the minions of the US Justice Department.

The son of George M. Black, one of Taylor's junior partners in the Argus venture, the youthful Conrad and his brother, Montagu Black, carried out an elaborate coup after McDougald's death, acquiring control of Argus with only a minority investment position but holding the proxies of the widows of two of the company's founding partners, including McDougald. Before long Conrad emerged as the dominant figure. Over the next few years he proceeded to dismantle Argus, selling off most of its member companies. This may not have been his initial intention, but the recession of the early 1980s revealed the competitive weaknesses of companies like Massey-Ferguson and Dominion Stores. In any case, Conrad Black seems to have had his sights set for a different goal. Even before his involvement with Argus, he and an associate, David Radler, had begun acquiring small newspapers and restructuring them, which usually entailed laying off staff and relying on wire services for news, in order to maximize revenues from advertising. By the end of the 1980s, more than 400 newspapers across the US and Canada had been folded into his empire, and to these were added the *Chicago Sun Times*, the *Jerusalem Post*, and a share in an Australian news chain in the 1990s.

In 1985, Black took a major step towards achieving his aspiration of becoming a British press baron in the mould of Lord Beaverbrook when he acquired the venerable Fleet Street newspaper, the *Telegraph*. A decade later he established a new Canadian 'national newspaper', the *National Post*, to challenge the *Globe and Mail*, whose editorials he regarded as too sympathetic to the Liberal Party. His increasing preoccupation with politics (the *Post* never was very successful financially and he sold most of his other newspapers in the late 1990s) culminated in a confrontation with Prime Minister Jean Chrétien when Black was offered a peerage. Chrétien invoked a 1919 measure that barred a Canadian citizen from accepting a noble title; Conrad then very vocally gave up his citizenship and was ennobled as Lord Black of Crossharbour in 2001 (a few years later, as his legal difficulties in the US loomed, Black set out to regain his Canadian citizenship).

Throughout this period Black had exercised control over his empire through Hollinger International, which had long since ceased to be a mining enterprise and was simply the holding company for his newspapers. After the crash of 2000–1 and the post-Enron scandals in the US, Black faced increasing pressure from shareholders in Hollinger and increased scrutiny from the US Justice Department over allegations that he and Radler and a few other insiders had siphoned money from Hollinger to their personal benefit. By 2005 the beleaguered Black had been forced to sell the *Telegraph* and *National Post* (the latter to CanWest Communications), as well as his opulent mansions in England and New York. The final blow fell in July 2007 when a jury in Chicago found him guilty of fraud and obstruction of justice. Black appealed the conviction, stalwartly protesting his innocence, but in the meantime he went to prison in Florida in March 2008 to begin

serving a six-year term. His fortune had dwindled considerably and his publishing empire was gone with the wind.[11]

One of Black's presumed role models was Roy Thomson, Lord Thomson of Fleet, whose son Kenneth, one of Conrad's contemporaries, proved to be more successful in managing his own empire. Roy Thomson had pioneered in the development of radio broadcasting in Ontario in the 1930s, then moved into newspapers. After World War II he migrated to England, establishing himself as a media baron with more than 200 newspapers, including the prestigious *Times* of London. In 1964 he was ennobled, giving up his Canadian citizenship in the process, as Lord Black was later obliged to do. But the most significant accretion to his wealth was a fortuitous investment with a US firm, Occidental Petroleum, in British North Sea oil fields shortly before the first energy crisis of 1973.

Three years later Sir Roy died, succeeded by Ken Thomson, who deployed the family fortune not only into expansion of the newspaper empire, including the Toronto *Globe and Mail*, but also into more diversified areas. In 1979 Thomson acquired controlling interest in the Hudson's Bay Company, which had previously gobbled up a variety of competing retailers, including Simpsons, making 'The Bay', as it was renamed, the largest department store chain in Canada. In contrast to the extravagant and extroverted Conrad Black, Ken Thomson was a self-effacing figure in the business community, who frugally shopped for bargains at Zellers, one of the discount stores he owned, although he also devoted himself to acquiring a remarkable collection of Canadian art and generously supported the Art Gallery of Ontario.[12]

Ken Thomson was not the only one to be caught up in the conglomeration fever of the era. The Reichmann brothers, who emigrated to Canada from Hungary via Morocco in the 1940s, established a foothold in the high-rise construction business in Toronto with their family firm, Olympia & York (initially a tile-making enterprise), then went into the skyscraper heartlands of New York, Chicago, and San Francisco in the 1960s and 1970s. At this point they decided to diversify beyond the boom-and-bust high-rise real estate market, although their first choice seems odd in retrospect: the pulp and paper giant Abitibi-Price was acquired in 1981, followed by attempts to expand further into the natural resources field with minority investments in Noranda and MacMillan-Bloedel. In 1986 they made their most dramatic moves, taking over Gulf Canada, jettisoning its refineries and gas station chain while retaining its stake in the Alberta oil fields. Later that year Hiram Walker was brought into the Olympia & York stable, with the distillery component discarded after a bitter struggle with the owners: the Reichmanns ended up with the oil and gas properties that Walker had acquired in its own bid towards conglomeration.

The Bronfman family, of Seagram distillery fame (see box, p. 226), produced two sets of rival acquisitors. Charles and Edgar, who had inherited control of Seagram, at the high point of the second energy crisis of 1979–80, sold off significant oil holdings that their father, Sam, had accumulated over the years. Flush with cash, they explored the US merger market, eventually settling on a bid for Conoco (Continental Oil), one of America's 10 major companies in the field and the former partner with Hudson's Bay Co. in Canadian oil and gas development. The struggle for Conoco pitted Seagram against much larger US companies, including Du Pont and Shell. In the end, Du Pont emerged triumphant, but the Bronfmans acquired a significant equity position in the American chemical giant.

Meanwhile, their cousins, Edward and Peter, who had been squeezed out of Seagram by 'Mister Sam', set up their own investment trust, Edper, and began shopping for companies, beginning in 1976 with Trizec Equities, a large Toronto property management company originally founded by the US high-rise developer Bill Zeckendorff. Their biggest acquisition, in 1979, was Brascan, successor firm to the Pearson/Mackenzie utility multinational Brazilian Traction. During the 1970s that company had sold off (under some pressure) its electric system to Brazil for $450 million and transformed itself into a diversified holding company. While engaged in a protracted struggle for control of Brascan, Edper also went after the even larger mining-cum-conglomerate, Noranda. Ultimately, both Brascan and Noranda, along with an array of manufacturers and insurance and trust companies, ended up in the hands of the Bronfmans.[13]

While the proprietary empire builders preempted media attention, among the largest of the era's conglomerates were two of Canada's oldest enduring corporate entities: the Canadian Pacific Railway and Bell Canada. After the expansion binge of the 1920s, CPR had retreated for a time from its earlier tradition of diversification. Apart from the creation of CP Air in World War II, the company stuck to railroading and managing its other established investments. During the buoyant 1960s, however, the company resumed its outward thrust, largely through the prodding of Ian Sinclair, who had joined CPR in 1947 as a lawyer representing the railroad in its perpetual freight-rate hearings before the Railway Commission, but soon displayed a talent for financial wheeling and dealing. In 1962, Canadian Pacific Investments (CPI) was set up to provide a vehicle for Sinclair's energies: non-transportation investments, including Cominco and CP Oil & Gas (established in 1957 to manage CP's mineral resource lands not already leased out), were assigned to CPI. In 1967, CPI began issuing its own public shares and embarked on a career of expansion through a subsidiary, Marathon Realty; telecommunications development (CNCP); and international investment in hotels, mines, and industrial acquisitions that included Algoma Steel, Maple Leaf Mills, and Canadian International Paper. When Sinclair took over as chief executive of the parent company in 1972, he arranged to remove the word 'Railway' from its corporate title. By the time he stepped down in 1981, more than half the company's earnings came from investments outside the transportation field.

THE FALL OF THE HOUSE OF SEAGRAM

Of all the family business dynasties in Canada, none have had the prominence and notoriety of the Bronfmans, who rose from shady origins in the Prohibition era to run one of the country's most successful multinationals, and whose domestic feuds were frequently chronicled by the media and celebrated in at least three novels, most notably Mordecai Richler's *Solomon Gundy Was Here*. Fittingly, the events that led to the final disaster and disappearance of the Seagram company, if not their fortune, was accompanied by melodrama and recrimination, making the Bronfmans a symbol of the hazards of family-controlled enterprise.

In the decades following World War II the Bronfmans ruled an empire of distilleries, vineyards, plantations, and sales agencies that virtually spanned the world, the largest global producer of alcoholic beverages as well as a substantial player in the Canadian high-rise real estate market and the oil business. The central figure was Sam Bronfman, who was as ruthless with other family members as he was with Seagram's competitors, driving his relatives out of management, dictating the division of profits among the family, and ensuring that his sons would inherit control of the business. But even at the height of his success, 'Mister Sam' fretted about the future: 'You've heard about shirtsleeves to shirtsleeves in three generations', he brooded. 'Empires have come and gone.'

To head off this disaster, Sam put his sons and heirs, Edgar and Charles, through a tough apprenticeship at Seagram, and as his hold on power loosened in the late 1960s, they carried out long-needed changes in the management of a company that had been run for many years as an absolute monarchy. They also demonstrated skills at dealmaking, parlaying investments in oil into a major stake in the giant US chemical company, Du Pont,

in 1981. For years the dividends from Du Pont provided earnings almost as large as the revenues from Seagram for the Bronfmans.

By the late 1980s Edgar had emerged as the key figure in the company, and he designated his son, Edgar Jr, as heir apparent. For a time Junior (also called 'Efer') carried out Seagram management tasks dutifully, but his heart was never in running an old-line alcoholic beverages enterprise. With his father's blessing, although with some grumbling from other shareholders (including Charles), the Du Pont stake was sold in 1994 to enable Efer to go into show business, acquiring the entertainment conglomerate MCA/Universal Studios and shortly thereafter Polygram, a European music company.

Despite a rocky baptism into the high-risk and personality-driven world of the entertainment business, Efer's commitment to the new course remained steadfast: the Seagram name disappeared after a few years, and eventually it was sold to a European rival, Diageo. But earnings from MCA/Universal lagged behind other entertainment companies, and did not match the Du Pont contributions of yore. By 2000, following the AOL-Time Warner merger, the Bronfmans sought a partner to help them exploit the supposed new era of 'convergence' of media and computer technologies. Their choice was the French company Vivendi, whose chief executive, Jean Marie Messier, had created a multimedia giant out of a sewer and water utility. Unfortunately, Messier's Napoleonic ambitions extended beyond his abilities, and the Bronfmans could only watch in horror as Vivendi sank into a morass of debt. By the time they were able to remove Messier from power, the value of the merged company's stock had collapsed to one-third of its initial value, and the Bronfmans fortune had halved, although still a healthy $4 billion (US).

The 'Founding Father': Sam Bronfman in 1938 with his sons, Edgar (on left) and Charles. (*Toronto Star/ The Canadian Press*)

Sources: Nicholas Faith, *The Bronfmans: The Rise and Fall of the House of Seagram* (New York, 2006); Michael Marrus, *Samuel Bronfman: The Life and Times of Seagram's Mister Sam* (Toronto, 1991); Rod McQueen, *The Icarus Factor: The Rise and Fall of Edgar Bronfman Jr.* (Toronto, 2004).

Bell Canada also turned to conglomeration in the 1970s, a novel move for what had traditionally been a profitable but conservative utility since its early years under Charles Sise. As in the case of CPR, the central figure in this transformation was a lawyer, Jean de Grandpré, who had been hired in 1965 to help persuade regulatory authorities to liberalize the legal formulas under which the utility's profits were determined, and later to combat Canadian Pacific's entry into the telecommunications field. In part to circumvent the reach of Canada's regulatory agencies over Bell's international activities, de Grandpré created a separate entity, Bell Canada Enterprises (BCE), which served as the legal parent of the telephone company. In 1983, de Grandpré became chief executive of BCE. Riding the mid-decade securities boom, BCE set out on an expansion strategy that led to the acquisition (among others) of Trans-Canada Pipelines and other remnants of Dome Petroleum, and the former Crown corporation, Teleglobe Canada. At the end of the decade Bell Canada and Canadian Pacific remained, as they had been 35 years before, the country's two largest non-financial enterprises, but both had been substantially transformed into 'diversified' companies operating in international markets.[14]

The economic downturn of the early 1980s had relatively little impact on the momentum of the conglomerators; the more substantial recession a decade later—the worst since World War II—was far more lethal, with many empire builders overly leveraged with debt as their companies fell on hard times. An early victim was Robert Campeau, yet another real estate tycoon who had acquired control over two major US retailing giants, Allied Stores (owners of Brooks Brothers, Ann Taylor, and Jordan March) and Federated Stores (owners of the Bloomingdale chain) in the mid-1980s. By 1990 he was overextended, with $10 billion (US) in debts and no prospects for a bailout. Two years later it was the Reichmanns who faced bankruptcy, largely because of their commitment to the huge Canary Wharf building project in east-end London that was premised on the erroneous (or at least premature) belief that Britain's financial houses would all relocate there. Edward and Peter Bronfman kept Edper afloat by increasing capitalization through new public issues of stock in 1989 and selling off MacMillan-Bloedel and Labatt over the next few years, but their days of expansion were largely over. Subsequently, CPR and Bell rediscovered the virtues of going 'back to basics'. William Stinson, a 'fourth-generation railroader' with CPR, became chief executive in 1981 and resumed a strategy of acquisitions of rail lines in the US. In 1996 the company headquarters relocated westward to Calgary from Montreal and it revived its original name, the Canadian Pacific Railway. Five years later, most of its non-railway subsidiaries were divested. BCE also sloughed off a number of 'non-core' businesses at the end of the 1990s, arousing controversy when it abandoned Teleglobe in 2002; that former Crown corporation was taken over by the Indian conglomerate, Tata Group.

One conglomerate that survived these upheavals was Power Corporation, controlled by Paul Desmarais. A French Canadian, born in Sudbury, Desmarais dropped out of Osgoode Hall Law School to take over a family investment in a nearly bankrupt local bus line in 1951. Building on success, he acquired more bus lines in Quebec and also invested in insurance companies and the media, notably Montreal's *La Presse*, which augmented his visibility as a rising francophone businessman during Quebec's Quiet Revolution. His greatest coup came in 1968 when he achieved a foothold in the utility company, Power Corporation, that had been established in 1925 by the Montreal investment firm of Nesbitt Thomson. By the time Desmarais arrived on the scene, Power Corp. had significant shares in the Quebec newsprint company, Consolidated Bathurst, and Canada Steamship Lines. In control of Power after 1970, Desmarais embarked on an expansionist policy, acquiring Great West Life Assurance, Montreal Trust, and Investor's Group, which became the centrepiece for an integrated financial services operation. A failed bid for control of Argus in 1975 precipitated a Royal Commission on Corporate Concentration, which, as usual, concluded that there was no danger of monopoly in Canada and, if anything, there was a need for larger consolidations to make Canadian enterprises more competitive globally.

During the 1980s Power Corp. disposed of its holdings in Canada Steamship Lines (which subsequently was managed for a time by Paul Martin Jr, en route to a political career) and expanded overseas, with an investment in a Swiss financial company, Pargesa Holding SA, paving the way for a new company, Power Financial (PFC), which raised substantial new capital and enabled Desmarais to maintain some of its more troubled subsidiaries, such as Consolidated Bathurst. In 1989 he sold Montreal Trust to BCE, and escaped the fate of most of his debt-ridden conglomerate brethren. Expansion in Europe and the US continued through the 1990s, and Desmarais formed a partnership with Albert Frere of Belgium: their jointly owned Groupe Bruxelles Lambert acquired large shareholdings in French companies, such as Total Petroleum and Lafarge Cement. When he stepped down as chairman of Power Corp. in 1996, Desmarais could boast of an increase in the market value of the company to $2.6 billion from $61 million in 1968. Desmarais's survival (and success) through the years could be attributed in no small part to his skill in disposing of assets in a timely manner as well as acquiring them.[15]

The crises of the early 1990s did not necessarily mark the disappearance of conglomeration. One persistent figure was Gerald Schwartz of Onex Corporation. A protege of the Aspers in Winnipeg, Schwartz honed his skills in the 1970s at the Harvard Business School and, perhaps more significantly, through contact with financiers of the junk-bond era like Bernard Cornfeld and Henry Kravis. After running an investment arm of Asper's CanWest, Schwartz relocated to Toronto and set up Onex in 1983. Drawing on the 'KKR model' of leveraged buyouts practised by the New York City equity firm of Kohlberg Kravis Roberts & Co., Schwartz focused on acquiring undervalued companies, reorganizing them, and then holding them as they revived, a formula not unlike that of Max Aitken earlier in the century. A takeover of Beatrice Foods in 1987 was an early victory. In 1999 his most ambitious venture, a $1.2 billion bid to merge Air Canada and Canadian Airlines International (formerly Pacific West Airlines of Calgary, which had taken over CP Air in the 1970s), was blocked, but the Onex empire included a wide range of companies, including Loews Cineplex, J.L. French (the largest die-cast maker in the auto industry), Magellan Health Services in the US, and the electronics manufacturer, Celestica, which he had acquired from IBM Canada in 1996, shortly after a lost bid for Labatt. Another westerner, Jimmy Pattison, built a diversified international conglomerate from his home base in Vancouver that included transportation companies, food packagers, financial services, auto dealerships, and 'Ripley's Believe It or Not', a franchised assortment of syndicated newspaper features, television series, computer games, and museums devoted to the bizarre and the unusual.

Critics of conglomeration saw much of this activity as simply 'sound and fury'—moving assets from one owner to another while creating little in the way of lasting value to the economy. Mergers and takeovers created work for numerous lawyers, accountants, brokers, and business consultants, but the 'restructuring' that usually followed eliminated managerial and manufacturing jobs in even greater numbers. The 1978 Royal Commission that followed the Argus–Power contest noted that the financial performance of conglomerates rarely matches expectations; and as the events of the early 1990s were to demonstrate, many of these companies carried huge debt loads that left them vulnerable to economic downturns.

A (PARTIAL) CHANGING OF THE GUARD

In 1975, the journalist Peter C. Newman, in the first of his numerous volumes on *The Canadian Establishment*, provided a portrait very similar to John Porter's *Vertical Mosaic* (1965). This was a picture of a business elite still carrying the legacy of their Anglo-Scottish forebears, who perpetuated networks of privilege and power through social and familial connections. Within this context, ethnic sub-communities formed their own limited business elites: a French-Canadian group in Montreal and Quebec centred on banking and the law; a Jewish business community, principally in Montreal but also found in places like Winnipeg. Oil and gas and related resource industries had spawned a new generation of aspiring capitalists in the Alberta and British Columbia, but they were at best a regional elite in the 1970s.

Even at this time there were changes in the political scene, with the emergence of Quebec and the West, the impact of immigration on Canadian society, and increased attention to the rights of women and Aboriginal communities. To some extent these changes were reflected in developments in the business world, although it would be an exaggeration to see the evolution of the business elite as a mirror image of broader trends in society. Nevertheless there were signs of increasing diversity among those who achieved great wealth if not necessarily the social prestige conferred by generations of reinvestment. Many of the conglomerate kings of the 1980s were 'outsiders' like Desmarais or the Bronfmans, if not 'newcomers' like the Reichmanns. Meanwhile, aspirants from communities of new immigrants were establishing more than a foothold in the upper echelons of the manu-facturing and financial service industries.

From the early twentieth century through World War II, much of the immigration to Canada came from either the British Isles or Eastern Europe, complemented by Chinese and Japanese immigration to the west coast. In the post-war era there was a fresh infusion of British migrants, as well as people from Central Europe whose homelands were disrupted by Cold War struggles. By the 1980s a tide of immigrants was coming into the country from the Indian subcontinent, the West Indies, Africa, and East Asia, the latter particularly from Hong Kong and Taiwan but also from Vietnam and the Philippines. By 2000, one-fifth of the population was foreign-born. These developments had wide-ranging effects on Canadian society, particularly since most of these immigrants settled in large cities from Vancouver to Montreal, and inevitably issues of 'multiculturalism' became a focus for political debate. At the same time, these patterns were affecting the business community, not just in terms of consumption and the workforce, but as a source of entrepreneurship.

The lands of the former Austro-Hungarian Empire provided an interesting mix of business-minded immigrants. The Reichmanns had originated in Hungary and spent time in Vienna as currency traders before fleeing in advance of the Nazi takeover in 1938. This same event precipitated the migration of another family. In 1894, Tomas Bata established a shoemaking factory at Zlin, in what was to become Czechoslovakia. Bata built a company town and experimented with new modes of industrial organization and social reform while promoting a vigorous export trade as far afield as India and Brazil, and building branch plants across Europe. Six years after Tomas's death in 1932, his son, Thomas Bata (Sr), arranged to set up a plant (and a company town, designated 'Batawa') in Ontario to avoid the anticipated calamities of Nazi rule and war. This proved to be an act of foresight as the Bata operation in Czechoslovakia was nationalized when the Communists came to power there in 1948. The Bata family was

embroiled for a time, however, in a power struggle between Thomas and his brother Jan Bata, who had remained in Europe. Meanwhile, the company, now operating from Toronto, rebuilt its international sales and manufacturing organizations.

In 1984, Thomas Bata Sr stepped down as chief executive, but after a few years there was increasing friction with his son, Tom Jr. In part, this reflected differences over marketing, as Bata faced new competition from cheap shoe producers in East Asia, and a need to reorganize the highly decentralized system of branch plants that had evolved in the early post-war years. After several changes in management, the company decided to close its Canadian plant at Batawa in eastern Ontario. Although Bata retained a retail presence in the Canadian market, most of its manufacturing operations had moved to Africa, Latin America, and India.

In contrast to the Batas, who moved an existing organization with them, Frank Stronach arrived in Canada in 1954 virtually penniless, and embarked on a genuine 'rags to riches' saga. Trained in his native Austria as a tool-and-die maker, Stronach recruited other Austrian mechanics to join him in 1957 when he set up an auto parts company, Multimatic. Later, he acquired control of a small electronics company, Magna, in the 1960s, which, rechristened as Magna International, became his vehicle for growth. Benefiting from opportunities presented to Canadian parts suppliers under the Auto Pact, Stronach won the loyalty of the American-owned automakers in Ontario by providing a version of 'just-in-time' delivery that had been a significant competitive advantage for the Japanese when they entered the North American market. In 1990, as the auto industry went into recession, Magna faced a crisis as a result of overexpansion of facilities to accommodate the needs of his clients; fortunately, Chrysler sustained contracts with Magna while Stronach downsized his operations, and by the middle of the decade the company had reduced its debts and expanded its clientele to include luxury carmakers like Jaguar and Rolls-Royce as well as Japanese manufacturers.

Stronach also invested in research and development, enabling Magna to come up with improved parts using lightweight materials and integrated assembly structures. In 1992, Magna began investing in Europe, acquiring the Austrian Steyr auto parts maker, which had the capability of assembling entire automobiles. Riding the auto boom of the 1990s, Magna's sales rose from $2 billion to $9 billion from 1990 to 1999, while profits increased from less than $100 million to $500 million. Stronach entered the pantheon of Canada's wealthiest individuals, although shareholders began to complain about his compensation level when the auto parts market began to cool down after 2001, particularly since Stronach had supposedly withdrawn from regular management responsibilities (his daughter, Belinda, had briefly run the company before embarking on a political career). Another source of friction was his growing preoccupation with horse racing, which led to the creation of Magna Entertainment in 2000, whose losses were offset by contributions from the parent company. But with control of the company through multiple voting shares, Frank Stronach was able to face down his critics. As the US auto industry lurched into crisis in 2007, Stronach joined forces with Gerald Schwartz of Onex in a bid to take over Chrysler.

While European immigrants like Stronach and his German-born contemporary, Robert Schad, who established Husky Injection Moldings in the 1960s, often moved into manufacturing, the 'new immigrants' of the 1970s and later were more likely to enter retail trade and services, establishing a range of small and medium-sized businesses in Canada's urban centres. On the west coast, particularly from the late 1980s, there was an infusion of wealthy expatriates from Hong Kong seeking a foothold in Canada in anticipation of the takeover of their haven by the People's Republic of China in 1996. Among the most prominent of these were the two sons, Victor and Richard, of Li Ka-shing, ranked by *Forbes* as one of the 10 wealthiest people in the world. Although the family members spent more time in Hong Kong than their new residences,

Li undertook some major investments in Canada, including major stakes in Husky Energy and the Canadian Imperial Bank of Commerce, and a dramatic albeit unsuccessful bid to acquire Air Canada in 2004.

A different path was followed by V. Prem Watsa, who emigrated as a young man from India to London, Ontario, in 1972, where he worked for Confederation Life. In 1984 he set up in business as an investment counsellor, acquiring a small, financially strapped trucking insurance company, Markel Insurance, which he renamed Fairfax, and broadened out into general property and casualty coverage. Over the following decade Watsa expanded the company by buying up other troubled insurance firms in Canada and the US; his most significant acquisition was the Skandia America Reinsurance Co. in 1996 after it had experienced serious financial losses after Hurricane Andrew, and he added other reinsurers based in Bermuda and Paris. Expansion was financed generally through new stock issues rather than debt, with Watsa holding a strong minority position. Stock analysts began comparing Watsa's investment strategies with those of Warren Buffett of Berkshire Hathaway. Although battered by losses from storms in Europe and the destruction of the World Trade Center in 2001, Fairfax survived, and in 2006 it was the third largest diversified insurance company in Canada, after Manulife and Sun Life.

In 2004 the Royal Ontario Museum, customarily the recipient of the charitable support of Toronto's social elite, received an astonishing gift of $30 million towards its ambitious renovation plans. The unexpected donor was Michael Lee-Chin, of Jamaican-Chinese parentage, who had come to Canada with a government scholarship in 1970 to study civil engineering at McMaster University (which also became the future beneficiary of a $5 million gift). Unable to find engineering work in Jamaica, he returned to Canada and worked as a financial adviser for the Investor's Group. In 1983 he set himself up in the financial services business with other investments in insurance and securities management. Four years later he acquired Advantage Investment Council, which he redesignated AIC and transformed into a major mutual fund. Lee Chin avoided entanglement in the dot.com boom of the 1990s, and AIC emerged after the debacle in that field as one of the best performing funds in Canada. As with Prem Watsa, there were comparisons with Warren Buffett. At this point, Lee Chin's philanthropic impulses moved to the fore, not only through his Canadian gifts but through more significant efforts to improve his homeland of Jamaica. He acquired 75 per cent of the shares of the National Commercial Bank of Jamaica, and established an AIC Caribbean Fund with the aim of raising $1 billion for investment in Caribbean businesses, including insurance, media, and health-related enterprises. In 2006 he stepped down as chief executive of AIC, although he continued to be active in shaping its overall investment strategy.[16]

The period from the 1960s on witnessed significant changes in the status of women in Canada, as in other industrialized societies. By the end of the century there were more women than men enrolled in universities, and their numbers in the professions rose, particularly in law and in the medical fields. Women also began to become more visible within the ranks of management, but at least in the upper echelons of business, there was a perception that a 'glass ceiling' prevented their rise to the top positions. To be sure, there were some prominent female chief executives, particularly among foreign-owned companies, such as Maureen Darkes, who was president of General Motors of Canada from 1997 to 2002, and Annette Verschuren, who as president of Home Depot Canada from 1996 expanded that company's operations from 19 to 150 stores across the country and into China. Nevertheless, several studies conducted in 2006–7 concluded that women remained under-represented in senior positions in Canada's largest corporations: only 13.5 per cent of board members in the top 100 companies were women, and only 7 per cent of the 500 highest-paid executives in Canada were

women. Even within this small cohort, there was a clustering in areas such as financial services and retailing, with relatively few in the industrial sector.[17] Belinda Stronach, whose sojourn in federal politics proved to be of short duration, returned to Magna and was an exception.

Looking beyond the realm of corporate top executives, there have been examples of women who have attained prominence in family or proprietary enterprises, and indeed this has been an area where barriers to women, such as restrictions on access to capital, have been attenuated somewhat. Some recent examples include Heather Reisman, who founded Indigo Books in 1996 and in 2001 acquired (with financial support from her husband Gerry Schwartz's Onex Corporation) a much larger chain, Chapters, making it the largest bookseller in Canada. Similarly, Wendy MacDonald, who inherited a relatively small Vancouver machine tool company, BC Bearings, when her husband died in 1950, expanded the firm across western Canada and into the US, Mexico, and South America by the 1990s; her company repeatedly earned the award as the 'best managed company in Canada' by the *Financial Post*.

Perhaps the most prominent example of an heiress-executive is Martha Billes of Canadian Tire. In 1922 two brothers, Alfred J. and John W. Billes, acquired an auto parts and service garage in Hamilton, which became the base for a chain of associated stores and a mail-order operation that established a dominant niche position in the auto parts market in Canada by the 1950s, when John W. died. His brother continued to run the company for the next decade, introducing 'Canadian Tire money' and other marketing devices that boosted sales. In 1966 he retired from active management, but continued to play a role in the company's strategic expansion. Upon his death in 1995, his two sons and daughter squabbled over the legacy (each had been given 20 per cent of the shares), with Martha emerging victorious, buying out her brothers for $45 million in 1996. Although the company was run throughout this period by professional managers, Martha assumed the role her father had maintained, as the company faced off competition from Wal-Mart and Home Depot, and acquired Mark's Work Wearhouse. It doubled its sales and profits between 1999 and 2006 and was one of the few major retail chains under Canadian ownership.[18]

Even more formidable obstacles to advancement in the business world faced Canada's Aboriginal peoples and Métis. For almost a century after the Indian Act of 1876, federal policies focused on the goal of assimilation and eradication of traditional tribal institutions and practices, particularly through education. But emphasis was not placed on generating entrepreneurial attitudes, even though Aboriginal people had traditionally been involved in trade; they were to be trained to be small farmers and labourers. This approach came increasingly under fire in the 1960s and there were proposals to devolve greater authority to Native communities, although there was resistance on the part of Native leaders to the elimination of their status under nineteenth-century treaties. In terms of economic development, the most significant measure of the era was the establishment of an Indian Claims Commission in 1969, which paved the way for negotiations by Native communities over compensation for access to their resources, although these processes were complicated by federal–provincial disputes over jurisdiction on these issues.

Among the most significant of these negotiations involved the Cree of the James Bay area in northern Quebec where, after years of litigation with the Quebec government over its hydro development plans, an agreement was reached in 1975 that provided for cash and royalty payments of $135 million, with an additional $90 million going to the Inuit of James Bay who set up the Makivik Corporation to manage investments that ranged from local fishing operations to shares in Nordair. Another large settlement was the Western Arctic Claim Agreement of 1984 that yielded $55 million to the Inuvialuit, who set up an Inuvialuit Development Corporation that invested in

transportation, real estate, and energy resources in the region.

These success stories largely benefited those Native communities fortunate enough to be sitting on highly desirable natural resources and who, because they had never been included in the treaty process of earlier years, were able to negotiate comprehensive agreements that included large cash settlements for portions of their traditional homelands. For the rest, conditions of poverty and marginalized development persisted. In 1981 the federal government introduced a Native Economic Development Fund, but by the end of the decade only a fraction of the $345 million promised had been allocated. Increasingly, Native leaders were looking to other means of promoting development, and for some this quest led to the world of gambling.

Gambling or 'gaming' was as much a part of traditional Native life as trading, and thus became a target for assimilation-minded reformers in the late nineteenth century, whose views on this matter were applied more generally: the 1892 Criminal Code strictly regulated all forms of gambling, including lotteries and raffles, although betting on horse races was exempted. Attitudes had begun to moderate after World War II, with the resurrection of government lotteries in the 1960s, but legalization of other forms of gambling, particularly casinos, continued to encounter resistance for another two decades.

Interest in casino gaming emerged among Native communities in Canada in the context of developments in the United States, where the concept of casinos as a vehicle for economic revival had been promoted by the experience of Atlantic City in the early 1980s. In that same time, the Seminoles of Florida had successfully challenged an effort by the state government to ban their bingo halls, with the court ruling that regulatory laws did not extend to Indian lands. This led to the establishment of a successful casino by the small Pequot community in Massachusetts, followed by a proliferation of Native gambling facilities in the US and a federal Indian Gaming Regulatory Act in 1988.

These events were observed closely by Native leaders in Canada, but efforts to follow a legal strategy similar to the Seminoles were thwarted by a court decision in 1990 that identified gaming regulation as falling under provincial jurisdiction—any plans by Native groups to establish gaming facilities required agreement with provincial authorities. Nevertheless, the casino commitment was pursued with some success, notably in Ontario and Saskatchewan in the early 1990s, and by 2006 there were 11 Native-owned casinos operating in Canada. While facing criticism for exploiting the weaknesses of problem gamblers (most users of Native casinos were not themselves Native Canadians) and promoting risks for the communities that owned them, the casinos were in a growth sector, with gaming accounting for 10 per cent of expenditures on leisure activities in Canada.[19]

CHAPTER 13

Into the Millennium

The 25-year period that bridged into the twenty-first century was an era of dramatic transformations in technology and the international economy, with concomitant effects on the Canadian business environment. Following a decade when inflation and energy crises had apparently demonstrated the inability of governments in the major industrial states to effectively manage their economies, the 1980s witnessed a revival of faith in the virtues of free enterprise, deregulated markets, and elimination of barriers to international trade and financial flows. By the end of the decade, even the centralized 'command' economies of the Communist world were collapsing. In this context there was a renewed emphasis on 'free trade', initially focused on the development of regional agreements and culminating in the 1990s with the establishment of a World Trade Organization, derived in part from ideas conceived at Bretton Woods a half-century earlier. Although various forms of 'non-tariff' and 'countervailing' barriers continued to plague trade relations among nations (including Canada and the US), in many respects the structure of the international economy had returned to the conditions that prevailed before the outbreak of World War I in 1914.

While the fall of the Soviet Union left the United States as the world's leading military power, it no longer exercised the kind of overarching economic influence that had prevailed in the years immediately following World War II. This shift was already taking shape in the early 1970s, exemplified by the termination in 1971 of the gold–dollar standard set up at Bretton Woods and by related protective trade measures. By the 1980s, Japan was challenging American supremacy in the auto, steel, and electronics industries, soon to be joined by countries of the European Economic Union and other East Asian nations, most notably China by the dawn of the millennium. US multinationals faced competition not just from traditional European rivals in oil and gas, chemicals, telecommunications, and electrical equipment, but also from new entities emanating out of Brazil, India, and South Korea. In 2001, only 12 of the top 50 non-financial multinationals were US-owned.[1]

The advent of the new era of globalization was not greeted with unadulterated praise in every quarter, although a mood of triumphalism pervaded the US and Europe in the period immediately following the end of the Cold War. Some critics argued that the benefits of trade and financial liberalization did not spread very deeply into developing countries, while others highlighted the propensity of multinationals to relocate operations into regions with cheap labour and inadequate social and environmental regulations. Another line of criticism focused on the cultural impact of globalization and its disruptive effect on traditional societies—an approach that had more resonance in the aftermath of the destruction of the World Trade Center towers in New York in September 2001. Although the terrorist attacks did not bring the international economy to a halt, they did lead to new security-driven restrictions that dampened to some extent the enthusiasm of the 1990s, and reflected, as well, renewed tensions over immigration, the movement of jobs from industrialized countries, and the prospect of a new era of international political rivalries.[2]

Underlying these shifts in the international economy were technological developments that began in the period of World War II and culminated in the 1980s–90s with the emergence of personal computers, satellite communications, and the Internet, all of which combined to usher in what some observers regarded as a 'post-industrial economy' (or the 'New Economy', as it was christened by US President Bill Clinton during the euphoric 1990s). In this changed economy, the manipulation of information would create more added value than the extraction of resources or the running of machinery. Just as the global economy of the nineteenth century rested on the technologies of the railway, steamship, and telegraph, the 'convergence' of computer and communications technologies accelerated the linkages of markets, facilitated the long logistic chains essential to 'just-in-time' production, and provided the virtually immediate transmission of images and ideas. As in the case of railway manias of the early 1900s and the recurring mining and petroleum booms of the twentieth century, a period of 'irrational exuberance' about the prospects of the new technology took hold as the millennium neared; and as in the past, the 'dot.com bubble' eventually burst. Nevertheless, the long-term impact of these technologies continued, threatened to some extent by challenges of environmental change but also offering the possibility of a more globally co-ordinated effort to meet these challenges.

'OPEN FOR BUSINESS'

Curiously, although the Canada–US Free Trade Agreement is associated with Brian Mulroney's Conservatives, the initiative for this undertaking came from the preceding Liberal regime. In 1982, with the country mired in recession, Prime Minister Trudeau followed the hallowed Canadian tradition of establishing a Royal Commission to consider Canada's economic prospects. The final report did not surface until long after the Liberals' departure from power, but in November 1984 the Commission's chairman, Donald MacDonald, began urging Canadians to take a 'leap of faith' and move towards comprehensive free trade with the Americans. MacDonald's call was quickly echoed by the Business Council on National Issues (BCNI), an organization set up in 1976 to represent the views of the country's large export-oriented corporations and banks, but it was also endorsed by the Canadian Manufacturers' Association, the traditional bastion of protectionist sentiment since the days of Sir John A. Macdonald.

Growing protectionism in the US stimulated the movement for free trade in Canada. Although the American government remained officially committed to multilateral tariff reductions under the General Agreement on Tariffs and Trade (GATT), during the 1970s US manufacturers, facing rising competition in their home markets from the Japanese and other foreigners, lobbied for non-tariff restrictions on imports, and the recession of the early 1980s increased these pressures. Particularly vexing for Canadian exporters were the actions of the International Trade Commission, an agency of the US Commerce Department that had authority to impose countervailing duties against countries deemed to be engaged in dumping or other 'unfair' trade practices. Rather than acting as an impartial tribunal to settle trade disputes, the ITC, in Canadian eyes, was perceived to be acting in the interests of American producers; a controversial ruling in 1986 against Canadian softwood lumber imports highlighted this problem. While Presidents Carter and Reagan rhetorically endorsed free trade ideas, the memory of the 'Nixon shocks' of the early 1970s lingered on and proposals for new protectionist measures circulated perpetually in the US Congress.

For MacDonald and other advocates of a US free trade agreement, growing American protectionism was not the only concern. With the emergence of regional trade blocs abroad, such as the European Economic Community, Canada ran the risk of becoming the only industrialized exporting nation without secure access to a market of more than 100 million people. The failure of Trudeau's 'Third Option' search for markets outside North America left Canada with few alternatives to the United States. Furthermore, it was argued, Canada's industries had to become more efficient and sales-oriented to survive in the globalized economy, and the 'cold bath' of competition in their own markets would hasten this process. Some critics, especially from the left wing of the Liberal Party and the NDP, perceived a hidden agenda in this line of argument, maintaining that the thrust for 'efficiency' would result in wage cuts for Canadian workers and undermine social welfare programs erected over the past generation. After the Mulroney government took up the initiative, Canadian nationalists saw free trade as part of the new regime's continentalist tilt. One of Mulroney's first steps was to change the name (and mandate) of the Foreign Investment Review Agency to Investment Canada, signalling to outsiders (especially Americans) that Canada was now 'open for business'.

Encouraged by a largely supportive business community, the Canadian government embarked on its free trade quest in 1985–6. The Reagan administration in the US seemed receptive—Reagan had talked vaguely of creating a 'North American Common Market' in the 1980 presidential campaign—and arranged for a 'fast-track' negotiating process that would circumvent congressional delaying tactics. But the American business community was divided on the issue. Financial service companies such as American Express saw in free trade an opportunity to penetrate the Canadian market more readily, and US oil

companies were interested in using an agreement as a means of blocking future NEP-type ventures by Canada. On the other side, American firms in direct competition with Canadians in fields such as lumber and food products were less receptive. The negotiations reflected these cross-pressures: the Americans pushed hard for inclusion of services and energy issues in the agreement but balked at Canadian efforts to establish a system of rules that would, in effect, exempt their exporters from ITC actions and shield them from quotas and other non-tariff restrictions.

The negotiations deadlocked in the fall of 1987, requiring intervention at the highest levels on both sides. In the ensuing Free Trade Agreement (FTA) the Americans achieved most of their objectives in the energy and financial areas, with further restraints on Canadian regulatory powers over foreign investment. The Canadians failed to get exemptions from countervailing measures but were able to secure agreement to a formal binational process for resolving trade disputes. Remaining tariff barriers between the countries would be phased out over 10 years; the Auto Pact remained in place. On one of the thorniest issues, the definition of 'subsidies' (the existence of which could be deemed justification for countervailing measures), both sides agreed to defer a final determination until a later date.

After the US Congress ratified the FTA, which would not come into effect until January 1989, Mulroney decided to make it the centrepiece of his re-election campaign in 1988—the first time a Canadian political leader had dared to risk his future on a trade agreement since Laurier's ill-fated reciprocity venture in 1911. In contrast to 1911, however, in this case the nation's business leaders were generally of one mind. The BCNI mounted a vigorous advertising campaign, combining assertions of confidence in Canada's competitiveness with ominous warnings of the economic chaos that would ensue if the Agreement were not approved. Opponents, including trade unionists, social reformers, and nationalists, mobilized their forces, exploiting familiar themes of patriotism and anti-Americanism. But their votes were divided between the Liberals and the NDP, facilitating Mulroney's victory with less than 45 per cent of the popular vote (except in Quebec, where all political leaders embraced free trade) but secure control of Parliament. When the FTA went into effect, it represented the most dramatic shift in the country's economic direction since the establishment of the National Policy more than a century earlier.

The onset of a new recession in the early 1990s complicated any assessment of the consequences of the FTA. Some American-owned branch plants closed down in Canada, but 'rationalization' was the order of the day in US industry as well. Cross-border shopping (mainly from the Canadian side) increased, but Canadian retailers blamed this development in part on the goods and services tax (GST) introduced by the Mulroney government in January 1991. Looking back from 1997, almost a decade after the free trade issue first emerged, Gordon Ritchie, who had figured prominently among the Canadian negotiators of the FTA, maintained that at that point it could be seen, on balance, as a success, particularly for Canada. Exports to the US had increased, which could be interpreted as increasing Canada's dependence on this one market, but this was 'a problem any other country would want to have'. Overall trade (imports and exports) had tripled since 1988, and this encompassed the 'high-technology and high-value added sectors' as well as resources. Also, between 275,000 and 400,000 new jobs had been created in Canada, directly attributable to the Free Trade Agreement (a neat riposte to the arguments that Sir John A. Macdonald had offered a century earlier on the benefits of the National Policy).[3]

The North American Free Trade Agreement (NAFTA) might seem to be a logical extension of the Canada–US Free Trade Agreement, but there was little direct connection between them. When the talks began in 1990, Canada was a somewhat reluctant participant, fearing that some old issues might be revived and changed yet again. The impetus came in large part from the Mexican

President, Carlos Salinas de Gortari, who saw a free-trade agreement with the US as a capstone to his efforts to modernize the Mexican economy. Canada's trade with Mexico was insignificant compared to its US connection; but the negotiations provided an opportunity for automakers to procure entry into the Mexican market, and this was to be a major gain from NAFTA. In Parliament, debate preceding the ratification of NAFTA reinvigorated the controversies over free trade, but the Liberal Party under Jean Chrétien, which came to power shortly thereafter, chose not to reopen the issue. In the US, NAFTA also proved controversial, with opponents raising many of the same issues about potential job losses and corporate relocations that had been raised by Canadian nationalists in 1988–9. The agreement was ratified in 1993 and came into force in 1994, with sideline arrangements to deal with issues related to labour and environmental issues.

Then, in 1995, Canada agreed to enter the World Trade Organization (WTO). This international body, empowered to make and enforce trade rules, had originally been conceived at the time of the Bretton Woods meetings in New Hampshire in 1944, but (ironically) it had been killed by protectionist interests in the US Congress in 1948. In its place had arisen the less-binding GATT, which had featured multilateral negotiations among countries, at first principally the major (Western) industrial nations, to reduce trade barriers over the following four and a half decades. At the conclusion of the Uruguay Round in 1993, GATT members, including Canada, agreed to the establishment of the WTO. Canada duly ratified it in 1995, following a relatively muted debate, reflecting in part the long-standing commitment of the country to participation in multilateral organizations, and possibly also exhaustion from previous trade controversies.

The auto industry was probably most affected by these trade agreements, with autos and auto parts accounting for one-fifth of overall trade in NAFTA between 1995 and 2005. The FTA had carefully left the Auto Pact untouched, and NAFTA brought Mexican imports and exports into the continental arrangements. The role of non-US-controlled auto companies in Canada, however, proved to be a thorny issue. During the 1980s, Japanese auto companies, including Toyota and Honda, had been encouraged to set up branch plants in Canada (mostly in Ontario) through duty-remission arrangements; this aroused hostility in the US, particularly in Michigan, and the elimination of these arrangements was one of the focal points for US negotiators in 1986–7. In the final negotiations for NAFTA, Canada agreed to phase out its duty-remission scheme, and the Pact was restricted to its original US participants (plus Volvo), excluding the Japanese, Korean, and other companies that were now operating in Canada. In 1998, after Canada had entered the WTO, the chickens came home to roost: Japanese and European automakers filed a complaint against the Auto Pact based on its discriminatory clauses, and the WTO ruled that it was in violation of international trade rules. In 2001 the Auto Pact expired.

Although several Canadian plants were closed, and there were warnings of the imminent disappearance of the industry in Canada, auto production continued to be the linchpin of Ontario's economy. To some extent this reflected the changes that had taken place in the industry over the preceding decades as automakers had reorganized plants to specialize in production of particular models for continental or international markets, which was, of course, one of the major goals of the Auto Pact. In addition, at least until 2006, currency differentials between the US and Canada worked to the advantage of the Canadian carmakers (as it did for Canadian exporters generally), and they benefited from new capital investments: GM's Oshawa plant, for example, was consistently ranked among the most efficient auto production sites in North or South America, with new equipment and good quality-control systems. The real danger for the Canadian auto industry lay in the declining competitiveness of the American parent firms: by 2007 all of the Big Three (GM, Ford, Chrysler) were facing substantial losses in terms of both sales and market share, aggravated by the high costs involved in funding corporate pension plans. At the same time, however, Toyota, which by 2007 had outpaced GM in sales to become the largest automaker in the world, and other East Asian companies continued to invest in branch plants in Canada, in part because of the proximity to well-developed auto parts makers like Magna, whose capabilities in turn had been fostered by the Auto Pact.

One of the most contentious issues for Canadians in the years preceding the Free Trade Agreement was the US habit of imposing countervailing duties and similar 'trade relief measures' on imports of products deemed by the US Secretary of Commerce to reflect 'unfair trade practices'. Consequently, Canadian negotiators fought to the bitter end for the establishment of binational trade dispute panels that were presumably to have final authority when these issues arose (initially, the Canadians had aimed for a set of agreed-upon rules covering trade disputes, but the US negotiators would not go that far). The dispute panel system also found its way into NAFTA and, in a somewhat modified version, into the WTO regime. On the whole, the dispute resolution process worked, at least in the sense of limiting the range and wider impact of these quarrels on trade relations. A 2003 study commissioned by Canada's Department of Foreign Affairs and International Trade found that 153 dispute panels had been set up since 1989, but they affected at most 4 per cent of all trade between the US and Canada and among the NAFTA partners. But the report acknowledged that 'these disputes are politically very visible and legitimacy of the overall trade agreement is clearly . . . impacted by perceptions as to the efficacy and fairness of the process.'

A prime example was the softwood lumber dispute, the origins of which predated the Canada–US Free Trade Agreement—indeed, the intransigence of the lumber dispute had helped generate pressure for the treaty in the first place. In 1982 the US lumber industry charged that Canadian producers, particularly in British Columbia, were given an unfair advantage by provincial governments whose allegedly low 'stumpage fees' charged for cutting on government-owned timber lands enabled the Canadian industry to undersell their competitors in the US market; in the US, fees for timber rights were determined by auction. The fact that the stumpage fees were set by government rather than markets gave the US producers the opportunity to present them as a form of subsidy. In this first round, the Department of Commerce did not support the US industry, but a second try in 1986 was more successful, resulting in the imposition of a 15 per cent countervailing tariff on Canadian lumber imports. The Canadian government, at this point eager to reach a broader trade deal, negotiated a 'phased-in' tariff. After the FTA was in place, however, Canada withdrew from this arrangement, setting the stage for renewed conflict, this time going before a trade dispute panel.

The panel's decision went against the US claimants, but this did not end the matter; the US Congress passed a law intended to close what was seen as a loophole used by the dispute panel (of whom a majority were Canadians) in its decision. After some posturing, the Liberal regime in Ottawa entered an agreement in 1996 to limit Canadian lumber exports over a five-year period. No sooner had this agreement run its course than the issue erupted again, with the Department of Commerce threatening a 27 per cent surcharge on Canadian exporters (some of which, like Weyerhaeuser, were themselves US-owned companies operating in both countries). Another trade panel, now under NAFTA rules, determined that the US countervail was too high.

Subsequently, yet another NAFTA panel ruled against the US claim altogether. But the American government, which had been collecting and holding over $5 billion in penalties, did not accept this ruling, and went separately to the WTO. Initially, the WTO panel ruled against the US, but then in 2005 the WTO reversed its position. Meanwhile, US lumber producers brought a lawsuit challenging the constitutional authority of the NAFTA dispute resolution process. By this time,

the Liberals had been replaced by the Conservatives in Ottawa, under Stephen Harper, whose government negotiated yet another agreement with the US, which essentially reduced the level of the countervailing duties and provided reimbursement of some (but not all) of the monies collected as penalties. Needless to say, some Canadians saw this as a resolution to a seemingly endless controversy, while others saw it as a 'sellout' that effectively undermined the trade dispute mechanism established in the FTA and NAFTA, for which Canada had fought long and hard.[4]

Despite these problems, the business community for the most part continued to see the free trade agreements as having positive benefits for all parties. The aftermath of the 9/11 attacks led to tighter security measures in patrolling the Canadian–US border that created bottlenecks in the flow of trade, particularly at Windsor/Detroit, a major crossing for auto products. Nevertheless, overall import–export trade between the two countries increased by 50 per cent in the period 2001–7, and Canada's exports to Mexico doubled in that same time.

THE CROWNS DEPART

As governments of all persuasions in the Western industrial nations seemed unable to overcome the effects of the Great Inflation of the 1970s, conservatives were emboldened to cast off their compromising ways and once again promote the virtues of free enterprise and untrammelled markets as well as free trade. The rise to power of Margaret Thatcher in Britain and Ronald Reagan in the United States heralded a new era in which the restraints of government regulation and control could be abolished in order to unleash the creative potential of private enterprise; and in Canada, the Mulroney regime embraced at least the rhetoric and to some degree the substance of this emerging conservative counter-revolution.

In the US, the focus of the free-market reformers was on deregulation, and their goals were not necessarily shared only by business leaders. During the

1970s even Democrats like Ted Kennedy criticized regulatory agencies such as the Civil Aeronautics Board and Interstate Commerce Commission, and the reduction of regulatory regimes, if not the elimination of the agencies themselves, predated the arrival of Reaganauts in Washington in 1981. In Britain, Thatcher's central targets were the nationalized industries that had been created by the Labour government in the aftermath of World War II, with a second wave in the 1970s. These were to be 'privatized', and forced to become more efficient and competitive, and, in some cases, dismantled. One of her most effective aides in this task of restructuring was Nova Scotia-born Graham Day, who arrived in Britain in the 1970s, where he reorganized an ailing shipyard, Cammell Laird. Under Thatcher, he took on similar tasks in managing the privatization of the government-owned companies British Shipbuilders, British Leyland (autos), and British Aerospace. Day was knighted for his efforts, and served as chairman of the board of Cadbury Schweppes and PowerGen, another privatized British electrical company in the 1990s, then returned to Canada where he was briefly involved in the controversial efforts to reorganize Ontario Hydro.

Mulroney was less of an ideologue than Thatcher, but he was determined to reverse what his political supporters deemed the worst excesses of the Trudeau era, including FIRA and the National Energy Program, which were duly transformed. But he was more circumspect on the privatization of Petro-Canada, mindful of Joe Clark's swift demise as Prime Minister in 1980, at least partly due to this issue. The government was eager to dispose of some of the 'investments in failure', such as Canadair and Devco, but wanted to avoid selling off Crown corporations at distress prices— although exceptions could be made for favoured firms like Bombardier, which acquired Canadair in 1985, leaving Ottawa with a substantial part of the company's debt. De Havilland was sold to the US company Boeing a year later, eventually passing into the hands of Bombardier as well. In 1987, Teleglobe, a little-known Crown created in 1950 to manage Canada's overseas cable systems, was sold, winding up with Bell Canada for a time.

The larger prey were targeted after the Conservatives were re-elected in 1988. Air Canada went on the auction block in 1989. Although institutional investors were wary, loyal Canadians patriotically bought shares, along with Air Canada employees. The timing was bad, however, as recession and the rising costs of financing a new fleet of airplanes forced cutbacks in service. By 1992 both Air Canada and its major domestic competitor, Canadian Airlines International, were in trouble and looking at possible American partners, although the US situation was equally bleak, with companies like TWA and Pan-American staggering into bankruptcy. Under Hollis Harris, a veteran manager of airlines in the US, Air Canada made deep staff cuts and invested in another near-bankrupt US company, Continental, gambling (accurately) that it would recover. In 1997 the Continental shares were sold at a profit and Air Canada formed a 'Star Alliance' with United Airlines, Scandinavian Airlines, Lufthansa, and Thai Airways.

Air Canada seemed to have surmounted its early growing pains as a private enterprise, but by 1999 it was facing disaster again, burdened by strikes and technological malfunctions. Another US manager, Robert Milton, came aboard, imposing a new round of austerity while fighting off a takeover bid by Gerald Schwartz. Milton orchestrated the oft-proposed takeover by Air Canada of Canadian Airlines in 2000, which for a time restored its near-monopoly as a domestic carrier, although Alberta and the Maritimes soon produced rivals for the domestic and US market, West Jet and CanJet. The melding of the two big companies was fraught with problems, and after 9/11, Air Canada, along with the airline industry in general, plunged into crisis: in 2003 it filed for bankruptcy. As it emerged a year later, a leaner Air Canada attracted suitors, including the Hong Kong tycoon Victor Li, but it was ultimately refinanced and reorganized as ACE Aviation Holdings, with Milton as chairman of the board.

Finally, in 1991, it was Petro-Canada's turn, although the government hedged its privatization with various safeguards, including retention of a 20 per cent share in the company and restrictions on foreign ownership to 25 per cent. As in the case of Air Canada, the timing for privatization was less than ideal: the oil and gas market had slumped badly since 1987, and Petro-Canada had to write down the value of its assets, so that even though the sale was scheduled to take place gradually, share values slumped and the company reduced its workforce by more than half, selling off its interests in Westcoast Energy and an oil sands company. The return of the Liberals to power in 1993 did not lead to a reversal of privatization; on the contrary, the new government accelerated the sale of its interest in the company. By 2005 Petro-Canada had rebounded, and was second only to EnCana among Canadian oil and gas companies, with a national retail network and positioning in new fields in the Caribbean and offshore Newfoundland. But its headquarters in Calgary was no longer regarded as 'Red Square' by other Alberta oilmen, although bitter memories of the NEP continued to linger there.

The Liberals proceeded as well with the privatization of Canadian National Railways in 1995 (again, with restrictions: no single shareholder could control more than 15 per cent of the stock, and corporate headquarters must remain in Montreal). Under its new aegis the company managed to realize the dream of Charles Hays back in 1910 of a North American railway system, taking over the Illinois Central Railroad in 1998, which gave it lines running from the American Midwest to New Orleans. This takeover was augmented by numerous other acquisitions. In 2003 there was some consternation in the Canadian media when the company sought to change its name formally to 'CN', although by this time Americans held a majority of shares in the company, and the logo change remained.

Privatization was also occurring among the Crown corporations in the provinces, although to a lesser extent than at the federal level. One of the most significant and successful privatizations involved Alberta Government Telephones, which had been set up in 1907 in the wake of controversies over Bell Canada's lack of service to rural users in the Prairie provinces. In 1990 the Alberta government of Ralph Klein privatized and renamed it Telus, which subsequently took over the municipally owned Edmonton telephone system. Telus diversified in the mid-1990s into cellular and wireless service and expanded geographically as well, merging with BC Telephones and moving its headquarters to Burnaby, BC, in 1999. A year later it went into competition directly with Bell Canada, acquiring Clearnet Communications and reorganizing it as Telus Mobility as well as taking over several Quebec telephone systems. Neighbouring Saskatchewan retained its telephone company as a Crown, which in the 1990s moved aggressively into digital television and Internet services within the province. Manitoba privatized its telephone system in 1996, and three years later Bell Canada acquired a 20 per cent stake in it as part of a partnership deal to create Bell West, which invaded the business market in Telus territory in Alberta.

The Potash Corporation of Saskatchewan was privatized in 1989. By this time it had accumulated massive debts, as demand for potash declined in the mid-1980s, and had become a target of US trade negotiators who maintained it was kept afloat through government subsidies, resulting in high duties on potash exports there, much like the softwood lumber industry. After privatization, the Potash Corporation benefited from a resurgence of demand, and acquired several companies in the US, including Texasgulf, one of the largest producers in that country, and in Brazil, Chile, and the Middle East.

Crown ownership of hydroelectric systems remained more or less sacrosanct in most of Canada's provinces. An exception was Nova Scotia, which privatized its power company in 1992, less than 20 years after it had been created through the amalgamation of government-owned rural services with the privately owned Nova

Scotia Light & Power that supplied Halifax. The most ambitious effort at privatization involved the venerable Ontario Hydro. Burdened by the costs of overexpansion, particularly into nuclear power in the 1970s and 1980s, the utility became the target of both the Conservatives and the NDP, which brought in Maurice Strong (of Petro-Canada fame—or infamy) to reorganize the company's finances during its brief period of power in the early 1990s.

The Conservative regime under Mike Harris that followed, however, pushed for deregulation of electric rates and privatization, forming a commission under Donald MacDonald (of free trade fame—or infamy), which duly recommended these changes in 1996. Two years later the Conservatives, buttressed by victory at the polls, introduced an Energy Competition Act, embodying the MacDonald Commission recommendations. In 2000, Ontario Hydro was reorganized as Hydro One, with plans for a private sale within two years. Further progress was derailed, however, when a coalition of unions brought a legal challenge that was upheld by the Ontario Superior Court in 2002. The subsequent electoral defeat of the Conservatives brought an end to any plans to privatize Hydro One, although the Energy Competition Act did allow for the emergence of new power generating companies in the province.[5]

The mid-1990s marked the apogee of the privatization movement in Canada. Although many of the tenets of market-oriented conservatism lingered on in a rejuvenated federal Conservative Party, which merged with the right-wing Canadian Alliance in late 2003 and dropped its 'Progressive' moniker, there were no major new privatizations after the turn of the century, aside from the aborted Ontario Hydro effort. While the vogue for Crown corporations may have run its course by 1980, these quasi-governmental entities continue to populate the Canadian business environment, as exemplified by the persistence of CBC, Via Rail, Canada Mortgage and Housing Agency, and assorted other federal and provincial Crowns. In 2001 the government of Nunavut, the

new territory and Inuit homeland in the eastern Arctic created in 1999, took over the assets of the Northwest Territories Power Corporation (itself a Crown), renaming it Qulliq Energy Corporation two years later: evidence of the continuing legacy of the Crown enterprise in Canada.

TRAVAILS OF THE 'NEW ECONOMY'

The evolution of what came to be known as the information technology (IT) industry took place in three general stages in the period after World War II. The 'mainframe era', from 1948 to about 1980, witnessed the commercialization of computer technology developed during the war. Owing to the large size and high cost of the machines (the UNIVAC, for example, weighed 29,000 pounds, took up 350 square feet of floor space, and cost over $100,000), the market was largely limited to big institutional buyers like government agencies and large corporations, particularly in the insurance industry. The development of integrated circuits using semiconductors in the 1960s and 1970s made possible the 'miniaturization' of electronic control systems and ushered in the era of the personal computer in the 1980s. In this phase the critical changes were not only in computer hardware but in the introduction of 'user-friendly' software elements that enabled personal computer manufacturers to sell their products to a mass market. The third phase, beginning in the early 1990s, involved the integration of the personal computer with improvements in communications technologies that culminated in the Internet and the World Wide Web, and many of the after effects of this development are still underway. While Canada was largely a passive recipient of technology in the first phase of the IT industry, both the Canadian government and entrepreneurs were to play a more active role as the technologies evolved.

In the mainframe era, one company, International Business Machines (IBM), came to dominate the industry by the end of the 1950s, and this was the case in Canada as well as many other industrial countries. IBM had set up a subsidiary in Canada in 1917 to sell its tabulating machines and similar devices, opening a plant in Toronto in 1952 that did not manufacture computers, although in the 1960s it was given the capability to build punch-card machines for the North American market—ironically, this was to be one of the early victims of the rapidly changing technology a decade later. In some respects, however, the Canadian industry benefited more from the activities of some of the smaller companies during this period, many of which were to disappear.

One of these was the British-owned company, Ferranti-Canada, which had been involved in the Royal Canadian Navy's effort to develop electronic surveillance systems in the early 1950s. After that project was terminated, Ferranti-Canada drew on its experience to develop digital electronic control systems for Canada Post, Trans-Canada Air Lines, and the Federal Reserve Bank of New York (the largest of the US central banking organizations). It also developed its own in-house computer, the FP6000, in the early 1960s; but like its counterpart Avro in the aircraft field, Ferranti-Canada had trouble finding buyers, particularly in competition with IBM and its ambitious 360 series computer. In 1964, the parent company, Ferranti UK, sold its data-processing operations to another British company. Another example was Sperry Canada, a subsidiary of the US company Sperry Rand (known in the trade as one of the 'Seven Dwarfs' to IBM's 'Snow White'), which set out to establish a foothold in the field of digitized automation of machine tools, and benefited for a time from support from Canada's Department of Industry, Trade and Commerce in the late 1960s. But larger competitors from Japan as well as the US largely overtook Sperry's position in the relatively small Canadian market by 1980.

Although the early history of the computer industry in Canada was marked by stillborn projects, the country was developing a technological cadre that played a role in the next phase of development of the IT field. In 1967, Mers Kutt and Don Parmenter, two veterans of

Honeywell, another one of the 'Seven Dwarfs', set up an enterprise in Ottawa called Consolidated Computer, which, among other innovations, introduced a 'key edit' system that would allow direct entry of data from a keyboard onto magnetic tape—this would eventually replace the punch-card system. Despite its technical success, the company went into receivership in 1972. At that point Kutt formed another company, Micro Computer Machines, and unveiled a desktop computer using a keyboard and a microprocessor developed by the American Robert Noyce, one of the inventors of the integrated circuit. Kutt's MCM 800 has since been recognized as the first personal computer, far in advance of the 'Altair' for which Bill Gates and Paul Allen designed their BASIC software, and seven years ahead of the first Apple personal computer. Unfortunately, Kutt had a falling-out with his partners shortly thereafter, and MCM went under in 1982.

A year after Kutt brought out his desktop computer, Terry Matthews and Michael Cowpland, two British-born engineers working for a subsidiary of Northern Electric (the future Nortel), set up an electronics company called Mitel, whose first product was a battery-operated lawn mower, but the company hit its stride with a touch-tone decoder for use with telephones. Mitel set up shop in Kanata, Ontario, in part because of its proximity to Ottawa, whose agencies both sponsored research and consumed expensive electronic products. Other companies, including Digital Equipment Corporation, subsidiary of a Boston firm that supplied equipment to Atomic Energy of Canada and the National Research Council, also relocated to Kanata, which eventually acquired the title 'Silicon Valley North' as the emerging centre of computer-related companies in Canada.

Mitel moved further into microelectronics, developing a miniaturized switching system, the SX-200, for internal office communications networks that became its signature product. In 1984 Mitel was bought by British Telecom; two years later, Matthews and Cowpland left the company after disagreements with the new managers (a recurring event in the history of the IT industry). Matthews set up Newbridge Networks, which developed networks for data transmission, with great success: in 2000, the French telecommunications giant, Alcatel, acquired Newbridge and Matthews became one of its largest shareholders.

Cowpland, who had always been the more flamboyant figure, established his own company, Corel, in 1985, focusing on software development. Corel's most successful product was a graphics design program, CorelDraw, and Cowpland's ambitions expanded in 1996 when he acquired the US word-processing company, Word Perfect. At this point his reach exceeded his grasp, as he challenged the industry's behemoth, Bill Gates's Microsoft. After this debacle, Cowpland was obliged to leave Corel in the wake of charges (which were eventually dismissed) by the Ontario Securities Commission that he had engaged in insider trading. A new management group was not able to stem Corel's decline, and it was acquired in 2003 by a private equity firm, Vector Capital, which delisted it from the stock exchanges, although a new public offering was floated three years later. Meanwhile, Cowpland bought Zim Technologies Ltd, a wireless technology company, and positioned himself for a return to the changing IT arena.[6]

In the 1990s no company better exemplified in the public mind Canada's aspirations in the high-technology field than Nortel. This company had begun its life in 1914 as Northern Electric, the manufacturing arm of Bell Canada. As such, it had benefited for decades from transfers of communications technology from its American counterpart, Western Electric, which also held shares in Northern, and from the innovations of Bell Labs, the research wing of American Telephone and Telegraph (AT&T). In 1956, however, under a consent decree negotiated by AT&T with the US Justice Department to settle an antitrust suit, Western divested itself of its holdings in Northern Electric, and by the 1960s Northern (now wholly owned by Bell Canada) no longer had access to the fruits of Bell Labs research.

Prodded by Robert Scrivener of Bell Canada, Northern Electric set about building up its own research and development program, which led to the creation of Bell-Northern Research as a joint entity in 1971. At an early stage the company decided to focus on the development of switches and related components for digital systems, which it anticipated replacing the analog-based systems that predominated in most telephone services. This proved to be a fortuitous move: during the late 1970s Northern sold its digital switches to the few independent US telephone networks; in 1984, another antitrust case resulted in the termination of AT&T's virtual monopoly, and Northern found new customers among the 'Baby Bells'— the local and regional telephone systems spawned by the breakup.

The entry into the US was not the only international venture for Northern (called Northern Telecom after 1976): Scrivener, who moved over from Bell Canada to be chief executive at Northern, pushed it into foreign markets to enable it to increase production and achieve economies of scale with its expensive new line of digital products. In 1978, Northern achieved a major coup when it secured a $3.5 billion (US) contract to supply a telecommunications system to the oil-rich kingdom of Saudi Arabia, outbidding much larger rivals such as International Telephone and Telegraph (ITT) and Philips. By the 1980s it had subsidiaries in Europe, Asia, and Latin America as well as the United States: Canada only accounted for 20 per cent of its business, and it had more employees overseas than at home. It was the second largest supplier of communications equipment in the US, with 130 plants and R&D centres in 11 states. Meanwhile, Bell Canada had begun to slowly divest itself of control of Northern, down to 50 per cent by the end of the 1980s, and Northern's public shares were traded in New York as well as Toronto.

At this point, Northern Telecom was beginning to lose its innovative sheen: technical problems with software alienated some overseas customers, and it faced competition, even in its home market, from a revived AT&T as well as from large foreign suppliers like Siemens and Ericsson. But more critically, the broader regulatory and technological environment in the communications industry was beginning to shift. In the early 1990s the Canadian Radio-television and Telecommunications Commission (CRTC), paralleling trends in the US and later in Europe, began removing barriers to competition between providers of communications services. This allowed companies like Bell Canada to acquire broadcasting licenses, and conversely, companies providing cable TV service, like Rogers and Shaw, to go into the telephone business. These developments triggered a period of frenzy over 'convergence' as a range of enterprises set out to build media empires through acquisitions: Bell Canada, for example, took over CTV and the *Globe and Mail*, setting itself up as Bell Globemedia; Rogers bought the magazine publisher, Maclean-Hunter, and acquired the former CNCP telecommunications venture—it later passed on to AT&T, which in turn sold Rogers its wireless communications operation in Canada, making Rogers, along with Telus, the largest provider of cellphone services in Canada; other cable companies, including Cogeco and Shaw, also moved into the telecommunications field.

Northern stood on the sidelines while Bell engaged in its shopping spree, but at the same time it was preparing to play a role in the emerging technology of the Internet. Based on a Cold War-era project in the US to develop a communications network that could survive nuclear war, during the 1980s the military origins of the Internet were increasingly overtaken by universities and scientific research labs, for which it provided a wide-ranging data-sharing system. By the end of the eighties there were around 300,000 Internet sites, but it was still a technology designed for a limited audience of high-end users, mostly scientists. That situation began to change in 1989 when Tim Berners-Lee developed a hypertext protocol that made the Internet more accessible to non-specialists. Two years later, Marc Andreesen, a student at the University of Illinois,

developed the Mosaic browser, which provided graphic, user-friendly features that opened the Internet to a mass market; Andreesen and an entrepreneur, Jim Clark, produced a commercial version, Netscape, in 1993. By 1995 the Internet had 16 million users, soaring to over 500 million within five years.

The commercialization of the Internet quickly spawned thousands of sites, ranging from elite institutions to entrepreneurs to pornographers and UFO enthusiasts. The major bottleneck in its early years, however, reflected its reliance on existing telecommunications systems: the sheer volume of data being transmitted could overwhelm all but the largest trunk-line systems, so breakdowns were frequent and even regular transmissions were time-consuming and costly. But a new technology based on fibre optics offered the prospects of significantly broadening the carrying capacity of systems and speeding up transmissions. The technology, based on glass fibres, was not exactly novel, and experimental work had begun in the 1960s in the US and Canada: Northern Telecom had been the site of early development in the 1970s, and it built a pioneer fibre-based network for Saskatchewan Telecommunications a few years later. By the mid-1990s most telecom companies had begun replacing or enhancing their major trunk lines with fibre optic cable; but it was still regarded as a high-cost technology for installation for the entire user market.

In 1997, John Roth, a veteran of Bell-Northern Labs, became chief executive of Northern Telecom and committed the company (soon to be renamed Nortel Networks) not only to the goal of extending the fibre optic system, but to becoming a major supplier of data-networking gear to Internet operators. To these ends Roth set out to expand Nortel's capital base and to absorb companies producing Internet-related technology, beginning with the takeover of a California company, Bay Networks.

Canadian investors were initially skeptical of what Roth called Nortel's 'right-angle turn' onto the Internet frontier. But, by 1999, demand for fibre optic networking was dramatically growing across the newly 'converged' telecommunications industry, and Nortel was highly competitive with the two major (US) suppliers, Cisco and Lucent (the former Western Electric). Furthermore, the stock markets, having recovered from the recession earlier in the decade, were entering the 'Roaring Nineties' phase of euphoria over the Internet and the 'New Economy'. Investors flocked to the high-tech companies listed on NASDAQ, and, in the spirit of the mining booms of the early 1900s, enterprises with non-existent assets but great prospects sprang up weekly. Nortel itself joined in the spree, picking up start-up companies with names like Qtera, Juniper Networks, Xros, and r3 Security Engineering AG. Nortel also bought out Bell Canada's share of Bell-Northern Research, and in 2000 Bell Canada reduced its holdings in Nortel from 39 per cent to 2 per cent, effectively ending the century-old relationship.

By this time Nortel's share price had surged from under $35 (Cdn) per share in 1999 to over $125 (Cdn) per share in early 2001, and at its peak, trading in Nortel accounted for more than one-third of the total value of transactions on the Toronto Stock Exchange. But then the bubble burst, not just for Nortel but the whole 'dot.com' speculative frenzy. By 2001 it was becoming clear that the era of e-commerce was not yet here, demand for optical fibre was saturated, and Nortel, it was discovered, had not made any profits since 1998. The share price plummeted, to less than $1 per share by August 2002. Roth left the company under a cloud, and his successors seemed unable to present even a clear statement of Nortel's accounts, repeatedly issuing earnings restatements that went back several years, meanwhile laying off more than 60,000 employees. Only after five years did the company seem to be stabilizing.[7]

The history of Canadian enterprises in the high-technology fields has been marked by episodes of promise followed by disaster, from Ferranti-Canada in the 1960s through Corel and Nortel at the end of the century. Nevertheless, by that time Canada was not exclusively relying on imported technology, and new champions emerged, including Research In Motion (RIM) and Open Text, both in Waterloo, Ontario, and Sierra Wireless of Vancouver (see box, p. 248).

RETURN OF THE 'OLD ECONOMY'

To the chagrin of Canadian nationalists, this country is best known to outsiders not for its highly educated workforce or its estimable quality of life but rather as a storehouse of natural resources. Even sympathetic critics like Michael Porter in his 1991 analysis, *Canada at the Crossroads*, observed that 'Canada's economy, and especially its export economy, is heavily based on natural resources', which is 'vulnerable to adverse shifts in technology, markets and international competition.' For a time in the 1990s that image, if not necessarily the reality, seemed to be shifting: the media featured stories of emerging high-tech companies like Corel and Nortel, juxtaposed with stories of declining fish stocks, abandoned mining towns, and bankrupt forestry companies. But with the new century, natural resources appeared to be experiencing a revival.

During the 1970s the gold-mining industry had thrived for a time because of the US devaluation of the dollar and unsettled economic conditions, but both the domestic supplies and international demand were declining by the 1990s. The new resource boom was triggered by the discovery in 1991 of diamonds in the Northwest Territories, and two years later, in 1993, vast deposits of nickel, copper, and cobalt were found at Voisey's Bay in Labrador, one of the largest base metal fields since those found in northern Ontario a century earlier. In addition, by the end of the decade plans were underway to revive the long-moribund uranium mines in Saskatchewan as the nuclear power industry began to show signs of life. Rising demand from industrializing countries such as China and Brazil drove up the prices of copper, nickel, iron ore, and aluminum.

But the most dramatic turnaround took place in the oil and gas fields of western Canada.

RESEARCH IN MOTION

Research In Motion (RIM) of Waterloo, Ontario, is virtually unique as a Canadian company: its main product—the BlackBerry—is better known internationally than the company itself. It is also, at least as of 2008, the country's prime example of leadership in high technology, an heir to the mantle once worn by Avro, Corel, and Nortel. Although it might be hoped that RIM will have a more enduring legacy than these companies, in recent years it has been battered by patent litigation, charges of stock option manipulation, and technical problems.

Much like the legendary beginnings of Microsoft or Apple, RIM was established in 1984 by two boyhood friends, Michael Laziridis and Douglas Fregin, initially as an electronics and computer consulting venture. Laziridis was so keen about the business that when they acquired a contract with General Motors for an industrial automation project, he dropped out of the University of Waterloo's engineering program two months before graduation (he later became chancellor at the university). The critical point for the nascent company was its entry into the wireless data industry in the early 1990s. Working with a wireless data network developed by the Swedish telecommunications company, Ericsson, Laziridis produced a small mobile pager with two-way communications capabilities, called Inter@ctive pager 950. Within a year, however, RIM, using the same basic hardware, came up with a far more versatile device that could handle interactive e-mail, mobile telephone, text messaging, faxing, and web browsing. This was the 'Black-Berry', introduced on the market in 1999 at the height of investor enthusiasm for Internet-related technology.

Laziridis had benefited from a significant amount of funding support from the University of Waterloo, the provincial government

Michael Laziridis and his BlackBerry. (www.bbhub.com/media/2006/02/laziridis.jpg)

(the Ontario Technology Fund), and the federal government (the Business Development Bank of Canada), and brought in Jim Balsillie, a Harvard MBA, to manage the business side of RIM. The company was not just another dot.com, but the market crash of 2001–2 sideswiped RIM, as investors abandoned high-tech stocks at the same time that the BlackBerry was encountering technical growing pains. Nevertheless, RIM survived as its signature product became the favourite of celebrities, ranging from GE's Jack Welsh to Pamela Anderson; more critically, the company's strategy shifted from marketing directly to consumers to sales to network carriers who would adopt the device for their entire organizations. By 2004 there were more than 2 million subscribers to the BlackBerry service, doubling the 2003 level, and this rose again to over 4 million in 2005 and to 8 million by 2007.

Inevitably, the new technology became embroiled in patent litigation. In 2001, RIM brought a suit against an Atlanta company, Glenayre Electronics, which they settled. But it was almost derailed that same year by a patent infringement charge by Thomas Campana of Chicago, who had begun working on pagers in the 1970s and took out a US patent for a wireless text-messaging system called Telefind in the early 1990s. RIM vigorously contested the claim, but its case in a Richmond, Virginia, courtroom presentation bombed. In 2003, a jury ruled against RIM, and the judge imposed additional penalties on the grounds that RIM had engaged in deceptive and dilatory tactics—most critically, he ordered a ban on further sales of the BlackBerry in the US market. The injunction was delayed pending appeals, but by 2006 RIM had exhausted that process, and agreed to pay Campana's company, NTP, $615 million to settle the suit—about 10 times the amount of the original award. Despite this setback, RIM continued to dominate the wireless pager field, and shifted its strategy again towards the licensing software related to its BlackBerry service, moving away from reliance on its lead in hardware.

RIM was the most prominent of a cluster of companies that included Open Text and Maple Soft in the emerging computer/communications industry located in the Kitchener–Waterloo area of Ontario. In part, this reflected the influence of the University of Waterloo, which had consciously set out to emulate Stanford University in California in nourishing new start-up firms in the high-tech field as well as focusing on the education of computer scientists. By the 1990s, community boosters were promoting the region as 'Canada's Technology Triangle', challenging the Ottawa region as the country's 'Silicon Valley North'.

Sources: 'Innovation in Canada: Case 7: Research in Motion Ltd.', at: <www.innovation.gc.ca/gol/innovation>; Erick Schonfeld, 'Blackberry Season', *Business 2.0 Magazine*, 1 Oct. 2004, at: <www.money.cnn.com>; Barrie McKenna, Paul Waldie, and Simon Avery, 'Patently Absurd: The Inside Story of RIM's Wireless War', *Globe and Mail Report on Business*, 28 Jan. 2006, B4–B6.

Albertans attributed many of their problems to the National Energy Program that led to the departure of American (and some Canadian) oil drillers, but the decline in international oil prices played a larger role: the drop was gradual for a time, but prices fell significantly in 1987. A brief spike occurred during the Gulf War of 1990–1, but prices then went back into the doldrums until the end of the decade. Recovery came after 2001, when prices that in the 1990s had been running below $18 (US) per barrel rose steadily to $50 (US) and higher. By mid-2008, the price had risen above $140 (US) per barrel.

Long years in the wilderness had produced a shakeout of the many smaller oil and gas companies that thrived in western Canada in the 1960s and 1970s, and when the new age of higher energy prices emerged, a more consolidated industry was there to exploit the situation. This included several of the multinationals, such as Imperial Oil, BP, and Shell Canada, but also some domestic players, among whom the largest was EnCana, the product of a merger in 2004 of Alberta Energy and PanCanadian Energy. Alberta Energy had begun life in 1973 as a somewhat novel form of provincial Crown corporation, in which the province held a 50 per cent interest, with the balance sold to Alberta residents; its mandate was to promote development of the province's oil and gas, petrochemical, forestry, and manufacturing capabilities. During the Ralph Klein era in the 1990s, the government divested itself of all shares in the enterprise that focused on oil and gas pipelines, merging in 1995 with CanWest Exploration Co. PanCanadian Petroleum was the heir to Canadian Pacific's investment in western oil and gas, going back to 1958: CP transferred mineral rights to 11 million acres, mostly in Alberta, to CP Oil & Gas in 1963, giving it a significant advantage in exploration and development of new oil fields over other companies holding five-year leases on Crown lands. During the 1990s PanCanadian moved overseas through joint ventures into Australia, Indonesia, and Russia, the latter investment proving to be particularly unprofitable. The company turned its attention homeward later in the decade, joining the Texas-based Hunt Oil in a Newfoundland venture and eventually returning to its roots in Alberta. The merger made EnCana the largest Canadian-owned oil and gas company, with $20 billion in assets, second only to Imperial Oil, the Canadian subsidiary of the American giant, Exxon.

By far the most dramatic development in this new era of western Canadian oil was the emergence of the oil sands, which sprawl across northern Alberta into Saskatchewan, as a viable source for exploration and exploitation. Estimates by the Alberta Department of Energy in 2005 indicated that the largest field, the Athabasca oil sands, held deposits of over 120 billion barrels of bitumen convertible to conventional crude oil using current technology, and the total amount of potentially recoverable bitumen came to over 2,000 billion barrels, making Canada second only to Saudi Arabia in terms of proven reserves. Oil sands mining, of course, went back to 1967 when Great Canadian Oil Sands, a subsidiary of Suncor, went into production. During the 1970s the Syncrude consortium undertook a larger project, but the collapse of conventional crude oil prices after 1981 brought further activities to a halt; no new oil sands mines were started until 2003, when Shell Canada commenced operations. Improvements in the technology of extraction and rising energy prices over the next four years lured new (and larger) players to the oil sands, including Imperial Oil, the French company Total, and a consortium set up by a Calgary company, Synenco Energy, with the China Petroleum Co.; companies from India were also showing interest in the Athabasca region.

Climbing energy prices also rejuvenated oil and gas exploration and development on the other end of the country. During the 1970s offshore drilling began in Nova Scotia and Newfoundland but a combination of factors—the high costs of operating in this harsh environment, the impact of the National Energy Program, and a disaster involving the *Ocean Ranger*, one of the large drilling rigs in the Hibernia field off Newfoundland in 1982—put a damper on initial expectations in the region for an Alberta-style boom. In ironic contrast to privatizations being undertaken in other cases, the Mulroney government set up a Crown enterprise, Canada Hibernia Holding Company, to partner with Petro-Canada and several multinationals, including Mobil, Chevron, and Norsk Hydro, to develop the Hibernia project. Production, principally by Chevron, commenced in 1997; meanwhile, Petro-Canada carried out explorations of other Newfoundland offshore fields, at Terra Nova and White Rose, again forming partnerships with Chevron, Mobil, and Husky Oil in the 1980s for development. The estimates for reserves were considerably smaller than in the oil sands—500 to 600 billion barrels for Hibernia, the largest field—but were sufficient to merit continued interest from the major oil companies in the context of apparently declining global petroleum reserves and political turmoil in the Middle East.

The new east coast oil and gas boom triggered by Hibernia in 1997 resurrected long-simmering disputes over royalty sharing—Newfoundland had no share in that project and its share of royalties was less than half that of the federal government. This issue was raised repeatedly by Newfoundland's political leaders with limited effect until the election of Danny Williams as Premier in 2003. Williams was a multi-millionaire in his own right, having constructed a cable television chain in the region, which he sold in 2000 to Rogers Communications for $250 million. Williams pressured the federal government into an agreement that left intact Ottawa's equalization payments to Newfoundland as a have-not province even as its revenues from offshore petroleum production rose. He then turned his

Trucks hauling bitumen from oil sands near Fort McMurray, Alberta. (Jeff McIntosh, AP, 2006)

attention towards the oil companies' consortium, which was in the throes of developing a new offshore project christened Hebron. Playing some members of the consortium (Husky and Petro-Canada) against others (Chevron, ExxonMobil, Norsk Hydro), Williams negotiated a 5 per cent equity stake for Newfoundland in Hebron, plus additional royalties and a pledge that the consortium would build a platform in St John's using local contractors. For a province that had suffered the indignities of Churchill Falls and the Come-by-Chance refinery, the Hebron deal was hailed as a significant achievement.

While the resource boom of the early twenty-first century resembled Canada's mining bonanzas of 100 years earlier, some new factors had to be taken into account by those seeking to exploit the country's remaining 'storehouse', particularly relating to Native interests and environmental issues. In both areas, controversies had erupted in the 1970s, and well-organized constituencies had evolved by the end of the century that businesses

ignored at their peril. The effectiveness of newly energized Native Canadians had been displayed by the Cree and Inuit in their confrontation with the Quebec government over the James Bay hydro development in the early 1970s. In this same period, a plan to build a natural gas pipeline from the Beaufort Sea in the Arctic through the Mackenzie Delta in the Northwest Territories was stalled by opposition from Inuit, Dene, and Métis communities, leading to a lengthy Royal Commission report in 1977 prepared by Justice Thomas Berger, which effectively established a moratorium on development; proposals for a new project (with some Native support) were floated again after 2000.

The Voisey's Bay mineral discoveries in Labrador in the 1990s led to protests from the Innu community over land claims. Although the Newfoundland government was not particularly sympathetic to Native claims, the project was bottled up until 2002, when a revenue-sharing 'interim agreement' was worked out. In this controversy, as in the case of James Bay and the Mackenzie Delta, issues relating to Native claims were intermixed with environmental concerns, although Native communities did not necessarily embrace all the values of their environmentalist allies. An example of the complexity of these issues is presented by the lengthy controversy over logging of Clayoquot Sound on Vancouver Island in British Columbia. In 1955, the BC government had opened the region to the forestry giant MacMillan-Bloedel, which aroused opposition from Native communities, who blockaded the company's entry to the area in the 1980s. Protests expanded after 1993 when environmentalists, enraged by MacBlo's commitment to clear-cutting, embarked on a lengthy campaign of civil disobedience, which attracted media attention abroad and led to a UNESCO designation of Clayoquot as a biosphere reserve. In 1999 an agreement of sorts was worked out among the parties, but within a few years environmentalists and Native groups were at odds over the latter's plans to harvest timber as part of their own development program.

The oil sands, however, would experience the most sustained criticism from environmentalists. Extraction of bitumen from the tar, like strip mining, damages the muskeg, and environmental critics argued that the Alberta government regulations did not require full restoration of the land to its original state. In addition, the oil sands operations required massive amounts of water diverted from the Athabasca River. These complaints surfaced when the earliest oil sands ventures began. But the most vigorous criticism emerged more recently in the context of increased public concern over global warming: the oil sands were estimated to produce 80 kilograms of greenhouse gases for every barrel of oil, and the high costs of energy involved in the extraction process also contributed to this output. As governments began to impose fuel emission limits on automobiles and encourage hybrid cars and ethanol production, not surprisingly, the oil sands operations could become a focal point for environmental wrath.[8]

'HOLLOWED OUT'?

For some of Canada's business leaders, including Peter Munk, Gerald Schwartz, and Dominic d'Allesandro, chief executive of Manulife Financial, one of the more alarming trends of the new century was the disappearance or transformation of the country's venerable business institutions, often through takeovers by foreign entities. Tim Horton's, the embodiment of Canada's love of hockey and doughnuts, had already been swallowed up by the US fast-food franchiser, Wendy's, in the 1990s. Eaton's self-destructed as well, leaving The Bay as the flagship of the country's retailers. Then, in 2006, The Bay was acquired by a South Carolina financier, Jerry Zucker. A year later Abitibi Consolidated, Canada's largest forestry company, merged with the US company, Bowater; and Alcan, Canada's largest mining multinational, after facing a takeover challenge from its former US owner, Alcoa, was acquired by the British mining giant, Rio Tinto, in August 2007.

Entire industries seemed to be swallowed up: in the 1990s Canada's major firms in the distilled spirits field, Seagram and Hiram Walker, were taken over by European companies. In the nickel industry, the long-time rivals, Inco and Falconbridge, fell in 2006, respectively, to Brazilian and Swiss entities. In that same year, Fairmount Hotels, which owned some of Canada's legendary hotels, such as Château Frontenac in Quebec and Banff Springs in Alberta, as well as Boston's Copley Plaza and many other international sites, was acquired by a consortium headed by a Los Angeles company, Colony Capital LLC. Later that year the Canadian luxury hotel chain, Four Seasons, founded by Isadore Sharp in Toronto in 1960, was taken over by Bill Gates of Microsoft in partnership with a Saudi Arabian prince.

By that time Canada's big steel companies were in play: Dofasco of Hamilton, long regarded as one of the country's best-run companies, had been acquired in 2006 by the European company Arcelor, which in turn was taken over by an Indian company, Mittal. A year later Algoma Steel, which itself had set out to consolidate with Stelco, was bought by another Indian company, Essar Group. Ipsco, the major representative of 'mini-mills' in Canada, was acquired by the Swedish company, Svenskt Stal AB, in 2007. Only Stelco remained of the once-formidable Canadian steel fraternity; and Stelco itself, having barely emerged from bankruptcy, was advertising its availability to foreign buyers.

A variety of factors were driving this trend. In some areas, particularly in the resource industry, this was an era of global consolidation, similar to the national consolidations that had been a feature of the early 1900s: Inco and Falconbridge, for example, had been seeking to amalgamate at the time of their separate takeovers to achieve a scale of operations that would make them competitive in the world nickel markets. Alcoa's pursuit of Alcan was triggered in part by the emergence of an aggressive Russian competitor, Rusal. Similarly, in the steel industry, the rise of Mittal as the world's largest producer capped a period of rivalry among international giants including Tata Group of India, the German firm ThyssenKrupp (which had bid against Arcelor for control of Dofasco), and companies in China, Japan, and South Korea. One of the characteristics of this merger wave—which may have attenuated traditional Canadian nationalist outcries—was that it was truly a global phenomenon: in contrast to the past, American companies were not the only, or even the most important, players in these takeovers of Canadian firms.

Another factor was the global availability of money from institutional investors, providing a pool that ambitious corporate and financial empire builders could draw upon for takeovers: an example of this dynamic at work was the proposed acquisition of Bell Canada in 2007 by a coalition of the managers of the Canada Pension Plan and the US takeover specialist Kolbert-Kravis-Roberts (KKR), later joined by Henry Kravis's old associate, Gerald Schwartz of Onex. Arrayed against them was the Ontario Hospital Pension Fund, allied with the US private equity company, Cerberus, fresh from a successful bidding war with Magna and Onex for Chrysler. In the end, the telecommunications giant was acquired by the Ontario Teachers' Pension Fund, allied with yet another US private equity firm, Providence Equity Partners Inc.

One of the interesting features of this contest was that the goal of the contestants in the bidding war was to buy out all other shareholders in Bell and essentially terminate it as a publicly listed company. This, too, was a trend of the times: several large multinationals were in the process of absorbing their own Canadian (and other) affiliates by buying out all minority interests, bringing a new meaning to the term 'privatization' as these companies were delisted from all stock exchanges. The process was augmented by legal changes in Ontario that removed restrictions on buyouts of minority interests. The US auto giant Ford proceeded to absorb its Canadian subsidiary in 1995, despite protests and legal actions by minority shareholders. Other big foreign-owned companies followed suit, including the US chemical company Du Pont and Royal Dutch Shell; it should be noted that these moves were not restricted to Canada, but reflected an emerging global strategy of consolidation by large multinationals.

On the other hand, there were examples of Canadian companies that were buying up large foreign entities. Power Corporation, for example, through Groupe Bruxelles Lambert, held the largest stake in such French companies as Total Petroleum and Lafarge. Manulife Financial acquired the US insurance company, John Hancock, in 2004. In 2007, Thomson International took over the global news service, Reuters. While the media focused on dramatic episodes of corporate struggles for control, analysts seeking to provide a broader historical context for these developments were drawing curiously differing conclusions.

In 2005, business historians Barry Boothman and Barbara Austin analyzed shifts in ownership and control of Canada's largest businesses dating back to 1973. Within that time frame, they presented a portrait of striking changes, particularly for the period since 1988 (the date, interestingly, when the Canada–US Free Trade Agreement was ratified). In the 1973–88 period, over 60 per cent of the companies ranked in the top 50 non-financial enterprises survived, yet only 42 per cent of the top 50 companies in 1988 were still there in 2003. Among the 25 largest industrial companies in Canada in 1973, more than two-thirds were still listed in 1988, but only half of the top 25 in 1988 were still listed in 2003. Relatively few of the companies that disappeared from the top rankings had gone bankrupt—most of them had been acquired by other Canadian companies or by foreign companies. In terms of take-overs, foreign companies accounted for only 22 per cent in the years 1973–88, but this doubled in the following 15 years. On the other side, the proportion of changes in the top-ranked companies accounted for by the entry of new Canadian companies doubled in the 1988–2003 period over the preceding 15-year period.

Boothman and Austin did not attribute the major shifts after 1988 to 'the rise of new technological services and sectors'; on the contrary, 'the sectoral mix of the biggest domestic companies did not fundamentally alter. Canadian firms remained clustered in the same industries.' On the other hand, they characterized this period as 'Armageddon for the most prominent closely-held corporations', particularly family firms. A number of factors were cited: Canadian firms were too small, 'ninety-pound weaklings', lacking the size and scale to compete effectively with larger global entities; Canadian companies failed to adapt well to changing markets, sticking to established practices, no matter how 'threadbare'; family firms were particularly vulnerable because of problems of generational transition of leadership. Echoing Michael Porter's warnings in *Canada at the Crossroads*, they noted that 'a greater proportion of the biggest non-financials now is located in the resource sector than at any time since 1930', and that 'technologically advanced activities usually

[are] dominated by foreign enterprises. Domestic firms, while they did attempt to build positions, rarely lasted more than a generation and never successfully displaced foreign first-movers.'[9]

In 2006, the Institute for Competitiveness and Prosperity at the University of Toronto's Rotman Business School released a study entitled 'Canada's Global Leaders 1985–2005', essentially covering much the same territory. Rather than drawing on traditional methods of ranking top Canadian companies in terms of assets, sales, etc. in comparison with other Canadian companies, the researchers at the Institute identified its 'global leaders' in terms of size based on revenue in comparison with other companies internationally 'in a specific market segment'. They then compared the overall number of 'global leaders' in 1985 and 2005, and assessed the number of companies that had 'departed' from that status or had attained it in that time period. They found that the number of Canadian 'global leaders' in specific markets or industries had increased from 33 to 72 over the 1985–2005 period; 17 of the 1985 'leaders' had departed (through mergers or takeovers) and 56 Canadian companies not listed as 'leaders' in 1985 had joined this elite group by 2005. The general picture, then, was of a rising Canadian phoenix rather than an Armageddon for Canadian firms.

Among the companies that had ceased to be 'global leaders' by 2005 were familiar names: Hiram Walker and Seagram, Hudson's Bay Company, Inco, Falconbridge, the Moore Corporation. The emerging 'global leaders' represented a wide variety of pursuits: Barrick Gold on the resource side; CN Rail (transportation); CHC Helicopters; Magna (auto parts); Manulife Financial; Research In Motion and Sierra Wireless in new technologies; and environment-oriented enterprises such as Tree Island Industries and SunGro Horticulture. 'Twenty years ago', a news story on the report commented, 'Canadian firms led in . . . spirits and wines, nickel, asbestos, solid waste management, and real estate. Today, according to the study, Canadians lead in environmental compliance technology, postage stamps, gastro-intestinal products and wollastonite, a mineral fibre used in ceramics, auto parts and concrete.' In this framework, corporate size in an absolute sense is less significant than size and performance within a niche, which may embrace a large field like financial services or a very small but high-value market.[10]

The difference between these two perspectives is not just a matter of seeing the glass half-full or half-empty: they rest on contrasting assumptions about which businesses are important. In that sense, the case could be made that both views provide an accurate picture of the current state of the Canadian business community. One of the reasons that corporations like Hudson's Bay Company or family dynasties like the Bronfmans have commanded attention is that they are exceptional: most enterprises have a relatively short life, disappearing into bankruptcy, sale, merger, or simply the retirement of the owner or the disinterest of investors. A trip to Henry Pellatt's Casa Loma or, for that matter, the Eaton Centre in Toronto provides a glimpse of the inevitable mortality of even the seemingly most entrenched business empires. It is worth noting that many of the companies whose fate in the hands of Americans or Russians or Brazilians is now a matter of public debate spent most of their history as subsidiaries to foreigners, only emerging into independence in the decades after World War II. The Canadian auto industry, the largest manufacturer and exporter of its products in the country, has always been under foreign domination.

At the same time, Canada has produced generation after generation of new entrepreneurs, in no small degree the result of immigration and social mobility. Even in the early nineteenth century, when Canadians were primarily hewers of wood and trappers of beaver for European consumers, a wide range of Canadian enterprises served local markets, created employment, and helped to build the communities that would eventually become major urban centres such as Halifax, Montreal, Toronto, Calgary, and Vancouver. Some of the strongest critics of the failure of leadership in Canadian business, such as Peter Munk and Ian Delaney, themselves exemplify this tradition of renewal. Whether their fears or the more optimistic perspective offered by the scholars at the University of Toronto represents the future direction of Canadian business is a matter that future readers of *The Rise of Canadian Business* will be better placed to judge.

Notes

Introduction

1. On Innis and the influence of the staple thesis, see Carl Berger, *The Writing of Canadian History*, 2nd edn (Toronto, 1986), 85–111. The standard survey of Canadian economic history for many years, reflecting the staple approach, was Hugh Aitken and W.T. Easterbrook, *Canadian Economic History* (Toronto, 1956). A more recent variant by a Canadian political economist is R. Tom Naylor, *Canada in the European Age 1453–1919* (Vancouver, 1987). The most ambitious effort to present an alternative to the 'staple' approach to Canadian business history is Michael Bliss, *Northern Enterprise: Five Centuries of Canadian Business* (Toronto, 1987).

2. Norman Gras's major work is *Business and Capitalism: An Introduction to Business History* (New York, 1939). The classic example of the 'robber baron' approach is Matthew Josephson, *The Robber Barons* (New York, 1934); see also Gustavus R. Myers, *The History of Great American Fortunes* (Chicago, 1910), and Myers, *A History of Canadian Wealth* (New York, 1914; repr. Toronto, 1972). A prominent example of the 'industrial statesman' view is Allan Nevins, *John D. Rockefeller: The Heroic Age of American Enterprise* (New York, 1940). The work of the 'entrepreneurial school' may be sampled in Hugh Aitken, ed., *Explorations in Enterprise* (Cambridge, Mass., 1967); also see Thomas C. Cochran, *Business in American Life: A History* (New York, 1972). The major works of Alfred D. Chandler Jr, the leading historian of large corporate enterprises in the twentieth century, include *Strategy and Structure: Chapter in the History of American Industrial Enterprise* (Cambridge, Mass., 1962); *The Visible Hand: The Managerial Revolution in American Business* (Cambridge, Mass., 1977); and *Scale and Scope: The Dynamics of Industrial Capitalism* (Cambridge, Mass., 1990).

3. On the history of multinational business and globalization, see Jeffrey Frieden, *Global Capitalism: Its Fall and Rise in the Twentieth Century* (New York, 2006); Geoffrey Jones, *Multinationals and Global Capitalism: From the Nineteenth to the Twenty-first Century* (Oxford, 2005).

4. A recent study of Australian business history is Grant Fleming et al., *The Big End of Town: Big Business and Corporate Leadership in 20th Century Australia* (Cambridge, 2004).

Chapter 1

1. Michael Bliss, *Northern Enterprise: Five Centuries of Canadian Business* (Toronto, 1989), 219; 'Donald Smith Drives the Last Spike at Craigellachie', The Canadian West Project, at <www.collectionscanada.ca>. The best-known popular history of the building of the Canadian Pacific is the two-volume work by Pierre Berton, *The National Dream* (Toronto, 1970) and *The Last Spike* (Toronto, 1972). See also W. Kaye Lamb, *History of the Canadian Pacific Railway* (New York, 1977); Hugh A. Dempsey, ed., *The CPR West: The Iron Road and the Making of a Nation* (Vancouver, 1984). On some of the principal figures involved, see Heather Gilbert, *Awakening Continent: The Life of Lord Mount Stephen* (Aberdeen, 1965); Valerie Knowles, *From Telegrapher to Titan: The Life of William Van Horne* (Toronto, 2004).

2. On the fisheries, see John Gilchrist, 'Exploration and Enterprise: The Newfoundland Fishery, 1497–1677', in David S. Macmillan, ed., *Canadian Business History* (Toronto, 1971), 7–26; Harold A. Innis, *The Cod Fisheries: The History of an International Economy* (Toronto, 1954); Rosemary Ommer, *From Outpost to Outport: A Structural Analysis of the Jersey–Gaspé Cod Fishery, 1767–1886* (Montreal and Kingston, 1991); Keith Matthews, *Lectures on the History of Newfoundland 1500–1830* (St John's, 1988).

3. Dale Miquelon, 'Havy and Lefebvre of Quebec: A Case Study of Metropolitan Participation in Canadian Trade, 1730–60', in Tom Traves, ed., *Essays in Canadian Business History* (Toronto, 1984), 24–46. See also John F. Bosher, *The Canada Merchants, 1713–1763* (Oxford, 1987); Graham D. Taylor and Peter Baskerville, *A Concise History of Business in Canada* (Toronto, 1994), chs 3–5.

4. Rare among Canadian enterprises, the Hudson's Bay Company has maintained an excellent archive

going back several centuries, and has made it accessible to historians. Among the most authoritative studies of the company are E.E. Rich, *History of the Hudson's Bay Company*, 3 vols (London, 1958–60), and a shorter volume by Rich, *The Fur Trade and the Northwest to 1857* (Toronto, 1967). See also J.S. Galbraith, *The Hudson's Bay Company as an Imperial Factor* (Berkeley, Calif., 1957). Popular histories of the company include Douglas MacKay, *The Honourable Company* (Indianapolis, 1936); and Peter C. Newman's three volumes: *Company of Adventurers* (Toronto, 1985), *Caesars of the Wilderness* (Toronto, 1987), and *Merchant Princes* (Toronto, 1991). On the company's relations with Native Canadians, see Arthur J. Ray and Donald Freeman, '*Give Us Good Measure': An Economic Analysis of Relations Between the Indians and the Hudson's Bay Company* (Toronto, 1978). On social dimensions of the fur trade, see Sylvia van Kirk, '*Many Tender Ties': Women in Fur Trade Society in Western Canada 1670–1870* (Winnipeg, 1981). On Simpson, see J.S. Galbraith, *The Little Emperor: Governor Simpson of the Hudson's Bay Company* (New York, 1956); James Raffan, *Emperor of the North: Sir George Simpson and the Remarkable Story of the Hudson's Bay Company* (Toronto, 2007).

5. Douglas McCalla, 'An Introduction to the Nineteenth Century Business World', in Traves, ed., *Essays in Canadian Business History*, 17–18.

6. David Macmillan, 'The "New Men" in Action: Scottish Mercantile and Shipping Operations in the North American Colonies, 1760–1825', in Macmillan, ed., *Canadian Business History*, 44–103. See also Gerald Tulchinsky, *The River Barons: Montreal Businessmen and the Growth of Industry and Transportation* (Toronto, 1977), chs 1–2. On William Forsyth, see David A. Sutherland, 'William A. Forsyth', *Dictionary of Canadian Biography Online*, at: <www.biographi.ca>. The *DCB* (also available in print form) is an excellent source of material on Canadian business and public figures up to c. 1930.

7. For a general overview, see Philip A. Buckner and John G. Reid, eds, *The Atlantic Region to Confederation* (Toronto, 1994), esp. chs 13–14. On Nova Scotia, see Julian Gwyn, *Excessive Expectations: Maritime Commerce and the Economic Development of Nova Scotia, 1740–1870* (Kingston and Montreal, 1998); Marilyn Gerriets, 'The Impact of the General Mining Association on the Nova Scotia Coal Industry, 1820–1850', *Acadiensis* 21 (Autumn 1991): 54–84. On the timber and shipbuilding industry in New Brunswick, see Eric W. Sager and Gerald Panting, *Maritime Capital: The Shipping Industry in Atlantic Canada, 1820–1914*

(Montreal and Kingston, 1990); Graeme Wynn, *Timber Colony: A Historical Geography of Early 19th Century New Brunswick* (Toronto, 1971).

8. Donald Creighton, *The Commercial Empire of the Saint Lawrence* (Toronto, 1936) [later editions shortened the title to *The Empire of the Saint Lawrence*]. See also Tulchinsky, *The River Barons*. On Upper Canada, see Douglas McCalla, *Planting a Province: The Economic History of Upper Canada, 1784–1870* (Toronto, 1993), esp. chs 6–8; Taylor and Baskerville, *A Concise History*, ch. 9. Studies of individual merchants of the era include: Bruce Wilson, *The Enterprises of Robert Hamilton: A Study of Wealth and Influence in Early Upper Canada 1776–1812* (Ottawa, 1983); Douglas McCalla, *The Upper Canada Trade 1834–1872: A Study of the Buchanans' Business* (Toronto, 1979). On the Boyd family, see Grace Barker, *Timber Empire: The Exploits of the Entrepreneurial Boyds* (Fenelon Falls, Ont., 1997). On the Welland Canal, see Hugh G.J. Aitken, *The Welland Canal Company: A Study in Canadian Enterprise* (Cambridge, Mass., 1954).

9. The classic study of this era is G.N. Tucker, *The Canadian Commercial Revolution 1845–1851* (Toronto, 1970). See also John B. Brebner, *North Atlantic Triangle: The Interplay of Canada, the United States and Great Britain* (Toronto, 1945); Peter Burroughs, *British Attitudes toward Canada, 1822–1849* (Scarborough, Ont., 1971); Michael Hart, *A Trading Nation* (Vancouver, 2002), chs 2–3. On the Reciprocity Treaty, see Donald C. Masters, *The Reciprocity Treaty of 1854* (Toronto, 1963); Ben Forster, *A Conjunction of Interests: Business, Politics and Tariffs, 1825–1873* (Toronto, 1986). For an American perspective, see Alfred Eckes, *Opening America's Market: U.S. Foreign Trade Policy Since 1776* (Chapel Hill, NC, 1995), 25–6, 67–8.

10. Andrew den Otter, *The Philosophy of Railways: The Transcontinental Railway Idea in British North America* (Toronto, 1997), provides a good overview of the development of railways in Canada in the period from the 1850s to the 1880s that goes far beyond the implications of the title. See also Peter Baskerville, 'Americans in Britain's Backyard: The Railway Era in Upper Canada, 1850-1880', in Douglas McCalla, ed., *The Development of Canadian Capitalism: Essays in Business History* (Toronto, 1990), 57–77; Douglas McCalla, 'Railways and the Development of Canada West, 1850–1870', in Allan Greer and Ian Radforth, eds, *Colonial Leviathan: State Formation in Mid-Nineteenth Century Canada* (Toronto, 1992), 192–229.

11. Bliss, *Northern Enterprise*, 194. For alternative views, see Stanley Ryerson, *Unequal Union: Confederation*

and the Roots of Conflict in the Canadas, 1815–1873 (Toronto, 1968); R.T. Naylor, *Canada in the European Age, 1453–1919* (Vancouver, 1987), chs 20–1.

12. Bliss, *Northern Enterprise*, 303–5. See also Ben Forster, 'The Coming of the National Policy: Business, Government and the Tariff, 1876–1879', in McCalla, ed., *The Development of Canadian Capitalism*, 124–40. On the issue of competitiveness of Canadian and US manufacturers in the 1870s, see Kris Inwood and Ian Keay, 'Bigger Establishments in Thicker Markets: Can We Explain Early Productivity Differentials between Canada and the United States?', *Canadian Journal of Economics* 38, 4 (Nov. 2005): 1327–63. On the 'Galt Tariff', see D.F. Barnett, 'The Galt Tariff: Incidental or Effective Protection?', *Canadian Journal of Economics* 9, 3 (Aug. 1976): 389–407.

Chapter 2

1. On investment banking in the US, see Vincent Carosso, *Investment Banking in America* (Cambridge, Mass., 1970), and Carosso, *The Morgans: Private Investment Bankers, 1854–1913* (Cambridge, Mass., 1987). On German banks and industrial investment, see Richard Tilly, 'Mergers, External Growth and Finance in the Development of Large-Scale Enterprise in Germany, 1880–1913', *Journal of Economic History* 42 (1982): 629–58. On British financial techniques, see R.C. Michie, 'Options, Concessions, Syndicates and the Provision of Venture Capital, 1880–1913', *Business History* 23 (1981): 147–64.

2. On the Bank of Montreal, see Merrill Denison, *Canada's First Bank: A History of the Bank of Montreal*, 3 vols (Montreal, 1966–7); on the Bank of Commerce (CIBC), see Victor Ross and A. St L. Trigge, *A History of the Canadian Bank of Commerce*, 3 vols (Toronto, 1920–34); on the Bank of Nova Scotia, see Joseph Schull and J.D. Gibson, *The Scotiabank Story* (Toronto, 1982); on Royal Bank of Canada, see Duncan McDowall, *Quick to the Frontier: Canada's Royal Bank* (Toronto, 1993).

3. On the early history of Canadian life insurance companies, see Joseph Schull, *The Century of the Sun: The First Hundred Years of Sun Life Assurance Company of Canada* (Toronto, 1971), and Schull, *The First Sixty Years: A History of the Manufacturers Life Insurance Company* (Toronto, 1947). More generally on the evolution of the life insurance industry, see Morton Keller, *The Life Insurance Enterprise, 1885–1910: A Study in the Limits of Corporate Power* (Cambridge, Mass., 1963).

4. On various Canadian capital-mobilizing institutions, see W.L. Marr and D.G. Paterson, *Canada:*

An Economic History (Toronto, 1980), 243–64: E.P. Neufeld, *The Financial System in Canada: Its Growth and Development* (Toronto, 1972): K.A.H. Buckley, *Capital Formation in Canada, 1896–1930* (Toronto, 1955); Ian Drummond, 'Canadian Life Insurance Companies and the Capital Market, 1890–1914', *Canadian Journal of Economics and Political Science* 27 (1962): 204–24. On banks' attitudes towards industrial investment, see R.T. Naylor, *The History of Canadian Business, 1867–1914*, vol. 1 (Toronto, 1975). For critiques, see L.R. Macdonald, 'Merchants against Industry: An Idea and Its Origins', *Canadian Historical Review* 56 (1975): 263–81; Paul Craven and Tom Traves, 'Canadian Railways as Manufacturers 1850–1900', Canadian Historical Association (CHA), *Historical Papers* (1983): 254–81; Kris Inwood, *The Canadian Charcoal Iron Industry* (New York, 1986), 5–7; Gerald Tulchinsky, 'Recent Controversies in Canadian Business History', *Acadiensis* 8 (1978–9): 133–9.

5. See James D. Frost, 'The "Nationalization" of the Bank of Nova Scotia', *Acadiensis* 12 (Autumn 1982): 3–38. Neil C. Quigley, Ian Drummond, and Lewis T. Evans, 'Regional Transfers of Funds through the Canadian Banking System and Maritime Development, 1895–1935,' in Kris Inwood, ed., *Farm, Factory and Fortune: New Essays in the Economic History of the Maritimes* (Fredericton, NB, 1993), 219–50, also find little evidence that banks in the region neglected or discriminated against local manufacturers.

6. On the Toronto and Montreal financial elites, see Christopher Armstrong and H.V. Nelles, *Southern Exposure* (Toronto, 1988), 3–23; A. Ernest Epp, 'Cooperation among Capitalists: The Canadian Merger Movement, 1909–13', Ph.D. thesis (Johns Hopkins University, 1973); Michael Bliss, *Northern Enterprise: Five Centuries of Canadian Business* (Toronto, 1989), 278–81. On the aspirations of the Maritime financial community, see T.W. Acheson, 'The National Policy and the Industrialization of the Maritimes, 1880–1910', *Acadiensis* 1 (1972): 3–29. On the 'French' banks, see Ronald Rudin, *Banking en français: The French Banks of Quebec, 1835–1925* (Toronto, 1985); Paul-Andre Linteau et al., *Quebec: A History, 1867–1929*, trans. Robert Chodos (Toronto, 1979), 51–5. On the social fabric of finance capitalism in late nineteenth-century Canada, see T.W. Acheson, 'The Social Origins of the Canadian Industrial Elite, 1880–1910', *Business History Review* 47 (1973): 189–217.

7. On the Canadian exchanges, see John F. Whiteside, 'The Toronto Stock Exchange and the Development of the Share Market to 1885', *Journal of*

Canadian Studies 20 (1985): 64–81; R.C. Michie, 'The Canadian Securities Market, 1850–1914', *Business History Review* 62 (1988): 35–73. On stock markets generally, see Michie, *The London and New York Stock Exchanges, 1850–1914* (London, 1987); Thomas Nevin and Marian Sears, 'The Rise of a Market for Industrial Securities, 1887–1902', *Business History Review* 29 (1955): 105–38.

8. On Canadian merger movements, see Epp, 'Cooperation among Capitalists'; Gregory Marchildon, *Profits and Politics: Beaverbrook and the Gilded Age of Canadian Finance* (Toronto, 1996): J.C. Weldon, 'Consolidations in Canadian Industry, 1900–1948', in L.A. Skeoch, ed., *Restrictive Trade Practices in Canada* (Toronto, 1966), 232-6.

9. On the changing role of the finance capitalists, see Louis Galambos and Joseph Pratt, *The Rise of the Corporate Commonwealth* (New York, 1988), chs 1–2. For various efforts to assess the Canadian business elite, see John Porter, *The Vertical Mosaic* (Toronto, 1965); Peter C. Newman, *The Canadian Establishment* (Toronto, 1975); Frank and Libbie Park, *Anatomy of Big Business* (Toronto, 1973); Wallace Clement, *The Canadian Corporate Elite* (Toronto,1975); Clement, *Continental Corporate Power* (Toronto, 1977); William K. Carroll, *Corporate Power and Canadian Capitalism* (Vancouver, 1986). For alternative viewpoints, see Jorge Niosi, *The Economy of Canada* (Quebec, 1978); Niosi, *Canadian Capitalism*, trans. Robert Chodos (Toronto, 1981); Bliss, *Northern Enterprise*, 358–78.

10. On US direct investment in Canada, see Mira Wilkins, *The Emergence of Multinational Enterprise* (Cambridge, Mass., 1970); Herbert Marshall et al., *Canadian–American Industry* (New Haven, Conn., 1936). On British direct and portfolio investment, see D.G. Paterson, *British Direct Investment in Canada, 1890–1914* (Toronto, 1976); Matthew Simon, 'The Pattern of New British Portfolio Investment, 1865–1914', in J.H. Adler, ed., *Capital Movements and Economic Development* (New York, 1967), 33–60; Gregory P. Marchildon, 'British Investment Banking and Industrial Decline before the Great War: A Case Study of Capital Outflow to Canada', *Business History* 33 (1991): 72–92.

Chapter 3

1. Christopher Armstrong and H.V. Nelles, *Monopoly's Moment: The Organization and Regulation of Canadian Utilities, 1830–1930* (Philadelphia, 1986), 63. On the international electrical utility industry, see Thomas P. Hughes, *Networks of Power: Electrification in Western Society, 1880–1930* (Baltimore, 1983);

on the electrical equipment industry, see Harold C. Passer, *The Electrical Manufacturers, 1875–1900* (Cambridge, Mass., 1953).

2. On the telephone industry in Canada, see Jean-Guy Rens, *The Invisible Empire: A History of the Telecommunications Industry in Canada*, trans. Kathe Roth (Montreal and Kingston, 2001).

3. On the electric power industry, see Armstrong and Nelles, *Monopoly's Moment*; H.V. Nelles, *The Politics of Development: Forests, Mines and Hydroelectric Power in Ontario, 1849–1941* (Toronto, 1974); John Dales, *Hydroelectricity and Industrial Development—Quebec, 1898–1940* (Cambridge, Mass., 1974); Ted Regehr, *The Beauharnois Scandal: A Story of Canadian Entrepreneurship and Politics* (Toronto, 1990); Patricia Roy, 'The Fine Art of Lobbying and Persuading: The Case of B.C. Electric Railway', in David S. Macmillan, ed., *Canadian Business History: Selected Studies 1497–1971* (Toronto, 1972), 239–54; Paul-André Linteau, 'Urban Mass Transit', in Norman Ball, ed., *Building Canada: A History of Public Works* (Toronto, 1988), 88–112. For an interesting study of the contrasting personalities of Mackenzie and Holt, see Ted Regehr, 'A Backwoodsman and an Engineer in Canadian Business', CHA, *Historical Papers* (1977): 159–77.

4. Christopher Armstrong and H.V. Nelles, 'A Curious Capital Flow: Canadian Investment in Mexico, 1902–10', *Business History Review* 58 (1984): 178–203 (the phrase is applicable to the entire process that Armstrong and Nelles describe in *Southern Exposure*); see also Duncan McDowall, *The Light: Brazilian Traction, Light & Power Co., 1899–1945* (Toronto, 1988); Jorge Niosi, *Canadian Multinationals*, trans. Robert Chodos (Toronto, 1985); 61–81.

5. On the CPR, see John Eagle, *The Canadian Pacific Railway and the Development of Western Canada, 1896–1914* (Kingston, 1988); W. Kaye Lamb, *History of the Canadian Pacific Railway* (New York, 1977); J. Lorne McDougall, *Canadian Pacific: A Short History* (Montreal, 1968); David Cruise and Alison Griffiths, *Lords of the Line: The Men Who Built the CPR* (Markham, Ont., 1988).

6. The quote about Canadian Northern's railroad building practices is from G.R. Stevens, *History of the Canadian National Railways* (New York, 1973), 177. The 'unconnected projections' quote is from Ted Regehr, *The Canadian Northern Railway: Pioneer Road to the Northern Prairies, 1895–1918* (Toronto, 1976), 55. On the history of Canadian Northern, in addition to these two sources, see R.B. Fleming, *The Railway King of Canada: Sir William Mackenzie, 1849–1923* (Vancouver, 1991).

7. Borden, quoted in Stevens, *History of the Canadian National* Railways, 278. See also Fleming, *Railway King of Canada*, 222–3.

8. Regehr, *Canadian Northern* Railway, 428–9; John Eagle, 'Monopoly or Competition: The Nationalization of the Grand Trunk Railway', *Canadian Historical Review* 62 (1981): 3–30. See also Michael Bliss, *Northern Enterprise: Five Centuries of Canadian Business* (Toronto, 1987), 375–7.

9. On the Beatty-Thornton years, see Stevens, *History of the Canadian National Railways*, 307–60; Cruise and Griffiths, *Lords of the Line*, 321–34; D.H. Miller-Barstow, *Beatty of the CPR* (Toronto, 1951); D'Arcy Marsh, *The Tragedy of Henry Thornton* (Toronto, 1935).

Chapter 4

1. See Robert Ankli, 'The Growth of the Canadian Economy, 1896–1920', *Explorations in Economic History* 17 (1980): 251–74, for a summary of this debate. See also the articles by E. Chambers and D.F. Gordon and by G.W. Bertram in Douglas McCalla, ed., *Perspectives on Canadian Economic History* (Toronto, 1987), 201–42.

2. On the wheat boom and the grain-handling industry, see C.F. Wilson, *A Century of Canadian Grain* (Saskatoon, 1978); Vernon C. Fowke, *The National Policy and the Wheat Economy* (Toronto, 1957); Charles W. Anderson, *Grain: The Entrepreneurs* (Winnipeg, 1991); A. Ernest Epp, 'Cooperation among Capitalists: The Canadian Merger Movement, 1909–13', Ph.D. thesis (Johns Hopkins University, 1973), 204–43.

3. On Massey-Harris and the farm implement industry, see Merrill Denison, *Harvest Triumphant: The Story of Massey-Harris* (Toronto, 1948); E.P. Neufeld, *A Global Corporation: A History of the International Development of Massey-Ferguson Ltd.* (Toronto, 1969); Peter Cook, *Massey at the Brink* (Toronto, 1981). Massey-Harris merged with the British manufacturer, Ferguson Company, in 1953, and changed its corporate name to Massey-Ferguson five years later.

4. Careless, quoted in H.V. Nelles, *The Politics of Development: Forests, Mines and Hydro-electric Power in Ontario, 1849–1941* (Toronto, 1974), 118–19. For other studies of the Canadian mining industry, see D.M. LeBourdais, *Metals and Men: The Story of Canadian Mining* (Toronto, 1957); Philip Smith, *Harvest of the Rock: A History of Mining in Ontario* (Toronto, 1986); Peter George, 'Ontario's Mining Industry,1870–1940', in Ian Drummond, ed., *Progress without Planning: The Economic History*

of Ontario from Confederation to the Second World War (Toronto, 1987), 52–76; Iain Wallace, 'The Canadian Shield: The Development of a Resource Frontier', in L.D. McCann, ed., *Heartland and Hinterland: A Geography of Canada* (Scarborough, Ont., 1982), 372–409; E.S. Moore, *The American Influence in Canadian Mining* (Toronto, 1941). On specific areas of the industry and companies, see Jeremy Mowat, 'Creating a New Staple: Capital, Technology and Monopoly in British Columbia's Resource Sector, 1901–25', *Journal of the Canadian Historical Association* (1990): 215-35; O.W. Main, *The Canadian Nickel Industry: A Study in Market Control and Public Policy* (Toronto, 1958); Leslie Roberts, *Noranda* (Toronto, 1956); articles by Alexander Dow and Robert Armstrong in Duncan Campbell, ed., *Explorations in Canadian Economic History* (Ottawa, 1985), 189–228; Alexander Dow, 'Finance and Foreign Control in Canadian Base Metal Mining, 1918–55', *Economic History Review* 62 (1984): 54–67.

5. Trevor Dick, 'Canadian Newsprint, 1913–1930: National Policies and the North American Economy', *Journal of Economic History* 42 (Sept. 1982): 659–87, reprinted in McCalla, ed., *Perspectives on Canadian Economic History*, 244–69.

6. On the lumber and newsprint industry, see A.R.M. Lower, *The North American Assault on the Canadian Forest: A History of the Lumber Trade between Canada and the United States* (Toronto, 1938); Nelles, *The Politics of Development*; Ian Radforth, *Bushworkers and Bosses: Logging in Northern Ontario, 1900–1980* (Toronto, 1987); G.W. Taylor, *Timber: History of the Forest Industry in B.C.* (Vancouver, 1974); Donald MacKay, *Empire of Wood: The MacMillan-Bloedel Story* (Vancouver, 1982); Patricia Marchak, *Green Gold: The Forest Industry in British Columbia* (Vancouver, 1983); J.A. Guthrie, *The Newsprint Paper Industry* (Cambridge, Mass., 1941); L. Ethan Ellis, *Newsprint: Producers, Publishers, Public Pressures* (New Brunswick, NJ, 1960); Carl Wiegman, *Trees to News: A Chronicle of the Ontario Paper Company's Origin and Development* (Toronto, 1953).

Chapter 5

1. See Alfred D. Chandler Jr, *The Visible Hand: The Managerial Revolution in American Business* (Cambridge, Mass., 1977), and Chandler, *Scale and Scope: The Dynamics of Industrial Capitalism* (Cambridge, Mass., 1990). On British business organization, see Leslie Hannah, *The Rise of the Corporate Economy: The British Experience* (Baltimore, 1976). Also see A.D. Chandler Jr

and Herman Daems, eds, *Managerial Hierarchies: Comparative Perspectives on the Rise of the Modern Industrial Enterprise* (Cambridge, Mass., 1980).

2. Craig Heron, 'The Second Industrial Revolution in Canada, 1880–1930', in D.R. Hopkins and G.S. Kealey, eds, *Class, Community and the Labour Movement: Wales and Canada, 1850–1930* (St John's, Nfld, 1989), 48–66; Glen Williams, 'The National Policy Tariffs: Industrial Underdevelopment through Import Substitution', *Canadian Journal of Political Science* 12 (1979): 333–68; Michael Bliss, *Northern Enterprise: Five Centuries of Canadian Business* (Toronto, 1987), 359–61; Barry Boothman, 'The Foundations of Canadian Big Business', paper presented at the Fifth Canadian Business History Conference (1998). See also Ben Forster, 'Finding the Right Size: Markets and Competition in Mid- and Late-Nineteenth Century Ontario', in Roger Hall et al., eds, *Patterns of the Past: Interpreting Ontario's History* (Toronto, 1988), 150–73.

3. On the 'revolution in retailing', see Ian Drummond, ed., *Progress without Planning: The Economic History of Ontario from Confederation to the Second World War* (Toronto, 1987), 274–93; Joy Santinck, *Timothy Eaton and the Rise of His Department Store* (Toronto, 1990); Peter C. Newman, *Merchant Princes* (Toronto, 1991). On resistance from the small retailers, see David Monod, *Store Wars: Shopkeepers and the Culture of Mass Marketing, 1890–1939* (Toronto, 1996).

4. A. Ernest Epp, 'Cooperation among Capitalists: The Canadian Merger Movement, 1909–13', Ph.D. thesis (Johns Hopkins University, 1973), 372. See also Barbara Austin, 'Life Cycles and Strategy of a Canadian Company: Dominion Textiles, 1873–1983', Ph.D. thesis (Concordia University, 1985); Austin, 'The State and Strategic Management of an Enterprise: A Life Cycle of a Symbiotic Relationship 1873–1997', *Business and Economic History On Line* 4 (2006), at: <www.thebhc.org>; *Report of the Royal Commission on the Textile Industry* (Ottawa, 1938). On the woollen textile industry, see Forster, 'Finding the Right Size', 154–8.

5. On the Canadian iron and steel industry, see W.J.A. Donald, *The Canadian Iron and Steel Industry* (Boston, 1915); Kris Inwood, *The Canadian Charcoal Iron Industry* (New York, 1986); Inwood, 'The Iron and Steel Industry', in Drummond, *Progress without Planning*, 185–207; William Kilbourn, *The Elements Combined: A History of the Steel Co. of Canada* (Toronto, 1960); Duncan McDowall, *Steel at the Sault: Francis Clergue, Sir James Dunn and the Algoma Steel Corporation, 1901–56* (Toronto, 1984);

T.W. Acheson, 'The National Policy and the Industrialization of the Maritimes, 1880–1910', *Acadiensis* 1 (1972): 3–29; David Frank, 'The Cape Breton Coal Industry and the Rise and Fall of Besco', *Acadiensis* 7 (Autumn 1977): 3–34; Gordon Boyce, 'The Manufacturing and Marketing of Steel in Canada: Dofasco Inc., 1912–1970', *Business and Economic History* 2nd ser., 18 (1989): 228–37.

6. Michael Bliss, 'Canadianizing American Business: The Roots of the Branch Plant', in Ian Lumsden, ed., *Close the 49th Parallel, etc.: The Americanization of Canada* (Toronto, 1972), 26–42. See also Stephen Scheinberg, 'Invitation to Empire: Tariffs and American Economic Expansion in Canada', *Business History Review* 47 (1973): 218–38.

7. Tom Traves, *The State and Enterprise: Canadian Manufacturers and the Federal Government, 1917–31* (Toronto, 1979), 101.

8. On the auto industry in Canada, see Tom Traves, 'The Development of the Ontario Automobile Industry to 1939', in Drummond, ed., *Progress without Planning*, 208–23; Howard Aikman, *The Automobile Industry of Canada* (Montreal, 1926); Robert Ankil and Fred Frederiksen, 'The Influence of American Manufacturers on the Canadian Automobile Industry', *Business and Economic History* ser. 2, 9 (1981): 101–13; Donald S. Davis, 'Dependent Motorization: Canada and the Automobile to 1930', *Journal of Canadian Studies* 21 (1986): 106–32; Mira Wilkins and Frank E. Hill, *American Business Abroad: Ford on Six Continents* (Detroit, 1964); Dimitry Anastakis, 'From Independence to Integration: The Corporate Evolution of Ford Motor Co. of Canada', *Business History Review* 78 (Summer 2004): 213–53; Heather Robertson, *Driving Force: The McLaughlin Family and the Age of the Car* (Toronto, 1995).

9. John Ewing, 'History of Imperial Oil' (1951), manuscript at Imperial Oil Archives, Toronto, ch. 8: 15. See also Peter McKenzie-Brown, Gordon Jarenko, and David Finch, *The Great Oil Age: The Petroleum Industry in Canada* (Calgary, 1991); Earle Grey, *The Great Canadian Oil Patch* (Toronto, 1970); David H. Breen, 'Anglo-American Oil Rivalry and the Evolution of Canadian Petroleum Policy to 1930', *Canadian Historical Review* 62 (1981): 283–320; Hugh M. Grant, 'The Petroleum Industry and Canadian Economic Development: An Economic History, 1900–61', Ph.D. thesis (University of Toronto, 1986); B.H. Wall and G.S. Gibb, *Teagle of Jersey Standard* (New Orleans, 1974); Graham D. Taylor, 'From Branch Operation to Integrated Subsidiary: The Reorganisation of Imperial Oil under Walter

Teagle, 1911–17', *Business History* 34 (July 1992): 49–68.

Chapter 6

1. On scientific management, see Harry Braverman, *Labor and Monopoly Capital: The Degradation of Work in the Twentieth Century* (New York, 1974). For other assessments, see Daniel Nelson, *Managers and Workers: The Origins of the New Factory System in the U.S., 1880–1920* (Madison, Wis., 1975), 55–78; David Montgomery, *The Fall of the House of Labor: The Workplace, the State and American Labor Activism, 1865–1925* (Cambridge, 1987), 214–56. On scientific management in Canada, see Bryan Palmer, *A Culture in Conflict: Skilled Workers and Industrial Capitalism in Hamilton, Ontario, 1860–1914* (Montreal, 1979), 216–22; Paul Craven, *An Impartial Umpire: Industrial Relations and the Canadian State, 1900–11* (Toronto, 1980), 93–100. On Knechtel, see Joy Parr, *The Gender of Breadwinners: Women, Men and Change in Two Industrial Towns, 1880–1930* (Toronto, 1990), 157–64.

2. On workers in the steel industry, see Craig Heron, *Working in Steel: The Early Years in Canada, 1883–1935* (Toronto, 1988), 53–72. On women and the development of clerical white-collar occupations, see JoAnne Yates, *Control through Communication: The Rise of System in American Management* (Baltimore, 1989); Graham S. Lowe, *Women in the Administrative Revolution* (Toronto, 1987).

3. On welfare capitalism generally, see Gerald Zahavi, *Workers, Managers and Welfare Capitalism* (New York, 1990); Stuart Brandes, *American Welfare Capitalism, 1880–1940* (Chicago, 1970). On welfare capitalism in Canada, see Margaret McCallum, 'Corporate Welfarism in Canada, 1919–30', *Canadian Historical Review* 71 (1990): 46–80. On Imperial Oil, see Graham D. Taylor, 'From Branch Operation to Integrated Subsidiary: The Reorganisation of Imperial Oil under Walter Teagle, 1911–17', *Business History* 34 (July 1992): 63.

4. On company towns, see Gilbert Stetler, 'Community Development in Toronto's Commercial Empire: The Industrial Towns of the Nickel Belt, 1883–1931', *Laurentian University Review* 6 (June 1974): 3–49. On industrial councils, see Irving Bernstein, *The Lean Years: A History of the American Worker, 1920–33* (Baltimore, 1966), 157–74; Bruce Scott, '"A Place in the Sun": The Industrial Council at Massey-Harris, 1919–29', *Labour/Le Travailleur* 1 (1976): 158–92; Robert Storey, 'Unionization versus Corporate Welfare: The "Dofasco Way"', *Labour/Le Travailleur* 12 (1983): 7–42. The Insull quote is in Bernstein, *The Lean* Years, 184.

5. On government policies towards labour relations, see Craven, *An Impartial Umpire*, ch. 11; Craig Heron, *The Canadian Labour Movement* (Toronto, 1989), 60–2.

6. For views of the Maritimes and regional disparity from 'mainstream' economists, see W.L. Marr and D.G. Paterson, *Canada: An Economic History* (Toronto, 1980), 418–38; Roy George, *A Leader and a Laggard: Manufacturing Industry in Nova Scotia, Quebec and Ontario* (Toronto, 1970). For the perspective of political economists, see Michael Clow, 'Politics and Uneven Capitalist Development: The Maritime Challenge to the Study of Canadian Political Economy', *Studies in Political Economy* 14 (Summer 1984): 117–40; Paul Phillips, *Regional Disparities* (Toronto, 1982).

7. For a summary of the history of Maritime industrialization and 'deindustrialization', see John Reid, *Six Crucial Decades* (Halifax, 1986), chs 4–5. On the achievements and problems of Maritime industrial entrepreneurs, see T.W. Acheson, 'The National Policy and the Industrialization of the Maritimes, 1880–1910', *Acadiensis* 1 (1972): 3–29'; Acheson, 'The Maritimes and "Empire Canada"', in David J. Bercuson, ed., *Canada and the Burden of Unity* (Toronto, 1977), 87–114; Eric Sager and Gerald Panting, *Maritime Capital: The Shipping Industry in Atlantic Canada, 1870–1914* (Montreal and Kingston, 1990), esp. chs 7–10; Kris Inwood, 'Local Control, Resources and the Nova Scotia Steel and Coal Co.', CHA, *Historical Papers* (1986): 254–82; L.D. McCann, 'Metropolitanism and Branch Businesses in the Maritimes, 1881–1931', *Acadiensis* 13 (Autumn 1983): 112–25. On the freight rate issue, see Ernest R. Forbes, 'Misguided Symmetry: The Destruction of Regional Transportation Policy for the Maritimes', in Bercuson, ed., *Canada and the Burden of Unity*, 60–86; Forbes, *The Maritime Rights Movement* (Montreal, 1979); Ken Cruikshank, 'The People's Railway: The Intercolonial and the Canadian Public Enterprise Experience', *Acadiensis* 16 (1986): 78–100.

8. On 'deindustrialization' in British Columbia, see John Lutz, 'Losing Steam: The Boiler and Engine Industry as an Index of British Columbia Deindustrialization, 1880–1915', CHA, *Historical Papers* (1988): 168–205. On prairie discontents, see chapters by Regehr and Bercuson in Bercuson, *Canada and the Burden of Unity*, 115–42; J.F. Conway, *The West: The History of a Region in Confederation* (Toronto, 1984); Gerald Friesen, *The Canadian Prairies: A History* (Toronto, 1987), chs 8, 12–13.

9. See Elizabeth Bloomfield, 'Boards of Trade and Canadian Urban Development', *Urban History*

Review 12 (Oct. 1983): 77–99; Alan F. Artibise, 'In Pursuit of Growth: Municipal Boosterism and Urban Development in the Canadian Prairie West, 1871–1913', in G.A. Stetler and A.F. Artibise, eds, *Shaping the Urban Landscape* (Ottawa, 1982).

10. On the west coast fishery, see Dianne Newell, ed., *The Development of the Pacific Salmon-Canning Industry* (Montreal and Kingston, 1989); Patricia Marchak et al., eds, *Uncommon Property: The Fishing and Fish Processing Industries in British Columbia* (Toronto, 1987). On the Great Lakes, see A.B. McCullough, *The Commercial Fishery of the Canadian Great Lakes* (Ottawa, 1989); William Ashworth, *The Late Great Lakes: An Environmental History* (Scarborough, Ont., 1986), 112–22. On the east coast fishery—which still awaits a full-scale history (except for Newfoundland, which is well chronicled)—see Harold Innis, *The Cod Fisheries* (Toronto, 1954), 425–43; Stephen Kimber, *Net Profits: The Story of National Sea* (Halifax, 1989); *Report of the Royal Commission Investigating the Fisheries of the Maritime Provinces* (Ottawa, 1928).

11. On farmers and 'businesslike practices', see Ian MacPherson and John H. Thompson, 'The Business of Agriculture: Prairie Farmers and the Adoption of "Business" Methods, 1880-1950', in Peter Baskerville, ed., *Canadian Papers in Business History* (Victoria, 1989), 245–69. On farm co-operatives and wheat pools, see C.F. Wilson, *A Century of Canadian Grain* (Saskatoon, 1978), 47–56, 211–26; Garry L. Fairbairn, *From Prairie Roots* (Saskatoon, 1978); Vernon C. Fowke, *The National Policy and the Wheat Economy* (Toronto, 1957), chs 8, 11–12.

12. On the issue of 'democracy' in the co-operative movement, see chapters by Christopher Axworthy, David Laycock, and Brett Fairbairn in Murray Fulton, ed., *Co-operative Organizations and Canadian Society* (Toronto, 1990). On the caisses populaires, see Ronald Rudin, *In Whose Interest? Quebec's Caisses Populaires, 1900-1945* (Montreal and Kingston, 1990); Paul-André Linteau et al., *Quebec Since 1930*, trans. Robert Chodos (Toronto, 1991), 369–71.

Chapter 7

1. For staple-oriented views of business–government relations in Canadian history, see Hugh G. Aitken, 'Defensive Expansionism: The State and Economic Growth in Canada', in Aitken, ed., *The State and Economic Growth* (New York, 1959), 79–114; W.T. Easterbrook, *North American Patterns of Growth and Development* (Toronto, 1990). The political economists' approach is reflected in R. Tom Naylor, *Canada in the European Age* (Vancouver, 1987),

parts IV and V; see also Wallace Clement, *The Canadian Corporate Elite* (Toronto, 1975), ch. 2. The 'corporate liberal' interpretation has been most fully developed for US history. See, for example, Louis Galambos and Joseph Pratt, *The Rise of the Corporate Commonwealth* (New York, 1989); and, for a left-wing version (probably more influential in Canada), the classic work by Gabriel Kolko, *The Triumph of Conservatism* (New York, 1963). Among Canadian studies often cited as reflecting this approach are H.V. Nelles, *The Politics of Development: Forests, Mines and Hydroelectric Power in Ontario, 1849–1941* (Toronto, 1974), and Tom Traves, *The State and Enterprise: Canadian Manufacturers and the Federal Government, 1917–31* (Toronto, 1979). A good succinct statement of this view is offered by Traves, 'Business–Government Relations in Canadian History', in K.J. Rea and Nelson Wiseman, eds, *Government and Enterprise in Canada* (Toronto, 1985), 8–19. Michael Bliss offers a radically different critique emphasizing the role of business 'adventurers' who exploited the ambitions of Canada's political leaders for rapid economic development through public subsidies in everything from canals and railways in the nineteenth century to the aircraft industry in the twentieth century. See Bliss, 'Forcing the Pace: A Reappraisal of Business–Government Relations in Canadian History', in V.V. Murray, ed., *Theories of Business–Government Relations* (Toronto, 1985), 106–19.

2. For a survey of regulatory initiatives among industrial countries, see Morton Keller, 'The Regulation of Large Enterprise: The US Experience in Comparative Perspective', in A.D. Chandler Jr and Herman Daems, eds, *Managerial Hierarchies* (Cambridge, Mass., 1980), 161–81. See also Keller, *Regulating a New Economy* (Cambridge, Mass., 1991). On US railroad (and other) regulation, see Thomas McCraw, *Prophets of Regulation* (Cambridge, Mass., 1984). On Britain's factory legislation, see Oliver MacDonagh, *Early Victorian Government, 1830–70* (London, 1977); A.J.M. Taylor, *Laissez-Faire and State Interventionism in Nineteenth Century Britain* (London, 1972).

3. For general overviews of Canada's experience with government regulation, see J.A. Corry, *The Growth of Government Activities Since Confederation* (Ottawa, 1939), a study prepared for the Rowell–Sirois Royal Commission; Carman Baggaley, *The Emergence of the Regulatory State in Canada, 1867–1939* (Ottawa, 1981), prepared for the Economic Council of Canada. See also G. Bruce Doern, *The Regulatory Process in Canada* (Toronto, 1978); Margot Priest and Aron Wohl, 'The Growth of Federal

and Provincial Regulation of Economic Activity, 1867–1978', in W.T. Stanbury, ed., *Government Regulation: Scope, Growth and Process* (Montreal, 1980), 69–149. On the regulatory conundrums of the insurance industry, see Christopher Armstrong, 'Federalism and Government Regulation: The Case of the Canadian Insurance Industry, 1927–34', *Canadian Public Administration* 19 (Spring 1976): 88–101. On the background to Radio Canada, see Frank Peers, *The Politics of Canadian Broadcasting, 1920–51* (Toronto, 1969).

4. On railroad regulation in the US, see Ari and Olive Hoogenboom, *The ICC* (New York, 1976); Gabriel Kolko, *Railroads and Regulation, 1877–1916* (New York, 1965). An alternative view that sees the ICC as both 'uncaptured' and ultimately a destructive force in the railroad field, see Albro Martin, *Enterprise Denied: The Origins and Decline of American Railroads* (New York, 1971). On railway regulation in Canada, see Ken Cruikshank, *Close Ties: Railways, the Government and the Board of Railway Commissioners, 1851–1933* (Montreal and Kingston, 1991); Baggaley, *Emergence of the Regulatory State*, 69–114. In *Monopoly's Moment: The Organization and Regulation of Canadian Utilities, 1830–1930* (Philadelphia, 1986), Christopher Armstrong and H.V. Nelles offer an equally complex interpretation of the growth of regulation in the electric utility industry in Canada.

5. On regulation of the Canadian telephone system, see Armstrong and Nelles, *Monopoly's Moment*, 270–92; on the provincial Crown companies, see Michael Denny, *Government Enterprise in Western Canada's Telecommunications*, Economic Council of Canada Discussion Paper no. 301 (Ottawa, 1986); Ronald Love, *Dreaming Big: A History of SaskTel* (Regina, 2003).

6. On antitrust in the US, see William Letwin, *Law and Economic Policy in America* (New York, 1965); Martin J. Sklar, *The Corporate Reconstruction of American Capitalism* (New York, 1988). On the combines laws in Canada, see Michael Bliss, 'Another Anti-Trust Tradition: Canadian Anti-Combines Policy, 1889–1910', *Business History Review* 47 (1973): 177–88; Carman Baggaley, 'Tariffs, Combines and Politics: The Beginning of Canadian Competition Policy, 1885–1900', in R.S. Khemani and W.T. Stanbury, eds, *Historical Perspectives on Canadian Competition Policy* (Halifax, 1991), 1–52; Paul Gorecki and W.T. Stanbury, *The Objectives of Canadian Competition Policy, 1888–1983* (Montreal, 1984); L.A. Skeoch, *Restrictive Trade Practices in Canada* (Toronto, 1966), part I; *The Report of the Royal Commission on Corporate Concentration* (Ottawa, 1978).

7. On the international dimensions of the Great Depression, see Charles Kindleberger, *The World in Depression, 1929-39* (Berkeley, Calif., 1973); John A. Garraty, *The Great Depression* (San Diego, 1986). On Canada, see A.E. Safarian, *The Canadian Economy in the Great Depression* (Toronto, 1970).

8. Christopher Armstrong, *Blue Skies and Boiler Rooms: Buying and Selling Securities in Canada, 1870–1940* (Toronto, 1997), esp. chs 11–14. For examples of the kind of sharp practices that occurred in the securities markets of the 1920s, see David Cruise and Alison Griffith, *Fleecing the Lamb: The Inside Story of the Vancouver Stock Exchange* (Vancouver, 1987); Douglas Fetherling, *Gold Diggers of 1929: Canada and the Great Stock Market Crash* (Toronto, 1979).

9. Depression-era economic policies are discussed in Baggaley, *Emergence of the Regulatory State*, 163–204; see also J.H. Thompson and Allen Seager, *Canada, 1922–39: Decades of Discord* (Toronto, 1985), chs 10–12. Pierre Berton, *The Great Depression 1929–39* (Toronto, 1990), presents a particularly acidulous view of both Bennett and King, not to mention the business community in this era. On Bennett's policies, see Larry A. Glassford, *Reaction and Reform: The Politics of the Conservative Party under R.B. Bennett, 1927–38* (Toronto, 1992), chs 5–6. On King's approach, see H. Blair Neatby, 'The Liberal Way: Fiscal and Monetary Policy in the 1930s', in Michiel Horn, ed., *The Depression in Canada* (Toronto, 1988), 257–73. On divisions in the business community, see Alvin Finkel, *Business and Social Reform in the Thirties* (Toronto, 1979); Michael Bliss, *Northern Enterprise: Five Centuries of Canadian Business* (Toronto, 1987), ch. 15; Richard Wilbur, *H.H. Stevens* (Toronto, 1977), chs 4–6. T.D. Regehr, *The Beauharnois Scandal: A Story of Canadian Entrepreneurship and Politics* (Toronto, 1990), presents a fascinating glimpse of the internal workings of politics and business in Canada. On US–Canadian trade relations, see Richard N. Kottman, *Reciprocity and the North Atlantic Triangle, 1932–38* (Ithaca, NY, 1968); Ian Drummond and Norman Hillmer, *Negotiating Freer Trade: The U.K., the U.S., Canada and the Trade Agreements of 1938* (Waterloo, Ont., 1989); Michael Hart, *A Trading Nation* (Vancouver, 2002), ch. 4.

Chapter 8

1. On economic mobilization in World War I, see Gerd Hardach, *The First World War 1914–18* (Berkeley, Calif., 1977); R.J.Q. Adams, *Arms and the Wizard: Lloyd George and the Ministry of Munitions* (London, 1978); Gerald Feldman, *Arms,*

Industry and Labor in Germany 1914–18 (Princeton, NJ, 1966); John F. Godfrey, Capitalism At War: Industrial Policy and Bureaucracy in France, 1914–18 (New York, 1987); Ronald Schaffer, America in the Great War (New York, 1991); Robert D. Cuff, The War Industries Board: Business–Government Relations in World War I (Baltimore, 1973). On World War II, see Alan Milward, War, Economy and Society, 1939–45 (Berkeley, Calif., 1977); John M. Blum, V Was for Victory (New York, 1976); Paul Koistinen, Arsenal of World War II (Lawrence, Kan., 2004); Arthur Marwick, Britain in the Century of Total War: War, Peace and Social Change, 1900–67 (London, 1968).

2. On Canada in World War I, see Desmond Morton, Canada and War (Toronto, 1981), ch. 3. On Hughes and the Shell Committee, see Ronald G. Haycock, Sam Hughes: The Public Career of a Controversial Canadian (Waterloo, Ont., 1986), 225–57. On Flavelle and the IMB, see Michael Bliss, A Canadian Millionaire: The Life and Business Times for Sir Joseph Flavelle (Toronto, 1978), 233–383; David Carnegie, The History of Munitions and Supply in Canada 1914–18 (London, 1925). On government economic controls, see J.A. Corry, 'The Growth of Government Activities in Canada, 1914–21', Canadian Historical Association Annual Report (1940): 63–73; Tom Traves, The State and Enterprise: Canadian Manufacturers and the Federal Government, 1917–31 (Toronto, 1979), chs 2–4. On Canadian–American economic relations, see Robert D. Cuff and Jack L. Granatstein, Ties That Bind: Canadian–American Relations in Wartime from the Great War to the Cold War (Toronto, 1977), chs 1–3.

3. On Canadian industrial mobilization in World War II, see C.R Stacey, Arms, Men and Governments: The War Policies of Canada, 1939–45 (Ottawa, 1970), 1–67, 485–528; Robert Bothwell and William Kilbourn, C.D. Howe: A Biography (Toronto, 1979), esp. chs 9–11; J.N. de Kennedy, History of the Department of Munitions and Supply, 2 vols (Ottawa, 1950); Morton, Canada and War, chs 4–5; John Schultz, 'Shell Game: The Politics of Defence Production, 1939–42', American Review of Canadian Studies 16 (Spring 1986): 41–57; H. Duncan Hall, North American Supply (London, 1955), chs 1–2. Bliss's comments on Howe are in Northern Enterprise: Five Centuries of Canadian Business (Toronto, 1987), ch. 16. On Maritime complaints, see E.R. Forbes, 'Consolidating Disparity: The Maritimes and the Industrialization of Canada during the Second World War', Acadiensis 15 (Spring 1986): 3–27. On wartime Crown corporations, see Sandford F. Borins, 'World War II Crown Corporations:

Their Function and Their Fate', in J.R. Prichard, ed., Crown Corporations in Canada (Toronto, 1983), 447–75. On Canadian Polymer, see Matthew J. Bellamy, Profiting the Crown: Canada's Polymer Corporation, 1942–1990 (Montreal, 1999).

4. On wage and price controls in World War II, see J.L. Granatstein, Canada's War: The Politics of the Mackenzie King Government 1939–45 (Toronto, 1975), 174–86; Joseph Schull, The Great Scot: A Biography of Donald Gordon (Montreal, 1979), chs 5-8. On wartime finance and US–Canadian arrangements, see Benjamin Higgins, Canada's Financial System in War (New York, 1944); Cuff and Granatstein, Ties That Bind, ch. 5; Granatstein, Canada's War, chs 4–5; Hall, North American Supply, ch. 7. On labour unions, see Desmond Morton, Working People, 4th edn (Montreal, 1998), chs 16–17; Craig Heron, The Canadian Labour Movement (Toronto, 1989), 77–93. On the Canol Project, see Mira Wilkins, The Maturing of Multinational Enterprise (Cambridge, Mass., 1974), 273-6; Richard J. Diubaldo, 'The Canol Project in Canadian–American Relations', CHA, Historical Papers (1977): 179–95.

5. On Canada–US economic relations in the Cold War era, see Lawrence R. Aronsen, American National Security and Economic Relations with Canada, 1945–1954 (Westport, Conn., 1997); R.D. Cuff and J.L. Granatstein, American Dollars—Canadian Prosperity (Toronto, 1978), esp. chs 4–6; Dan Middlemiss, 'Economic Defence Co-operation with the United States, 1940–63', in Norman Hillmer, ed., Partners Nevertheless: Canadian–American Relations in the Twentieth Century (Toronto, 1989), 167–93; B.W. Muirhead, The Development of Postwar Canadian Trade Policy (Montreal and Kingston, 1992). On stockpiling, see Alfred E. Eckes Jr, The United States and the Global Struggle for Minerals (Austin, Texas, 1979), chs 4–8; Melissa Clark-Jones, A Staple State: Canadian Industrial Resources in Cold War (Toronto, 1987), chs 3–4. On Canada's 'industrial strategy', see Senate of Canada, Special Committee on Science Policy, A Science Policy for Canada (Ottawa, 1970), ch. 4.

6. Marsha Gordon, Government in Business (Montreal, 1981), 66–78, presents a jaundiced view of Air Canada's relations with the Air Transport Board. On Richardson, see Shirley Renders, Double Cross: The Inside Story of James A. Richardson and Canadian Airways (Vancouver, 1999). For other views on TCAL/Air Canada and other Canadian airlines, see John W. Langford, 'Air Canada', in Allan Tupper and G. Bruce Doern, eds, Public Corporations and Public Policy in Canada (Montreal, 1981), 257–84; David Corbett, Politics and the Airlines (Toronto,

1965); Garth Stevenson, *The Politics of Canada's Airlines: From Diefenbaker to Mulroney* (Toronto, 1987), which also examines the growth of smaller regional carriers.

7. On Avro, see James Dow, *The Arrow* (Toronto, 1979); Greig Stewart, *Shutting Down the National Dream* (Toronto, 1978); J.L. Granatstein, *Canada 1957–67* (Toronto, 1986), 105–17, reflects the view that the Arrow was too costly to be sustainable. For an alternative argument, see Palmiro Campagna, *Requiem for a Giant: A.V. Roe and the Avro Arrow* (Toronto, 2003).

8. John N. Vardalas, *The Computer Revolution in Canada* (Cambridge, Mass., 2001), chs 1–2 (quote on p. 74). See also David Thomas, *Knights of the New Technology* (Toronto, 1983), 82–4.

Chapter 9

1. On the development of the oil and gas industry, see Ed Gould, *Oil: The History of Canada's Oil and Gas Industry* (Vancouver, 1976); George de Mille, *Oil in Canada West: The Early Years* (Calgary, 1969); Earle Gray, *Wildcatters: The Story of Pacific Petroleums and Westcoast Transmission* (Toronto, 1982); Philip Smith, *The Treasure Seekers: The Men Who Built Home Oil* (Toronto, 1978); Eric Hanson, *Dynamic Decade* (Don Mills, Ont., 1958); Peter Foster, *The Blue Eyed Sheiks: The Canadian Oil Establishment* (Toronto, 1979); Peter McKenzie-Brown, Gordon Jarenko, and David Finch, *The Great Oil Age: The Petroleum Industry in Canada* (Calgary, 1991). On Alberta business in the 'pre-Leduc' era, see Henry C. Klassen, *Eye on the Future: Business People in Calgary and the Bow Valley, 1870–1900* (Calgary, 2002). On the economic and political orientation of Alberta's oil community, see J.D. House, *The Last of the Free Enterprisers: The Oilmen of Calgary* (Toronto, 1980); John Richards and Larry Pratt, *Prairie Capitalism: Power and Influence in the New West* (Toronto, 1979), chs 3–4, 7, 9. On the business and development views of Social Credit, see Alvin Finkel, *The Social Credit Phenomenon in Alberta* (Toronto, 1989), esp. chs 4–6. On the oil sands, see G.D. Taylor, 'Sun Oil and Great Canadian Oil Sands Ltd.: The Financing and Management of a "Pioneer" Enterprise, 1962–74', *Journal of Canadian Studies* 20 (Autumn 1985): 2–21; Larry Pratt, *The Tar Sands: Syncrude and the Politics of Oil* (Toronto, 1976). On Saskatchewan, see Richards and Pratt, *Prairie Capitalism*, chs 5–6, 8, 10–11; Jeanne Kirk Laux and Maureen Appel Molot, 'The Potash Corporation of Saskatchewan', in Allan Tupper and G. Bruce Doern, eds, *Public Corporations and Public Policy in Canada* (Montreal, 1981),

189–220; Laux and Molot, *State Capitalism: Public Enterprise in Canada* (Ithaca, NY, 1988), 107–14. On Ipsco, see David Margoshes, *Against All Odds: The Story of Ipsco's First Fifty Years* (Regina, 2006).

2. On British Columbia generally, see Jean Barman, *The West Beyond the West: A History of British Columbia* (Toronto, 1991), esp. chs 12, 14. On Bennett, see David Mitchell, *W.A.C. Bennett and the Rise of British Columbia* (Vancouver, 1983), esp. chs 8–9; an alternative view is offered by Patricia Marchak, 'The Rise and Fall of the Peripheral State: The Case of British Columbia', in Robert J. Brym, ed., *Regionalism in Canada* (Toronto, 1986), 123–59. On BC industries, see G.W. Taylor, *Builders of British Columbia: An Industrial History* (Victoria, 1982); G.W. Taylor, *Timber: History of the Forest Industry in British Columbia* (Vancouver, 1975), esp. chs 13–15; Donald McKay, *Empire of Wood: The MacMillan-Bloedel Story* (Vancouver, 1982); Patricia Marchak, *Green Gold: The Forest Industry in British Columbia* (Vancouver, 1983).

3. On Quebec generally since World War II, see Paul-André Linteau et al., *Quebec Since 1930*, trans. Robert Chodos and Ellen Garmaise (Toronto, 1991). On the French-Canadian business community, see Jorge Niosi, 'The Rise of French Canadian Capitalism', in Alain Gagnon, ed., *Quebec: State and Society* (Toronto, 1984), 186–200; Niosi, *Canadian Capitalism* (Toronto, 1981), ch. 3; Matthew Fraser, *Quebec Inc.* (Toronto, 1978); Paul-André Linteau and René Durocher, *Le retard du Québec et L'infériorité économique des Canadiens français* (Montreal, 1971); Pierre Fournier, *Le Capitalisme au Québec* (Montreal, 1978); Norman Taylor, 'French Canadians as Industrial Entrepreneurs', *Journal of Political Economy* 68 (1960): 37–52; René Prevost and Maurice Chartrand, *Provigo* (Scarborough, Ont., 1988). On Duplessis, see Conrad Black, *Duplessis* (Toronto, 1977). On the Quiet Revolution, see Dale C. Thomson, *Jean Lesage and the Quiet Revolution* (Toronto, 1984), esp. chs 10–12; Kenneth McRoberts, *Quebec: Social Change and Political Crisis*, 3rd edn (Toronto, 1993). On particular Crown enterprises and projects, see Pierre Fournier, 'The National Asbestos Corporation of Quebec', in Tupper and Doern, eds, *Public Corporations and Public Policy*, 353–64; Laux and Molot, *State Capitalism*, 114–21; Carol Jobin, *Les enjeux économiques de la nationalisation de l'électricité* (Montreal, 1978); André Bolduc et al., *Québec: un siècle d'électricité* (Montreal, 1984), chs 17–23.

4. On Maritime economic affairs after World War II, see James P. Bickerton, *Nova Scotia, Ottawa and the Politics of Regional Development* (Toronto, 1990),

which goes well beyond its title in covering the region. See also Roy George, *A Leader and a Laggard: Manufacturing Industry in Nova Scotia, Quebec and Ontario* (Toronto, 1970); Henry Veltmeyer, 'The Restructuring of Capital and the Regional Problem', in Bryant Fairley et al., eds, *Restructuring and Resistance: Perspectives from Atlantic Canada* (Toronto, 1990), which offers varying views of the roots of the region's problems. See also chapters 11-13 in Ernest Forbes and Del Muise, eds, *Atlantic Provinces in Confederation* (Toronto, 1993). On IEL, see Roy George, *The Life and Times of Industrial Estates Limited* (Halifax, 1974); Garth Hopkins, *The Rise and Fall of a Business Empire: Clairtone* (Toronto, 1978); Harry Bruce, *Frank Sobey* (Toronto, 1985), ch. 9. On Peter Munk and the rise of Barrick, see Richard Rohmer, *Golden Phoenix: The Rise of Peter Munk* (Toronto, 2002). Other studies of provincial development debacles include Philip Mathias, *Forced Growth* (Toronto, 1971); Sandford Borins and Lee Brown, *Investments in Failure* (Toronto, 1986); Tom Kent, 'The Brief Rise and Early Decline of Regional Development', *Acadiensis* 9 (Autumn 1979): 120–4.

5. On Newfoundland generally, see James Hiller and Peter Neary, eds, *Newfoundland in the Nineteenth and Twentieth Centuries* (Toronto, 1980); Peter Neary, ed., *The Political Economy of Newfoundland, 1929–1972* (Toronto, 1973); David Alexander, 'Development and Dependence in Newfoundland, 1880–1970', *Acadiensis* 4 (Autumn 1974): 3–31; Brian C. Bursey, *A Half Century of Progress? A History of Economic Growth and Development in Newfoundland, 1930–1980* (St John's, 1980); Richard Gwyn, *Smallwood: The Unlikely Revolutionary* (Toronto, 1972); Gerhard Bassler, *Valdmanis and the Politics of Survival* (Toronto, 2000); J.D. House, *Against the Tide: Battling for Economic Revival in Newfoundland and Labrador* (Toronto, 1999); Forbes and Muise, *Atlantic Provinces in Confederation*, ch. 10. On Brinco, see Philip Smith, *Brinco: The Story of Churchill Falls* (Toronto, 1975); Thomson, *Jean Lesage*, 248–88. On the problems of the fisheries, see David Alexander, *The Decay of Trade: An Economic History of the Newfoundland Saltfish Trade, 1935–65* (St John's, 1977); Rosemary Ommer, 'What's Wrong with Canadian Fish?', *Journal of Canadian Studies* 20 (Autumn 1985): 122–42; *Navigating Troubled Waters: A New Policy for Atlantic Fisheries* (Ottawa, 1983) [Kirby Report].

Chapter 10

1. General comparative analyses of government economic policies in the post-war era include

Robert Lekachman, *The Age of Keynes* (New York, 1968); Andrew Shonfield, *Modern Capitalism: The Changing Balance of Public and Private Power* (New York, 1965). See also Robert Collins, *The Business Response to Keynes* (New York, 1981).

2. On macroeconomic policies in Canada, see David A. Wolfe, 'The Rise and Demise of the Keynesian Era in Canada: Economic Policy, 1930–82', in M.S. Cross and G.S. Kealey, eds, *Modern Canada, 1930s–1980s* (Toronto, 1984), 46–80; Robert Bothwell, Ian Drummond, and John English, *Canada Since 1945: Power, Politics and Provincialism* (Toronto, 1981), chs 19, 23, 27, 33; Richard Phidd and G. Bruce Doern, *The Politics and Management of Canadian Economic Policy* (Toronto, 1978). On bailouts, see Marsha Gordon, *Government in Business* (Montreal, 1981), 83–7, 150–4; Sandford Borins and Lee Brown, *Investments in Failure* (Toronto, 1986). On reorganization of the fisheries companies, see Stephen Kimber, *Net Profits: The Story of National Sea* (Halifax, 1989), chs 15–17; Jeanne Kirk Laux and Maureen Appel Molot, *State Capitalism: Public Enterprise in Canada* (Ithaca, NY, 1988), 135–9; Gordon Pitts, *The Codfathers: Lessons from Atlantic Canada's Business Elite* (Toronto, 2005), 198–205.

3. For varying views on the rise of multinational enterprises and their impact on economic and political affairs, see Raymond Vernon, *Sovereignty at Bay: The Multinational Spread of U.S. Enterprises* (New York, 1971); Richard Barnet and Ronald Muller, *Global Reach: The Power of the Multinational Corporations* (New York, 1974); Stephen Hymer, *The International Operations of National Firms* (Cambridge, Mass., 1976); Mira Wilkins, *The Maturing of Multinational Enterprise* (Cambridge, Mass., 1974), chs 12–14. Among many critiques of multinationals in Canada, see Kari Levitt, *Silent Surrender* (Toronto, 1970); I.A. Litvak and C.J. Maule, *Dual Loyalty: Canadian–US Business* (Toronto, 1971). A.E. Safarian, *Foreign Ownership of Canadian Industry* (Toronto, 1973), examines the internal structures and perspectives of Canadian subsidiaries; Eric Jackson, *The Great Canadian Debate: Foreign Ownership* (Toronto, 1975), looks at different viewpoints.

4. On the Auto Pact, see Dimitry Anastakis, *Auto Pact: Creating a Borderless North American Auto Industry* (Toronto, 2005); Michael Hart, *A Trading Nation* (Vancouver, 2002), 240–7.

5. On Canadian policies vis-à-vis foreign direct investment, see Michael Bliss, 'Founding FIRA: The Historical Background', in J.M. Spence and W.P. Rosenfeld, eds, *Foreign Investment Review Law in Canada* (Toronto, 1984), 1–11; Charles McMillan, 'The Regulation of Foreign Investment in Canada',

Journal of Contemporary Issues 6 (Autumn 1977): 31–51; Richard D. French, *How Ottawa Decides: Planning and Industrial Policy Making, 1968–80* (Ottawa, 1980). On the pipeline debate, see William Kilbourn, *Pipeline* (Toronto, 1970).

6. On the issue of foreign ownership in the banking sector, see John Fayerweather, *The Mercantile Bank Affair* (New York, 1974). On the TSE, see Christopher Armstrong, *Moose Pastures and Mergers: The Ontario Securities Commission and the Regulation of Share Markets in Canada, 1940–1980* (Toronto, 2001), 281–99.

7. On the origins and growth of Petro-Canada, see Larry Pratt, 'Petro-Canada', in Allan Tupper and G. Bruce Doern, eds, *Privatization, Public Policy and Public Corporations in Canada* (Halifax, 1988), 151–210. On the National Energy Program, see G. Bruce Doern and Glen Toner, *The Politics of Energy* (Toronto, 1985). For an acerbic view of the government's energy policies, see Peter Foster, *The Sorcerer's Apprentices: Canada's Super-Bureaucrats and the Energy Mess* (Toronto, 1982); for different assessments, see David Crane, *Controlling Interest: The Canadian Oil and Gas Stakes* (Toronto, 1982); James Laxer, *Oil and Gas* (Toronto, 1983).

8. On deindustrialization and union responses in the US and Canada, see Steven High, *Industrial Sunset: The Making of North America's Rust Belt, 1969–1984* (Toronto, 2003), esp. ch. 6. Also see Desmond Morton, *Working People*, 4th edn (Montreal, 1998), chs 27–9.

Chapter 11

1. 'Think, Act Globally, Alcan CEO Urges', *Globe and Mail*, 5 Oct. 2006, B1; Michael E. Porter and the Monitor Company, *Canada at the Crossroads: The Reality of a New Competitive Environment* (Ottawa, 1991), 21–2.

2. 'Canadian Outward Foreign Direct Investment to the World', *Asia Pacific Business*, 9 Oct. 2006, at: <www.asiapacificbusiness.ca/data/trade/general>; Industry Canada/Strategis, 'Special Report: Canadian Foreign Direct Investment Trends in the 1990s', July 1998.

3. James L. Darroch, *Canadian Banks and Global Competitiveness* (Montreal and Kingston, 1994); P. Nagy, *The International Business of Canadian Banks* (Montreal, 1983); Geoffrey Jones, *British Multinational Banking 1830–1990* (Oxford, 1993). For individual banks, one of the best recent studies is Duncan McDowall, *Quick to the Frontier: Canada's Royal Bank* (Toronto, 1993). Also see Merrill Denison, *Canada's First Bank*, vol. 2 (Toronto,

1967); Joseph Schull and J.D. Gibson, *The Scotiabank Story* (Toronto, 1982).

4. On Sun Life, see Joseph Schull, *The Century of the Sun* (Toronto, 1971). On Manulife, see R.V. Ashforth, *'And All the Past Is Future'* (Toronto, 1987).

5. Jorge Niosi, *Canadian Multinationals*, trans. Robert Chodos (Toronto, 1985), 83–124; I.A. Litvak and C.J. Maule, *Alcan Aluminum Ltd.: A Case Study*, Royal Commission on Corporate Concentration, Study no. 13 (Ottawa, 1977); Duncan C. Campbell, *Global Mission: The Story of Alcan*, 2 vols (Montreal, 1990); John Deverell et al., *Falconbridge: Portrait of a Canadian Mining Multinational* (Toronto, 1975); J.H. Bradbury, 'International Movements and Crises in Resource Oriented Companies: The Case of Inco in the Nickel Sector', *Economic Geography* 61, 2 (1985): 129–43; Jacquie McNish, 'The Great Canadian Mining Disaster', *Globe and Mail*, 25 Nov. 2006, B8–17.

6. Jonathan C. Brown, 'Jersey Standard and the Politics of Latin American Oil Production, 1911–30', in John D. Wirth, ed., *Latin American Oil Companies and the Politics of Energy* (Lincoln, Neb., 1985), 1–51.

7. 'Talisman Energy Inc.', at <www.fundinguniverse. com/company-histories>; Madelaine Drohan, *Making a Killing* (Toronto, 2003), 243–89; Tamsin Carlisle, 'Calgary Oil Firm Talisman Pays Painful Price for Sudan Investment', *Wall Street Journal*, 17 Aug. 2000.

8. Douglas MacKay, *Empire of Wood: The MacMillan-Bloedel Story* (Vancouver, 1982); Ilan Verlansky and Rachana Raizada, 'MacMillian-Bloedel: Foreign Investment Decisions and Their Welfare Consequences', in Steven Globerman, ed., *Canadian-Based Multinationals* (Calgary, 1994), 367–420.

9. 'Abitibi-Consolidated Inc.', at: <www.fundinguniverse.com/company-histories>; Barry Boothman, 'A Bond of Sympathy: The Receivership of Abitibi Power & Paper', paper presented at annual meeting of Canadian Historical Association, 2005, London, Ont.

10. E.P. Neufeld, *A Global Corporation: A History of the International Development of Massey-Ferguson* (Toronto, 1969); Peter Cook, *Massey at the Brink* (Toronto, 1981); Michael Bliss, 'Last Harvest', *Report on Business Magazine* (Aug. 1988): 48–53.

11. Nicholas Faith, *The Bronfmans: The Rise and Fall of the House of Seagram* (New York, 2006); Michael Marrus, *Mister Sam: The Life and Times of Samuel Bronfman* (Toronto, 1991).

12. 'CHC Helicopter Corporation', at: <www.fundinguniverse.com/company-histories>; Gordon Pitts,

'Craig Dobbin, Aviation Executive 1935–2006', *Globe and Mail*, 12 Oct. 2006, S9.

13. Henry C. Klassen, *A Business History of Alberta* (Calgary, 1999), 195–9, 214–15.

Chapter 12

1. Russell Knight, quoted by *Globe and Mail* reporter Jan Wong, in J.R. Colombo, *Dictionary of Canadian Quotations* (Toronto, 1991), 52.

2. Family Business Centre, Sauder School of Business, UBC, at: <www.sauder.ubc.ca>; 'Facts and Perspectives on Family Business Around the World', Family Firm Institute, Boston, Mass., 2005, at: <www.ffi.org>.

3. 'Top 1000 Companies 2006', *Toronto Globe and Mail Report on Business*, at: <globeinvestor.com>; 'World's Largest Family Businesses, 2005', *Family Business Magazine*, at: <familybusinessmagazine.com>.

4. On issues relating to family business, see Kelin Gersack, *Generation to Generation: Life Cycles of the Family Business* (Boston, 1997); articles on 'Family Capitalism' in *Business History* 35 (Oct. 1993); Gordon Pitts, *In the Blood* (Toronto, 2000), 1–17.

5. On the early years of the Molsons, see Merrill Dennison, *The Barley and the Stream: The Molson Story* (Toronto, 1955); Douglas Hunter, *Molson: Birth of a Business Empire* (Toronto, 2001); Karen Molson, *The Molsons: Their Lives and Times 1780–2000* (Willowdale, Ont., 2001).

6. Paul Brent, *Lager Heads: Labatt and Molson Face Off for Canada's Beer Money* (Toronto, 2004); Pitts, *In the Blood*, 185–203; Allen W. Sneath, *Brewed in Canada* (Toronto, 2001).

7. On the Westons and Loblaw, see Charles Davies, *Bread Men: How the Westons Built an International Empire* (Toronto, 1987); Anne Kingston, *The Edible Man: Dave Nichol, President's Choice and the Making of Popular Taste* (Toronto, 1994). On the Steinbergs, see Anne Gibbon and Peter Hadekel, *Steinberg: The Breakup of a Family Empire* (Toronto, 1990). On the Woltes, see Pitts, *In the Blood*, 151–70; Dave Mote, 'The Oshawa Group Ltd.', in Tina Grant, ed., *Canadian Company Histories* (New York, 1996), 201–2. On the Sobeys, see Gordon Pitts, *The Codfathers: Lessons from the Atlantic Business Elite* (Toronto, 2005), 148–88; Jeffrey Covell, 'Empire Company Ltd.', in Grant, ed., *Canadian Company Histories*, 100–2.

8. For a highly critical analysis of the collapse of Eaton's, see Rod McQueen, *The Eatons: The Rise and Fall of Canada's Royal Family* (North York, Ont., 1998). A more sympathetic treatment of the family (written before the company's decline) is offered in Mary-Etta MacPherson, *Shopkeepers to a Nation: The Eatons* (Toronto, 1983).

9. A.D. Chandler Jr, *Scale and Scope: The Dynamics of Industrial Capitalism* (Cambridge, Mass., 1990), 18–31; Robert Sobel, *The Rise and Fall of the Conglomerate Kings* (Briarcliff Manor, NY, 1984).

10. On the origins of Argus, see Richard Rohmer, *E.P. Taylor* (Toronto, 1978); Frank and Libbie Park, *Anatomy of Big Business* (Toronto, 1973), 162–91; Peter C. Newman, *The Canadian Establishment* (Toronto, 1975), 20–31.

11. Conrad Black (a prolific author of biographies of Maurice Duplessis, Franklin D. Roosevelt, and Richard Nixon) provided a view of his career in *A Life in Progress* (Toronto, 2002). Other perspectives are offered in Peter C. Newman, *The Establishment Man* (Toronto, 1983); Richard Siklos, *Shades of Black: His Rise and Fall* (Toronto, 2004).

12. See Russell Bradon, *Roy Thomson of Fleet Street* (London, 1968); Susan Goldenberg, *The Thomson Empire* (Toronto, 1984).

13. Among the many accounts of these conglomerators of the 1980s and 1990s are Susan Gittins, *Behind Closed Doors: The Rise and Fall of Canada's Edper, Bronfman and Reichmann Empires* (Englewood Cliffs, NJ, 1995); Anthony Bianco, *The Reichmanns: Family, Faith, Fortune and the Empire of Olympia & York* (Toronto, 1997); Peter Foster, *Towers of Debt* (Toronto, 1993); Patricia Best and Ann Shortell, *The Brass Ring: Power, Influence and the Brascan Empire* (Toronto, 1988); Diane Francis, *Controlling Interest* (Toronto, 1986).

14. Susan Goldenberg, *Canadian Pacific: A Portrait of Power* (Toronto, 1983); Lawrence Surtees, *Pa Bell: Jean de Grandpré and the Rise of Bell Canada Enterprise* (Toronto 1992); 'Canadian Pacific: A Brief History', at: <www.cpr.ca>.

15. On Desmarais's early career, see Newman, *The Canadian Establishment*, 43–87; 'Power Corporation of Canada: Seventy Five Years of Growth, 1925–2000', at: <www.powercorporation.com>.

16. On the Batas, see Thomas J. Bata and Sonja Sinclair, *Bata: Shoemakers to the World* (Toronto, 1990); Pitts, *In the Blood*, 41–59. On Stronach, see Wayne Lilley, *Magna Cum Laude: How Frank Stronach Became Canada's Best Paid Man* (Toronto, 2006); David Olive, *No Guts, No Glory: How Canada's CEOs Built Their Empires* (Toronto, 2000), 161–82; Jeffrey L. Corvell, 'Magna International Inc.', in Grant, ed., *Canadian Company Histories*, 159–62. On Watsa, see 'Fairfax Financial Holdings Ltd.', at: <www.fundinguniverse.com/company-histories>.

On Michael Lee-Chin, see <www.aic.com/fund_managers>.

17. Roma Luciw, 'Corner Office Headcount: Women 3, Men 97. Go Figure', *Globe and Mail*, 12 Jan. 2007; Janet McFarland, 'More Women Take Seats in the Boardroom', *Globe and Mail*, 15 Jan. 2007.

18. Pitts, *In the Blood*, 101–15; Rod McQueen, *Can't Buy Me Love: How Martha Billes Made Canadian Tire Hers* (Toronto, 2000).

19. See Olive P. Dickason, *Canada's First Nations* (Toronto, 1992), 402–16; Yale D. Berlanger, *Gambling with the Future: The Evolution of Aboriginal Gaming in Canada* (Saskatoon, 2006).

Chapter 13

1. See Jeffrey Frieden, *Global Capitalism* (New York, 2006), chs 16–17; A.G. Kenwood and A.L. Lougheed, *The Growth of the International Economy* (London, 1999), chs 19–20; Geoffrey Jones, *Multinationals and Global Capitalism* (New York, 2005), ch. 2 and Appendix 1.

2. For critiques of globalization, see, for example, Pat Marchak, *The Integrated Circus: The New Right and the Restructuring of Global Markets* (Montreal and Kingston, 1991); George Stiglitz, *Globalization and Its Discontents* (New York, 2002). On the cultural impact of globalization, see Benjamin Barber, *Jihad versus McWorld: How Globalism and Tribalism Are Reshaping the World* (New York, 1996).

3. The best recent overview of the Canada–US Free Trade Agreement is in Michael Hart, *A Trading Nation* (Vancouver, 2003), ch. 13. Blow-by-blow accounts of the negotiations are provided in Bill Diamond and Colin Robertson, *Decision at Midnight: Inside the Canada–US Free Trade Negotiations* (Vancouver, 1994), and Gordon Ritchie, *Wrestling with the Elephant: The Inside Story of the Canada–US Trade Wars* (Toronto, 1997). The quote from Ritchie on the benefits of the FTA is on p. 260. See also G. Bruce Doern and Brian W. Tomlin, *Faith and Fear: The Free Trade Story* (Toronto, 1991); Gilbert R. Winham, *Trading with Canada: The Canada–US Free Trade Agreement* (New York, 1988).

4. On NAFTA, see Hart, *A Trading Nation*, 393–7; Ritchie, *Wrestling with the Elephant*, 181–92; Richard G. Harris, 'The Economic Impact of the Canada–U.S. FTA and NAFTA Agreements for Canada: A Review of the Evidence', in John M. Curtis and Aaron Sydor, *NAFTA @ 10*, at: <www.international.gc.ca/eet/research/nafta-en.asp>. The quote is from Harris, p. 35. On the auto industry, see Dimitry Anastakis, *Auto Pact: Creating a Borderless North American Auto Industry* (Toronto, 2005),

172–9. On the softwood lumber dispute, see Daowei Zhang, *The Softwood Lumber War: Politics, Economics and the Long U.S.–Canadian Trade Dispute* (Baltimore, 2007).

5. On Air Canada, see Robert Campbell and Leslie Pal, 'Air Farce: Airlines Policy in a Deregulated Environment', in Robert Campbell, ed., *The Real Worlds of Canadian Politics* (Peterborough, Ont., 1994), 83–141; Wayne Skene, *Turbulence: How Deregulation Destroyed Canada's Airlines* (Vancouver, 1994). On Canadian National, see Harry Bruce, *The Pigs That Flew: The Battle to Privatize Canadian National* (Vancouver, 1997). On hydro power, see Neil Freeman, *The Politics of Power* (Toronto, 1996); Gordon Laird, *Power: Journeys Across an Energy Nation* (Toronto, 2002).

6. For general overviews of the evolution of the IT industry, see Martin Campbell-Kelly and William Asprey, *Computer: A History of the Information Machine* (New York, 1996); Wade Rowland, *The Spirit of the Web: The Age of Information from Telegraph to Internet* (Toronto, 1997). On the early history of the computer industry in Canada, see John Vardalas, *The Computer Revolution in Canada* (Cambridge, Mass., 2001); Beverley Bleackley and Jean LaPrairie, *Entering the Computer Age* (Agincourt, Ont., 1982). On IBM Canada, see Manuel Cote, Yvon Allaire, and Roger Emile Miller, *IBM Canada: A Case Study*, Royal Commission on Corporate Concentration Study #14 (Ottawa, 1976). On Mers Kutt, see Z. Stachniak, 'The Making of the MCM/70 Microcomputer', *IEEE Annals of the History of Computing* 25 (Apr.–June 2003): 62–75. On Cowpland and Matthews, see David Thomas, *Knights of the New Technology* (Toronto, 1983), 39–56.

7. For very different perspectives on Nortel, see Larry Macdonald, *Nortel Networks* (Etobicoke, Ont., 2000); Douglas Hunter, *The Bubble and the Bear: How Nortel Burst the Canadian Dream* (Toronto, 2002). On 'convergence', see Matthew Fraser, *Free For All: The Struggle for Dominance on the Digital Frontier* (Toronto, 1999); Gordon Pitts, *Kings of Convergence: The Fight for Control of Canada's Media* (Toronto, 2002). For background on the telecommunications industry since the 1960s, see Laurence Mussio, *Telecom Nation: Telecommunications, Computers and Governments in Canada* (Montreal and Kingston, 2003).

8. For a particularly scathing view of the environmental effects of the oil sands, see William Marsden, *Stupid to the Last Drop: How Alberta Is Bringing Environmental Armageddon to Canada* (Toronto, 2007).

9. Barry Boothman and Barbara Austin, 'Another One Bites the Dust: Turnover and Failure among

Leading Canadian Firms', *ASAC Conference Proceedings* 26, 24 (Toronto, 2005), 32–44.

10. Institute for Competitiveness and Prosperity, Rotman School, University of Toronto, 'Canada's Global Leaders, 1985–2005', at: <www.competeprosper. ca/research/GlobalLeaders>; Heather Scoffield, 'Is Canada Hollowing Out? Actually, It's a World Beater', *Globe and Mail Report on Business*, 5 Dec. 2006, B1.

Further Reading

For discussion of many of these works, as well as additional readings, see the Notes.

General
Michael Bliss, *Northern Enterprise: Five Centuries of Canadian Business* (1987).
Douglas McCalla, ed., *The Development of Canadian Capitalism: Essays in Business History* (1990).
Joe Martin, *History of Canadian Business* (2008).
Kenneth Norrie and Douglas Owram, *A History of the Canadian Economy* (1991).
Graham Taylor and Peter Baskerville, *A Concise History of Business in Canada* (1994).
Tom Traves, ed., *Essays in Canadian Business History* (1983).

Business in Canada to 1885
John F. Bosher, *The Canada Merchants, 1713–1763* (1987).
Donald Creighton, *Empire of the St. Lawrence: A Study in Commerce and Politics* (1956, 2002).
Julian Gwyn, *Excessive Expectations: Maritime Commerce and the Economic Development of Nova Scotia, 1740–1870* (1998).
Douglas McCalla, *The Upper Canada Trade, 1834–1872: A Study of the Buchanans' Business* (1979).
———, *Planting the Province: An Economic History of Upper Canada* (1993).
Dale Miquelon, *Dugard of Rouen: French Trade to Canada and the West Indies, 1729–1770* (1978).
Tom Naylor, *Canada in the European Age, 1453–1919* (1987).
Eric Sager, *Maritime Capital: The Shipping Business in Atlantic Canada, 1820–1914* (1990).

The Fur Trade
John S. Galbraith, *The Hudson's Bay Company as an Imperial Factor, 1821–1869* (1957).
Peter C. Newman, *Company of Adventurers: The Hudson's Bay Company* (2005).
James Raffan, *Emperor of the North: Sir George Simpson* (2007).
Arthur J, Ray, *Indians in the Fur Trade* (1998).
———, *The Canadian Fur Trade in the Industrial Age* (1990).
Sylvia Van Kirk, *Many Tender Ties: Women in Western Fur Trade Society, 1670–1870* (1980).

Railways
Pierre Berton, *The National Dream/The Last Spike* (1974).
David Cruise and Alison Griffiths, *Lords of the Line* (1988).
John Eagle, *The Canadian Pacific Railway and the Development of Western Canada* (1989).
R.B. Fleming, *The Railway King of Canada: Sir William Mackenzie* (1991).
Valerie Knowles, *From Telegrapher to Titan: The Life of William Van Horne* (2004).
W. Kaye Lamb, *History of the Canadian Pacific Railway* (1976).
Donald Mackay, *The People's Railway: A History of Canadian National* (1992).
Ted Regehr, *The Canadian Northern Railway* (1976).
G.R. Stevens, *A History of the Canadian National Railways* (1973).

Banks, Finance, and Investment
Christopher Armstrong, *Blue Skies and Boiler Rooms: Buying and Selling Securities in Canada, 1870–1940* (1997).

———, *Moose Pastures and Mergers: The Ontario Securities Commission and the Regulation of Share Markets in Canada, 1940–1980* (2001).

Kenneth Buckley, *Capital Formation in Canada, 1896–1930* (1955).

James Darroch, *Canadian Banks and Global Competitiveness* (1994).

Duncan McDowall, *Quick to the Frontier: Canada's Royal Bank* (1993).

Gregory Marchildon, *Profits and Politics: Beaverbrook and the Gilded Age of Canadian Finance* (1996).

E.P. Neufeld, *The Financial System of Canada* (1972).

Ronald Rudin, *Banking en français: The French Banks of Quebec, 1835–1925* (1985).

———, *In Whose Interest? Quebec's Caisses populaires, 1900–1945* (1990).

Utilities

Christopher Armstrong and H.V. Nelles, *Monopoly's Moment: The Organization and Regulation of Canadian Utilities, 1896–1930* (1986).

——— and ———, *Southern Exposure: Canadian Promoters in Latin America and the Caribbean, 1896–1930* (1988).

Duncan McDowall, *The Light: Brazilian Traction, Light & Power Company, 1899–1945* (1988).

Laurence Mussio, *Telecom Nation: Telecommunications, Computers and Government in Canada* (2001).

Jean-Guy Rens, *The Invisible Empire: A History of the Telecommunications Industry in Canada*, trans. Kathe Roth (2001).

Natural Resources

Ed Gould, *Oil: The History of Canada's Oil and Gas Industry* (1976).

D.M. Le Bourdais, *Metals and Men: The Story of Canadian Mining* (1957).

———, *Sudbury Basin: The Story of Nickel* (1953).

Gordon Hak, *Capital and Labour in the British Columbia Forest Industry, 1934–1974* (2007).

Henry Klassen, *Eye on the Future: Business People in Calgary and Bow Valley, 1870–1900* (2002).

Patricia Marchak, *Green Gold: The Forest Industry in British Columbia* (1983).

David Massell, *Amassing Power: J.B. Duke and the Saguenay River, 1897–1927* (2000).

Peter McKenzie-Brown, Gordon Jarenko, and David Finch, *The Great Oil Age: The Petroleum Industry in Canada* (1993).

H.V. Nelles, *The Politics of Development: Forests, Mines and Hydro-Electric Power in Ontario, 1849–1941* (1974).

Ian Radforth, *Bushworkers and Bosses: Logging in Northern Ontario, 1900–1980* (1987).

G.W. Taylor, *Timber: A History of the Forest Industry in British Columbia* (1975).

Manufacturing

Michael Bliss, *A Canadian Millionaire: The Life and Business Times of Sir Joseph Flavelle* (1978).

Craig Heron, *Working in Steel: The Early Years in Canada, 1883–1935* (1988).

Kris Inwood, *The Canadian Charcoal Iron Industry* (1986).

William Kilbourn, *The Elements Combined: A History of the Steel Company of Canada* (1960).

Duncan McDowall, *Steel at the Sault: Francis H. Clergue, Sir James Dunn and the Algoma Steel Corporation, 1901–1956* (1984).

Bryan Palmer, *A Culture in Conflict: Skilled Workers and Industrial Capitalism in Hamilton, Ontario, 1860–1914* (1979).

Joy Parr, *The Gender of Breadwinners: Women, Men and Change in Two Industrial Towns, 1880–1930* (1990).

Retailing

Donica Belisle, *The Rise of Mass Retail: Canadians and Department Stores, 1880–1940* (2006).

Nicholas Faith, *The Bronfmans: The Rise and Fall of the House of Seagram* (2006).

David Monod, *Store Wars: Shopkeepers and the Culture of Mass Marketing, 1890–1939* (1996).

Peter C. Newman, *Merchant Princes* (1991).

Joy Santinck, *Timothy Eaton and the Rise of His Department Store* (1990).

Government and Business

Carman Baggaley, *Emergence of the Regulatory State in Canada, 1867–1939* (1981).

Matthew Bellamy, *Profiting the Crown: Canada's Polymer Corporation, 1942–1990* (1999).
James Bickerton, *Nova Scotia, Ottawa and the Politics of Regional Development* (1990).
Robert Bothwell, *Nucleus: The History of Atomic Energy of Canada Ltd.* (1988).
———, *Eldorado: Canada's National Uranium Company* (1984).
——— and William Kilbourn, *C.D. Howe* (1979).
Ken Cruikshank, *Close Ties: Railways, the Government and the Board of Railway Commissioners, 1851–1933* (1991).
Alvin Finkel, *Business and Social Reform in the Thirties* (1979).
Ted Regehr, *The Beauharnois Scandal: A Story of Canadian Entrepreneurship and Politics* (1990).
Greig Stewart, *Shutting Down the National Dream: A.V. Roe and the Tragedy of the Avro Arrow* (1978).
Tom Traves, *The State and Enterprise: Canadian Manufacturers and the Federal Government, 1917–1931* (1979).
John Vardalis, *The Computer Revolution in Canada* (2001).

Trade Policies

Dimitry Anastakis, *Auto Pact: Creating a Borderless North American Auto Market, 1960–1971* (2005).
John B. Brebner, *North Atlantic Triangle: The Interplay of Canada, the United States and Great Britain* (1945, 1968).
Robert Cuff and Jack Granatstein, *Ties That Bind: Canadian–American Relations from the Great War to the Cold War* (1977).
Ben Forster, *A Conjunction of Interests: Business, Politics and Tariffs, 1825–1879* (1986).
Michael Hart, *A Trading Nation: Canadian Trade Policy from Colonialism to Globalization* (2002).
Randall White, *Fur Trade to Free Trade* (1989).

Index